TYPE T

Andy Guest

COPYRIGHT

ISBN-13: 978-1985327542

This work depicts actual events in the life of the author as truthfully as recollection permits. Occasionally, dialogue consistent with the character or nature of the person speaking has been supplemented. All persons within are actual individuals, and only a few names have been changed for security purposes.

Author: www.andy-guest.com
Editor: www.elainedenning.com

To Mum and Dad, for your endless love and support. You're with me always.

To Ken and Pete, for sharing the adventures. It wouldn't have been the same without you.

And to Alison, Westleigh and Daniel, for being the most important part of my journey.

CONTENTS

INTRODUCTION

It's been more than a decade since the idea to write a book first sparked within me, a few years since my friends started telling me to stop sharing my stories on Facebook and to just write the damn thing, and about ten months since a friend on the drop zone told me he knew an editor he could put me in touch with. And now here I am, sitting with a cup of tea (you'll find I do that quite a lot), with the final words written. There are equal measures of excitement and fear in my belly at the thought of the book being 'out there'. I'm not a seasoned writer and I have no idea how the book will be received but, as with all the journeys I've taken in my life, if I don't step outside my comfort zone I'll never find out.

The process of getting the words from my brain to the screen was harder than I'd anticipated. I discovered early on that merely listing my accomplishments in chronological order wasn't going to cut it; I needed to dig deep and find the emotion, and leave the reader with a real sense of who I truly am. That's easier said than done considering I've spent a lot of my life burying emotion (through necessity rather than choice). There have been times when I've had tears of laughter streaming down my face – and revisiting those moments has been great - but there has been emotional pain, too. For someone who is a private person, who has had it drilled into him to never let his guard down or to show vulnerability, recalling these latter events and laying them out bare for all to see has certainly been an experience.

Everything I have embarked on in my life has been for the sole purpose of discovering who I am. So, you may ask, who am I? I guess you'll have to read the book to find out but, if you're looking for the quick answer, I'm just as the book title states. I'm a Type T. I know that my insatiable desire to feel alive, to set my inner spirit free, to walk the untrodden path and to be 'me' will always remain.

If I have one hope or intention for this book it's that you, the reader, will have the courage to step outside your comfort zone to discover who you truly are. You only live once, so make sure you have the ride of your life.

Pour yourself a tea and join me on my journey. Photographs to accompany every chapter of the book can be found at my website: www.andy-guest.com

Let the voyage begin …

THE SEED IS SOWN

As I evaluate my day, my concentration is broken by the voice of Kevin Mcllwee, our parachute instructor.

"Okay, listen up. The first three students will be Andy Guest, Carol Medley, and Neil Harrison."

The excitement and apprehension is palpable as I, along with the others, climb into a parachuting B4 harness. I can sense the atmosphere has changed as our nervous laughter tries to disguise the fear but, for all the bravado, our eyes cannot hide it.

It's not long before we're inspected and head over to the aircraft, a Cessna 180. The engine bursts into life and emits a cloud of smoke that embraces us with the smell of Avgas. It's stimulating, intoxicating, and I wonder whether it would work as some sort of perfume.

There's something exhilarating in knowing I'm about to challenge myself, and I feel all the senses in my body coming alive; an electricity running through me. I'm not a cocktail drinker but this concoction of excitement and apprehension, of feeling my blood being pumped harder, stirs something inside of me. At this moment in time I'm not sure what it is.

The aircraft roars down the runway, the wind sweeping into the plane, and eventually the tyres depart from the tarmac. It dawns on me, suddenly, that this is a one way journey. They've positioned me as the first student to jump and I'm kneeling up by the door, but there is no door, just a large gaping hole that allows me to see the landscape below, which retreats at an alarming rate as we climb higher. There's a beauty in the landscape but it doesn't register. I'm going into myself. I am here but not here. My mind and body are becoming detached.

It's fair to say there is no smile on my face. I've never flown before, and having a fear of heights coupled with no barrier separating me from the abyss are not the best ingredients to generate one. The empty space where the door should have been causes my pupils to enlarge. Something is calling me towards that hole but I don't particularly want to look. The adrenalin kicks in with a vengeance and it feels as if it's surging through my body; either that, or it's my nervousness making me tremble. My grasp on the pilot's seat is more like a death grip and my knuckles are turning white. It's a fact I'm not aware of until the pilot pushes me away from him; I had started to encroach on him without realising I was leaning away from that gaping hole and onto his lap. My heart thumps for all its worth, my mouth is going dry, and I try to moisten it. My head buzzes with so many messages hurtling through it and I try to evaluate each one. I never realised it was possible to have so many voices in my head at the same time. Strangely, the voices are in opposition to each other. Some calmly try to convince me that this is a foolhardy error while others tell me this is where I prove my metal and to not listen to the rest. My head drifts into a reflective mood and I ponder how on earth I got here.

I'm convinced that for a large percentage of people who have a thirst for adventure, the force that drives them is genetic. My father, at aged twenty-one, was fighting in the jungles of Malaya as a police officer. So, perhaps it's he who is responsible; it's his fault that I'm having to test myself, all the while terrified that the grim reaper's hand is outside this aircraft, ready to snatch me away.

Having missed the end of his formal education at Dulwich College - a very prestigious school founded in 1619 - my father, at aged seventeen, chose to join the Royal Marines under the 'Y Entry Scheme'(Y standing for Youth). He wanted to be a pilot but the RAF were winding down recruiting, however, the Fleet Air arm were still recruiting so there was a possibility he could get in via the Royal Marines.

That dream didn't work out and my father left the Royal Marines at the age of nineteen. It was at a time when the armed forces were meant to help arrange work for former military servicemen, and companies were offered cash incentives to take them on and give them training. My father, looking at his options, elected to join a firm of architects, as that's what he wanted to be at that point in time, knowing the door to a flying career was closed as he wasn't able to finance it himself. But he became disillusioned when it was apparent the company he was with, like many others, were taking the cash incentives but treating staff as cheap labour rather than as apprentices, and giving them no proper structured training.

At the Union Jack Club in London, accommodation run for the ex-military forces, he heard that the Royal Federation Police in Malaya were advertising for recruits. He immediately chased it up, went for the interview and was accepted. As a result, he found himself flying out on a British transport aircraft – an Avro York – with the first group of recruits at the age of twenty-one. His adventure had begun. Little did he know that, in time, he would develop and excel, and rather than stepping *out* of his comfort zone into each unknown environment, he would actually step *in* to it.

When trouble broke out in Malaya in June 1948, when three European plantation managers were killed by three young Chinese men, it was described as a guerrilla war, however the conflict was only labelled as an 'emergency' because insurers would not have compensated rubber plantation and tin mine owners whose livelihoods were under attack from communists insurgents had it been labelled a war.

As a civil emergency it was the responsibility of the police to deal with incidents; the military would be acting purely in a supporting role and not leading. This meant the rule of law still applied, so every incident and every contact was subject to a full police report. To make this work the Royal Federation of Malaya Police had to radically increase in size, and some of that expansion would be dedicated to direct action against 'the bandits' - the name given to the enemy to make them appear to be nothing more than criminal gangs. However, those 'gangs' were actually forces, mostly Chinese, who had been trained by the British to fight the Japanese. They were organised into eleven regiments and divided into companies (much smaller than normal military forces), each with an independent platoon that was more heavily armed. This meant that in the early stages they fielded sizable units, at times two or three hundred men in size - definitively more than 'bandits'. They were savage in deployment, terrorising the population into submission and carrying out barbaric executions. Police officers who were captured would be tied up and forced onto their tip-toes while a wire was placed around their neck. As they tired, the wire would cut into their neck resulting in a slow death. The term of reference was soon changed from 'bandit' to Communist Terrorist (CT for short).

I was born a colonial child in Batu Gajah in 1958, and my brothers, Pete and Ken, in Kuala Lumpur. As young children we were oblivious to the risk my father was under on a daily basis. In later years I would see a black and white photograph on the first page of my father's album. It was a picture of the police officers dressed formally for an evening dinner. As I delved further into the album I realised that 40% of those in the first picture would be killed in action. I looked at their faces, smiling at a moment in time when they were unaware their fate was approaching, and sadness washed over me.

As boys, we lived what some would consider to be the dream, in a house by the sea. We would take a few running steps in our bare feet across the warm, sandy dirt track and under the coconut trees to arrive at the balmy sea, where we would splash and laugh and play, tasting the sea salt on our lips. This tropical location awoke my senses: the smell of spicy curries drifting from cooking stoves, and floral scents of the undergrowth wafting through the breeze. At another property at a different location where my father was deployed, we had a baby elephant that we looked after for a short period of time. Not an everyday pet for a European child.

But not all properties we lived in were safe. At one property, a shot rang out in the evening. My father grabbed his Sten gun and shouted to my mother to fetch him a magazine as he tried to identify where the shot came from. My mother returned with a magazine of the reading type, much to the dismay of my father.

This environment - living in colonial houses in a tropical country with beautiful coasts and ponds, where we would catch turtles, and where local nannies helped our mother look after us - was an adventure. We were living it and loving it. I must admit, having locals wanting to rub my tummy for luck as they considered me to be a little Buddha was all very strange, though my parents assured me it was okay.

As for my father, his working environment was very different, having to live on the edge, not knowing if something was about to kick off. On one occasion he was leading a patrol through the jungle when they were ambushed. The CT, numbering around one hundred, had initially allowed his patrol to pass through. The CT were positioned on the high ground, their eyes undoubtedly peering out from the undergrowth, not a muscle moving as they controlled their breathing, as they would have been taught. Once the column was in front of them the CT triggered the ambush, hitting the centre of the column as well as the cut off group. My father told me the jungle noise was drowned out as weapons erupted and rounds cracked through the air, rifle flashes spitting out death. There were cries of pain, not only from the men but from the elephants that were carrying supplies, which were now stampeding and crashing through the jungle to escape the hell they had just walked into, as birds and other wildlife fled the scene.

My father, realising what had just happened behind him, regrouped his small band of men and issued orders for a flanking manoeuvre, and instructed each of his men to scream as if they were ten men. With the flanking manoeuvre completed they charged, firing from the hip, ducking and weaving through the jungle, which was not easy to move through as feet had to be raised high to avoid tripping over. The CT, realising they were being attacked from the flank and hearing all the commotion, assumed a reinforced patrol had arrived on the scene and took flight. It was only after interrogating one of the captured and wounded CT did my father realise how close he had come. All that time patrolling the jungle, having lost so much weight and being tanned, the CT had mistaken him as one of the natives.

After Malaya declared their independence my parents weighed up their options and, with three children to think about, they chose to return to the UK. Our passage back was on a cargo ship called the Mombasa, where the crew had made up a makeshift swimming pool for me and my brothers, the only children on the ship.

On arriving on UK soil with their future uncertain, my parents settled in a village called Wrotham, in Kent, where I was soon to be introduced to the wonder of the white stuff that fell from the sky, something I had never seen or felt before.

Though I understood English at school when asked a question by the teachers, for some reason I preferred to answer in Malay, which resulted in one of my brothers often being called into my class to find out what I had replied. It was easier for the school in those days to summon my parents and inform them they must stop interacting with me if I spoke Malay and to only respond if I spoke English. Thus, over a period of time, I lost my ability to speak the language. It's a real shame that rather than encourage a child to be fluent in two languages, the school chose the easy option to suit them.

This colonial child was different from the rest of the boys and one day, for no reason, I was set upon by two boys while walking through the village. It was quite clear I was losing this battle as I took their punches but, even at the age of eight, I remember evaluating my options and saw an opportunity to alter the odds. A lorry was driving towards us and without hesitation I grabbed the youngest of the boys and swung him into the path of the lorry, which swerved to avoid us, with the angry driver beeping his horn. The older boy had the fright of his life and ran away in tears. This encounter left me with two black eyes and tears running down my own face. Where it came from - that I was able to evaluate my options and make a decision while under attack - I do not know. Nor did I know that in the future I would find myself in different circumstances and under intense pressure, where time would not be on my side, and where the consequences of my decision would result in either life or death, and not just tears rolling down a schoolboy's cheeks.

Due to financial circumstances my parents were on the move yet again, and this time my brothers and I moved to Scotland with our mother to a village called Aberdour, while my father worked in London. At the time I never understood why my father worked away; a nine-year-old boy does not comprehend that a parent has to do what he can to provide for his family and that sometimes he has no choice.

I have fond memories of Aberdour as a child. The village was friendly and set in a lovely location with a small harbour. At school the boys preferred to play football, while I preferred to hang out with a girl called Alison Brown, whom I had a crush on. My parents bought me a fishing rod so I could fish in the harbour, and my eldest brother, Pete, decided to join me. It wasn't long before I hooked a fish.

"Don't be too keen to reel it in … let it take the line to tire it out," he said. So I did, and we both watched as the last bit of line fell into the water as it hadn't been tied off. It goes without saying that as we both turned and headed home, I was not impressed.

As a family we were again on the move, this time to Chelsea in London to live with my father, and for someone who had been raised in villages this was a shock to the system. On my first day at Park Walk school the other boys surrounded me, demanding to know which football team I supported. For a boy who had no interest in football it wasn't an easy question to answer. They kept pushing for one and were not going to leave me alone until they had one. My answer was the first thing that came into my head, and probably the only team I had heard of at the time: "Queens Park Rangers." This was obviously the wrong answer for the Chelsea boys and over the next few weeks I found myself in three fights. Two of the fights I'd been dodging until my father, realising something was wrong, gave me a pep talk about standing up to bullies. So, I took his advice and met the boys on different days. However, something was missing from his pep talk – the fact that I would take a beating and lose. But I was left alone after that, so in a way it worked.

On one boring evening one of my friends mentioned there was a youth club at Chelsea School so we went to check it out, and it was there I was introduced to table tennis. I fell in love with the sport and would spend hours practicing and improving my skills. The table tennis coach entered us as a team to represent the youth club in the Wandsworth table tennis league, and in our first season we won our division. I was the top table tennis player with 92% wins. My competitive drive had been brought to life and I liked the feeling of it within me. From that day on, being average wasn't enough for me ... I wanted to aim higher.

The only other interest I had was fishing, and I'd struck up a friendship with Neil Harrison who lived in the same street as me in Edith Grove, Chelsea's World's End. Mick Jagger had once lived in our street, not that we had ever met him. Often, we would walk around the corner and fish in a small creek behind Chelsea Power Station that most people had thought polluted, but we knew otherwise. We would go to this tidal stretch and have some amazing catches ... one time I caught a 3/4lb fantail goldfish. The coal fields behind the power station – now all converted to create Chelsea Harbour – were where we used to dodge the security man with his bulldog.

Spending my teenage years in Chelsea certainly helped me become more street wise; like most areas it had a good side and a bad side. Kings Road had gone through a change and punk had become all the rage, so there were some very strange people walking around wearing odd outfits and make-up. It became the norm to see all sorts of people donning peculiar fashions, trying to find their identities. Earl's Court had a pub where Teddy Boys used to hang out, and the Rocky Horror Picture Show was playing in Kings Road, the billboards depicting men in women's underwear.

Education is a gateway to a child's future but for someone who, by then, loved nothing more than kicking a football around in the playground and playing table tennis, I didn't understand that, and I quit school at the age of fifteen. I had a gift when it came to maths, so, in the fourth year when we had to choose a specialist subject I asked to study Applied Maths. Unfortunately,

I didn't get it. I spoke with the math's teacher who said I had his support to join his class and he advised me to see the headmaster. It's quite daunting for a young boy to stand outside the headmaster's office, waiting to speak to him. The last time I had stood there I was about to be punished for going into a sweetshop outside of school hours on my way home as, unbeknown to me, the school had put it out of bounds. The other boys and I thought it was quite funny until we realised we were about to be caned, and that soon wiped the smiles from our faces. I entered his room with a sense of dread, was told to bend over, and then there was an agonising moment when it felt like the clocks had stopped. I remember telling myself to show no fear as the other boys were watching. And then the door closed. He didn't hold back; in fact it felt as if he took some pleasure in it. As the first blow hit my backside the pain shot through me and, as a rush of adrenalin surged, I gritted my teeth when all I wanted to do was swear. *You bastard!* I muttered in my head as the second strike hit me. One boy swore out loud and received an extra strike for his defiance. Thank god I'd kept my mouth shut. Strangely, later in life when I read about how Royal Navy seamen in Lord Nelson's time would receive so many lashes as punishment, I felt I could relate to it on a small scale.

At last the waiting game was over. The headmaster's door opened and I was summoned in to this room of deadly silence, so quiet I could have heard a pin drop. The feeling was akin to entering a graveyard at night on my own when I really didn't want to, though I could see daylight was bursting through the window. I took a few steps to enter his domain and realised the moment was too important to feel intimidated. So I spoke up, laying down my case as to why I should be allowed to study Applied Maths. It took the headmaster a fraction of a second to refuse my request; I was to continue with British Constitution (politics). As I left his office, in my head I had already left the school. It felt as if there was nothing there for me. I soon learned the art of forging my father's signature for sick notes and I was rather good at it, in conjunction with using his typewriter. I worked out how to beat the school system by turning up at the lunch time registration and apologising for being late for the morning one, and as soon as I was ticked off

I turned around and walked right back out of the school gates.

This was the first time I had thought about predictable patterns and the fact they highlight weaknesses in a person or a system. This would come into play later in life. Those first signs of being strong-willed were emerging and I was changing from a boy to someone who was capable of standing on his own two feet. The school had no interest in me so I would show I had no interest in the school. It was a foolish mistake, but at the time it felt right.

I wasn't an idle child who sat at home doing nothing and feeling the world owed me; instead I was working in a self-service restaurant in DH Evans, a department store in Oxford Street. More out of curiosity, I enquired how to do each person's job in the restaurant, including the supervisor's, intrigued by how he knew how much food to order. This soon came to the attention of the restaurant manager and I found myself at the age of sixteen overseeing the restaurant when the supervisor was on holiday. The restaurant staff were good and accepted my instructions, probably because they saw I worked hard and covered them for breaks without taking any breaks for myself. This was during the time when the IRA was planting bombs in London: Chelsea Barracks, Knightsbridge, Oxford Street, and the Post Office Tower - all the places along my bus route and around my work place. When a bomb goes off the noise travels, and I remember hearing three detonate on different days. It never took long for information to trickle through as to what has taken place, and hence the staff at DH Evans were told to be more vigilant. This seemed to have paid off as, one day, a suitcase was spotted having been left in our restaurant. Everyone was nervous, including the manager, and rather than clear the restaurant for safety I was tasked with taking the suitcase to lost property two floors below. My guess is that, as a young boy, I was more likely to obey such an order as opposed to an adult. I carried the suitcase as if it contained the most fragile china that existed, eventually arriving at lost property and explaining this item had been left in the self-service restaurant. I could see the concerned looks on their faces, their brows rising, their eyes opening wide. They refused to accept the suitcase and instead sent me back to the restaurant with it. Having been delighted that I'd made it to the lost property office I was now backtracking, walking so slowly as if I were at a funeral, and trying to keep calm and control my breathing. On arriving back at the restaurant the owner of the suitcase appeared and, as it turned out, it belonged to a nun. There were smiles all around, starting with the manager and the rest of the staff, but it stopped at me. I was still feeling slightly peeved that I'd been sent off with the suitcase, which everyone had thought was a bomb.

I had applied to join the Royal Marines at the career's office in Holborn and was on their books waiting for a vacancy to arise. It was at this time that something happened which nearly curtailed my dream of joining them. I was with some friends - kids with nothing to do but roam the streets in Chelsea's World's End - when we came across a smashed up moped in a derelict street. As kids do, we picked it up and found that the pedals worked, so we took turns to peddle it, all the while laughing and fooling around. No sooner had I sat on this broken moped, a police car came around the corner and the other kids ran off. Within minutes I found myself being driven to Chelsea police station to give a statement.

I was about to learn an important lesson in trust, which would stand me in good stead for the future, and in later life I would learn to be more selective but, alas, lessons have to be learned somewhere. At the station the police sergeant informed me he would write the statement on my behalf as he didn't want any spelling mistakes. After verbally giving my statement I was asked to sign it, and I pointed out that I couldn't read his writing, whereupon, in an aggressive voice, he told me it only said what I had told him. So I signed it only to find out later, much to my shock, that he had altered a few of the things I'd told him. I'd been brought up to believe the one person you could trust was a policeman. This lesson in trust was to see me attend the Crown Court in Knightsbridge.

It transpired that the moped had been stolen and my father, a former colonial police inspector, had taken in all the facts and decided to support me by employing a barrister to defend me. In court, in front of a jury and sat next to my jailer, it was pointed out that the night the moped was stolen I'd been playing a table tennis final at Fulham Town Hall, which was verified. It was also pointed out that my only previous time in a police station was when I'd walked in of my own accord at aged fourteen, after traipsing three miles to find the place, to hand in a purse I'd found that contained fifty pounds, which was recorded in the police records. Sadly, after the jury went out twice to deliberate because they were unable to reach a decision the first time, they found me guilty of being on the moped without the owner's consent. I'll never understand why pictures of this wrecked moped were not shown to the jury to enable them to understand why we thought it had been dumped. They would have seen half the number plate was missing and all the wires had been pulled out, as well as a smashed headlamp. The judge, to his credit, turned to the jury.

"You find this young man guilty, yet his only previous time in a police station was to hand in a purse, which shows his good character." At this point the majority of the jury stared at the floor. "I am somewhat surprised," he continued, "but, nevertheless, I have to accept your decision." My barrister pointed out I was in the process of joining the Royal Marines and a police record would prevent it. The judge smiled at me and replied, "Royal Marines and outstanding military service with a long and proud history; I wish you well in that profession," whereupon I was found guilty with forty pounds costs, but with no criminal record to be kept.

I felt I had let my parents down and yet I also knew I'd done nothing wrong. Not only had the policeman twisted the statement to suggest I knew the moped had been stolen, he had also told the owner where I lived. My father had the drunken owner turn up one night who admitted he'd seen the culprits steal his moped and confirmed I was not one of them. My father commented on how disappointing it was to see the police being unprofessional and giving away confidential information.

Life is a never-ending learning curve and I was starting to learn the hard way that trust is a rare quality and one must tread very carefully, yet I would still be knocked for six at various times in my life when dropping my guard.

My parents moved to Rustington in West Sussex having purchased their first home, with me and my brothers helping to contribute to the deposit. I was now one of the many commuters travelling to London on the Brighton line. It's a strange life, spending four hours a day travelling back and forth. The trains were more like cattle trucks, as people were herded on, and there were never enough seats so many people had to stand. I was fortunate as I boarded the train either at the beginning of its journey or at the second station, so most of the time I could travel in comfort. I would always try and fall asleep so the journey would go quicker and not drag out. At times I found myself in embarrassing situations, once falling asleep and waking up to realise my head was on a woman's shoulder. I removed it, still pretending to be asleep, not wanting to open my eyes for fear of the humiliation. I suppose, at being only seventeen, I got away with it.

Often I would finish work and dash off to play my table tennis league match, and the clock would be ticking as I raced off afterwards to catch the last train home. For a young person who looked a couple of years younger than he was, the train stations at night were not a safe environment. Men would beckon me over to sit next to them and talk with them. No one had to tell me the dangers because I would feel them and then apply common sense: stay close to a crowd of people and not go into an empty train carriage. These attributes I found within me would surface again later in life.

Some nights I failed to catch the last train home and could only catch a train to East Worthing, leaving me six miles short. I would run those six miles home, occasionally being stopped by the police who only saw a person running with a bag. "Are you the lad who plays table tennis in London?" they would say, and when I said "yes" they would just drive off. I didn't realise at the time that all this running, whether trying to get back home or sprinting to catch the train, would eventually help me.

One particular night at about 1:00 a.m. while running back from East

Worthing, I noticed a car trailing me. Each time I looked at the car the driver would put his main beam on and blind me, then drive past only to return again moments later. Each time I spotted the car returning I would dive and hide behind some bushes, my heart pounding, my fists clenched, and my eyes large. I sensed danger and felt vulnerable on this dark, open road with nothing but empty fields on either side of me. Once the vehicle had passed I would start to run again. This cat and mouse game lasted for over five miles, and the relief I felt when I reached my front door confirmed how intense this encounter had been for me. I told my parents about it and they informed the police about the incident but we heard nothing back. How close I had come to being a statistic I will never know.

In 1976, a heat wave had the whole of the UK in its grip. Everywhere was parched, like a tinderbox. During this period I changed jobs as it made no sense to see most of my salary go on train fares; as far as I was concerned it was a temporary thing as my goal was still to join the Royal Marines. I took a job in a factory washing pots and pans, nothing glamorous, but I had saved four hours of travelling a day and had more money in my hand.

One day I was at home when my brothers, who were both serving in the Royal Marines, arrived.

"Andrew," Ken said. "There's a skydiving school four miles down the road. We're off to do a jump. Do you want to come and watch?"

Both my brothers at the time were part of the Royal Marines Free Fall Parachute Display Team. My answer was no, I was watching the football. Before I knew it they had dragged me into their car, which felt like a well organised abduction. As I arrived at Ford airfield, a throwback from World War Two, I took in my surroundings. There was a small hangar, a six-berth caravan, a Cessna 180, tarmac runways, and an orange wind sock that wasn't moving.

Like any teenager who doesn't get his own way, I paced up and down, totally unimpressed. I told my brothers how good that football match was and how much I'd been enjoying it, but it fell on deaf ears.

It wasn't long before they were in the aircraft and climbing to seven thousand feet. It was a perfect blue-sky day as I watched them exit and free fall down before opening their parachutes. Something within me sparked and I strolled over to Bob Swainson, the chief instructor. I asked how long I would have to wait if I wanted to do a parachute course and, to be honest, if Bob's reply had been three or four weeks I would have walked away. As a typical teenager I had little patience. Instead he said, "Turn up next Saturday and you're on the course." That got my attention and I felt a frisson of excitement run through my body. This upcoming adventure ticked more than one box for me - it would answer a question I had often asked myself: Could I step outside of my comfort zone? If I could, it would show my brothers that I, too, could challenge myself and succeed.

Once my brothers and I were at home I called my close friend, Neil Harrison from Chelsea, and informed him I knew what we'd be doing the following weekend. "We're doing a parachute jump," I said, ready for the onslaught of comments. Instead, Neil replied, "Okay." We had made a commitment and I liked this feeling of adventure that made my heart pound.

The following Friday Neil arrived with his girlfriend, Diane Fenner, who I'd actually known longer than I'd known Neil, as we both attended the same year at Park Walk primary. Even at nine years of age girls were catching my eye and I had thought Diane the prettiest girl at the school.

On the morning of 24th September 1976 we arrived at the airfield on another blue-sky day, the heat wave continuing having started in April. Everywhere the ground was parched and hose pipe bans were in place. It hadn't occurred to me this would mean not only the tarmac runways, but the ground was going to be rock hard. The number of students on the parachute course only amounted to ten, and we all seemed to be feeling the same, experiencing equal amounts of excitement and apprehension. The course was conducted in a small hangar with aircraft parts and mechanical things strewn around. There were no Power Point presentations in those days, there wasn't even a whiteboard, but it made no difference as we knew no better. Bob was very enthusiastic in his instructing and Kevin, his colleague, a little quieter. Whenever the question was asked by either of them, "Do you understand?" we all nodded, not wanting to be the one to admit that we weren't entirely sure we'd grasped everything.

When I reflect back to 1976 the scene resembles something from the 1920s, where there was little regulation and control in comparison to how skydiving courses are conducted today.

At the end of the day our parachute course was finished, and all the jumping around and rolling over was done and dusted. It all seemed pretty exciting but the reality of what I was embarking on didn't sink in. Why would it feel any different up there than on the ground? Clearly, I hadn't processed the enormity of it.

There wouldn't be enough time for everyone on the course to jump that evening as darkness was descending. Names were scrawled on a piece of paper for the first aircraft load to be drawn. We all eagerly waited for the names to be read out - no one wanted to have to wait overnight. It was a relief when my name was called; I didn't understand then the mind games I would have to put myself through in the aeroplane. Another name was called but it wasn't Neil, and I felt for him. But then there was a 'eureka' moment as the instructor read out his name. We would, after all, share this unique experience together, and nobody could have wiped the smiles from our faces.

There's a sudden jolt that brings my senses back to where I am, right now.

The jumpmaster is moving around, not that there is much space as we're all squashed in. The aircraft is still climbing as I find myself staring out of that gaping hole again at the coast below me. The aircraft turns and Arundel Castle comes into view. On another day, and not in the position I find myself in now, I would have remarked at how beautiful it looks, but words and beauty are the furthest things from my mind.

We're passing through one thousand feet and the jumpmaster informs us we're half way there. In my head I hear a voice shouting, *Is he kidding?*

Half way? I realise some serious thought needs to be had here as I ponder my situation. I'm not liking this height and the sense of that drop past the edge of the door. *It's not a big thing if I don't jump,* I tell myself, *I can just laugh it off.* But then I look over my shoulder to assess where the jumpmaster is in case we have to come to an understanding, and notice the person to jump after me is a girl and, oh my god, this changes things.

Time is running out as we're approaching our run in height of two thousand feet, and my brain accelerates, evaluating my predicament. I visualise the instructor moving me back and the girl taking my place. I see her jump in my mind's eye. It feels awful. Horrendous. God … the embarrassment and shame I'd feel if she were to succeed after I had backed out. People may say there would be no shame, and for anyone else in a similar position they'd be right. But not for me. For me it would be mortifying. I'm aware that the voice in my head telling me I have no choice but to jump is nothing but my ego talking. Another voice tells me I'm doomed. "It was nice knowing you, in the brief eighteen years you've been around," it says.

I feel the aircraft turn sharply and level off, and there is a loud shout, "Cut!" The pilot starts to throttle back, reducing the speed of the aircraft. Suffice to say, my senses are in turbo-mode, and in my chest cavity my heart thumps so hard I swear I can hear it. I could glance over my shoulder and smile at Neil, pretend to look cool, but I know my face will look far from it so I remain facing forward. That dreaded voice comes again from the jumpmaster. "Out you get!" To add to this madness I can't just jump, but I have to climb outside the plane and hang onto the strut with my foot on the step. I turn to that gaping hole that has been taunting me on the journey up and, with my right hand against the back of the door frame, I focus on the step and not what's beyond as I place my left foot on it. The slip stream tries to blow my foot off the step as my left hand reaches for the strut. *For God's sake, don't slip now!* I tell myself. It's an effort to push against the slipstream that's coming through at sixty-five knots. I tell myself to breathe, to get a lungful of air, when a voice in my head screams, *Forget breathing… just make sure you grab that bloody strut!* Before I know it, both hands are holding on and my right foot is trailing.

I'm in position and my last action is to look at the jumpmaster who screams, "Go!" *Was that go or no?* I think, faltering; wishful thinking on my behalf. My eyes stare ahead. So, is this to be my kismet? Let no one ever say I bottled it.

With a deep intake of air combined with the energy charge that has built up within me, I channel it for an aggressive push off, throwing my body into a stable spread position as my hands leave the strut. I snap into the moment instantly, screaming the safety count out that actually helps to release the tension I've been feeling. "One thousand, two thousand, three thousand, four thousand, check canopy." I feel myself being pulled upright, above me the C9 round parachute is blossoming, and there is no noise but peace all around me. There's a huge smile on my face, I just can't believe how wonderful it felt, and is still feeling, as I'm floating down.

I reach up and grab my steering toggles and start to steer the parachute. The art of going with the wind, facing into the wind, and judging how far I've travelled across the ground seems like maths, and I adapt to it very quickly. The ground is approaching and I check the windsock, ensuring I have the parachute facing into the wind, resulting in a slow speed across the ground. My feet and knees are together and then make contact with the ground as I complete my parachute roll.

There's no hiding my euphoria. So many emotions course through me that I can't stop grinning. It was so intense, my head is close to bursting with the sheer amount of thoughts racing through it, and my senses are in overdrive. I'm buzzing. I'm feeling so alive.

I watch Neil as he floats down and lands, and soon we're both walking back together, talking, beaming, desperate to do it again. That evening in the pub we're both still buzzing and I can't wait for the morning to come.

I've learned something about myself today; something has triggered inside of me. This stepping outside of my comfort zone, this adrenalin adventure, has my inner spirit screaming, "This is me! Don't lock me away!" I like how I feel and we – my inner spirit and I - are going to be good friends.

I just know it. Mentally, I've been pushed. Challenged. The adrenalin that surged through me when I left the aeroplane - when I let go - brought about a sense of excitement, of freedom, that allowed the 'real me' to emerge. I know there's no going back from this, and I promise myself that when I'm old there will be no regrets. I will look back at my adventures, at my life, and I'll smile.

The 1976 heat wave marches on and for this up-and-coming skydiver it's a blessing. Each weekend a blue sky hangs over the drop zone. It's not long before I'm cleared for free fall with a three second delay which means, unlike the times before, I will be deploying my own parachute. There will be no static line – the safety net that I've grown to love, to rely on, and to trust. I'm over the moon with excitement but at the same time I know when I leave the aircraft and have to pull the ripcord myself there will only be two outcomes: life or death. If I fail, I'll be walking towards the bright light to see the person waiting to sign me in. There will be no appeal; no second chances. He'll be well rehearsed, I'm certain of it. "Shit happens; move on." I know what's at stake and I'm nervous. More than nervous. I tell myself not to dwell on what may not happen, but to concentrate on the job in hand and focus on my drills, my free fall position, and nothing else.

As I go up for my free fall jump, that cocktail of excitement and apprehension is overflowing and, strangely enough, I feel that I need it. Something is sparking within me. I have no doubt if I have to find the strength of Hercules, that ripcord will be pulled. I am not going to die.

The time has come and I walk out to the aircraft with two other students who will be doing a static line jump. I feel slightly undressed, something is missing, and I realise it's because I'm not holding onto a static line. I'm envious of the other two students … they only have to have one thought and that is to jump, whereas I have to remember to pull. I will be the last student to jump and I'm pushed back into the corner of the aeroplane.

Once the other students have jumped the plane climbs up to two thousand eight hundred feet, giving me a little more height. At this moment in time my thoughts are mine and no one else's. No other voices are permitted to enter my head. This is now a dictatorship, the decision has been made, and I'm in charge of my own mind games.

The command at the door is bellowed out and, without hesitation, I move myself into position. The word "Go" echoes in my head. That voice wasn't asking, it was demanding, so I launch myself into the world below, screaming my count. One thousand: I arch hard and spread my legs and arms. Two thousand: I manoeuvre my arms, grasping the ripcord which my eyes have locked onto. Three thousand: I pull the ripcord. It doesn't move. The hand above my head follows down and, with two hands on the ripcord, I give another tug, this time with success. I'm elated as I find myself under a fully inflated parachute.

The day's skydiving is over and Neil and I head to the local village, Yapton, to have a celebration T-bone steak meal and a beer. Dancing Queen by Abba is playing on the juke box, cigarette smoke is drifting around the room, and there's much laughter as the day's activities are recounted. I feel content; pleased with myself that I had the bottle to go free fall.

At the factory I'm working in at Brighton, the secretary of the social club pays me a visit while I'm washing pots and pans. It transpires that he used to parachute and he shows me a picture of himself under a Para Commander parachute. We chat for ten minutes or so and, just before he leaves, he shows me a lapel badge. I ask him what it is.

"Gold Wings," he says, "for a thousand jumps. Something you will never have."

I don't dispute it.

In time, I qualify for Category 8. I'm no longer classed as a student parachutist but as an experienced skydiver. The reality is different as all Cat 8 means is that I can fall through the air and open the parachute safely, but the advantage is that I can now jump a high performance parachute, the Para Commander. I inform my brothers. Pete tells me there's a Para Commander in our parents' loft, and Ken adds that he has a front mounted reserve up there, too. The thought of having my own parachute feels like I've won the pools and I can't climb the ladder quick enough to check it out. Tomorrow I'm off to Ashford with Neil and a couple of others to jump, so I'm excited when I find what I'm looking for.

The car follows the road, twisting and turning its way to the new drop zone, and soon we're in the plane and climbing to seven thousand feet. I'm no longer scared of the height; the landscape just looks like a painting below me. To my joy, I jump the Para Commander and am thrilled with how much more responsive it is compared to the student C9 parachutes. I can't wait to tell my brothers and as soon as I'm through my parents' front door I'm on the phone to Pete. He mentions something about repacking the parachute. I find this confusing and point out to him that the parachute was already packed. Only now do I find out that reserve parachutes should be repacked every four months, and the main parachute repacked virtually every week, subject to weather conditions. Both the parachutes I'd used, which had been sitting in the attic, hadn't been touched for eighteen months.

My parents are visiting my brothers at Dunkeswell and I decide to tag along to see a new drop zone. As I climb out of the car Pete calls out to me.

"Andrew, get your kit on, we're on the next aircraft load."

I wasn't expecting to jump but I call back, "Does anyone need to see my documents?"

"No, just get yourself ready."

The girls complain about why I'm allowed to have so much hair hanging outside my helmet when they can't. Soon, I'm in the Cessna 185 and climbing to ten thousand feet - a height I have never been to before.

"What am I doing?" I ask Pete.

"Just jump out, get stable, and we'll come and get you," he says.

Before I know it I'm hanging outside the plane and I hear Ken shout, "Give him room," as I depart. It's a wonderful sight to see someone in free fall and flying towards me. Pete grabs hold of me and, the next thing I know, Ken is docking onto us. I didn't even see him coming. Here we are, three brothers linked in free fall - a first for the UK. Mike Oulton, an Irish friend of my brother's, also docks on us before Bob Scoular, a member of the Royal Marines Free Fall Parachute Display Team that my brothers are a part of, hits us like skittles and sends us flying. I don't care – I'm buzzing, and my huge grin tells the story of how much I'm enjoying it.

Back on the ground my mother comments that it's the first time she has had all three sons in the air at the same time. The point is missed and I fail to understand what it meant for her emotionally. It'll be a while before I finally comprehend the magnitude of it.

A few days later, a long-awaited letter drops onto the doormat. I've been accepted by the Royal Marines and have a date to roll up at the Commando Training Centre at Lympstone in Devon. Another adventure is about to start, to challenge me both physically and mentally. I'm to be the fourth in my family to join them.

THE PATH WE CHOOSE

It's taken fifteen months to reach the beginning of this new path I have chosen to take, the one which leads me to the Royal Marines. I visualise a smiling drill instructor, waiting to greet me with an embrace as he welcomes me. I take comfort in thinking like this, as opposed to picturing a scary man who rubs his hands as he bellows, "Welcome to hell! You're all mine!"

The time has come and my parents take me to Angmering railway station. The platform isn't too busy, it's only a small station, and I hear a few people chatting quietly and the occasional sound of a passing car. My friends from London, Neil and Diane, have come to see me off. I'm aware that my life is changing and that something is drawing me to this, but I'm not sure whether it's just a desire to be considered an equal to my brothers or a yearning to discover who I am. One thing is for certain: I have no idea of the challenges I'll face, both physically and mentally, in order to become a Royal Marine Commando, but that word, 'Challenge' holds a certain appeal to me.

The train arrives and before I know it I'm on my way, sitting in a half-empty carriage and feeling very alone. The countryside flashes past me in a blur of images as the vibration of the train lulls me, quieting my thoughts. I have to change trains at Portsmouth, Salisbury, then Exeter, before I arrive at Lympstone Commando Station, next to the River Exe.

The Devon fields spread out beyond the river and the sun is high in the sky when I step off the train. It's a beautiful day. There's excitement in the air, right up to the moment when I see a Royal Marine with a clipboard under his arm who is staring straight at me. It's clear he's not smiling. He asks for my name and I tell him, "Andrew Guest."

"It's Andrew Guest, Corporal," he replies, his voice chilling me as he escorts me through the gates. I question what I have let myself in for.

Throughout the day more individuals arrive looking like young lost sheep, not sure if they have arrived at the slaughter house. But one thing is for sure - we're in this together, and we soon introduce ourselves.

The following day we line up at the barber's on the camp. As soon as I sit in the chair I'm asked how I would like my hair to be cut but I realise my reply is pointless as the barber retrieves the No. 1 shears and shaves it off. There's no doubt about it, I think, as I stare at my reflection in the mirror; I am now in the Marines.

We're marched from place to place, collecting stores. Back at the accommodation we have to strip naked and are shown how to shower, iron, and pack our clothes, including our underpants, to the size of the Royal Marines' magazine, the *Globe & Laurel.* They also give us long johns, or passion killers, as we instantly name them. Who the hell would want to undress in front of a girl wearing those? The drill instructor hammers home the importance of personal hygiene, cleanliness, and keeping on top of everything. Our troop 106 photograph is taken, showing we're sixty-five strong. I don't know it yet but this photograph will be on the inside of my locker door, and in time it will motivate me. At the end of each week, as individuals drop out of the Royal Marines training, a black marker pen will colour the faces out of those who have quit.

The first three weeks is a transition period from being a civilian to being military, and there's a lot to learn.

I'm looking forward to our first night on Woodbury Common which, I imagine, will be nothing more than a camping trip, until I see the crude tent we've been issued. After an introduction on how to put up a bivvy we move on to cooking and are shown a twenty-four-hour ration pack. I'm given chicken curry and chocolate sponge pudding and feel as if I've hit the jackpot. There's a quietness in the woods. Rays of sunshine burst through the branches, and the smoke from my cooker drifts straight up as the wind is sleeping today. I'm chosen to demonstrate how to cook, with one of the instructors talking me through it. All is looking good as I see my chicken curry bubbling away. I inhale the spices, the aroma taking me back to my childhood days and enticing me. My stomach rumbles as I anticipate how great it's going to taste, but then the spell is broken.

"Guest, add your pudding to the curry."

I hesitate.

"All food goes down the same way - down your throat. Time is of the essence. You'll never know how much time you'll have, so put everything into the same pot."

So, my chocolate pudding is added. Much later, there will be times when I'm so hungry that I really won't care. It's just food after all.

It's not long before we're back on Woodbury Common doing another exercise. We patrol to a hill and are told to dig in and, eight hours later, working in pairs, we're still digging. This trench will be our home for the next three days. Half the trench is covered and camouflaged as a shelter. At night, one person stays guard while the other tries to sleep, but we're not allowed to use sleeping bags. The nights are cold and the skies are clear and at any other time I would be in awe of it, but when the only warm part of my body is my balls and I can't stop shivering, I really don't care about how pretty the night sky looks. The webbing behind me is white and stiff due to the frost on the ground. I can't believe how cold I am and my body continues to shake, my teeth chattering. I struggle to do star jumps to warm up. Time seems to slow down as if the second hand is being dragged backwards. I long to see sunrise, knowing it will warm up the temperature somewhat.

On the second night I hear a voice shouting, "Help me, help me." It's clear one of the guys on sentry duty has fallen asleep and has been dragged out by the training team. I'm all too aware that one of the training instructors is approaching me.

"Guest, what do you hear?" he asks me.

"It appears, Corporal, that the enemy has captured one of our men and he's somewhere over there in the darkness," I reply.

"So what are you going to do about it?" he asks.

"Nothing, Corporal. It's better to lose one man than more," I tell him.

"Guest, you heartless bastard," he replies, then all I hear is footsteps crunching in the frosty ground, fading away in the darkness.

The days pass, and we enter the phase between weeks four and ten of learning elementary military skills in a progressive manner. Personal admin and hygiene continues to be hammered home. The training team are hot on this, with numerous crash inspections being carried out and punishment being issued for failing in the form of press-ups and sit-ups. The physical training is ongoing, the PTIs exhausting us in what they call 'warming you up' before training us hard, hence the term *beasting* is often used.

Between weeks eleven and fifteen we consolidate the skills we have learned and progress onto more advanced aspects of military training. We're introduced to live grenade throwing, and the idea of it sounds great; I recall the war films I've watched that show the hero tossing grenades as he charges forward. The reality is different and, as I insert the detonator, the knowledge that this grenade is now extremely fragile settles within me. I find myself constantly checking the safety pin each time I move.

One of the guys steps forward to throw his grenade, and we hear a bit of a commotion and see the training instructor drag him back around the corner before there's a large explosion that impacts on our eyes. It takes us all by surprise. "Fucking hell," someone shouts. My heart races and I check my safety pin once again. Judging by the expressions on some of the guys' faces, I can't help but think they have, perhaps, encountered another surprise in their underpants. When someone's comment mimics my own thoughts it causes everyone to chuckle, except the training instructor, who gives verbal abuse to the individual involved.

I'm soon called forward to throw my grenade and as soon as I do so my survival instinct kicks in. I immediately duck into the trench, whereupon the training instructor pulls me up by the collar. I'm nearly peeing my pants when he tells me I need to watch to see where it lands. I swear blind that I did - I would swear to anything right now to be honest - and we both duck together before the grenade explodes.

A few days later we're introduced to chemical warfare and taken into the gas chamber wearing our gas masks. We observe the instructor setting off the CS gas and watch as the vapours rise. The small room is cramped and my vision through the mask is restricted. I can feel my heart racing, thumping in my chest, and tell myself to slow it down. One at a time we're asked to remove our mask and to state our name and military service number. Having seen the effects the gas had on the first person, it's clear that this was never going to appear on my bucket list. As soon as I remove my mask my eyes are hit with the CS gas and immediately start to sting. Tears stream down my cheeks as I try to rush my sentence, only for the instructor to tell me to repeat it. I only manage to state my name when my throat starts to burn and the coughing begins. At this point I'm allowed out into the fresh air. It's a horrendous experience and, twenty minutes later, after stupidly touching my clothes and then my face, inadvertently rubbing the gas into my pores, I have a rather nasty reaction.

The weeks seem to pass quickly, and at the end of each one it is now routine to take my marker pen and colour out the faces on the group photograph as more individuals drop out. I don't feel any sadness when they leave; they made their choice, they lost their mind-game battle. And it *is* a mind-game battle at times, where I have to dig deep to focus to stay on track. I get a feel-good factor seeing all the faces disappear, knowing I'm still here. It inspires me to want to be here at the end.

Another week passes by with more physical training thrown at us. It's not something I look forward to as I often hear the words 'no pain, no gain' but I'm conditioned to it now and just take each day as it comes. There's still a feeling of dread when I encounter new things, or repeat things I dislike, but an aggressive attitude is growing inside of me and it shouts, "Let's get this bastard over with."

There is something different about today as we head off to the gym, because boxing has come up on the agenda and we're to have an internal troop boxing match. We're paired off by weight and there are three of us in the featherweight category: myself, George Mathieson - an ex Royal Navy guy who transferred to the Royal Marines - and Carl Thomas. I watch George and Carl box and, clearly, George is too strong for Carl and wins the fight. George approaches me and prods me in the chest.

"I'm going to kill you!" he yells.

I turn to the guy next to me and say, "He's taking this a bit too seriously." The guy just laughs.

Half a dozen fights later, I'm called up to face George. I'm not a boxer and have no interest in fighting; I'm a peaceful guy. I have two choices: take a beating, or show what a Royal Marine is all about and fight. I know that's what the training team is looking for. I quickly conclude my best option is to go on the offensive and throw as many punches as I can for each of the three, three minute rounds.

The bell rings and George and I launch into our attacks. It appears that George has the same idea as me but is taken by surprise. I have no style at all; I resemble a windmill swinging boxing gloves as I try to rain in as many punches as I can so he can't see his target. At the end of the three rounds I'm declared the winner, and George is sent to sick bay for some ice packs, but not before we're both congratulated and praised by the training team for getting stuck in. I'm just happy to have survived the encounter.

My reward for winning is being put forward for the inter Commando Training Centre boxing matches against other boxers who, I think, are probably not boxers at all but individuals like me who have been pushed into it. I win two more fights only to discover I advance to the inter Commando Unit Boxing Championships. I now see the predictable pattern: If I win the fight I'll get another one, if I lose the fight there'll be no more. As tempting as it sounds, the idea of throwing the fight doesn't enter my head as my competitive streak, which emerged and intensified in table tennis, wants to compete to the best of my ability.

The next fights have me concerned as I'm now up against trained Royal Marine Commandos, and I fear there will be only one outcome. I'm just wondering how much damage is going to be done to me. My style hasn't changed at all and any tips are wasted on me. As soon as the bell rings I just move into survival mode and start swinging. I'm up against an individual from 40 Commando who tells me he's going to beat me and, funnily enough, I believe him. All I have to do is lose and this journey will be over. But this 'windmill swinging the leather gloves' re-emerges and, to my surprise, I'm declared the winner. The same is repeated on my next fight, and people congratulate me as I reach the final of the Royal Marines Boxing Championships. I'm in disbelief and not exactly overjoyed, as this means yet another fight. I'm sent to sick bay to have ice packs put on my face to get the swelling down so I'll be more presentable on the big night in two days' time. I chat to my mother on the phone and update her as to how the boxing is going. She asks me if I'm enjoying it.

"Mum," I tell her, "being punched in the face is not what I'd call an enjoyable experience."

My troop sergeant is concerned about me, worried that any injuries I sustain could affect my training, and he asks me if I still want to go ahead. I tell him, honestly, that I have no interest in boxing but if I have to then I'll give it my best effort. He disappears and returns later to tell me he has had a word with the Commanding Officer of the Commando Training Centre. The CO's decision is that I will box and represent the unit.

On the day of the championships I find myself alone in my room, posing in front of the mirror. *All these fights I have won*, I say to myself. *Do I have some sort of natural talent that I'm not aware of?*

I'm about to have that question answered as before long I'm standing in the ring, and it certainly looks like a big occasion. On one side of the ring all the officers are in their first dress uniforms with their wives and girlfriends alongside them, and the other three sides are full to the brim. There's an atmosphere as the noise of people chatting booms around the gym. It's not really any different from the days the Romans built amphitheatres to entertain the crowds with a battle, I think. At least this is not 'to the death'. Well, I bloody well hope not, I tell myself.

My opponent is opposite me, staring me down. I'm not fazed as I've been in this situation before, and I've decided to stick to the same tactics that have seen me through to this final. The bell sounds and I'm off, straight at him. I start raining down the punches and he covers up and backs into the corner. The crowd cheer as punch after punch lands on his defensive wall, and there's a sense that all is going to plan. Sweat is already pouring off me under the bright lights, and my lungs suck in air as fast as they can when, suddenly, he side steps me and with one punch I'm sent cart wheeling backwards. I hit the canvas, the moment a blur. This has taken me by surprise. I quickly jump to my feet, telling myself I must have slipped and lost my balance. The referee checks me over and I'm cleared to continue to fight. *Right then, let's be showing him,* I tell myself, as I go on the offensive again, gritting my teeth and swinging punch after punch, forcing him to back up to the corner again and cover up. I'm feeling good, feeling in control, when boom! My head is thrown back and my body slams into the canvas for the second time with a bang.

It's all too clear that he can box, and the thought I'm in deep shit enters my head. When our eyes meet he's looking very pissed off with me.

I'm still in the first round and hit the canvas for the third time. *What the hell has he got in those gloves?* I ask myself. I'm thinking horse shoes. I'm on my feet but the referee continues to count me out, and my boxing match is over. I should feel disappointed, heartbroken, but I don't. I'm just surprised that I reached the final in the first place. When I've been given my runner's up trophy I walk out of the arena knowing my boxing career has ended. The bright lights above the boxing ring fade away behind me, and I'm happy about that.

The following day I re-join my troop with two black eyes. The training team soften their approach for a few minutes to say 'good effort', and then we're back to normal.

"Guest, get your arse over here and give me twenty press-ups."

It's good to be back with the troop.

During weeks sixteen to twenty-five we seem to have one exercise after another as we learn operations and all transitional phases of war. I can't say I enjoy it as I'm constantly wet and cold and suffering from lack of sleep, but I understand that's the aim - to see if we can still function to achieve the objectives.

In one exercise, each section is given a live chicken to look after for three days. We're told to give it a name and look after it, to feed it and make sure it has access to water. We name her Sally and grow attached to her, and on the last day we're told we have to kill her and eat her. The lesson? Don't give your live food a name as it affects your appetite.

We start training for the Commando physical phase in week twenty-five and I have to do a load carry, which involves carrying a heavy water container on my back and marching for twelve miles. It's very uncomfortable to carry, and this task soon gives me blood blisters on the soles of my feet. This happens within the first four miles, which is not what I need. Unable to stride with the troop I'm reduced to running small steps to keep up. One of the training team asks me if I have blisters. "Yes, Corporal," I reply.

"Just keep up; don't drop behind," he says.

Eventually there are four others in the same situation as me. Once back at camp we're sent straight to the sick bay to have a medic insert a needle into the soles of our feet to withdraw the blood from the blisters.

We are soon introduced to the speed marches which involve running and fast walking, carrying 32lbs of weight, including a weapon. Everything is weighed to ensure we're carrying the correct weight and not cheating. After the first speed march I learn to tie down my webbing to prevent it from moving, as this had chafed my skin and caused painful sores around my waist and back. All those six mile runs I did when I used to miss my last train home in London are now paying off. Speed marches never trouble me and I'm thankful to have something I excel at.

In weeks twenty-six to thirty-one we move into the phase where the recruit is professionally prepared for life in an operational Royal Marine unit, is at a Commando level of fitness, and has the requisite qualities of determination, courage, unselfishness, professional skill, and cheerfulness under adversity.

The famous Royal Marines six mile Endurance Course on Woodbury Common is next on the agenda, and we're told to stay as a four man team until the last obstacle, whereupon we can run the last phase back to camp on our own. Each team is sent off at intervals and my heart thumps as I wait my turn. With a stop watch in his hand, one of the training team calls us forward. I have just enough time to check my webbing is on tight and my weapon is slung across my back when he shouts, "Go."

We're off, and all my thoughts are suppressed, my brain focussed now on the job in hand. We dive into the pitch black darkness of the first obstacle, the Double Tunnels, as quickly as we can, one after the other, scrambling forwards on our hands and knees. The pebbles are digging into me when my head hits a dead end. Clearly, I have to do a ninety degree turn in this tunnel, which I manage, and when daylight appears I note how much pain my knees are in.

We scramble down a steep incline, taking leaps to keep the momentum going. As I enter Peter's Pool, a small pond, I am reminded that it's October as my testicles beat a hasty retreat, my breath is shortened, and I see my exhaled air fading away across the water. I continue to wade through it, noticing it's getting deeper until it stops at my chin, which I lift as high as I can. While wading forward I hold my weapon up to keep it clean as it has to function at the end.

I'm soaking wet - my webbing, pouches and boots full of water, when I encounter a hill that zaps all my strength. It feels as if my lungs are about to burst, I can hear my laboured breaths in my ears, and my weight seems to have doubled as I push on. In my head all I see is the stopwatch ticking as my feet pound the track and I continue to suck in as much air as I can.

The scenery around me is a blur as another tunnel comes up but we are soon in and out, and the run continues under an overcast sky. I still drip water and gasp for breath while a voice inside my head screams, *Push harder!*

Further down the course we encounter the Sheep Dip. I jump in and duck under the water while someone pushes me into the tunnel as far as he can. At the other end, someone reaches in and grabs what little hair I have left to try and pull me out. The pain I can blank out - I really don't care as long as he gets me out of here - and there's relief when my lungs take a sharp intake of breath. The team completes the obstacle and I move off once again, trying to empty the water from the pouches on my webbing.

We encounter more tunnels, one called the Smartie Tube, which is a concrete tube full of gravel and mud and half-full with water. It's a tight squeeze. I'm the second person in, following my team mate, and I'm about to get an unpleasant surprise. He has been pushing the water forward like a bow wave and, at the other end when he stands up, a tidal wave flows back and completely submerges me. Alarm bells ring in my head as I know I'm trapped in the tunnel and under water. I can sense a slight panic as I hold my breath for what seems like an eternity but in reality is no more than a second or two before the water level drops and I continue my crawl through this claustrophobic environment.

With the last obstacle completed I'm now on my own. I open my legs and, during the downhill phase, extend my stride, pretending I'm running back from the railway station to my parents' house. I'm aware I've left the other three guys behind and this makes me feel good as I'm not going to be last. I enter Heartbreak Lane, the road is flat and deserted, my footsteps pound a beat and my shadow keeps me company. My lungs are on fire and the voice in my head yells, "Don't slow down!" I pass the sign in the tree that tells me there's only five hundred metres to go. The finishing line is close but, even so, it seems to take an eternity to get there and the pain worsens. Finally, I cross the finishing line at the main gate of the Commando Training Centre to be greeted by Sergeant Smith.

"Guest, you lazy bastard, where the hell have you been?" he screams at me.

"Running, Sergeant," I reply.

"You better sort out your act, Guest, and find some determination and push harder," he tells me.

I'm sucking in air, sweat is pouring off me, I'm wet, covered in mud and I'm not looking my finest. Sergeant Smith looks confused as he can't find my name on the list.

"Guest, where did you start?" he asks.

I take a deep breath. "Second team from the end, Sergeant."

Now realising I must have passed individuals in teams ahead of me, Smith finds my name on the list. "Bloody hell, Guest, I take back everything I said. Bloody good effort. Take the afternoon off."

The allocated time to complete the course is seventy-two minutes. Some guys have failed but I've completed it in sixty-three. Dave Alexander has beaten my time and there are less than sixty seconds separating us. It seems unfair, though, because Dave has to work this afternoon. However, I don't care as I'm escaping from the Commando Training Centre to head up to Dunkeswell Airfield to go skydiving, as I have done on all my days off.

All through training I'm tested both physically and in military skills and am only able to advance once the tests have been passed. I have another weekend pass and prepare everything in my locker: shirts and trousers are ironed, boots are polished, and I'm good to go. I race out of the camp as fast as I can to head to Dunkeswell again. It's a great weekend and a welcome break from the Royal Marines training.

On Monday morning we parade outside for an inspection and the training instructor, Corporal Scobie Brice, steps in front of me.

"Have you been skydiving, Guest?"

"Yes, Corporal," I reply.

"Well you shouldn't go skydiving if you can't turn up immaculate, Guest," he says.

I'm confused as to where this is going so I hit back with, "I don't understand, Corporal."

"Look at your boots."

I look down and see polished and gleaming boots, only for Corporal Brice to wipe his boots on mine. *This has to be a wind up*, I tell myself, whereupon I'm told to go around the corner to see the troop officer, Lieutenant Booth.

He tells me to sort myself out and focus on training and not skydiving, and that it's been reported that my skydiving equipment has just been thrown into my locker.

"Sir," I say, "if your life depended on your parachuting equipment, would you look after it or just throw it in the locker?" I know it doesn't matter what I say as this situation has been engineered. I am given galley (cook house) fatigues on the following weekend, and I'm gutted to miss out on two days' skydiving when my whole troop has been given the weekend off.

More weeks pass and we reach the Critical Phase towards the end of the Commando Phase. Individuals are getting nervous about picking up an injury and being back-trooped, where you re-join another troop that started training behind you. We have formed a bond as a troop, having gone through all the hardship of the training together, as well as dealing with the crap that has been thrown at us, and we all want to finish together. The Commando tests now come up thick and fast. All four tests have to be completed in five days, allowing some to retake a Commando test on the last two days of the week if they have failed.

The first Commando test comes on the Saturday: The Endurance Course. Dave Alexander and I are given a couple of individuals who failed the practice run, and we're told this time we must finish the test as a team. Our hearts sink. Dave and I were on a high, knowing we finished last time with nine minutes to spare. Now we have to get those that failed the practice through on the allocated time of seventy-two minutes.

Once our team start our focus is to encourage each other, all the time shouting, "Push, push." Finally, all the obstacles on Woodbury Common are completed and we hit the main road for the four mile run back to camp. I'm alarmed to see the slow guy wanting to stop to catch his breath. We shout at him, "Don't stop! Keep pushing!" I tell him to let the downhill take him and to extend his strides but he's struggling, so I take his weapon and carry it for him. Another guy grabs hold of him and keeps pushing him. At last we hit

Heartbreak Lane, and I shout encouragement. "This is it… the final bit. Give it your all, keep pushing, and focus fifty metres pass the finishing line." I'm concerned that some people, when they see the finishing line, will start to slow down, so I imply the finishing line is actually fifty metres further on. I give him back his weapon as I don't want the training team to see I've been carrying it, and I can see the pain in his face. We're all pouring sweat and digging deep to find that bit extra to carry us through. But it's running, and once again I thank all the times I missed the last train and had to run those six miles back home from West Worthing.

We cross the finishing line and hear a time of seventy minutes. We've done it, we're in time, but it's not over yet. All this work and it's now straight down to the firing range where we each have to hit the target six out of ten times. Fail this, and we fail the Endurance Course. I clean my weapon quickly, take a deep breath, hold it, squeeze the trigger, and repeat. All my team's aims are true, and we pass. With one Commando test now ticked off, I sense the relief. Dave Alexander's section passes, too.

Sunday is a day of rest and, having cleaned all our gear the day before, we carry out a few admin jobs. With laundry completed, everything ironed and put away, clothes, webbing, and boots checked in the drying room, and spare boots polished, the day is spent resting the body.

On Monday we're all dressed and ready for the second Commando test: the 9-Mile Speed March, to be completed in ninety minutes. It consists of a combination of fast marching and jogging, while wearing 32lbs of weight. I'm not concerned about this test but I'm aware that some of the bigger guys are. Half way through, I'm in the middle in the front line of three and it's going well; I'm feeling comfortable. Looking around, I can see others seem to be struggling and this has a knock-on effect in boosting my confidence. The training team try to encourage those who are finding it difficult in their own unique way: "Don't you fall back… I will have your arse, you little dip shit." Is there any greater thing than to see the finishing line at the end of a physical challenge? Heads rise up, a new surge of energy resurrects the body, and on crossing the line a voice shouts out, "Yes!" My second Commando test is ticked off, although some have failed.

It's Tuesday and we're all nervous as we have another test to pass. I'm carrying no injuries but I know there are a couple of obstacles where at times I've struggled and it plays on my mind. I'm at the Tarzan assault course, trying to relax and to control my breathing, as my nervousness is making me feel tired. *You can do this,* I tell myself.

The Tarzan course starts off with a high death slide, and how I hate climbing up that forty foot ladder, as my fear of heights sinks into my stomach. A small rope with a loop at either end is thrown over the line, and I place my hands into the loops before stepping off into the abyss from this too tall tower, carrying my 32lbs of equipment. The death slide is followed by a series of high rope crossings through the trees, using different techniques. I'm envious of the tall guys as I struggle at times to reach some of the ropes.

I complete the Tarzan course and sprint down to move on to the Bottom Field assault course. There is no let up, the clock is ticking and I'm gasping for breath, but there's no time to catch it as those dreaded obstacles are looming. "Get aggressive, get mad," the voice in my head shouts. I snap out of my negative thoughts and hit the obstacles with force; I have no wish to repeat this test. *Put the bloody thing to bed,* I tell myself. As I succeed in getting through each one, the voice in my head shouts, "Yes! You got that bastard out the way!"

At last the final obstacle is cleared and I have a short uphill run to the thirty foot wall. As tired as I am, I can feel my determination coming through. "You passed those bloody obstacles, don't fail now, push for all you've got," the voice demands, but nothing seems to be happening. I can't increase the pace as I'm already giving all I have. I reach the wall, which has to be climbed with all my equipment. Time is of the essence but there are no clocks on display to inform me how I'm doing. When I reach the top of the wall I jump down and hear no other sound other than the air filling my lungs. My eyes are glued to the mouth of the training instructor. I'm trying to catch my breath and hold my breath at the same time, and the sweat is running into my eyes, stinging them. Finally, the training instructor informs me of my time: ten minutes thirty-five seconds, which is under the thirteen minutes allocated. "Yes, you beauty!" I yell. I'm relieved, ecstatic, but now it's time to shout encouragement to those who are still running. My third Commando test is ticked off, I'm smiling, and I'm very, very happy.

My body is feeling bruised, sore and stiff, and the last Commando test is tomorrow morning. It's the one I dread the most. The thirty mile march across Dartmoor is a load carry, wearing 50lbs of equipment as well as other safety items. The fact that I suffered on a previous load carry that was only just over a third of this distance, which gave me the blood blisters, plays on my mind. The taller guys seem to find it easier - they're carrying twenty-five percent of their body weight whereas I'm carrying thirty-three percent, and I'm envious for a moment, but I can't let it linger. I need to be positive. This is the last Commando test and all negative thoughts are banned from my head. *I can almost touch the finishing line,* I tell myself. *It's going to hurt; I'm going to be in pain, but just focus on that finishing line and think of nothing else.* All that work, blood, and sweat, all the highs and lows for the last thirty-one weeks has brought me here, to this final challenge. I look around and can see the other guys in my troop are also deep in thought. No one is talking.

The time has come and we're told to line up as a troop with our Bergens on. I have an instant dislike of the weight of this rucksack on my shoulders but I'm pleased I'm carrying my SLR rifle and not the General Purpose Machine Gun (GPMG), which someone else has been given. In a loud voice the command, "Right turn" is issued by the training instructor. My heart rate shoots up as I know I'm in for a rough ride. This is a continuous march for the next eight hours over Dartmoor, where the landscape is undulating. I know I'm heading for pain. The order, "Quick march," is given and we're off. In some ways I'm pleased to start as I've had enough of thinking about this. I'm here now, at the climax of all my Royal Marine training. I've reached this phase of being able to undertake these physical Commando tests and I have passed three. This is it, the last one, and it feels like a positive. I cling onto that thought. I want this so badly and tell myself there is no such word as 'can't'. In my head I picture my brothers and my father, all Royal Marines, but that picture is not complete. I know I am the missing piece and I will not let them down.

It doesn't take long before I'm sweating. I'm in a rhythm, moving one leg in front of the other, my arms swinging, and my mind in neutral. Each step is one step closer to the finishing line, I tell myself, desperately trying to create positives that I can cling onto, as I'm sore from the webbing and tired of this relentless pace. The training team ensure we don't drop the pace as we only have eight hours to get this finished.

As the miles pass and the rolling hills come and go, everyone's faces tell a story, and I have no doubt mine is doing the same. A couple of the guys are struggling with the pace and are given verbal abuse to keep up. The GPMG is being shared around and soon I hear my name being called to swap my rifle for the GPMG. I'm not happy but I have no choice, and I immediately notice the extra weight. It's uncomfortable to carry and hangs over my neck, and I can sense the negatives in my head sneaking their way in which makes me angry, as I didn't give my permission for them to be there. A debate takes place in my mind, a stronger voice telling the negatives to piss off. I'm all too aware it's a slippery road if the negatives are allowed to get louder. The training team tell John Fraser to take the GPMG from me and it's music to my ears. I feel my spirits lift, and I'm only too happy to hand it over and take an SLR rifle in its place. Instantly, I notice how much lighter it is. It's not a massive amount of difference, just a few pounds, but it's a huge amount in my head and enough to make me feel buoyant.

We've only marched three hundred metres since I handed over the GPMG when John Fraser suddenly steps away from the troop and sits down on a rock. A training instructor instantly descends on him.

"What the fuck do you think you're doing, Fraser?"

"I quit," he says.

Some of us look on in disbelief at what he has done at this stage of training, though we're aware he was struggling to pass a couple of the other Commando tests, but even so. He used the word 'quit' and the conversation is over. He's told to get back into the Landrover and I feel sorry for him until

I hear, "Guest! Grab that GPMG." I cannot protest; I have to do as I'm told. I'm pissed off…very fucking pissed off with him, and the anger within me rises. *What a wanker*, I think, and my sympathy for him dissipates.

Fatigue had set in many miles back and I look around and glance at people's faces. Most are blank, their eyes just staring, while their bodies go through the motion of one foot in front of the other. Some are clearly in deep trouble, their stress apparent. I grab that picture as a positive. As tired and sore as I am, I tell myself the others look worse, though deep down I know it's a lie.

It's been a long march and as we come over the crest of a hill and see ahead of us, parked to one side, our two four-ton trucks, morale rockets up. "We've done it, lads!" someone says, but something isn't right and the voice of Ken, my brother, enters my head.

"The finishing line is not always what it seems," he'd told me.

We approach the vehicles and continue to march straight past them. Morale goes into free fall and heads drop. I can hear a few men moaning whilst it seems a couple have started to cry. So, Ken was telling the truth and this is a massive blow. I'm also feeling the gut-wrenching disappointment and I wonder just how many more miles are left to do. *It can't go on forever*, I tell myself. *Just keep going.*

We march eight hundred metres down the track and we're suddenly told to halt, about turn, and quick march. Confused as to what is going on due to the tiredness, I'm slow to pick up what has just happened, and then it hits me. That was the finishing line.

There's no sign of joy or happiness when I get there, just relief it's all over. When told to drop the Bergen I'm only too happy to do it and don't have to be told twice. It doesn't sink in what this means, I'm just so exhausted.

Once in the truck we head back to the Commando training centre and a voice pipes up.

"That's it, lads! We've just earned our Commando Green Beret."

I remember when I started this journey hearing that only one percent of people who apply to the careers office will complete their training, and I feel a sense of achievement; pride at what I've accomplished. No one speaks but there are smiles appearing on people's faces, including mine, and as our weary heads drop down the only noise is the rumble of the tyres on the road. The smell of exhaust fumes and the rocking motion of the truck send me to sleep.

We are now the King's Squad of the Commando Training Centre and every new recruit looks at us with envy. I feel great knowing we have earned their respect. Our King's Squad Pass Out Parade is due to take place at the end of the week but it has been postponed. The UK fire service is on strike and the military have been tasked to provide the fire cover. Before long we're all dispatched to various parts of the country, but before we go we are awarded our Green Beret. It's a very proud moment for me - a symbol that I am now a Royal Marine Commando and have joined the elite.

The Marines send me to Edinburgh to do a two day course on fire fighting before sending me on to Glasgow to join 40 Commando. I'm based in Strathclyde and staying at a nursery school on a camp bed. It's a strange environment; all the walls are decorated with kids' paintings and the rooms have tiny chairs. On Christmas day some of the locals visit and hand food to us, not because we're not being fed but to show appreciation for what we're doing, and the gesture is appreciated.

When the first alarm goes off we grab our gear, jump into our Green Goddess fire engine and race to the scene. The initial rush of adrenalin is short-lived as we arrive at the location to see a sports car on fire, the owner of which had set the petrol tank alight while working underneath it with a blow torch. Over the next two weeks we're called to a burning washing machine and a derelict house, set on fire by kids. My time as a fireman is over within three weeks, as the fire service vote to return to work.

We're informed that 106 & 107 troops are to have a joint King's Squad Pass Out Parade and we return to the training centre feeling rather strange, as we've already been working as trained ranks. We have an intense week of drill, polishing our brasses and boots, and ensuring our blues (a ceremonial uniform) are fitted correctly by the tailor for the big day. Our King's Squad photograph is taken and reveals that 106 squad, which started with sixty-five recruits, has finished with just twenty. My pride at having made it is evident.

With only a couple of days to go, the training team announce the awards that will be given on the day. There are two up for grabs: The King's Badge is awarded to the best section leader, of which there are four, and judged by a panel. The Commando Medal is awarded to the recruit who has best displayed the following qualities: Determination, Courage, Leadership, Unselfishness and Cheerfulness. This award is decided by the training team.

"The King's Badge is awarded to Simon Last," states Sergeant Smith. There's no surprise there for any of us as we all felt he would get it.

"The Commando Medal goes to Andrew Guest."

It's not the name I was expecting to be read out and it knocks me sideways. I'm in a daze as the other lads start to congratulate me. Later, I reflect on this and think about how nice it's going to be for my parents and brothers to see me receive it. The stress I caused them by leaving school at fifteen and having to attend Knightsbridge Crown Court has always weighed heavily on me, but now I feel I have turned things around. I can't wait to see their faces when they find out. I also feel I'm now equal to my older brothers, and it's a good feeling.

The big day arrives. We're all excited and immensely proud that we've reached this moment. It feels like a carnival day: smiles and laughter fills the air, the sun is shining, and the joy amongst families and friends is palpable. None of us in 106 can stop grinning; we busted a gut to get here and we're going to wallow in this incredible feeling. As our families are given a presentation to understand what we have gone through, we dash off to get ready for the parade.

My parents and brothers take their seats and the Royal Marines band starts off the parade with *A Life on the Ocean Wave* as 106 & 107 troops march on. We're taken through our drills and the crowd enjoy it as much as we do - loving this climax of our thirty-two weeks of training. Half way through the drill we stop as the Exeter Mayor has been invited to present the medals.

When my name is called I come to attention and march out. The Commando Medal is presented to me with a hand shake, and it's a moment I treasure knowing that my parents and brothers are looking on. As I march back to re-join my troop, I see again that picture of my father and brothers in the Royal Marines, and I am now stood alongside them. The picture is complete. My heart is bursting with pride; I have not let them down.

After the parade we meet up with our families to enjoy the rest of the day together. It's now that I understand what the training team were doing when I lost my weekend off – they were concerned I could have been injured in a skydiving accident when I was so far into training, and they didn't want to see that happen. Realising I wasn't ever going to stop skydiving they finally accepted it, as they couldn't keep giving me galley fatigues.

As the day closes we go on our well-deserved leave, having been informed which Commando unit we're joining. I'm being sent to 42 Commando based at Bickleigh in Plymouth. I can sense my parents are thinking, 'The boy did well'. It's true, I was a boy when I arrived, but I'm feeling very grown up now. It's just a shame I'm still baby-faced and look about fifteen-years-old, even though it's my birthday today and I've just turned twenty.

I have learned a lot about myself both physically and mentally during the last seven months. There will be more to learn, I know, through challenges that will have me looking deep inside of myself, searching for answers. I can't help but wonder if I'll find something that disappoints me.

LIFE CAN BE TAKEN IN A SECOND

I arrive at 42 Commando based at Bickleigh Barracks in Plymouth, Devon, to join Lima Company. The weather is atrocious.

It's become apparent that most of us don't relish the idea of carrying a heavy weapon, and the new guys and I joke that they've already lined us up to be the GPMG gunners, which would see us doing exactly that, but we wait in anticipation to see what's in store for us.

The Commando unit are gearing up to depart for Norway as they are an arctic warfare unit and, as I've missed the arctic training, I'm told I'll remain behind to do rear party guard duties. It's ironic that, unusually, 42 Commando find a lack of snow in Norway in 1978, and I find myself doing foot patrols around the camp in Plymouth in deep snow, with most of the Devon roads cut off by the terrible conditions.

When the unit returns from Norway we launch straight into Northern Ireland training, with two objectives. One: to get the Commando unit up to speed in the environment we will be working in and, two: to understand how the Irish Republic Army (IRA) terrorists operate. These are the same people who were responsible for planting bombs in London amongst civilians when I worked there after leaving school, and now I'll be in their territory. It's something I'm looking forward to - it will no longer be an exercise but the real thing, and with high stakes, which will give me the opportunity to put into practice what I've been trained to do.

I'm aware that I'm starting to be considered a bit of an odd-ball in the troop. During the week when the guys head into Union Street in Plymouth to drink and chase women, I remain on camp. I'm saving my money for skydiving but they don't know this. At the weekends I head up to Dunkeswell, not only for the skydiving but for the social scene which, at times, gets pretty wild – often far more outrageous then a normal 'run ashore' in Plymouth.

Before long I'm asked by the chief instructor at the skydiving club if I'd like to take part in a water jump parachute display. Even though I don't have a lot of experience I relish the opportunity, eager to learn, and join two other skydivers.

We arrive over the Isle of Wight in a Cessna 185 and circle above Cowes, peering down at a thousand boats that have gathered for the Daily Express Power Boat Race. We're unable to pick out the safety boat that's been tasked with retrieving us from the sea but, with a schedule to adhere to, we decide to jump anyway, certain that the boat will make its way to us as we descend.

The three of us exit and I pull my ripcord. I spot the boat, which appears to be trying to get to us, but it doesn't look promising. Not wanting to be stranded in the middle of the English Channel, I quickly sum up my options. There are many yachts sailing below me but one appears to be drifting. What's more, there are five women on board in bikinis, sunbathing on the deck. It's a no-brainer. I splash down right next to it, they lift me aboard, and within minutes I'm presented with a glass of Champagne. When Andy and Jackie, the other two skydivers join us, the skipper very kindly sails us to Portsmouth and drops us off at a Royal Navy base where we explain who we are.

Cold and wet, we pack our parachutes into dustbin liners and climb out of our jumpsuits, and I glance across at Jackie, noticing all eyes are upon her.

"Jackie," I say, strolling over to her. "You just did a water jump, right?"

"Yeah," she says, looking a bit baffled.

"And you chose to wear a white T-shirt with no bra?"

Her eyes drift down to the see-through material doing a dire job of covering her chest while I, of course, try not to look at her ample assets. It's obvious she didn't intend to take the words 'display team' to a whole new level.

Back at Dunkeswell I've formed good friendships on the drop zone: Dave Grindley - Royal Navy, and Bonnie Wilkens - a university student, to mention just two. But there are many others I've bonded with and we have much laughter.

I'm keen to improve my skydiving to maximise my fun. My one hundredth jump has come up but the weather prevents any skydiving from taking place, however, we wait in hope. Meanwhile, we drink tea or coffee and tell stories, plan future skydives, and look forward to the night-time activities to be enjoyed later.

By mid-afternoon it seems the clouds have lifted in height slightly, and a few of us debate whether it's safe for us to jump. Eventually, four of us decide to give it a go. As we walk out to the aircraft I pass Aussie Frances, the skydiver who packed the parachute I'm about to jump with.

"You haven't packed me a malfunction, have you?" I jokingly ask him.

Aussie laughs and shouts back, "I've never packed a malfunction in my life!"

Other skydivers watch us walk out to the plane and the peace is broken when the pilot fires the engine up. The smell of Avgas is strong as we push through the prop blast to climb into the aircraft. Even though not much free fall will be had, we're happy we've got the opportunity to jump.

As we climb away from the airfield the dark clouds above us move closer and the aircraft bounces in the turbulence as the engine continues to roar. Unexpectedly, we hit cloud lower than expected and are disappointed when we level off at fifteen hundred feet. A discussion pursues and one person announces they're not happy to jump from this height. The other two latch on and decide they're staying on board, too. I evaluate the situation and conclude I'm okay with it, and tell the others I'm getting out.

I instruct the pilot to keep the power on. Normally we reduce power to exit, but I want that extra power to speed up the opening of my parachute. As I dive out the slip stream hits me at eighty knots, and there's a sense of exhilaration as I use the airflow to turn and smile at the others on board as I fall away. The air accelerates past me and the pressure pushes against my whole body, rapidly increasing. I deploy my parachute, the lines play out and the parachute grabs the air, but I come to a halt only to find I'm stalling backwards and going into a spin. I know immediately that something isn't right; the square parachute shouldn't be doing this and the feeling isn't familiar. I'm surrounded by a silence that's only disturbed by my own thoughts as I hang under this misbehaving parachute above the beautiful Devon countryside, which is getting closer and closer. I look up to check the parachute and identify the problem. A cascade - where a rigging line divides into two - has caught my wooden steering toggle and taken it up, causing one side of the parachute to be in the stall. The seriousness of the situation hits me. *This is bad. Very bad,* a voice in my head says. I quickly check my altimeter to see what height I have and see I'm at one thousand feet. *This isn't good at all.* There is no discussion to be had; there are only two outcomes in this, one of which is death. As I have a hunger for life, I choose option two.

There's no time for fear; seconds passing is altitude evaporating and my brain engages with the emergency drills I've been taught. I know I need to break away from my main parachute before I can use my reserve – at the risk of it getting tangled up - so I grab my capewells, which attach the parachute to my harness, go through the motions of releasing the rings and inserting my thumbs into them, and I jerk hard. My main parachute disengages from my harness and I fall in silence, plummeting to the earth below me, aware that I'm accelerating in speed. My eyes drop down and I focus on the reserve handle, grasp it, and pull it as hard as I can. The reserve parachute unfolds away from me. My job is done and there's nothing more I can do now; it's just a question of what fate has decided for me. It's a helpless feeling, and I'm really hoping that today is not the day. As I continue to observe the reserve deploying it crosses my mind that this reserve must have the world's longest lines because nothing is happening. It seems like a lifetime ago I was at one thousand feet and I know all too well what this could mean for me – I am rapidly running out of time and height in order to make a safe landing.

Suddenly, the reserve pulls me upright and blossoms above my head. It's a wonderful sight, and there's a rush of elation. I float down, steering into an open, green, freshly-cut field. With feet and knees together I impact with the ground and carry out my parachute roll, noticing the grass is still wet from an earlier rainfall. It's a sweet feeling to be safely back on land, and only now it hits me that I've just had my first malfunction and I've dealt with it. My heart didn't have time to miss a beat as my brain was too busy going through what needed to be done. I know, should I find myself in this situation again, I'll be able to deal with it.

In the bar the beers flow, people chat loudly trying to be heard, and there's laughter in the air as local residents look on. Cigarette smoke fills the room and creates a haze. Dave Tylcoat tells me I have to buy a round of drinks for my one hundredth skydive, which I do. Then, he tells me, peering at the empty glasses minutes later, I have to buy another round for my first malfunction. It's a skydiving tradition, he says, to buy beer when you complete a first, and so I oblige. The two rounds empty the wallet of this young Marine and tomorrow, due to being broke, I'll have to stay on the ground. But strangely, it's been a good day. I know I'll never forget my one hundredth skydive. Today I've learned a little more about myself and I'm feeling good.

Back at camp, Northern Ireland training continues night and day. We hit the firing range and I'm confused as to why some guys are keeping live rounds for when we get there. Surely we'll be given enough rounds to defend ourselves in a hostile environment, I think, but no one offers me an explanation.

My father, brothers and I hatch a plan to keep my mother in the dark, not wanting her to know where I'm going and to worry. My brother, Ken, is living in Scotland so we tell her I'm on a big exercise there. The plan is for me to write to my mum from Northern Ireland, send the letter in another envelope to Ken, whereupon Ken will send it from Scotland and my mother will see a Scottish postmark, and all, according to her, will be well.

A few months down the road the unit is deployed to Northern Ireland at various locations in County Armagh, nicknamed 'bandit country'. I arrive at Forkhill, a small village close to the border of Southern Ireland with a population of around four hundred. It reminds me of sleepy villages in Devon and I find it hard to contemplate there could be any trouble here.

The company creates three activities for us: patrolling within the village, as well as on an observation post at the top of a hill that looks down onto the village; patrolling in the surrounding area outside the village; and lastly, staying on the base to do galley fatigues and man the watch towers. The company has been briefed to keep vigilant, especially after week two when the terrorists will have had an opportunity to observe us to see if we display any predictable patterns that they can exploit.

The camp duties I find boring. Galley fatigues are bad, but doing sentry duties in the observation towers on the four corners of the camp is worse still. Eventually, it's my turn to go into the observation tower again. It's a quiet sunny day, birds are singing, a few of the local residents are working in their gardens, and time drags.

It's not long before I notice a woman is waving at me from one of her upper floor windows and appears to be holding up a sign. It crosses my mind that perhaps she's trying to warn me about some sort of IRA activity on the quiet. I peer through the binoculars so I can see the sign, and read the words, *The show starts in five minutes*. Oh my God, I think, the guys were telling the truth! I'd heard some rumours but had dismissed them as a wind-up.

I watch curiously as the woman positions a chair in the centre of the room, strips naked, then lowers herself into it. Slowly, she runs her hand seductively over her breasts and her belly, before sliding it down between her thighs. Tilting her head back, she spreads her legs on the chair and…

They made no mention of this in the Marine's training, and I certainly won't be writing to my mother about this unexpected experience.

I find foot patrols in the village quite strange. I could be patrolling in a Devon village, with the countryside here a mirror image of the place I've just left. The only difference, I notice, is that the villagers ignore us during the day, and at night if we cross their path they apologise for not being able to speak to us during daylight hours as they can't be sure the IRA are not watching.

I understand this, as the IRA have been known to carry out 'kneecappings' - where they put a pistol just behind the knee and pull the trigger, crippling the person for life. I find it so sad that people here have to live under this constant threat in such a beautiful country.

It's nice to be out of camp and on patrol; it breaks up the boredom. As expected, I've been made the GPMG runner and I enjoy it. I patrol as Tail End Charlie, keeping an eye on the rear and watching for any unusual movements that might set off alarm bells in my head. I've mastered carrying the GPMG on a sling; I can throw it forward and simultaneously cock the weapon and, if need be, fire a burst from the hip should we come under opportunistic sniper fire.

It's the 17th August 1978 and another foot patrol has come to an end, so we head back to camp. On arrival we pass the next patrol going out, led by Corporal Robert (Dusty) Miller, who has just returned from four days' leave. I remark to Dusty that his short haircut is a high price to pay for leave, and he smiles as he passes me.

Back in my room I rack my weapon, put my ammunition and webbing away, and lie on my bed, closing my eyes. Within seconds the whole building shakes from a huge explosion. I hear footsteps running in the corridors and people bellowing - this temporary base is made up of portakabins so sounds travel freely. I grab my webbing and the GPMG and race outside to the RV point to see smoke rising to the sky. We've been hit but the explosion is outside the camp, and it's clear to see it's close to our main gate. There's confusion as to the cause; mortar round or car bomb? It dawns on me the other patrol has only just exited, and there's concern for Dusty and his men. Soon, the news we were dreading reaches us when the medic returns, and it's devastating. The IRA had driven a vehicle and parked it close to our main gate, and the driver walked off without being spotted. I'm told the foot patrol spotted the vehicle as they exited and did a registration plate check, which came back as being a local car that is seen regularly throughout the week. As the patrol continued to walk down the road, still opening out, Dusty stopped to peer inside the vehicle from the passenger window. The IRA trigger man was watching and pressed the trigger, detonating the car bomb, with Dusty catching the full blast from his chin to his waist. It killed him instantly. The radio operator was on the other side of the road and the blast took him over a wall. With shrapnel in his leg and in considerable pain, he gave a contact report the best he could, expressing that he couldn't see anything as he was on the other side of the wall.

The warning we were given has come true. We've been hit in week three and, without knowing it, we gave away a predictable pattern. This was seized by the IRA who observed how we exited as a group and then panned out as we walked down the road. The IRA had come up with a plan and attempted to try and kill the whole patrol at its weakest point, close to our main gate.

Everyone in the company is visually upset, the shock embedded in their faces, their eyes glazed and widened. Its disbelief all round. Dusty was just twenty-two-years-old.

The high brass brings in outside patrols from another regiment to give us a cooling off period and we're confined to camp, the payphone now out of bounds. It makes sense to confine us as its unclear which of the locals are a part of, or a supporter of the IRA, as opposed to living in constant fear of them. All we have are details of the more high profile members, such as Martin McGuiness, on our list. Along with the list we have to carry the Yellow Card that details the rules of engagement, which is a sore point as many servicemen disagree with them. If a gunman opens fire we can return fire, but if he stops and runs away we have to cease fire. This doesn't make sense as it will mean the gunman will return another day, putting more lives at risk.

During the afternoon the television news reports that a Royal Marine has been killed in Forkhill. I'm aware that my family, like other families, will be concerned as his name has not been released. The ban on the payphone is lifted and we're limited to five minutes each to make a call. I call home to find my father is out and I speak to my mother. I tell her the exercise in Scotland is going well, and to tell my father I will phone again at the exact same time tomorrow, which is six o' clock in the evening. I know my father will realise the phone call came after the explosion in Forkhill and that I'm safe.

After a few days we return to duty and start patrolling again in the village. Local residents, under the cover of darkness, express their sadness over the death of Dusty Miller and again apologise that they can't be seen to be talking to us during the day. It brings it home - the environment they are living in. As we patrol around the village we have to walk past the spot where Dusty was killed, and we can see the blast damage on the pavement. It's a constant reminder to us of a popular colleague liked by all, and an image of his smiling face as he passed me in the corridor is etched in my mind.

The wreckage of the car is dumped outside the camp on some waste ground for all to see; there's isn't much left of it. I no longer enjoy patrolling in the village as it means I have to walk past many cars, and I find myself holding my breath, not that I'm going to know anything about it should a bomb detonate, but it plays on my mind.

Outside the village there are signs reminding us there is hostile intent in the area and one has to be vigilant. One of the signs painted on the road does make me smile. *Join the IRA and see the world. Join the Brits and see the next one. Drumintee is Provo land.*

We pass the Three Steps pub where Captain Robert Nairac, with his cover broken in the bar, was abducted by the IRA and murdered. The bad guys are around and I could be walking past one of them and not even know. It's for that very reason I have to adopt a mistrust of the people I see on patrol and constantly evaluate their behaviour as they go about their business.

The company decides to send out two-man, low profile patrols, armed with just a pistol and under the cover of darkness with their faces blackened out. Their task is to sneak behind the pub outside the toilet window on the off chance they may hear any IRA personnel talking with loose lips, which may be helpful for us to gather information. It's only been going for a short time when I find myself patrolling through the village at night and hear footsteps approaching me. A lady looks down, avoiding eye contact, and as she passes me she says, "They know about your two-man teams," before she walks away under a dim street light and fades away. This takes me by surprise and I report back what I've heard to my section commander who, in turn, reports back to the operations room. The danger of a two-man team being abducted while on a mission is too high, so the senior officers scrap the idea. I can't help but think it's a prudent decision and, clearly, some of the locals do care about us.

I find myself on my four days R & R leave after completing three months of the Northern Ireland tour, and it's a welcome break. When I hit the mainland I head for Dunkeswell; it's an opportunity to do some skydiving and socialise. I'm surprised at how much I've missed talking to girls – making eye contact, and smiling and laughing with them. I'll also have the opportunity to meet up with my parents who are travelling to Dunkeswell to see me, and I'm looking forward to it.

It's early afternoon at Dunkeswell, we're drinking tea and having a chat when one of the guys walks past.

"Andy, how's Ireland?" he shouts.

"All good," I shout back. Inside I'm horrified that he's given the game away.

My mother looks at me, puzzled, with a frown on her face. "Ireland?"

"No, Mum. He said, 'how's the island'. Shetland Islands," I say, with no hesitation. It just so happens the Royal Marines have been reported in the newspapers as carrying out an exercise there, and my mother accepts this answer. It's a close call.

Being able to relax, chat, and laugh with friends makes me realise how isolated we are in Northern Ireland. The rest of the world has carried on living; for them time has not stood still. They seem happy being in their world, and the last thing I want to do is bring sadness into their lives by talking about the brutality I've witnessed and the grief of losing a colleague, so I keep it to myself. The alcohol helps me to unwind and soon I forget about Northern Ireland. I'm in this time zone now, and not in the past.

On returning to Northern Ireland it's back to the normal routine of carrying out foot patrols. We set up a vehicle checkpoint on a bend, where we stop vehicles and carry out a search for arms, and a very irate driver tells us he's pissed off ... that he's been stopped twice now, the first time by the checkpoint on the other side of the bend two hundred metres back, by guys wearing black balaclavas. We race to the bend only to discover the IRA have legged it, probably having been told by the driver who we let go previously that we were doing a checkpoint on this side.

Later, we walk into Jonesborough, which is one kilometre from the border. The patrol is staggered with half a patrol on each side of the road. We're in what was considered to be a 'no-go' area by the previous regiment, and can sense this by the deep, cold stares we receive from people going about their normal routines.

I lie down on the pavement on the corner of a street, my GPMG covering the road behind me, and I can feel something isn't right. My senses spark onto high alert and my brain searches for the reason I'm feeling this way. The street is deserted, people are peering from their curtains looking down at us, and *that*, I think, is the answer. People have deserted the street for a reason. Logic says they've been tipped off that something is about to go down. I'm not the only one to sense this as the troop sergeant asks me what I can see. I tell him that's the problem, I don't see anything. We all agree there's a high chance we're about to be hit so we move quickly to vacate the area - not by the main road where we could be hit by an IED or a sniper, but by climbing over people's garden walls. It's bloody hard work with the GPMG and at times I curse my bad luck for having to carry it. However, I'm also aware if we get into a fire fight and when I let fly with this GPMG, firing short concentrated bursts, I'm going to be the most popular person here. I've discovered why some Marines kept rounds from the firing range back in Plymouth. Here, for each lost round, we are fined £200, which isn't good considering when we jump down from walls the rounds have a tendency to pop out of the magazines. It seems crazy, as the threat of a fine has guys taping up their magazines, which would delay them in changing a magazine in a fire fight. As the GPMG gunner, this rule for me is a nightmare as my rounds are exposed. I've already had a situation while climbing through a hedge when a belt of five rounds snagged a twig. By chance, I spotted the rounds were missing and went back and retrieved them. So, as I scale each garden wall, I pray I haven't lost any.

I'm back at my accommodation at Forkhill and try to pass the time by writing a letter to my mother, describing my environment. This is quite difficult to do because she thinks I'm in Scotland, but I figure most bases are similar and the countryside is green no matter where I might be. Here, there isn't much in the realms of entertainment, just a TV room showing the standard programmes but everyone has different tastes so, instead, guys might do some physical exercise, sit on their beds and read a book, or put pen to paper to write a letter home.

My room is an old portakabin that is looking very tired. It has four sets of bunk beds sleeping eight men and there's no privacy. We're cut off from the real world with one payphone serving all the men in Lima Company, hence we're limited to how much time we can spend on it.

I look up from my letter and notice that Mike, one of the Marines, has just posted a letter on the notice board and is walking back to his bunk with a solemn face. It's obvious it's a 'Dear John'. It's standard practice for guys to post their break-up letters so we can go up to read them one at a time, which may seem like a strange thing to do but it makes us aware they may be going through a hard time, as they can't do anything about their relationship until the tour is over or when their four days' R & R comes up. Also, they may not want to talk about the situation straight away, so it's easier to post the letter on the board instead. Often, the letters are viewed as entertainment; emotional stuff is made light-hearted, and that's the best way for the guy in question to deal with it. Sadly, quite a few 'Dear Johns' are sent as the tours last for six months and girlfriends back home get bored waiting.

I make my way to the notice board to read Mike's letter.

Dear Mike, I didn't want to finish with you but my mother made me. I've just found out I'm pregnant and I don't know what to do. What should I do? Love Annabel.

A week later, Mike posts another letter on the board and the guys are curious to know how this is going to pan out, so once again go up to read it. This letter takes everyone by surprise. It's not from Annabel, but from her mother.

Dear Mike, I've just found out I'm pregnant and my husband, who's in the Royal Navy, is due back from sea. I don't know what to do. What do you suggest? Tracy.

It makes sense now why the mother put pressure on her daughter to ditch Mike. Through boredom, I find myself at times trying to work out what the relationships between them all will be if both mother and daughter decide to have the babies. Talk about complicated.

We're two weeks from the tour being completed and I've been told to see the company commander who informs me he has two options for me. I have no idea what's going on as I listen in. He tells me I'm doing well and promotion may not be too far away, so I could stay with the unit and see the tour to the end. Or, my second choice, I'm on the four o'clock helicopter flight out to Bessbrook, where I'll be transported to catch a ferry back to the UK to join the Royal Marines Free Fall Parachute Display Team who are about to go to Cyprus for a training camp.

"Sir," I say. "Did you say four o'clock?"

He smiles, and I'm told to do my leaving routine and hand back my stores. I'm about to do the one thing I enjoy with a passion, and they're going to pay me to do it. I can't believe my luck.

At the base in Poole, I meet up with the guys on the free fall team, all of whom I've met before as a weekend skydiver, and am greeted by each one with a smile: Gary Lawry - a very close friend of my older brother Pete, Pete himself, Bob Scoular, Derrick White - our display team leader, and Andy

Grice, who has just joined the team. We discuss what our parachute display will consist of, which will be free falling and then linking up while in free fall, trailing smoke from grenades attached to our ankles in order for the crowd to see us. Linking up our parachutes involves one guy hooking his feet around another guy's rigging lines. I'm happy about the free fall part, that's just going to be fun, but the thought that my safety could be jeopardised as someone is going to grab my parachute has me concerned. Stan Wood has been chosen to be my partner.

In Cyprus we jump from six in the morning, but when the winds are too high we hit the beach. In the evenings we go out for meals and drinks. The team bonds well, with the guys accepting Andy and me.

We hear on the news that 42 Commando have had another person killed by an explosion in Northern Ireland, with only a week to go before their tour is over. I feel a bit guilty that I didn't complete the last two weeks of the tour but, at the same time, I couldn't turn down this dream opportunity to do what I enjoy.

The training jumps go well, with Stan and me working well as a partnership. I understand what Stan wants from me: I need to position my parachute to make it easier for Stan to grab it, all the time keeping an eye on where we are in relation to the landing area. Once Stan has hold of my parachute he becomes the pilot and steers us to the landing area. At times it's difficult, depending on how much cloud is around and at what height we're at.

Back in the UK I head to Dunkeswell for another fun weekend. The day's skydiving has been good, with much laughter. In the evening in the bar I find myself chatting to Dave Tylcoat, one of the older skydivers who is serving with 59 Commando, an army unit. The banter between us is constant, with me holding my own against this old sweat. The beers flow, along with my retorts, and I feel really pleased with myself until Dave starts to laugh at me.

"What's so funny?" I ask him, intrigued as to why he's so amused.

"Justa," he says.

"Justa what?"

"Justa boy," he answers, with more laughter.

The next morning, Dave tells my team what he'd said to me and my fate is sealed. We can't have two Andys on the team as its causing confusion under the parachutes, so I have now been given a nickname.

I'm standing outside the Sergeant Major's office when he pokes his head out of the door and calls out for two volunteers for a military parachute course, and it's like sweet music to my ears when, five minutes later, I walk out having been booked onto it. I'm chuffed to bits, not only because I'll receive my military para wings but because, as I'm on the parachute display team, I'll now get 'para pay' and have an increase in salary.

I attend the course at No 1 Parachute Training School at Brize Norton, which is run by the Royal Airforce, along with two guys, Ian Graham and Greg Andrew, who are due to join the Royal Marines Free Fall Parachute Display Team at a later date. The course is broken down into syndicates and our Airforce parachute jump instructor (PJI) introduces himself as Dave Hart. He tells us his background, along with the fact he has logged sixty jumps. We're then asked to introduce ourselves and tell the group of our experience. Many of the guys have completed just one jump, and some have no experience at all, while Ian and Greg have around sixty jumps each. I introduce myself and tell the group I have logged one hundred and sixty jumps and this seems to surprise the PJI.

As we start our training, the PJI gives incorrect information about the safety of some of the manoeuvres in order to boost confidence in the inexperienced jumpers, and he tends to look in our direction in the hope we won't say anything. We don't, but just smile.

We have a week of going through landing techniques and leaping from fan trainers, and at last we start jumping, much to the relief of my stomach muscles. The balloon jump is unusual and I'm made all too aware of how much lower we are jumping from at eight hundred feet, compared to sport parachuting from two and a half thousand feet. Having height always brings a sense of comfort.

The jumps from the C-130 (Hercules) are a buzz ; it's fun jumping out of such a large aircraft, and I use my free skills to pivot in the slip stream and watch other people exiting after me, giving me great visuals. The C-130 has doors on both sides from which people exit on hearing their number being called, but often the PJIs lose count, resulting in jumpers exiting at the same time. On my fifth jump, as I approach the door over Weston on the Green, I'm aware that jumpers on both sides have started to exit at the same time; however, time is of the essence so I leave the aircraft. As my parachute starts to deploy I notice another parachute over my right shoulder that's approaching me fast. I adopt a large body spread position, like a star jump, as I hit the other guy's rigging lines. There's no sense of fear as I've already got used to canopy stacking and grabbing parachutes, however in this case there's a sense of dropping and a feeling that something is seriously wrong. I feel a jolt and notice I'm looking at a paratrooper recruit's eyes that are the size of saucers, while his hand is grasping his reserve handle. One of the draw backs of the PJI losing count as jumpers exit from both doors is that they get sucked underneath the plane and risk a collision.

"Seriously mate, that reserve is not required," I shout at him, even though he's only a few feet away from me. I look up and notice that I'd entered his lines and, unfortunately, I've emerged on the wrong side of one of them, but both parachutes are flying. As we descend it's just a question of chatting to him to reassure him, but he stays transfixed on me while continuing to grip his reserve handle as if his life depends on it. All the while I'm pulling on a lift web (riser) and trying to keep our parachutes apart. We touchdown, and land safely, and a PJI races over to ask if I'm okay before he starts to yell at the other guy. I can only assume he could hear what was being said up there, but it's time for me to walk away.

We make some jumps with containers which, after the parachute opens, we attach to our harness with a carabiner. We then release the container so it lands first. Some guys forget to attach the carabiner and when they release the container it becomes an earth-bound missile. Others forget to release the container and take a hard landing, a mistake they won't make twice.

With eight jumps completed, one of which was a night jump, I'm awarded my military para wings and can now display it on my uniform. More importantly, the extra pay I'll receive while I'm on the Royal Marines Free Fall Parachute Display Team will come in very handy indeed.
The team now has some funding to send us out to Pope Valley in California for a final training camp before the display season starts. As Andy and I walk around San Francisco, we're shocked when two guys approach us and ask if we'd be interested in a foursome. The more we walk the more we seem to be hit upon by men, and I can't fathom out what's going on. Later, in a bar, I'm irritated when a man keeps staring at me, and I'm curious when he asks the bar tender for two beers, as he's alone. My curiosity soon disappears when he strolls over to me with a smile and offers me one, which I decline. It is then promptly swiped by another Marine who tells him, "He'll have another one." I'm happy when we move on to another bar in case the guys get the idea of selling me, which could go horribly wrong. The place is packed and a piano is playing in the background. I chat up a waitress who asks me if I'm straight. "Yes I am," I reply, and she tells me that she isn't, and walks away. Okay, I am now very confused about San Francisco; it's a very strange place.

On the Pope Valley drop zone we practice the display routine continuously and are consistent in having three pairs of parachutes linked up and flying down to the landing area. The Royal Marines Parachute Display Team hold the British stack record of five parachutes linked together but the team is now six and it's decided we should attempt to build a six stack. The more experienced guys decide the docking order of the stack and I'm given the third slot, something I've never done before. Pete gives me a pep talk about 'angles' and 'sight picture', and no sooner has he done that I find myself in the plane climbing to altitude. I'm nervous, I don't want to let the team down, and I'm anxious in case this goes badly wrong and I end up wrapping my parachute around Andy Grice. *Deep breath,* I tell myself, *stop thinking negatively and focus on the job in hand.*

It's time to exit and as I hit the slip stream my nervousness has gone;

I'm too busy concentrating and trying to get myself into the correct position. Derrick and Andy have got together, and now it's time for the weakest link in this whole attempt to do what he has to, which is me. I fly towards them, searching for that sight picture, and hear my brother's voice. *Get slightly lower, think sight picture, and put Andy in between your centre lines, the leading edge of your parachute just above his waist.* I have it - the sight picture Pete said to have. My parachute makes contact with Andy and he grabs it.

"He's on! He's bloody well on!" I hear Pete shouting in the distance.

The last three - Stan, Pete and Gary - dock on and we now have a new British CRW six stack record flying over the skies of California. Rod Boswell, a Royal Marine officer who came on the trip but isn't part of the team, is flying his parachute around and taking pictures.

That evening I don't know whether I'm feeling proud of myself or just relieved that I did what was asked of me. What I do know? The cold beers are going down all too easy and our laughter gets louder.

A few days later we're approached by some Americans who were part of the world record nine stack and they ask if they can join us on a big stack attempt. Our attempt builds to an eight stack with Gary becoming the first British person to dock eighth, and the rest of us the first British to be in an eight stack. We're awarded the Canopy Crest Recipient 8-Stack Award.

Back in England I return to Dunkeswell and that evening, while watching Whicker's World - a documentary that reports on stories of social interest - I hear how San Francisco has the biggest gay community in America. That clarifies why we were approached, but it doesn't explain why it happened so many times. Surely their 'gaydar' must have picked up on the fact that I and the other guys were giving out zero signs of being that way inclined? But then the penny drops when Alan Whicker goes on to explain that in wanting to identify as being gay, it's common for men in San Francisco to wear some kind of adornment, which hangs down one side of their trousers. As skydivers we use a cord to close our parachute containers and, to ensure it isn't lost, guess where we hang it? It's nice to know the reason, although I'd have been happy to believe it was nothing other than my exceptional good looks that had them all flocking. Just a shame it wasn't the women.

The time comes to have a beat up at Wroughton, where the whole show is put together. The Royal Marines Free Fall Parachute Display Team is part of R Company, which consists of the abseil and unarmed combat teams, as well as the Royal Navy helicopter crew. A high ranking official has to give his approval for the team to go on the road and to give displays. Approval is granted, and we're good to go and start the season. Before we can carry out displays we have to do a dress rehearsal in front of the high brass. The display goes well and we are given a green light to go on the road.

My first display is at Oldswinford School in Stourbridge, Birmingham, and we board the helicopter in the arena. Normally we would climb to two thousand feet where the jumpmaster would throw the wind drift indicator, but today Gary has thrown it from a thousand feet due to the low, overcast clouds. The wind drift indicator is made of crepe paper, twenty-two feet long with three ounces of plasticine, and its descent rate mimics that of a round reserve parachute, which is exactly what we have in our containers. Where this lands will let the jumpmaster know the wind direction and strength, and enable him to work out where we should depart the helicopter.

The weather isn't looking too clever; there are low, black clouds at eighteen hundred feet looking like a monster that's about to get angry. Birmingham city is stretched out below me and there are no green, lush fields to welcome me. It's a landscape that's looking very threatening should I fail to reach the landing area - a concrete jungle, some of which reaches to the sky - and there are cars everywhere. I have in my head that on displays we have to jump from higher than two thousand feet.

"From Drop Zone Control, the winds are gusting 25mph," one of the helicopter aircrew shouts, and I feel myself relax, although I'm slightly disappointed we don't have the height and the winds are too high to jump.

I turn to Andy Grice. "Andy," I say, "I'm gutted. I was really looking forward to this."

"Me too," he replies.

The helicopter suddenly jerks and I flick my head towards the door, where it's looking very much like Gary is spotting the parachute load, as the helicopter seems to have made a correction. He's trying to calculate if the aircraft is in the right position in order for us to exit and get safely to the landing spot.

I turn to my brother. "Pete, what's Gary doing?"

Pete looks at me. "We're running in," he says.

My heart rate shoots off the scale and there's a surge of adrenalin racing through me as if I've just injected it into my arm. I'm in disbelief. "Pete, we're only at eighteen hundred feet, and DZ said the winds are over the top."

"Welcome to the parachute display team, Andrew," he says with a smile.

The next thing I hear is Gary shouting out, "Here we go," and bodies start throwing themselves out of the Wessex Mk 5 helicopter. It's my turn and, in a panic with a hundred things going through my head, I launch myself out of the helicopter door but not in a good body position and I find myself upside down. I honestly don't care right at this moment in time, my parachute is coming out. I throw the deployment pilot chute out, which triggers the main, only to observe it deploying between my legs. My mouth opens wide, my eyes widen from saucers to dinner plates, there's a snap, and I'm thrown around to see the opening has just given me twists. I kick out of the twists like a deranged lunatic as I know the parachute is running off the landing area. No sooner are the twists out I have to hang onto my front risers, trying to hold my ground against this strong wind. I make it to the arena … just, and my heart is pounding out of my chest, my pupils dilated as I try to catch my breath.

"Hey, you did alright," Pete says, walking over to me. I'm still hunched over as I look up at him.

"Is it always going to be like this?" I ask.

He smiles. "I'd be lying if I said no."

My learning curve on this parachute display team has just gone vertical.

We do one or two shows at one location and then move onto the next. Every night seems to be a party night. We go out and eat, and then drink, telling stories and reliving the day's display jump with much laughter. I enjoy changing locations, not knowing what the next one will bring, how tight the arena is going to be, and what the hazards are likely to be that will set my pulse accelerating. I know one thing for sure - this is not your normal skydiving on a standard drop zone. The stakes are high, and the risk of a serious injury that could see me being paralysed or even killed is real.

It's another display day and I'm over Newcastle city, looking down from ten thousand feet, and thinking today is a very bad day to have a round reserve parachute ride. The winds are high - around 20+ mph - and I have a round reserve that has limited steering capabilities. I'm looking mostly at streets, some extremely busy with traffic and tall buildings, and our landing area is a postage stamp five miles away. The shout is given and we climb into our positions in the doorway, some people hanging outside while others are inside pushing against the outside jumpers. On the word 'Go!' we exit the helicopter and hit the slipstream, and all other thoughts are blanked out as we focus on flying together and linking up in free fall. As soon as the parachutes are open we move into the next phase in linking up the parachutes. Everyone is concentrating as we fly the stacks into the arena while mentally being on high alert in case something starts to go drastically wrong. We all land safely, it's a job well done, and there is satisfaction throughout the team on our performance.

The following day we're at the East of England showground. The Royal Airforce Falcons Parachute Display Team has cancelled due to the weather. A few hours later, the Red Devils Parachute Display Team cancels, too. When our slot comes up I look at the senior guys on the display team but I don't even have to ask the question and start getting into my jumpsuit. Due to the weather conditions we can't do our canopy stacking, and the jumpmaster screams out, "Everyman for himself," an indicator of how risky it's going to be as we exit the helicopter.

This is the reason, I think, why the free fall team party hard with a 'not a care in the world' attitude. It's certainly true in my case and I take each day as it comes. It seems that sometimes being in a military free fall parachute display team has its advantages, as it attracts a fair few women. Most of them are no different to me - they're out in the evening wanting to have a fun night, which ends, more often than not, with no strings attached sex. Some days I wake up and try to piece together my memories of the previous night, but the alcohol has made everything hazy and leaves me wondering who the hell this naked woman is lying asleep next to me. As I stagger out of bed, my head throbbing, I wonder where the hell I am as I search for my clothes.

We arrive at Pebble Mill Studios to show them our display of hooking up parachutes, which makes us different to other teams as we are consistently doing it to a high standard. As I step out of the minibus I observe that the building is an L shape, and trees close the front lawn off by forming another L shape. What I do notice further down the road is a park.

"Are we landing down by the park?" I ask the producer.

"No," he replies, and points to the front lawn.

"Really?" I laugh.

"The Red Devils landed there," he says, sealing my fate.

Suddenly, my free meal doesn't feel quite as appetising and my nerves kick in. I tell my partner, Stan, if there was ever a day I would want him to land me, today is the day. I have more faith in Stan than being by myself in this tight landing area that offers no overshoots.

We exit the helicopter over the TV studios in Birmingham. It's a perfect sunny day with light winds, and when Stan grabs hold of my parachute I sense the relief inside of me. My eyes are large as I constantly evaluate my fate, and I lift my legs up to avoid part of a high building. We're on finals and there's nowhere else to go. Stan nails it and we both have a soft landing in the centre of the lawn. I feel reborn, and I supply Stan with unlimited beers later in the evening as a thank you.

Another display, and it's in Rotherham. We ditch our gear in the sports centre as we're sleeping there on camp beds, and once showers are out of the way we head into town to grab a beer. We enter a pub and casually walk over to the bar. I sense something isn't right because the conversation in the pub quietens. I feel like we're on someone else's patch and we've just encroached on it. One of the guys orders a round of drinks and my brain tells me to look around to find the threat so I'm able to evaluate the situation we're in. All I see are groups of women in twos, threes and fours, sat at tables and staring at us.

"Gary," I say, "the bar's full of women; there's no men."

"It's Rotherham, mate. The women here outnumber the men by seven to one. In Nottingham it's five to one."

Now I understand why so many of the Marines on R Company were looking forward to coming here.

David Waterman, a photographer and videographer, has been tasked with making a BBC two minute filler and has approached us. He jumps with us on a number of locations, filming both free fall and canopy stacking. High over the skies of Southport we build our British CRW six stack record with Dave flying around us and capturing everything on film. On one jump we decide to land the six stack in the arena and Stan does an outstanding job; all six of us land safely in the arena on the beach to hear the Red Devils had pulled up in their vehicle, watched us, and then driven away. There's nothing like friendly rivalry between the Parachute Regiment Display Team and the Marines.

I've formed a good friendship with Ian Graham and Greg Andrew, who are training up to join the team next year with Paul Austin and Dave Wildman. The guys for this season are part of the unarmed combat team, but are getting a good insight as to what is expected of them next year.

At the Doncaster race course we recce the landing area, and the senior guys opt to land in the winners' enclosure as it will be right in front of the crowd where the stadium is. All that grass and we choose a small landing area, but this is what gives our team the reputation of being the best in the UK.

The Wessex Mk 5 helicopter climbs to altitude; it's a sunny day and there's no wind. The free fall goes well, followed by the parachute hook ups. We have three pairs flying but Stan notices that one pair has caught up with us as their stack is descending faster than ours.

"Justa," Stan shouts, "I'm gonna let the other pair go in first and follow behind."

"Yeah," I shout back.

I'm admiring the scenery as we approach the arena. My thoughts are interrupted when Stan calls out again.

"Justa, two of us aren't going to make it."

"Yeah," I say, and then, "What?" when I realise what he's just told me. I look up to see his feet have just released me and I'm suddenly on my own. There's no wind so I'm travelling at 20mph when I flare my parachute to slow my descent, which would normally result in a small run on landing, but I can only take one step. I'm short of the arena when my chest hits the fence, shortly followed by my chin.

I wake up at a bed and breakfast with a sore head, with no recollection of the night before. I turn my head on the pillow and see no naked woman next to me. I feel this is one really bad hangover and I swear I'm not going to drink so much again. As my hand touches my head I realise I have a bandage around it, and am horrified I got so drunk that the guys have dressed me in this bandage. This is embarrassing. My tongue touches a tooth that divides into two and causes me to sit up. I probe a tooth on the other side and it does the same. I'm not sure what's going on so I pinch myself to confirm I'm awake. At that precise moment Stan walks through the door.

"Stan, what the hell happened last night?" I ask. Why do I have shattered teeth?"

Stan explains to me what happened. Apparently, after I hit the fence, I staggered around and told everyone I was alright with blood pouring out of my mouth. A few seconds later I repeat the question, asking Stan what happened, as I'm still concussed. Stan brings out a tape recorder from under my bed, records me repeating myself, and plays it back to me. Upon hearing myself ask the same question over and again, it snaps me out of it.

Later that day I'm taken to a Royal Air Force base to see a dentist; he pulls my teeth out and I hear them clang into a tin. I can't help thinking that the military dentist, due to costs, may have just taken the easy option and rather than repair my teeth made the decision to pull them instead. I grab hold of his arm and say, "You don't mind if I take a look?" Sure enough, in the tin are four halves of my teeth. He had no choice; I can see that.

A little while later we're in Minehead and Andy, Derrick, Stan and I try to build a parachute diamond formation, which has never been successfully built before in the UK. Three of us have linked up - we have Derrick on top hooked up to Andy and me, his feet inserted into the corners of each of our parachutes, so from the ground it looks as if he is standing on top of us. All of a sudden my parachute gains lift due to rising air. Due to Derrick's foot being hooked into it, my parachute swings round and dives into the centre. Andy's does the same, so Andy and I are bouncing next to each other. We look up and see both parachutes have completely wrapped up Derrick. This isn't good at all. Minehead town is below us, as well as the sea close by, and in a very English manner Andy and I offer the other the opportunity to jettison their parachute first, as neither of us are keen to find ourselves under a round reserve parachute over Minehead, though the likelihood is we will both be under one.

"No, after you," I insist, when suddenly Andy falls away and his parachute opens. *The lucky bastard* comes to mind, and I'm feeling envious. I look up and shout to Derrick to hurry up and climb out of my parachute and, to my surprise, he succeeds. I fall away, my parachute re-inflates, and I take a much needed breath.

My first parachute display season comes to an end. It's been fun, scary at times, mentally challenging at others, but my skydiving ability has shot up. I'm all too aware that I'm starting to get respect from my fellow skydivers. I feel I haven't let my team mates down and it's a great feeling. My only regret is that I can't quite remember all those nights out, but I'm pretty sure I had a good time.

THE ULTIMATE TEST

It's the start of the year, 1980, and I'm just approaching my twenty-second birthday. The British Parachute Association is holding its Annual General Meeting in Leicester and skydivers throughout the UK are attending, including me. For the hardcore party people it's going to be a thirty-six hour piss-up.

After a heavy Friday night on the beer we gather on the Saturday for more drinks and to watch the latest skydiving films; it's an opportunity to see world class skydivers at their best. When one film finishes a tall guy stands up and asks if we'd like to watch his film, and as soon as the opening titles have rolled we stare at the screen in confusion because there isn't an aircraft in sight. Instead, the camera pans around and focuses on a group of backpackers at the bottom of a huge cliff.

"What a wanker," somebody remarks. "He's put on a climbing film at a skydiving convention."

Half the audience get to their feet and start to make their way outside. I remain seated as the alcohol is having an effect, and I'm thinking it's wise to stay here for a bit as there's a second night of heavy partying ahead of me.

The next scene shows the backpackers chilling out around a bonfire, and it isn't until the camera zooms out that we notice they're wearing skydiving gear. The room stills; this now has everyone's attention. Next, we see two skydivers standing on the edge of El Capitan - a three thousand feet high vertical rock formation in Yosemite National Park. One of the guys on the film looks over his shoulder; those that are still in the room are glued to the screen. The jumper runs to the edge of the cliff, quickly followed by a second, and there's a huge cry of, "No way!" in the room as the two jumpers leap off the cliff. They're filmed altering their body positions to track positions that allow them, once they've reached a certain speed, to move horizontally over the ground and, more importantly, away from the cliff face, before they open their parachutes half way down. There's a huge buzz, the atmosphere is electric, and people try to rush back into the room to see what's going on.

I watch this short film half a dozen times and try to imagine what it must feel like to stand on the edge of that cliff. Terrifying, I conclude, my fear of heights hitting home, but I can feel my senses coming alive, nudging the part of me that craves adventure.

I rejoin my friends in the bar and those crazy guys leaping off the cliff is the topic of the evening. This film has triggered something deep inside of me; it's awoken something. I feel different and ponder whether it's due to the alcohol, but deep down I know my inner spirit is screaming at me to be set free.

A couple of pints later the film has been forgotten. We're in full swing again as stories are rehashed and the banter escalates. My chances with the ladies are zero tonight; the alcohol wins.

Back at the camp my issue with transport plays on my mind. I no longer want to catch trains, hitch-hike, or rely on friends, so it makes sense to take driving lessons. I do a crash course and book three hours at a time, simultaneously applying for my driving test. I'm given permission to disappear for a while during work hours, hence I'm still in my Royal Marines uniform on the day of my test. My driving instructor picks me up and we do a practice run-through before heading to the test centre, and when we arrive he strolls off to grab a coffee, leaving me waiting for the examiner.

I spot the examiner marching out of his office with a clipboard under his arm. John Cleese comes to mind, from Fawlty Towers. It's a strange thing to see as this examiner is a civilian but, seeing his march, I wonder if he's ex-military. He stops right in front of me, looks at my shoulder flashes with the words *Royal Marine Commando* adorned there, and shoves his face six inches away from mine, which causes me to lean back.

"My son is in the army," he says, looking me straight in the eyes.

Without hesitating, the words, "That's his problem," flow from my mouth. I know instantly from the expression on his face that this was a mistake.

At the end of the test he tells me I've failed. I can only reply, "What a surprise."

I'm so pissed off that I decide to buy a motorbike. I've never been on one before but it's a bicycle with an engine, how difficult can that be? I head into Exeter to a motorbike shop and a second-hand one catches my eye - a silver Honda Superdream 250cc. I purchase it, along with a full face helmet, and while I'm filling out the paperwork the mechanics take the bike outside ready for me to ride it away.

I approach the bike like a matador to a bull, only to see the mechanics have gathered outside with their coffees to watch. I really don't need this added pressure. Helmet on, I straddle the bike and turn the key. It comes to life and my heart rate soars. Off the stand, clutch in, push into first gear. Simple. Then I make the mistake of letting out the clutch too quickly. The bike surges forward, I pull the clutch in and swerve, and narrowly miss the parked car opposite me. I don't have to look; I just know the mechanics are howling with laughter. My stress levels shoot through the roof. This isn't a bicycle with an engine; it's a beast with a roar, this clutch is unleashing it, and I'm sat on the bloody thing.

I head out of Exeter and try my best not to stall it. The miles pass, the scenery is a blur, traffic accelerates past me, and I feel as if I'm being taunted by all the other vehicles on the road. My concentration is high as I focus on the lane in front of me but it soon becomes clear I'm heading in the wrong direction when I see a sign for Plymouth. *Bollocks.*

I eventually arrive at Dunkeswell and park the bike up, relieved the journey from hell is over and that I've survived it. Exhausted, I grab a tea to chill and slump down in a chair. "What the hell have I done?" I ask myself. Yes, I have the freedom to come and go as I like now, which is excellent, but it's just a question of living to tell the bloody tale. All that money spent but clearly there's a lot of learning to be done. The plus side is I'm on an airfield, which is mostly deserted, and it's a good place to get the hang of that clutch control.

The Royal Marines Free Fall Parachute Display Team has changed - members have left and new members have joined, which has increased the team to eight. Pete Lambson is in the process of taking over as team leader by rank, but is actually the least experienced skydiver of us all. Pete has a presence about him and his approach to the team wins him respect.

"Though I'm going to be team leader," he says, "the more experienced guys on the team will dictate the skydiving side on displays." I revere the fact he's using common sense.

The team have two training camps: Kingsfield in Cyprus, and Pope Valley in California. As a team we go out for a few beers at different locations, and one night in San Francisco we give the Irish bar a try. As I'm looking around I spot a very large jar on the counter with a label on it which says, *Support the IRA*. I'm not sure we'd be welcome if they knew they had eight Royal Marine Commandos drinking in the bar, so it seems prudent to move on. We try a few different establishments, and all in all it's an enjoyable evening. There's a huge difference in our experiences on this trip to San Francisco than in the previous year but, then again, none of us are hanging anything from our trousers.

The display routine has changed and we're now going to link four parachutes to build a four stack. Greg Andrew and Ian Graham will build the pin and base, and Andy Grice and I will fight for the third and fourth position. The other four will link two pairs.

It's April, and the display season doesn't start for another two days so I head up to Netheravon in Wiltshire to do some fun jumping. On the drop zone there are a few other people who have the same interest in stacking their parachutes like the Marines. We chat and decide to jump together to link eight parachutes and form a stack. One of the guys expresses an interest to dock eighth for the first time, and we all agree as that will mean he has to buy the beers tonight. The eight stack goes well and we're in high spirits after landing when we're approached by Geordie Laing, the Chief Instructor, who's been observing us. He asks us to do it again but we politely refuse, telling him we're going to do a long free fall jump instead. That's when he offers us a free jump, something we're never going to say no to, so we change the positions around and build another eight stack.

When we land, Geordie Laing asks us to repeat it, again for free. So we change positions and for the third time build another successful eight stack. Geordie tells us to follow him into his office, whereupon he explains he's an FAI (IPC – International Parachuting Commission) international judge, and has timed us on our last three jumps.

"You probably don't know this, but you've just broken the world record three consecutive times for the fastest eight stack ever built," he tells us.

We're dumb struck, and it appears we're all going to have buy the beers tonight in the bar. That's not so bad; the vibes are going to be brilliant. He also informs us there's a stacking competition coming up in America at the end of the year - the Canopy Relative Work World Cup - and his aim is to put an invite out for anyone in the UK to compete against us. If no one beats us or comes forward to challenge us then, with the British Parachute Association's support, we'll go to America to represent Great Britain.

The Royal Marines Free Fall Parachute Display Team's season begins and we head to Eastbourne to take part in our first display at Hamden Park School. The risks have increased as we'll now be landing a four stack into the arena - the more people in a stack, the greater the speed, and the higher the risk. Although I've been part of an eight stack several times, these were never landed; the stack, after joining up, separated in the air.

Andy Grice and I soon realise the fourth person in the stack at the bottom is going to hit the ground hard and, what's more, at times it's going to hurt. Most of the time we debate in the air whether or not to land it. The stack pilot at the top will say yes, as will the second person from the top, as they'll get a soft landing. The third person knows his landing will be firm, but not as hard as the fourth person's, so he'll say yes to please the crowd. The end result is that Andy and I will race against each other, the aim to not end up being the fourth person at the bottom.

The Devon County Show is the first show this season and we build a four stack, but the turbulence in the air is making one of the parachutes misbehave.

"Hold it, hold it," a shout goes out.

"More brakes," another voice calls.

"Number three is starting to collapse, clear your nose of your parachute."

The adrenalin increases and it pumps harder the closer we get to the ground as the safety margin in height has gone. All eyes in the stack closely watch the stack pilot's approach. If he messes up some of us are going to be in deep shit, so we scan the ground to see what hazards could be there. It's May, a sunny day, the show ground is buzzing, and helium balloons have escaped and rise to the sky in a graceful waltz. Music plays in the background and the smell of burgers wafts through the air. The four stack is the last group to land and the applause of the crowd echoes around the arena. We have achieved our aim and we all walk out of there to see another day.

I enjoy being on the parachute display team. It's challenging at times when the risks are high, especially at some shows where they place farm machinery adorned with spikes close to the arena ... it's just another potentially fatal hazard to think about. I love it when my heart rate increases though, and the mind-games start playing in my head, the loudest voice telling me I have to win. It's a wonderful feeling to have pride and to be involved in something so special.

In the evenings it's back to the bar after overcoming difficult weather conditions and unexpected dangers, and I'm left feeling reborn at having been given the chance to walk out of the arena. It's like a drug – each narrow escape and successful landing giving me a hunger for more.

Nobody knows what tomorrow will bring and it gives us an excuse to party hard. We've put our necks on the line, our expertise has been tested, and so much energy that has built up within us during the day has to be released. There's a deep respect between all the team members, not only because we've all passed the Royal Marines training but because we take things to the limit on a daily basis, not knowing what the outcome will be.

We tell stories that evoke laughter, but hidden within a lot of them are opportunities to learn. As it's my second season on the display team I'm now one of the more experienced team members and able to pass on my knowledge to the new guys so they can shorten their learning curve. I relate a couple of stories of displays I did with Stan Wood, my stacking partner from the previous season.

On one demo, Stan was flying me in a two stack and started to make his approach. I was scanning the arena we were landing in when I noticed a man floating in the middle of it, which confused me. Suddenly it hit me and the alarm bells went off.

"Stan!" I screamed, "there's a high wire act in the arena… we only have half an arena!"

"What?" Stan shouted back.

"The arena … we only have half of it … there's a wire going across the middle!"

Stan altered his approach and we landed safely, but we were both left shaking our heads. The show's organisers hadn't thought to tell us when the recce was carried out.

On another display we wore smoke bombs and, after free fall, the stack pilot had to take his off and tie it around his chest straps. We were high in the air when something silver flashed past my face.

"What the fuck was that?" I muttered, yanking my head back.

"Justa, I've just lost my smoke bomb!" Stan yelled.

"I know Stan, I'm watching it. Fucking hell, mate, it's somersaulting over the crowd." The spectators numbered around ten thousand. "Someone's going to wear that," I told him. I was horrified, my eyes glued to this silver smoke bomb. I watched with bated breath as it bounced on the grass in the arena, only four feet away from them, which caused some of the crowd to jump back in panic.

"That's why only the ones at the bottom of the stack wear smoke bombs," I tell the new guys. Everyone likes a good story and it goes down well.

For men whose testosterone is running high, the perfect location to be is at a Butlins holiday camp and we've just arrived for four days of shows. Our vehicles are parked up, the HGV1 lorry has 'Royal Marines Britain's Commandos' painted on the side - a huge advertisement - and another smaller lorry arrives with stores.

Our first job is to build a cliff and assault course, a static display that the public can have some fun on. As we're climbing up scaffolding and connecting the pieces, and the structure is coming together, there's a sense of being watched. A quick glance down and my eyes meet a group of about eighty women who are sitting on the grass and watching us. Some are quiet, just looking up at us, and others are chatting, but we don't need to hear what they're saying as we've carried out displays at Butlins before. One can only assume they're discussing which men they're going to get acquainted with over the next four days.

After the day's work and having completed a show it's back to the chalet to grab a shower and hit the bars, and the women are out in force. There's a mixture of Butlins' staff and holiday makers and they're out to score. Most of the display team stick together as we drink round after round; the rest of the company - the unarmed combat and abseil teams - spread out to different bars in their little groups.

The bar closes and, as I stumble back to my chalet, a hand grabs my collar. For a moment I assume a punch is coming my way and I brace myself for it, wondering what I've done wrong. Instead, I turn to see a girl who just says, "You're coming with me." I offer no resistance and she leads me back to where she's staying. There's no conversation; all she wants is some physical action.

In the morning my head is a bit hazy, my mouth is dry, and I try to piece together the events of the previous night. Again, there's no real conversation but more of a 'you can go now' vibe emanating from her. I almost feel I've been used but I don't mind. We part company and go our separate ways.

Later in the day I've recovered and we perform another parachute display. Trust is paramount when you're in a four stack and the guy at the top is doing the steering for all of you. It's not an easy task steering a four stack, and as we approach the arena I can see we're hot and high when I feel myself swinging forward. Instantly, I know this is bad because it means the stack pilot has applied brakes, which causes the stack to sink faster. This means the bottom guy is going to have a rough landing, and I just happen to be at the bottom. I curse, but nothing is going to change as we approach the ground. I adopt the 'feet and knees together' position, bending my knees for suspension, and sure enough I hit hard and it winds me. I look at Andy who is also picking himself up.

"That was fucking hard," I say, getting to my feet.

"You're not wrong there, "he replies.

I'm not too impressed as I limp away.

That night I'm oblivious to who is around me as I chat to a girl in the bar. After a few drinks I suggest we go back to my chalet, she agrees, and we head off with a bottle of wine. Back at the chalet I place the wine on the floor, and we both strip off and climb into bed. We chat for five minutes or so before things start to heat up but then, from the corner of my eye, I see the cupboard door open slightly and a hand appears. It takes me by surprise and I watch as the hand grabs my bottle of wine and disappears back into the cupboard. I'm not into giving a show so I climb off the bed and open the cupboard door to find two giggling Marines.

"Out!" I yell, and they both emerge, laughing. The next thing I know, a third amused person crawls from beneath the bed. I push all three out of the door and when I turn around the girl is pulling up her knickers.

"I have to go," she says, and beats a hasty retreat, clearly thinking I've engineered this. I'm even less impressed with the guys now.

The next morning I confront them and they think it's even funnier that she left. It appears they overheard me in the bar inviting this girl back, and rushed down to my chalet to find the small window open that allowed them to stick a hand in and open the door.

Another location, and this time we're in Sheffield, climbing up to altitude over the city in the Royal Navy Wessex Mk5 helicopter. Each skydiver is deep in thought; it's just the noise of the helicopter and the vibration going through us. I gaze around and look towards the pilot, who sits higher up, so all I can see is a pair of black boots under his seat. My eyes flick across to the co-pilot and wander down, so again, I'm looking just below his seat. I turn away and suddenly it hits me what I've just seen. In a split second, my eyes are focussed back to where they were. I hadn't imagined it ... I'm staring at a pair of high heels. My curiosity gets the better of me and I head to the door, telling the crewman I'm going outside. The rest of the team look on, obviously wondering what the hell I'm doing. All the time this Wessex Mk5 helicopter is clawing its way up to ten thousand feet.

I have to climb around the wheel strut carefully, grabbing hand holds and foot holds, as this isn't the time to slip and fall off over Sheffield with its buildings reaching towards the sky, and traffic like ants spreading out for miles. *How embarrassing would that be?* I think. Eventually, I arrive outside the pilot's window and knock on it, and he slides it back.

"Hello, sir," I say with a grin. "Thought I'd just pop up to admire the view. What a beautiful day it is." I look over to the co-pilot's seat and see this rather attractive lady in a skirt who is peering out of her window. She turns towards us, sees me outside the helicopter at eight thousand feet, and her jaw just drops. The look on her face is priceless and is well worth the trip up there. As I climb down I realise my team mates have closed the door and so, for the rest of the journey to altitude, I'm stuck outside the helicopter and freezing my nuts off, cursing my team mates, and slowly turning blue.

The jump goes well and, later, even I can see the funny side of what they did.

I never did catch that lady's name.

As the season comes to an end, my friend and colleague on the display team, Ian Graham, approaches me and asks what plans I have for leave. Ian is a Scottish lad and one of life's nicest and most genuine people. I consider myself fortunate that we've become good friends.

"Ian," I say. "You know the film at the AGM that showed skydivers jumping of that El Capitan cliff face?"

"Yes," he replies.

"Well, mate, I have to find out what it's like to be stood on the edge of that cliff. It has to be the ultimate test for someone like me who's scared of heights, right?"

Non-skydivers may be baffled at how someone who has a fear of heights can leap out of an aeroplane. It's hard to convince people who haven't jumped that you just don't register the height; it's nothing more than a picture of a landscape because you're so high up.

Ian, without hesitation, replies, "Well, I haven't got anything arranged so I'll come with you."

Getting information is hard as most of it is by word of mouth; however, I manage to find out that the Yosemite Park rangers were issuing permits which allowed people to jump off El Capitan. I reach the conclusion that if we go to Perris Valley Skydiving Centre in California, it will be close enough that we should be able to gather more information there as to how to go about things.

We arrive at Perris Valley mid-week, late in the day, so the drop zone is not too busy. As soon as our log books are checked the manifester calls on the tannoy system for Doc Johnson to 'get his arse over here'. Ian and I watch as Doc bursts through the door.

"What's up?" he says, panting from his run over.

"We have a couple of CRW guys here, that's what's up."

Doc Johnson, we soon find out, is a man with a passion for stacking and he's pleased to meet us. Ian and I are invited on the CRW sunset load and we tell him that as much as we'd love to join them our skydiving gear hasn't been checked. Before we know it, Doc has grabbed our gear and tagged it as checked and we're gearing up for the jump. They had planned to do a seven stack and we're asked where we'd be happy to dock.

"We're happy to dock wherever, Doc" I reply.

"Okay, you guys are eight and nine," he says.

To our surprise they actually build a seven stack, and Ian and I dock completing a nine stack. Beers flow that night as some guys had never been in anything that big before.

We carry on jumping for a few days and it's proving difficult to find any information on El Capitan. On our third day on the drop zone I'm approached by an American who mentions it hasn't gone unnoticed that we've only been jumping as a pair, and he asks what experience level we are. As soon as we mention the amount of jumps we've logged we're invited to join their group but we decline, telling him we've just completed a display season and are happy just doing fun two-ways.

On the very next jump Ian and I decide to do a shorts and T-shirt jump as it's so hot. We exit the DC3 at thirteen thousand feet and are laughing so much in free fall when I notice Ian's expression has changed and he's pointing behind me. At the same time I become aware of something tapping on my foot. To me it's obvious what's happening - the Americans have followed us out and have joined our jump to have some fun. There's a huge grin on my face as I look over my shoulder, however, rather than Americans, I'm staring at my partially inflated parachute, which soon wipes the grin from my face. I take one look at Ian and think, *Get the pilot chute out before I have a horse shoe* - a nightmare scenario where the parachute won't inflate due to the pilot chute being stuck in your pocket, causing a risk of the reserve entangling with the main. It's not something anyone wants to have. Before I can pull out the pilot chute, there's a loud crack and my parachute opens instantly. My knees shoot past my ears and I yelp in agony, and the air exhales from my lungs as if a professional boxer has punched me in the guts and kicked me in the balls at the same time. As I raise my head my vision is blurred, stars flash in my eyes, and my arms and legs just hang down limply. I'm open at seven thousand feet and it's proving painful to raise my arms to steer due to the pain in my chest.

I finally land next to Ian, who landed five minutes previously, and I cry out in pain.

"Mate, was that opening hard?" Ian says.

"Fucking hard," I gasp, trying to get air into my lungs.

"One moment you were in front of me and then, kapow, you were gone," Ian replies as I slowly stagger away.

For my following jumps I alter my body position on opening to 'feet to earth', all the while howling in pain, and find that it helps. In the evenings the alcohol seems to ease my discomfort unless I laugh too much. The only problem is, there's lots of laughter as we've met up with three Irish girls and we're having a great time.

Over the weekend more jumpers arrive and I make the point of circulating amongst them, eventually meeting some who have jumped off El Capitan. I'm informed that the park rangers had issued jumpers with three permits each, though some were happy just to jump it once. By luck I come across two skydivers who are willing to give us their spare permits and I rush off to tell Ian before calling the rangers to double check this will be acceptable, explaining we've travelled from England to do this. The female official tells me they'll allow us to use the permits, but I express my concern about whether we'll be able to arrive on time in order for the rangers to check our logbooks. To my surprise, she gives me her home number and says, "If you guys arrive late, don't hesitate to give me a call. I'll drive out to check your logbook and permits."

Ian and I are on our way. To reach Yosemite we have to travel all day and catch two greyhound coaches. The first one drops us off on a deserted city road in the early hours of the morning. We pace up and down, unsure where our connecting bus stop is, but luckily spot a police car across the road.

"Who better to ask than a friendly policeman?" I say to Ian.

We start to head over to him – it looks as if he's reading something -

and as we get closer he looks up, sits bolt upright, and shouts, "Freeze!" as he reaches for his pistol. And that's exactly what we do. We freeze. He no longer looks like a friendly policeman from England.

"One man approach," he shouts.

There's a slight debate between Ian and I as to who is going to approach first, and then Ian pushes me forward.

"I'm sorry to trouble you," I say, "but…"

"Are you English?" he interrupts.

"Yes," I reply, aware I've just made Ian an honorary Englishman, no doubt much to his disgust. The policeman heaves a sigh of relief and his hand comes off the pistol. Soon, he's given us directions and we head off, wondering what sort of neighbourhood we're in.

On arriving in Yosemite, the excitement of the adventure starts to kick in. The beauty of Yosemite is incredible; it has to be one of nature's most beautiful creations, and our noses are pressed against the coach window trying to take it all in.

We head straight over to the ranger's office and on entering I give the heartiest, 'Good afternoon' I can in my best British accent, knowing how much the American women love it. The lady behind the desk looks up.

"You must be the British guys! Nice to see you made it on time."

The documents are quickly checked and she wishes us a good jump. As Ian and I head off to find a campsite we spot a lot of signs warning us of the danger of bears, which mostly relate to not leaving food around. We have no food on us, but we're both in agreement it would be better to pitch our tents in the middle of some others - common sense, really, as the bears would reach the outer tents first, meaning we'd hear someone else's scream first as opposed to our own.

A map is purchased and we study the route to the top of El Capitan. Skydivers had previously talked about it being an eight hour climb and we'd just smiled. Eight hours for civilians, perhaps, but as young Royal Marines we felt four hours would be about right for us.

We work out the timings, ensuring we have enough daylight to reach the top. There's no time to enjoy our surroundings as our permits to jump El Capitan are for the following morning at 08:00 a.m., so we need to hike today. We grab the bare essentials we need but, as we'll be jumping, sleeping bags are out of the question.

We hike down the road in silence. For seven months I've dreamed about this and now I'm on my way to the top of El Capitan. We decide to try and hitch a lift to the starting point and the very first vehicle we see pulls over. It's an excellent start. As the vehicle drives down the road, El Capitan comes into view and I can feel the butterflies in my stomach as I picture myself standing on the edge of the cliff. The driver drops us off and we thank him for his kindness. Ian and I look at each other.

"Four hours, mate, and we'll be up at the top. Let's do it!" Ian says, and I nod with a smile on my face.

The walk through the forest is incredibly scenic and the path just keeps going up and up. Every so often we come to a fork, or a crossroads of paths, which tests our map reading skills. I remember what one of the skydivers who had jumped El Capitan said to me: "Look for the cairns on the path as they'll show you which route to take." Ian and I walk all the paths for a short distance and, sure enough, we spot them. What a brilliant idea! We're both extremely grateful to those skydivers who took the trouble in laying out the cairns, as it's helping us enormously.

The going gets tougher as the weight of our gear seems to increase, and it's such a relief when the path flattens out. It's an opportunity to try and catch our breath but the rest-stop doesn't last long and we're soon climbing up again.

According to our map we reach the half way stage and find the log with skydiving carvings on it that we'd been told about, so we decide to take a short break.

"Ian," I say, turning to him, "we've been hiking uphill for four hours and we've only reached the half way stage. How the hell do civilians do this in eight hours, bearing in mind all the training we've done?" By assuming we could do the hike in half the time, we've badly underestimated how long this is going to take.

We continue the hike through the forest and it isn't long before night falls upon us, making our navigation task that much harder. Disorientation is a real concern, as is the odd steep drop. The light from the torch feels like a life jacket in this sea of darkness. We scour the paths, trying to locate cairns at each junction we come across and breathe a sigh of relief when we find them. The air is still as there is no wind, and the sweat trickles down my forehead as my lungs try to grab as much air as possible. My legs begin to feel heavy and it becomes an effort to keep putting one foot in front of the other. At various times the silence of the night is broken by the crashing sound of a bear charging through the undergrowth and a voice in my head shouts, *Shit. What was that?* With eyes like saucers I scan the darkness where shadows take on strange shapes. I no longer have problems filling my lungs as my heart is beating that much faster. I know nothing about bear attacks but the thought of two Royal Marines running and tripping through the undergrowth, screaming in fear, would be enough to alert every bear in the neighbourhood.

The torchlight starts to fade and this is a real concern as we won't be able to see the cairns, so we cut out the rest-stops. I'm exhausted, my whole body is hurting, but our permits are only valid for 08:00 a.m. so we need to keep pressing on. To come this far and miss the window of opportunity is not an option. Ian takes everything in his stride and forges ahead.

As the torch finally dies we break out from the forest canopy and it's surprising how light it is under the stars. We can see the path and, some distance ahead of us, the sudden drop to the valley below. Even through the tiredness it kicks off the butterflies again.

We finally make it to the top of El Capitan and Ian spots a bonfire just below us. There's a deep satisfaction that we've made it to the top; the hike in itself in darkness is feeling like an achievement. As we amble down the slope, a voice from the glow of the fire calls out, "Hey! We have another two jumpers." It's an effort to introduce ourselves but we do, and slump onto the ground. A member of the group asks how long it took us and, on checking my watch, I tell him eight hours.

"That's about right. Did you start off by the log with the carvings on it?"

"No," I say, slightly confused. "That's the half way mark."

"Wow. You mean you started from the valley floor?"

It soon transpires we left the vehicle way too early and it could have dropped us within four hundred feet of the log. Ian and I are too tired to feel annoyed with ourselves, we're just happy that we've made it to the top. We crash out close to the open fire for warmth, and soon the temperature plummets. When we can't stand the cold any longer we search for more wood, and ensure the piece we add to the fire is closest to us.

Daylight arrives and bodies stir. It wasn't the best of sleeps but I'm happy there are no more hills to climb. We chat with the other skydivers and stretch our limbs as the sun rises higher, and eventually someone suggests we start heading down to the edge of the cliff face. Once we've put on our parachute gear we make our way down the slope, and my brain tries to take all of this in. I'm heading to the edge of El Capitan, and the questions I have to ask myself are about to be answered. The vastness of the valley and the sense of this huge depth just seem to keep growing. I can see the mountains in the distance on the opposing side and feel the sheer size of the cliffs. It's breathtaking.

We stop about thirty feet short of the edge to wait for 08:00 a.m., and there's complete silence as each man goes within himself for a bit of soul searching. As I look towards the edge I no longer feel the thrill of the excitement but just an overwhelming sense of dread. My fear of heights is all too real and makes me feel queasy. I no longer want to take photographs; I'm not in the mood. I dig deep into my thoughts and put my camera inside my jumpsuit. My heart is pounding and I take deep breaths, asking myself, *Why?* This has to be one of the stupidest ideas I've ever come up with. It all sounded so good back in England but now, faced with the enormity of what

I'm supposed to be doing, I question the logic of it.

"Oh my God!" someone shouts out, "he's just gone over the edge!" Heads scan around and, yes, it's true, we're one person down. This starts my heart pounding faster. Another jumper steps forward and says he's going, he can't wait any longer, and we all just stare as a climber from the group walks to the edge to watch him disappear. One moment he was there and then he was gone, and my ears strain to hear the sound of his parachute opening. The climber jumps up and down. "Wow, that was awesome!" he yells. The fact he has no safety harness on and is so close to the edge is making me feel physically sick.

Out of the blue, Ian turns to me. "Andy," he says, "I'm not going to wait any longer, I'm going now."

My head turns to face him and my brain is saying, "Hey, it was my idea, I go first," but the words, "Okay," come out of my mouth instead.

I watch Ian take those steps towards the edge, my eyes transfixed on him, and very calmly Ian launches himself off. My heart sinks. The climber confirms he's okay and then all eyes turn towards me.

"I suppose you'll be wanting to go next?" a voice pipes up.

I'm having a complete coordination problem with my brain and tongue. My head is thinking, "Hey, what's the rush?" but a resigned, "I suppose so," comes out instead. With a deep breath, I walk towards the edge.

All the senses in my body are at fever pitch, my mouth has gone dry, and my brain feels almost numb as I step up to the launch platform, which slopes steeply towards the edge. No one needs to tell me my pupils have enlarged. Yosemite National Park is all around me and the view is magnificent. I can't look down, but I focus on the horizon to try and control my fear. This is the moment; I can't have any more questions in my head. There are people watching, and this means the backdoor has closed. I pause to analyse the situation. I'd seen in the film how far it was possible to get away from the cliff face. Quite a few skydivers have taken this plunge ... I've just seen three of them do it and they were okay. It really is just a question of conquering the fear within me, not what's out there.

But can I do it?

There's no sound; just silence. I look at the blue sky, the stunning landscape before me, and it's a beautiful day, I think. I'm at peace with myself. I take a deep breath and many thoughts and pictures flash through my mind, but the answer is yes. Yes, I can do it. With my legs bent, I take two steps down the slope whereupon I leap, as hard and as far as I can, over the edge.

My body position starts to go head down and this wasn't in the plan. I throw my legs and arms back into the tracking position, which should see me move away from the cliff face, but it has no effect. I look over my shoulder, my concern building, the cliff face so close, and I can see the speed accelerating as the side of the cliff races past me. I'm five seconds into my free fall jump off El Capitan when I suddenly feel and visually see myself accelerate away from the cliff. "Yes! Yes!" my brain screams out as it continues to count the seconds. The valley below me is looking even more beautiful as the distance between me and the cliff face grows. Ten seconds, and I can see I'm half way down. It's time to open the parachute. I throw out my pilot chute and feel myself being tugged upright. The parachute opens and I swear I have never seen it look so beautiful. There are countless emotions running through my body and my mind. This is such a massive high, created by a natural rush of adrenalin, and I feel euphoric.

I have a soft landing in the valley next to the crowd who have come to watch, and they clap and cheer for the entertainment I've just provided them. My equipment is dropped to the ground where I've landed, and Ian walks over to me. We're both speechless.

A ranger on horseback rides up to ask to see my permit and I pull it out of my pocket. I then have to sit down; I'm still trying to take it all in. I look up to see the next jumper leap off El Capitan and watch him in awe. Chuck lands and walks up to me.

"You know, Andy, that was the most terrifying piece of cake," he says.

"What do you mean?"

"When I was stood up there on the edge I was terrified, but once I'd leapt off it just became another skydive."

I feel so alive. My body is buzzing, that free spirit deep inside me is thanking me for allowing it to breathe, and I feel – as strange as it sounds – as if I'm me … the me that I'm *supposed* to be.

Ian and I party until the early hours, starting off in the restaurant, and money is no object. We order the finest food and drink so many beers that it impairs our walk back to the tents, but who cares? We've just jumped off El Capitan.

On my return to England my chest is still giving me pain, so I go to see the doctor who sends me for an X-ray. The doctor informs me I actually cracked my sternum from that hard opening at Paris Valley.

Two weeks later I'm jumping again at Netheravon. We're going to the World Cup to represent Great Britain, so the team starts training in speed eight stacks. During the training we break the world record a few more times for the fastest eight stack to be built. More skydivers show an interest in trying this stacking, and there's a real bond building between those that do it. Other skydivers consider us slightly crazy for grabbing each other's parachutes and sliding down the rigging lines.

We take a break from doing a training jump as we notice we now have enough CRW guys to try for the world record for the biggest stack. Everyone on the jump is allocated a slot of when to dock and we walk it through, making sure each person knows what's expected of them. When we board the aircraft I can sense the excitement. We're all up for this. As the aircraft climbs up to altitude, everyone is in deep thought and going over in their heads the job they need to do.

We start to exit the two planes, leaving a trail of parachutes opening up. Now it's just a question of getting into the right position. I watch the stack building, making sure I lose height and stay below the stack, as it starts to descend faster the bigger it gets. The guy I'm docking on to makes his approach and I start mine, lining myself up under him. Two years later I can still hear my brother's voice telling me to get my sight picture and keep it there.

My parachute hits the bottom guy and I'm on. I've done my job having docked seventh, and everything goes smoothly as each person joins the stack. Finally, the last person docks thirteenth. We've just set a new world record for the biggest stack ever built, and the cheers ring out both in the air and on the ground. We reach our break off height and start to peel off one at a time; it's now a safe journey down to the ground. I can't stop smiling and shout to myself, "We've got it! We've got the world record!"

The atmosphere in the bar that night is electric, with the participants in the stack and those that watched it celebrating. For the first time the world record biggest stack has been taken away from America, and it's a wonderful feeling.

A week later, Andy Grice, Mike McCarthy, my brother Pete, and I are doing a four man stack rotation jump, where each time the person at the top of the stack comes off and docks on the bottom, the team score a point, and we're working against the clock. We soon notice that when the top person comes off the three stack will surge, so we come up with the idea of the second guy applying brakes by using his steering toggles.

Andy Grice has just docked on me, I'm starting to slide down his two front-centre rigging lines, and my brother is above me, when Mike comes off the top. I hear my brother shout, "Whoa!" and the next thing I know I have a falling sensation. I know it's bad - very bad - and as I go through Andy's rigging lines my brain evaluates that the stack has stalled. I suddenly go from daylight to darkness; I'm completely wrapped up by a parachute. My brain races as I struggle to get it off me. Daylight appears, but instead of joy I see the horizon is spinning out of control, and the reality of my dire situation hits me. It's not just Andy I am entangled with, but also my brother, and the three of us are spinning and falling to earth. My heart rate goes through the roof. *Focus! Work it out!* I tell myself. I grab rigging lines and lift them over my head; it's a struggle and time is not on my side, but I seem to find extra strength and lift a couple more rigging lines over to see Andy fall away.

"One gone, one to go," I hear my brother shouting to me. "Don't jettison your parachute."

I shout back, "Seriously, Pete? Do I look like I'm in the position to do that?"

We've stopped spinning out of control, my parachute is fully inflated above my head, Pete is hanging off me, but I've bought some extra time. At last I manage to clear the last couple of lines, Pete drops away, and his parachute re-inflates. There's damage to mine, though - I have torn cells. I call my brother over to fly his parachute next to me, so I can evaluate my rate of descent compared to his, and my decision is made… I'm landing it. Pete follows me down and lands next to me.

I'm thankful that Andy and my brother kept a cool head, having seen I was wrapped up in their parachutes. They stayed with theirs and bought me time to get out of that predicament, so the beers are on me tonight and I gladly buy them.

Geordie Laing, the Chief Instructor at Netheravon, asks to see us concerning the CRW World Cup, and apparently it's to do with finances. The team is a joint military team and we've come up with a name, 'Mountain Men'. Geordie explains that the Army are paying for the Army lads to go, the Air Force is paying for their guy to go, but the Royal Marines have refused to pay for the four Marines - Andy Grice, Gary Lawry, Pete and me - to go. Geordie goes on to say that the Army have run a couple of parachute courses to help raise some funds for the four of us but have failed to raise enough, and he apologies that he has to ask us to contribute £350.00 each towards the trip. There are no complaints from us, I'm over the moon to be going to the World Cup and representing Great Britain.

We arrive at Zephyrhills in Florida and can see other teams are already there and doing practice jumps. We gear up to do ours and notice the other teams have come out with clipboards and stopwatches to time us. It appears word has got around. The Americans are considered the favourites but they've heard we've not only broken the world record for the fastest eight stack, but we also hold the record for the biggest stack ever built at thirteen.

In the aircraft we decide not to do an eight stack but a free fall jump instead, just to wind the other teams up who really want to see us perform.

Later, our team win the CRW speed eight stack and secure gold, and now we just have the four stack rotations team event left. We're around five points in the lead, and things are looking promising that the Mountain Men may well be taking home two golds.

The weather changes and the four stack rotations event is put on hold. The Americans try to encourage us to go out drinking but we decline. There's a further two days of bad weather and plenty of hanging around and getting a bit frustrated. On the third day the weather improves and we receive a phone call at 05:45 a.m. to inform us the competition is back on. We load up the vehicles but notice two of the guys are missing, and we question where on earth they could be. One of the team spots them and says, "I don't believe it." We look over to see both men staggering; they have only just left the bar. Shaking our heads, we tell them the competition is back on.

Over the next few jumps the Americans pull back as the two hung-over guys perform below their normal standard. The Americans have it - they win the gold. Our 'A' team has the silver, and our 'B' team comes fourth and misses the bronze. The four of us in the Marines feel let down, and we make a decision that we will never again compete in a joint military team, it will be all Royal Marines next time.

Back in the UK we hear the Royal Aero Club have decided to award us the Prince of Wales trophy for our achievement, which will be presented by the Prince of Wales.

I'm currently on a notice engagement with the Royal Marines. I've considered my options and, as I'm enjoying my time with them, I decide to sign on and extend my time with them. I head over to the Sergeant Major's office to sign on and, as I approach, he looks up at me.

"Guest, you were on that trip to America. There's a Major on the phone who wants to speak to someone who was on it."

It dawns on me it's probably someone who wants to congratulate us on our achievement. I pick up the telephone and introduce myself. "Marine Guest speaking, Sir."

"Were you on that trip to America?" he asks.

"Yes, Sir," I reply.

"Who the fuck gave you permission to go?" he shouts.

This doesn't sound like a congratulatory call. "My company commander gave me permission to go, Sir," I reply.

"What's all this nonsense about representing Great Britain?" he asks.

I'm irritated by his aggressive tone. "Quite simple, Sir. Prior to going to the CRW World Cup, we'd broken the world record a number of times, as well as getting the world record for the biggest stack. We've brought back gold and silver from the CRW World Cup and have been informed that the Royal Aero Club have awarded us the Prince of Wales trophy, which will be presented by the Prince of Wales," I reply.

"You'll hear more about this," he snaps, and slams down the phone.

I'm disappointed. Angry at his response. I reflect back to the beginning of the year when a few of us were awarded our Royal Marines Sporting Colours and were asked if we thought we deserved it. Andy Grice came to attention and replied, "Well, Sir, I could represent the Royal Marines in boxing and be knocked out three times but I would still be standing before you receiving my Royal Marines Sporting Colours. However, Sir, in this unique situation, you have before you six people who hold a British record. I believe we're the only Marines at this time to hold one."

There was no reply from the colonel; not even a hand shake.

I step out of the office into the corridor and look towards the Sergeant Major. "Sir, regarding my notice," I say to him as he looks up. "I'll take it."

Normally it takes between three to six months to leave the Royal Marines but, four hours later, I drive out of the camp on my silver Honda Superdream. I stop the bike and look back at the camp. "Bloody hell, I'm a civilian," I tell myself. It's still sinking in as I accelerate and head to West Sussex.

The open road stretches out before me. Although I know where this one leads, I have no idea where my life's path is going to take me. But I do know what my free spirit wants, and that's to take a big step outside of my comfort zone. I reflect back on the year: six world records, a brilliant time on the parachute display team, a gold medal at the CRW World cup representing Great Britain, and that incredible jump off El Capitan. I wonder if I'll ever have a year like it again.

HELL ON EARTH

My brother, Ken, has just returned from his travels and I note he's looking gaunt and tired, but I'm intrigued to know what he's been up to. He has centre stage in my parents' living room and we're all captivated, listening in awe to his exploits. It's clear this has been no ordinary journey for him.

Ken has just spent four months working in Afghanistan alongside the mujahideen, filming their war with the Russians. His words enthral me and I'm riveted to the chair as he speaks, wondering what on earth it must feel like to be in such a volatile situation. The questions in my head pop up thick and fast. Would I handle it? Woul I have the balls, the courage, to enter the fields of death? Would my thought processes be quick enough to keep me safe? The stakes would be high - make one wrong decision or hesitate at the wrong moment and it would be all over. The biggest question is: What would I learn about myself? I had my Royal Marines training to prepare myself for such a situation, but I never had the opportunity to find out.

Later, in the kitchen and when we're alone, Ken asks me what my plans are now my military service has come to an end.

"I'm thinking of the oil rigs. The government run a course to learn how to be a floor man, and I've just taken the pre-application test."

"Not heard anything yet?" he asks.

"No, not yet."

"And in the meantime?"

I shrug my shoulders.

"Well, I'm going back to Afghanistan to film the war and I need someone to give me a hand with all the camera gear. Fancy it?"

My first reaction is to say yes, but the word doesn't leave my mouth. Instead, the reality of the world I'd be entering hits me with full force. This isn't a movie script where the good guys always win and ride off into the sunset; I'd be in an environment where most things would be out of my control, where anything, literally, could happen. I ask Ken to tell me more of his plans so I'm able to see the bigger picture and understand the risks, and as I listen to his words a debate takes place inside my head. Yes, I'll be stepping outside of my comfort zone, but I won't be on my own. There will be dangers that will test me, but I've had first-class training. I could die but, then again, I might not, and what an adventure I'd have to reflect on in years to come. The overwhelming feeling I'm left with after the voices in my head fade away is that there's something for me to learn from this. I'm not sure what it is, and that's why I know I need to find out.

"Why not, Ken? It sounds like an adventure," I tell him.

There's no turning back. I've made a commitment that I have to honour, and my brother is delighted. *How bad can it get?* I think.

The weeks leading up to our departure feel strange. I spend my time skydiving, laughing, and having fun with friends, and I embrace it all even more as I contemplate whether I'll ever get the opportunity to do it again. Ken dashes around putting everything in place for our trip, and there's only one thing left for me to do. I write a letter to my parents. I tell them, in the past tense, how lucky I was to have them as my parents; that I can't thank them enough for their support. It's crucial they understand why this journey was so important to me and that I fully understood the risks, and so I explain it all. And then I write to my brothers, and tuck all the letters inside a single envelope.

I travel up to London and ask my friend Diane to look after it and, should the worst happen, make sure my parents receive it. I can see this request makes Diane feel uneasy but I tell her she's doing me a huge favour and she agrees.

The time for me to journey into the unknown arrives, and Ken and I board the aircraft. As it climbs into the sky I look down and wonder if I will ever see these green pastures again. I don't think I've ever seen England looking so gorgeous.

On our arrival at Islamabad airport, the first thing I notice is the overpowering stench in the air. This is my first time in Pakistan and it already feels like an adventure. Ken sorts out the transport and we squash into a small minibus that's heading to Peshawar. It's hot, cramped and smelly, and the minibus swerves to avoid other vehicles on the road. I can't help thinking I misjudged the risks on this journey as I hadn't put this road trip into the equation, with the driver quite clearly not caring if he lives or dies. The odd bang as we hit a pothole sets my nerves on edge, and the shockwaves shudder through my spine and make me grimace.

We finally reach Peshawar and it's like a wild frontier. Tuk tuks zoom around like dodgems with their horns beeping; car horns join in and the drivers rev their engines - it sounds as if an orchestra has lost its composer. The sun beats down, creating a haze through the smoke and dust rising in the air, and beggars peer up from the dirt roads at this crazy world in the hope of a kind heart. Steely eyes pierce me wherever I look, wanting to know who this foreigner is who's ventured into their domain. I haven't shaved since leaving the Marines and I felt the beard may have helped me to blend in on this trip, but now I'm not so sure.

We arrive at our hotel - The Khyber, which is to be our base until we've made the right contacts to enter Afghanistan – and it's like nothing I've ever seen before. Ken promised me no luxuries as the budget was tight, but even so…

This run down building hosts unsavoury, spaced-out characters who loiter on the landing and stairways, and our room houses not much more than two very old sun loungers acting as beds. I observe Ken as he pours a line of DDT powder around his bed, and he advises me to do the same.

"Why?" I ask.

"It'll stop the ants climbing up and feasting on you."

On that note, I have no wish to question his wisdom and pour the powder in a circle around my bed, just outside the boundary of my mosquito net.

We have the window open, the air is thick and warm, and the voices of the unsavoury characters I'd seen earlier float into the room, which makes sleeping difficult. Sweat trickles down my body but tiredness helps me to drift off, where, for brief moments I escape my surroundings. I really hadn't thought this part of the trip through, either. The night is long, and the sounds seem to echo and create images in my head of things that will do me harm.

In the morning we're up early. The shower isn't great and I'm even less than impressed with this hole in the floor they call a toilet. I realise it's something I'm missing from England: just a normal toilet to sit on to ponder the meaning of life.

We head out, stopping at a street stall for some green tea. Flies are everywhere, swarming around the food and turning my stomach, and making the thought of using a street vendor for sustenance unappealing, but it's still likely to be safer than the hotel food.

I notice I'm receiving a lot of attention - men openly stop and stare at me - and it's apparent they're not accustomed to seeing someone walking around in shorts. The way they stare reminds me of how some men ogle women, and I begin to feel uncomfortable. I tell Ken I want to change into long trousers so we head back to the hotel, and the relief I feel when we step back out again confirms it was a good decision.

As we pass the people on the stairs and out on the street at the front of the hotel, it's clear they're from Europe, and I ask Ken why they would be here. Ken explains there used to be a hippy trail that some westerners followed in the late sixties and seventies - most in search of adventure, fun and travel - but some failed to make it back to their homeland after getting hooked on drugs. They create a sad image: lost souls who cannot see the light and escape their entrapment.

The main road is filled with little cottage industries, people making and selling all manner of things. We stroll down the street and watch a guy in the process of ageing furniture and other items to make them appear antique. Copies of the Russian AK-47 rifle are cheap but unreliable and on sale at every corner, along with pistols and military webbing equipment, all of which is under par. The streets are crowded and noisy with cars, lorries and tuk tuks that race around haphazardly, and the stench from open sewers clings to my nose, only occasionally replaced by the aroma of pungent spices from the street vendors' food.

Ken chases a contact that was suggested to him back in the UK as someone who could guide us into Afghanistan, and we head to the address to discuss the possibilities. We arrive at the house, which is secured in a compound with security on the gate, and are escorted inside. I sit back and let Ken do the talking.

Professor Majroor is delighted. It is no problem, he tells us. Everything will be laid on. His own nephew will be there and leading mujahideen to the fight. Afghans were born expert guerrilla fighters, he goes on… expert marksmen from birth, and fitter and faster than mountain goats. Ken is already seasoned to the way Afghans think and the things they say, and tells me not all will be as promised, but still we strike a deal.

On the day of our journey I change into local clothes to try and blend in and hope my beard will aid me in the process. I very quickly realise this is going to be a long, uncomfortable ride as we're crammed like sardines into a minibus with all our kit, along with the mujahideen.

We head north from Peshawar, winding uphill to Charsadda. Slowly, the arid dust of the Peshawar Plain gives way to trees carpeting the mountain slopes. Cramped in this minivan, with the curtains partially closed, the landscape passes by in a blur. All I can focus on is the pungent smell of petrol from a can at the back, and the sweat from those on board.

From Charsadda the road continues to climb uphill and we head east, towards Mardan. From there the road swings north and we make our way towards Swat, via Jalala and Sakhakot. Along this stretch we have a brief stop, which is a welcome break to stretch the legs. We stand by the side of the road next to a *Chai Khana*, a tea house. Lunch is a naan dipped into a plastic bowl of watery goat stew, accompanied by a swarm of flies, and the meal is washed down with a steaming glass of *shire chai*, a sweetened milk tea.

It's a long, uncomfortable journey when we set off again and at numerous times cramp sets in. The space on the minibus is limited, there's no way to get comfortable, and my knees smack against the seat in front of me with every bump and pothole on the road. At checkpoints we encounter bored frontier police who wear black uniforms and berets and hold AK-47 rifles. As they enter the vehicle I pretend to be asleep, my *pawkul* pulled down over my eyes, my scarf around my neck and face, my head bowed down.

There are an increasing number of military checkpoints as the road slowly draws closer to the Afghan border, and I'm aware that at any one of these we could be arrested for being in the tribal area, where outsiders are not permitted. This adventure could have many outcomes, I think.

Eventually, darkness falls and the journey comes to an end. We arrive in the Dir Valley, where we climb from the bus with stiff, aching limbs. I look up, stretching my neck, and note how bright the stars are. With no electricity here there is no light pollution.

Our accommodation for the night is a house built of concrete. Not all the windows have glass, some just have cardboard, and it's very basic with no furniture, no carpets. We'll be sleeping on the dusty floor but I'm glad to be off the bus.

A meal is brought and we eat communally on an oiled cloth. There are no knives and forks; it is not their way, so we use our fingers. I soon realise there's a skill to it. We're given *blastans,* thick cotton quilts, and *pertous,* blankets, and as I settle down on the hard floor I'm conscious that tomorrow we'll be heading into Afghanistan. Professor Majroor's nephew boasts of his prowess and physical stamina, and his determination to kill Russians. He jokes we will not be able to keep up with him. Time will tell, I think, as I close my eyes.

I awake after a restless sleep and, from now on, we're on foot. We start to climb a mountain that forms part of the Hindu Kush – a formidable mountain range that stretches close to the Afghan-Pakistan border - which towers above us and touches the clouds. A rough path snakes its way up the mountainside and will eventually take us over the top and into Afghanistan. It's an endless climb and at times I find it hard to catch my breath. I ignore the views as I put one foot in front of the other and suck in air as the sweat trickles down my forehead and into my eyes. My brother and I pace ourselves, drinking from our water bottles, not knowing when our next opportunity to top them up will be.

The top of the mountain is barren and a bitter wind cuts through us. We spot a lonely tent in this harsh environment, full of holes, its loose material flapping. The occupants, we discover, are an Afghan family who decided to flee when the Russians bombed their village.

The owner of the tent invites us to join him for some green tea and we accept his kind offer; it's an opportunity to escape this cold wind and get something warm inside us. Our tea arrives with a lump of brown sugar, which we bite into before taking a sip of our hot drinks. The man apologises that he has no food to offer us and seems embarrassed about his predicament. I look around the tent and see he has two small daughters, aged around five and seven, and a wife who is hiding, as strangers are not permitted to see the Afghan women.

Before we leave Ken suggests that we give this family our rations as we'll undoubtedly be able to pick up food along the way. I agree wholeheartedly. The gesture is welcome and the man is very emotional, close to tears. It's a clear indication they haven't eaten for a while. If ever I thought life was treating me hard, this encounter puts things into perspective for me, and I realise how blinkered I've been at various times in my life when I've felt sorry for myself.

Tashakor, we tell the man, thanking him for his kindness, and begin our descent down the mountain. It's only now, feeling refreshed and walking downhill, that I take in the view that spreads out before my eyes. It's a beautiful, idyllic landscape.

My brother decides it's the right time to mention to me that the Russians have a tendency to drop 'butterfly' anti-personnel mines over mountain passes, so to keep my eyes open and watch where I put my feet. The mines, designed for use against humans rather than vehicles, were given the name 'butterfly' because of their shape, which unfortunately attracts children to them who think they are toys. In a single sentence, the words 'idyllic landscape' are erased from my mind; it just disguises the horror - the pain and death - of this war in Afghanistan.

The first village we enter is quiet; it's Ramadan - the month of fasting - and people we were expecting to meet are not here. We trudge on and, again, find no food. We're in Kunar and following a mountain river which, in parts, originates from the melted snow in the mountains. As we walk the Afghans tell us stories of how they blew up a thousand tanks and killed thousands of Russians. Even I can see how farfetched these accounts are. Ken tells me for every tank the mujahideen destroy they claim to have destroyed hundreds more.

As we continue to follow the path running alongside the river we come across a scene where an ambush has taken place and the atmosphere changes instantly. Although it's a bright and sunny day without a cloud in the sky, it feels as if a dark cloud has descended over this spot. It's an eerie and sinister picture, just like a flashbulb memory where everything, in minute detail, has been captured and preserved in a snapshot.

I see panic, where men have tried to build small stony walls to hide behind, but there is nowhere to escape. Rations, along with personal items, are scattered on the ground. I hear voices, men screaming out in pain, others calling for their mothers. And I sense fear; there's an overpowering stench of death in the air from the unburied bodies which lie under cairns of stones. The ones left out in the open are normally eaten by dogs, and there is evidence of this.

I look up from the windy track of the gorge to the mountains that tower over us. It's a horrendous place to be caught in an ambush and I don't understand why anyone would lead their men through here without dominating the high ground. The phrase 'lambs to the slaughter' comes to mind.

As we haven't eaten for three days, Ken suggests we collect some of the tinned rations that are strewn around us. As much as I don't like the idea it makes sense because we have to keep our strength up. I eat Bulgarian beans from the dead Russian and Afghan armies, trying not to picture the scene of the ambush, and am happy when we move on, leaving the smell of death, fear and panic behind us. As I walk away voices scream out to me, yet it is silent.

The following day it's all too clear that our escort party haven't a clue what they're doing and we're not actually heading towards any fighting at all. Professor Majroor's nephew has already left us; he turned out to be more of an 'urban softie' than the 'man mountain' he professed to be - in a knackered sulk by end of day one, and miserable and morose by day two. Having not eaten for two days he decided to leave. Ken and I discuss our options and agree we're wasting our time with this group, so we push to be taken back to Peshawar. Three men are tasked to escort us and one of them has a rifle, which appears to be an old British Lee Enfield that dates back many years.

Not long into our journey things take a sinister turn. Ken listens to the three men talking, who are unaware he speaks a little of their language. Ken tells me they've been discussing how much money we could be carrying and how much our camera equipment could be worth. Also, one of them has noticed a gold ring I'm wearing which I'd forgotten about. We talk about what pre-empted action they may take and it's felt likely the man carrying the rifle will ambush us, laying the blame on the Russians. So, we come up with a plan. If the rifleman disappears at any point, we will each latch onto one of the other guys and stay very close, shoulder to shoulder.

Sure enough, at various times the rifleman disappears as we make our way up the mountain. We put our plan into operation and I stick to my designated man like glue. Should a shot be fired, I will tackle him and take him out in whatever means possible, most likely with a rock. It would be brutal but necessary, considering my life would be at stake.

As we descend back into Pakistan it's obvious that one man stands out as the person who has been in charge, and Ken decides it would be a sensible idea to give him his watch as a thank you, in the hope it will increase the odds in our favour of getting back alive. Thankfully, it all works out, and we arrive safely in Peshawar. The unsavoury characters are still on the landing of the Khyber hotel, smoking weed or injecting heroin.

Ken meets an Australian/Afghan journalist who has just come out of Afghanistan and takes pity on us. He gives us a contact that comes to fruition.

On our second trip back into Afghanistan we find ourselves placed into one of two groups that will be travelling together. The other group consists of French doctors and nurses from the Médecins Sans Frontières (Doctors without Borders), an organisation that sends qualified medical professionals into areas of conflict. The French aren't too impressed to see us as what they do is supposed to be kept a secret and, viewing us as journalists, they choose to ignore us.

After a lengthy ride in the vehicles we arrive at our destination. We walk along a short path, heading into a compound, and as we approach the main building two Chinese people in suits appear. Our eyes meet, a voice shouts out, and suddenly Ken and I are bundled into a room. Three hours later we're allowed to come out and are escorted into the main building where we're given green tea. All around the room there are open packing boxes with Chinese writing on the sides which contain AK-47s and mines. It's clear we were not supposed to see that the Chinese are supplying arms.

Eventually we continue our journey on foot along flat ground, passing the odd village where women hide behind closed doors so as not to be seen.

After a long, hot journey and as we climb the mountain, Ken and I pace ourselves on our water as we know we're only half way up. I'm approached by one of the Afghans who asks for my water bottle and then asks for my brother's. We pass them over, assuming that a couple of them are thirsty, but we watch as they're handed over to the French who promptly guzzle it all and return our empty bottles without even a thanks. I'm furious, especially as I'm thirsty myself and have been holding back. The French don't even have the decency to give us an acknowledgement of a thank you, having clearly seen that the water came from us.

We descend into Afghanistan and I'm happy not to be hiking up that twelve thousand feet mountain; the downhill stretch is far easier. We arrive at a bombed out village where the locals have fled and see the mujahideen have taken up residence in small numbers. We're sweaty and tired and, to be fair, we stink. There's a mountain river two hundred feet below us, flowing fast. The mujahideen organise some food and Ken suggests we go down to the river to freshen up, which sounds like a brilliant idea.

The river water is freezing but the opportunity to wash with a bar of soap and feel like a new man makes it so worthwhile. When we return to the bombed out property we find that the mujahideen had brought the food while we were gone and the French have eaten it all, leaving us with nothing. Though I admire they are volunteers, and what they do putting themselves at risk is noteworthy, their arrogance and rudeness is too much.

Due to exhaustion I sleep soundly that night, and in the morning we continue our descent. As we follow the track along the river I notice that an Afghan, ahead of us, is picking up rocks and dropping them into the water. My curiosity gets the better of me and I wonder if is this some sort of Afghan fishing technique, so I approach him and look to see what he's doing. I see no fish but, instead, a Russian anti-personnel mine on a boulder, sticking out of the water. The man's rock bounces off the boulder, narrowly missing the mine, and I leap back in horror. What the hell is he thinking? Had he hit the bloody thing it would have detonated, injuring if not killing the both of us.

Further down the trail a shot rings out. Everyone is startled and jumps for cover before realising it's one of our mujahideen who has accidently pulled his trigger with the safety catch off.

We come across a trader with a small hut along this track, which comes as a surprise. He's selling green tea and some food, and Ken treats me to a boiled egg. I take small bites to make it last longer, and it tastes wonderful.

As we reach the plains where the ground flattens out we see black smoke rising on the horizon; Russian attack helicopters are bombing and shooting up a village. Ken curses and says had we been a day earlier we could have been in that village and filming the attack which, funnily enough, are the exact opposite of my thoughts, as taking cover would seem to be to be the more appropriate action.

The French depart with their group and we set off in different directions. Personally, I'm thinking 'good riddance' as they were a bunch of miserable people.

A while later we reach a village and settle down to eat. It's not long before we hear explosions in the distance and venture outside onto the terrace to see what's going on. Again, we see Russian attack helicopters strafing another village, and there are more explosions and black smoke rising. I become aware of a whizzing sound and ask Ken if he can hear it, which he confirms. Suddenly, the dust kicks up all around us. The penny drops: it's shrapnel cutting through the air, so we retreat indoors. An hour later we venture outside again to find chunks of shrapnel - some weighing a couple of pounds and with razor sharp edges - laying on the terrace where we'd stood, which are still extremely hot to touch.

The Afghans spot a patrol on top of the hill behind them and plan a quick attack. We haven't got the time to set up the 16mm cameras but tag along, just to observe. On top of the hill I see a couple of vehicles and some men walking around, and the mujahideen engage them by opening up with their rifles. There's a return of fire which cracks above our heads. It's only a brief fire fight because as soon as the sound of a Mi-24 gunship is heard, the mujahideen take flight. I've never seen them move so fast but know they must be doing so for a very good reason so I increase my sprint so as not to be left behind. Clearly, this is a case of every man for himself.

A few days pass and we continue to walk in the Nangarhar Province, being passed from group to group. In one village we come across two Russian prisoners and enquire what is to become of them.

"We may kill them tomorrow, or the day after," we're told. There's a blasé attitude about it, as life is cheap in this country.

A couple of days later we depart the village to continue our journey in the hope of finding some fighting taking place, and hear that the day after we'd left the two Russians were executed.

At another village we discover the mujahideen are planning an attack on a fort while supper is being cooked, and it's our first opportunity to film so we tag along. The mujahideen carry out a small attack, and Ken is able to film them using a heavy machine gun that fires 50 calibre rounds. Meanwhile, I use my stills camera to capture Ken filming this. It's only a short fire fight exchange and then it's back to the village to have supper. The Afghans seem to have a predictable pattern: they always launch their attack when breakfast or tea is cooking, but never at lunchtime because it's too hot under the sun. My only surprise is that they – the Russians or Afghan army - haven't seized on this opportunity and set up an ambush.

The sun begins to set and Ken has a conversation with the mujahideen leader. Voices are raised and this increases my curiosity, so I approach my brother and ask him what's happening.

"They're planning an attack tonight and were going to put us right at the back of all their action, so I told him 'no way, we'll go with the front man', and reluctantly he's agreed."

"I didn't know you could film at night," I reply.

"I can't," Ken tells me.

I'm completely dumbfounded so I push as to why we're going.

"To show the Afghans we're not scared," he says. I'm glad my brother has confidence in me but that's not how I'm feeling.

That night we head out into the darkness. I'm struggling to see the person in front of me so there's no chance of spotting any anti-personnel mines. I can only hope the path is clear.

We hit a point where the riflemen break off and we follow a guy with a Chinese recoilless rifle, that's better described as a bazooka. We crouch down and edge forwards towards the fort, and the man drops us off just in front of a building that has two shallow scrapes to lie in. Ken crawls out about twelve feet to set up a tape recorder to record the action. As we lie there we can hear voices from the fort on this clear sky night, as everything else appears to be silent.

There's a huge bang from our left as the recoilless rifle is fired, followed by an explosion on the fort. All hell lets loose as the mujahideen riflemen on our far right open up, and those in the fort return fire. The sky lights up in red and green as tracer rounds fly through the air, and it's mesmerising, as if someone has put on a rather spectacular but noisy firework display.

I hear the sounds of two mortars being fired and mention it to Ken. Time passes and the explosions can be heard some distance away. A few rounds crack above our heads as they go past as a reminder this is no kiddies firework display. I pick up that three more mortars have been fired and tell Ken. They seem to be in the air a long time and it hasn't dawned on me that it means they're going to land closer to where we are. It's now that I hear the sound of an incoming mortar that rattles through a tree sixty feet away from us before exploding. It only just sinks in what's just happened when there's the most terrifying screaming noise right above our heads, like a German Stuka plane, which is getting louder. There's a deafening explosion thirty feet from us and the instant smell of cordite, and dirt and gravel rains over us, followed by dust. In a split second my brain evaluates that there were three mortars fired, the first that landed sixty feet away, and the second just thirty feet away. I'm curled up in the smallest foetal position I can get into, and turn to Ken.

"There's a third mortar," I tell him. The silence is smothered by rounds going past at supersonic speed, and rifles exploding, spitting out bullets of death.

"Brother, kiss your arse goodbye," Ken says, in a perfectly calm voice.

"You what?" I squeal.

I cannot curl up any tighter, and my only thought is to cling onto life, knowing that when the shrapnel carves up my body it's going to hurt. The waiting seems to last an eternity and leaves me feeling my journey has come to an end. Sadness gushes through me; my life has been far too short.

I hear an explosion four hundred metres away on the far side, and it's the third mortar. *Thank God!* No sooner have I had this thought, we notice a tracer round has just set a bush on fire, highlighting our position. Ken slides out to retrieve his tape recorder and we beat a hasty retreat as the bush fire grows.

Later, we listen to the tape, and the sounds picked up confirm the terrifying noise I heard of mortars incoming. It's a great recording, only ruined by my rather effeminate and embarrassing high pitched shriek.

We move to another location, and hiking during the day in the fifty degree heat with no water is hard work. The Afghans annoy me because they won't give me a truthful answer … the last time I asked when we would have water, they replied, "Yes yes, soon", and that was six hours ago.

We're with another group and being led by Khomeini, and this second trip is hugely different than the first trip with the professor's nephew. We've been in Afghanistan on this second trip for a month, and the highlight of the day for Ken and me is talking about food, taking turns to select fictitious meals for breakfast, brunch, lunch, and tea. We're both aware we have lost a considerable amount of weight, which only makes these fantasy banquets even more delicious.

The night falls and we lie on the track and sleep under a sky filled with so many stars its breathtaking. I close my eyes and escape my environment, drifting to somewhere that fills me with happiness. My dream is wonderful; there are women. I haven't spoken to the opposite sex for six weeks now, so I wallow in their company. Suddenly, I feel a nudge. As I wake up the women disappear and I feel robbed. People around me are grabbing their gear and running, and Ken and I grab ours and chase after the Afghans in a full sprint.

"Stop!" Ken yells. I'm in mid-flight, my foot is about to make contact with the ground, and my heart sinks as I think he's spotted an anti-personnel mine. The second that passes seems to go on forever but when my foot strikes the ground nothing happens.

"What do you hear?" Ken asks.

"Vehicles," I reply.

"Yes, and the only people with vehicles is the Russians. We're going the wrong way."

We catch up with Khomeini and ask him why we're running in the opposite direction.

"Because the Russians very, very bad, they kill you," Khomeini tells us.

It's like a scene from a comedy as a discussion takes place, but soon we all turn around and race towards the vehicles amid the sounds of machine gun fire and the odd explosion. I'm at Tail End Charlie, trying to keep up with a day sack on my back and as we run in front of a building, loud supersonic cracks fly past me. Without thinking, I hit the dirt. An Afghan in front of me does the same, but he suddenly jumps up and sprints around the corner as another burst from a machine gun explodes, ripping up the corner of the building.

I'm all alone and more incoming rounds crack above my head. I notice the fall of the shots are hitting the building I'm next to and the rounds are getting lower. To my right I can see the Russian BMP armoured personnel carrier, and I'm aware that my day sack is sticking up. *Shit!* They're using the building to see their fall of shots as they zero in on me. During the next lull in the burst of fire I jump up and dart around the corner, whereupon I hear a huge machine gun burst which impacts on the corner of the building just behind me.

Okay, I think, I'm in the middle of a village and there's no one to be seen. I have no idea where everyone has gone or whether the Russians are using ground troops. What I do know is my adrenalin is pumping and my mind is very much focused.

"Where have you been?" Ken says, appearing from nowhere, and it feels as if I'm being told off for skiving off work. Ken asks me to hand him a lens, and I follow him up a narrow path that leads to a building close to the road. I can see that the ground to my right above the embankment is a bit higher. We're ahead of a number of Russian BMPs who are spraying the whole area with heavy machine gun fire, and it reminds me it's the sort of thing the Americans would do.

Khomeini crawls out into open ground with an RPG. We're within a hundred and fifty metres of the Russian BMPs, Ken has his camera out, and I have a 16mm camera in my hand.

"Start rolling the film! "Ken shouts.

"It's rolling!" I tell him.

Khomeini kneels up and fires his RPG and I watch as the rocket screams through the air, only to see it rise and go over the top of the BMP. The Russian fire power drops – they're quite clearly looking to see where the RPG was fired from.

We go to ground and I hug the embankment. There's a huge bang close to me and I see another RPG has been fired. That, too, misses its target because the Afghans are not using the sights. My worst fears are about to become a reality. The back blast from the second RPG has kicked up the dust, giving our position away.

I have just entered hell on earth.

Three Russian BMPs position themselves to put cross fire into my location, and as each machine gun fires eight hundred rounds a minute, I now have just under two thousand four hundred incoming rounds ripping, tearing, and shredding everything around me. The sand at my feet dances, as rounds impact inches away from them. As I try to turn my feet ninety degrees to reduce the chances of them being hit, twigs land on my head from the tree I'm next to as it starts to disintegrate. The noise is deafening and I blink rapidly as some of these rounds are inches away from my ear.

"This is more than fucking bad, you're in deep shit. Think, and bloody well think quickly!" the voice in my head screams.

I can hear one of the Russian BMPs is on the move. I know it's only about a hundred and fifty metres away and time is running out. I have two options: Stay, and I'll be looking at a Russian BMP machine gun barrel, and shouting "BBC" is not going to prevent the guy from pulling the trigger. The second option is to run, but with so much shit coming through and disintegrating everything in its path, it's unlikely I'll survive. However, it feels as if it's the only choice I have and time is of the essence.

The noise is deafening. I grit my teeth as I'm expecting to be hit in the back, I turn and take one step, and there's a 'boom' that sends me airborne. I complete a summersault, landing on my back. I have no idea what's happened, all I know is this hell I am in is erupting. Jumping to my feet, I simultaneously focus on my escape route and run the gauntlet through three heavy machine guns that don't let up. As I cross the open courtyard camera lenses and other items fall out of my pockets but I don't care. Rounds crack past my ears, and dirt explodes all around me as they impact with the ground. I see Afghans standing still and holding their heads, and I'm baffled as to how they think this will save them. My legs stretch out and I catch up with a young Afghan, about eighteen-years-old. He's too slow, he's blocking my route, so I opt to jump in a ditch to my left. The moment I sidestep him I hear him being hit. His body exhales all the air that was within him and he goes down, the dust rising where he lies, before he is picked up by two men. I cannot believe I've made it this far but my head screams, *You're out of time!*

The path turns ninety degrees to the left. I've reached the conclusion that my time is up. I no longer have four steps, so on my third step I launch myself at a wall, hitting the top of it with enough momentum to carry me over, and land on the other side. Are the Russian ground troops sweeping through? I have no idea, but I need to put more space between me and the Russian BMPs. I see some of the mujahideen have retreated in a compound so I join them, as I feel it will give me some support. From the look on their faces it's quite clear, like me, they're in deep shock.

When Khomeini arrives I'm gobsmacked that he has survived after firing that first RPG from open ground.

As I kneel down and try to regroup my thoughts it dawns on me that Ken is missing, and a sense of dread comes over me. I approach Khomeini and, using sign language, ask about my brother. He calls over one of his men who looks at me and shakes his head. My thoughts are immediately with my mother, and how on earth I'm going to explain this to her. I indicate to Khomeini that I need to go back, to have eyes on and confirm the worst. To his credit he agrees, and three of us start to head back to hell on earth.

As I approach the bend in the path, my brother pops out from the cornfield.

"Where the hell have you been?" I ask, relief flooding through me.

"Did you see what was coming in?" Ken says.

"Did I see it? Of course I bloody well saw it; I was in the fucking middle of it! Did I see it? Unbelievable!"

We establish that the Russians are not on foot so we're able to stay in the compound to regroup and catch our breath, and our heart rates take some time to come back down. I reflect deeply on this incident and turn to my brother.

"Ken, we very nearly got wasted back there," I say, my words trying to hit home how lucky we've been.

"Andrew," Ken replies, "you say that, but if you think about how many bullets were fired in World War Two and compare it with how many people were hit, the odds were on your side."

I look at my brother in disbelief. "Ken, ten minutes ago I didn't think it was bloody well in my favour."

I know his comment was intended to make me feel better by down-playing the incident, but I'm not in the mood for it. I'm too busy analysing what happened, and the actions I took.

One of the Afghans approaches me and points to the camera strap around my neck. Three quarters of it has been sliced through by shrapnel. We're all now aware of how lucky I've been; in fact, we've all been lucky … only one person has been hit. As to his situation, it remains a mystery as we don't see him again. The likelihood is he would have been transported back to Peshawar in Pakistan which would have taken two days, providing he survived.

I reflect deeply on this whole adventure, knowing I've had far more than I bargained for. I think of my skydiving friends in England and how things would have been had I been killed, had Lady Luck not been shining on me.

"Whatever happened to Andy Guest?" I imagine someone on the drop zone asking. "I know he went off to Afghanistan but he never came back."

The conversation would then change, and the laughter would continue in the bar. It makes me realise how quickly I'll be forgotten, and I know I want the fun again, and the laughter; to be able to talk to the girls instead of being in this environment with a culture that's alien to me.

We return to Peshawar and those unsavoury characters on the landing of the Khyber hotel no longer seem threatening to me. Ken tells me he wants me to go back to the UK to sell the film to the news network and announces he is going back into Afghanistan. I feel I'm letting him down by not going with him but, at the same time, inside I feel the adventure is over for me and I'm happy to return to England's green pastures.

On my return to England I discover my weight has dropped to eight stone, and I wonder how Ken is faring. I pray that he's safe.

The film footage is sold to ITN news for the first showing in the UK, and they screen it that night. In my opinion they did a poor editing job as they tried to grab all the best footage and squeeze it in two minutes. However, our payment is £400. 00.

The following day I go back to ITN to collect our footage and discover that ITN, instead of copying the film and editing the copy, have butchered the original. I'm shocked at what they've done.

"Do you realise what my brother and I went through to get that footage?" I tell the guy. "We were nearly killed."

"Perks of the job, mate," he says.

I lose my temper." Perks of the job? I'll give you perks of the job… I should drop you on your fucking arse, mate, and say those are the perks of *your* fucking job." I become aware that everyone in the background at ITN who were working have stopped, and are looking over at me.

I walk out of ITN with our butchered film. I'm not looking forward to explaining this to Ken, that now we can't sell to Europe, North America or Asia.

Ken returns safely two months later, and when he tells his story I relate to it far more as I'm no longer just an avid listener; I've witnessed it.

The Royal Marines Free Fall Parachute Display team brought my older brother, Pete and I closer together because of the risks we encountered together. This Afghan trip and the dangers Ken and I were faced with have brought us closer together, too.

BOYS IN BLUE

It's good to be back from Afghanistan. Although I was keen to return to the UK to catch up with friends and to get out of that hideous environment, there was something else pulling me back. Just prior to Ken and I leaving on that hellish adventure, Pete had returned from a skydiving holiday in Florida and I'd asked him how he'd got on.

"I did thirty-five jumps from an aeroplane," he said.

I looked at him curiously, his words sounding strange, and it stopped me in my stride.

"Pete," I said, "why would you emphasise the word 'aeroplane'? You wouldn't, you'd just say you did thirty-five jumps. What's going on?"

"Well," he said, "I also jumped an antenna. Eleven hundred feet high."

I was shocked at the height. "You're mad," I told him, unaware at the time he'd sown a seed, and my inner self had nurtured the thought.

Shortly afterwards I bumped into Frank Donnellan at Netheravon, and it didn't take long for the two of us to talk about our separate jumps off El Capitan and what amazing experiences they'd been. Frank showed me a letter he'd recently received from America. Carl Boenish - a freefall cinematographer who had filmed the first jumps from El Capitan - along with his wife and two friends, had formed an organisation called BASE. Intrigued, I continued to read the letter. BASE, it said, is an acronym that stands for four categories of fixed objects from which one can jump: Building (a manmade structure, which can include monuments), Antenna (TV mast), Span (a bridge or a structure that 'spans' canyons, gorges or rivers), and Earth (a cliff, or natural formation). Carl Boenish had developed a BASE number system whereby anybody who accomplishes a jump is recorded in a notebook. Once they complete one jump of each type, they're assigned a

BASE number, in sequence of the people who have completed all four types before. Carl was BASE number 4.

Pete's decision to jump from an antenna suddenly didn't seem like such a crazy idea, and as soon as he told me that TV antennas existed in the UK it triggered something within me. I used a pilot's map that listed all the TV antennas in the UK and went searching for one on my motorbike. A few times I found the journeys to be fruitless as the antennas or towers turned out to be unsuitable. Once, I covered six hundred miles in a day. But, when I came across Mendlesham TV antenna in Suffolk, with Boston's *More Than a Feeling* blasting in my ears from my Sony Walkman, I knew I'd found the one, and so did my body as my nerve endings began to prickle. At a later date, after scaling the perimeter fence and negotiating the barbed wire surrounding the mast, and then climbing thirty feet up the ladder, I came across a sign: 'High Radiation – Danger to Life'. It seemed prudent, at the time, to make my retreat.

Although I wanted to be the first to BASE jump in Britain it had to be put on hold because Afghanistan was calling, but it played on my mind while I was there that someone in the UK was going to beat me to it.

On returning to England I meet up with Frank again, and the conversation soon returns to this new thing called BASE. Frank mentions that he's heard I'd found a TV antenna and that it's jumpable. I explain to Frank what the problem is, and that I'm trying to find out more about the warning sign I saw. Frank says that his friend, Mike knows all about antennas due to his job in military signals, and will be able to help us. The following Saturday we decide to hit the road and drive to Suffolk.

We pull up in the lay-by, exit the vehicle, and walk around the outside of the compound. I explain the point of entry, the route to the tower, and the importance of being concealed from anyone working in the main building. We're soon back at the lay-by and I turn to Mike.

"So, what do you think about the warning sign? Do you think it's safe to climb?"

"Andy," he says, "I work with thirty feet radio antennas, not one thousand feet TV antennas."

Regardless of his comment, the weather isn't suitable to jump anyway, so we agree to meet up and return the following Friday. But back at my parents' house I pace up and down as it dawns on me that Frank had suckered me into revealing the location of the antenna. Would the guys wait until Friday? I so badly want to be the first in the UK to achieve this so I decide to make the trip a few days earlier on my own.

I head off to the library to research TV antennas, and on my way ponder my problems. I'm unemployed, broke, and my motorbike is also in need of repair. I know someone who is interested in buying my main parachute, and this would enable me to buy a train ticket to Suffolk, which would work out cheaper than repairing the bike. But this just creates another problem as I then wouldn't have a main parachute to jump with. I think hard for solutions.

I have a reserve parachute, and if I can't trust it to open from eight hundred feet if the main one fails, then I shouldn't be jumping in the first place. I take my gear out into the garden, remove the main parachute and open the reserve compartment. My mind is at war with itself, going through the pros and cons of each solution I come up with. I drink a cup of tea, staring at my kit, and then suddenly the answer is there.

I leave my reserve rigging lines stowed in the reserve compartment, place the reserve in the main compartment, and attach the throwaway pilot chute onto the reserve. I ensure the loop is not too tight for the curve pin as I want very little pressure to open the container so the reserve parachute can start its journey. I can't see why it wouldn't work, but weather conditions on the day would have to be good as it's a round reserve with limited performance. The TV antenna has four supporting wire guide lines attached to it on all sides, and with limited steering capabilities on the reserve parachute any wind would have to be straight down the middle of two sets of the guide lines, otherwise I'd run the risk of getting tangled up, so I note that I'll need to take paper to drop from the tower to ascertain the wind direction.

The following day I sell my main parachute, pack my gear, and buy my train ticket. I stay overnight with a friend in London who I haven't seen for a while and who's keen to hear about Afghanistan, and I continue my journey in the morning. On arriving in Ipswich, I track down the stop for the bus to Norwich. The TV antenna is in the middle of nowhere with no bus stop in sight, but I ask the driver if he could stop there, telling him it's close to my farm and would save me walking a few miles. Thankfully, the lie pays off and he agrees.

As the bus trundles down the road, I stand and look up at the TV antenna with butterflies in my stomach and my heart racing. *What was the attraction?* I think. *This overpowering urge that was driving me? I can walk away now and nobody will be any the wiser - nobody knows I'm here.* Again, I realise the biggest challenge is not overcoming the fear of the TV antenna, but the fear within me, and the urge that drives me is my need to know, when the time comes, if I can do it. If I walk away, *I* will know.

As the night draws in the wind howls and its clear the conditions are against me, so I pull out my sleeping bag and sleep in the field.

The following day I walk around the lanes to pass the time and come across a house in the village which seems to double-up as the local pub. I buy a coke and sit in the living room for a while, but it doesn't seem right that I'm spending what could be my last night in the company of strangers. I leave, and stroll down the unlit lanes back to the field. It's another night when the weather is against me; the wind continues to howl and, for good measure, it rains. With no suitable cover I'm soon soaking wet.

With the arrival of dawn the rain has moved on, and at any other time I would have said it was a beautiful day, if a little windy. But I'm feeling rough from lack of sleep, dirty, and hungry. I take account of the situation and it's obvious I need to go back to Ipswich, grab something to eat, have a shower, and take a nap to be in the right frame of mind for this.

I manage to find a B & B on the main Ipswich to Norwich road, with a Chinese take-away opposite. I pay up front in the knowledge I'll be leaving early, wash the dirt and grime away, and head to the Chinese where I buy too much food and struggle to eat it all. It's early afternoon and the bed is so comfortable that I drift off in no time.

I have no idea what wakes me but I sit bolt upright, knowing something is wrong. It's dark and I run to the window. With no watch, I can only guess by the deserted roads it's the early hours of the morning and I've overslept.

I grab my gear and run outside. How on earth am I going to get to the TV antenna now? *Idiot!* As I cross the road, cursing myself, a single lorry appears that's heading in my direction and I throw out my thumb. To my amazement and relief the lorry pulls over.

As we drive out of Ipswich and into the darkness my eyes scan the area, looking for any indication of wind in the trees caught in the headlights. Eventually we arrive at Mendlesham TV antenna and I ask the driver to pull over.

"You're out in the sticks here, mate," he says, and I explain that I live on a farm a short distance away. We part company and as I cross the road and make my way over to the lay-by, I spot two parked cars. *Is this Frank and Mike?* I think. As I approach, a face lunges at one of the car windows and it's not one I recognise. *Keep walking,* I tell myself. I'm all alone out in the countryside and feel slightly vulnerable, and as I continue, quickening my pace, I glance over my shoulder. No one has exited the vehicle. Out of sight, I hurry to one of the guide lines, pull out my parachuting rig and gear up. It's strange because I have no idea what the time is. My only concern was to try and get to my launch site at the top of the TV antenna by dawn.

I creep up and take a quick glance around to make sure it's all clear, and then navigate the barbed wire fencing. Soon I'm inside the compound and my heart is thumping as I'm in a place I know I shouldn't be. I hurry over to the TV antenna and start to climb. There's more barbed wire to manoeuvre over, but soon the task is complete. Now there is only one way to go, and that's straight up.

I'm soon at thirty feet and already feeling scared. My knuckles are white from gripping the ladder so hard, and my cheeks blow out with each step I take. My fear is so intense it reaches deep inside of me, causing me to feel slightly sick. It's impossible to quash this fear of heights and it has an effect on my body that causes my muscles to tighten, while noisy voices in my head express things I don't want to hear. My arms ache due to leaning back while climbing, so a new technique is required. Using my legs one step at a time is the key, treating the rungs like steps instead of pulling up with my arms. I prefer this as it enables me to hug the ladder more, taking the strain off my biceps.

I keep up a running commentary - *look at the horizon, do not look down, this isn't so bad* - but mentally I'm not going to win this battle. I continue to grip the ladder with all my strength and finally reach the first rest platform at two hundred feet, which enables me to step off the ladder. I get to my hands and knees and welcome the break, reaching behind me to check my throw away pin; the last thing I need is for the container to burst open and for my parachute to deploy through the side of the tower. I've visualised this climb a thousand times, and the fear I'd have doing it, and the intense feelings my body and mind are going though is exactly what I'd expected. I'd always thought this would be my biggest challenge ... my only surprise is that I haven't peed myself in fright.

With a deep breath I crawl back to the ladder. Each rest platform is something to look forward to and is like a reward for all my hard work. I finally reach six hundred feet and still prefer to be on my hands and knees, hugging the rest platform, too frightened to move because I can feel the tower swaying in the breeze. I know I'm getting closer to my objective, but as I look across the countryside I can see that dawn has beaten me and I'll have to jump later then I wanted to.

Many thoughts go through my head, and I can't shake this overwhelming feeling of being all alone. Maybe the pioneers would understand this craving I have, this passion for a dangerous adventure. There are certainly many skydivers who don't understand, perhaps because they're unable or unwilling to face their own fears. Whatever their reasons it doesn't matter. This isn't about them, it's about me.

As I start to climb the ladder again a body shoots past me and a parachute snaps open. I cling onto the ladder for dear life, the shock of seeing something so unexpected scaring the hell out of me. Shortly afterwards, a second body shoots past, then a third. So, there's three of them. Frank, Mike, but who's the third? It has to be Nigel, I think, our getaway driver from the previous week. I watch the parachutes drift down to the field and it soon becomes apparent that the two vehicles in the lay-by are their getaway team, and I watch as they race away.

There's a huge disappointment. I'd wanted so badly to be the first person in the UK to parachute off a fixed object, according to the BASE Association rules, and now I've been denied. But I shrug it off and continue my climb with a bit more energy due to the surge of adrenalin I've just been given on seeing the guys jump. I spot a couple of workmen at an industrial site next to the TV antenna who keep running in and out of their building to check on my progress, and at eight hundred feet I reach another rest platform. The next climb will see me reach the top of the mast. As I peer up the tower I notice the structure changes shape, and I spot cables. Perhaps, I think, I'm now actually looking at the transmitter. I'm not sure, but it feels as if I could be entering into dangerous territory with very little knowledge on the effects it could have on my body, and I decide this will have to be my exit height instead. I hadn't anticipated jumping lower than one thousand and thirty feet but, hey, I have a reserve, and if I can't trust it to work from this height, why has it been part of my equipment these last few years?

With no more ladders to climb I begin to feel calmer. Wow! I think. I've actually climbed an eight hundred feet ladder, which in itself is a massive achievement for me. I sit and catch my breath and, in the distance, I hear a police siren which is getting closer. I'm also aware, as I peer down at the industrial area, that a crowd of around forty people have gathered and they're all looking up at me. The sound of the siren increases and I watch as the police car turns into the road that leads up to the TV antenna. I stare at the crowd, wondering who has taken the pleasure in being a snitch. The question is, what do I do now? Would the police actually climb the ladder, or get one of the TV antenna work crew to climb it, to get me down? It would be funny, I think, for me to jump just as they reached me; they would have to climb all the way back down again.

The police car drives off and my eyes follow its every move. It comes as no surprise to see it turn into the industrial site. I release some torn up white paper and watch it float away with the wind, straight down the middle of two sets of wire guide lines. It's perfect. The police climb out of their vehicle and two people from the crowd run over to them and point me out. I try to visualise what their reaction will be if I jump – they'll likely be gobsmacked at not ever having seen anything like this before. The parachute will open and they'll watch me drift away. It'll be only by the time I'm landing that they'll think about giving chase and, by then, I'll be running with a head start.

My mind is now at peace and it's time to go. I've reached a tranquil moment where a complete calm takes over. There are no more crazy voices in my head, just the one which says, "Andy, this is what you've dreamed about, and the method you're using to deploy the parachute is good. You know it is."

For the first time I stand on the rest platform. I give myself a once over safety check and place the pilot chute in my hand, ensuring there's no slack bridle line to snag on anything, and then climb outside the grey steel structure that has imprisoned me for the last two hours. My mind is crystal sharp and my hearing is finely tuned. All the senses in my body have come alive. I take one last look at the countryside and, having seen the sun rise this morning, the world looks amazing.

My head runs through the jump once more. *Concentrate on the exit*, I tell myself. I take one last look at the crowd and hear the policeman shout for me to get down. It makes me smile and I give them all a wave.

The moment has arrived. My legs push hard, my arms extend, and my head is pushed back as I dive for the sky. I can sense I'm falling away from the tower and it's a serene feeling. The altitude I'm at questions all my skydiving training and in a split second it clouds my judgement. I throw my pilot chute but it's a mistake; I have no speed yet. With speed, the pilot chute would have snatched the pin and caused the container to open and drag the parachute out. By throwing it out too early, the pilot chute tows behind me. As I look down I see the red lights next to each rest platform; the first one has gone past and I'm just reaching the second set, which I know is the half way mark. I was sure it would have opened before now, and I start to question whether something is going to go terribly wrong. Suddenly, I'm yanked upright to see my reserve parachute fully inflate.

The wind takes me away from the antenna and as I hear the policeman shout, "Come back!" I drift across the main road and spot a set of power cables, so pull hard on the steering toggle to avoid them. I land softly, do my parachute roll, and am fully elated that I've done it, but the race is on. Quickly, I gather my parachute and run towards a mound of earth, which I dive behind. I stare at the sky, fully expecting the boys in blue to suddenly appear and look down at me, and I'm all ready to say, "Hi, how's it going?" but I hear nothing.

It feels as if I've been lying here for an enormous amount of time but it's only been a few minutes. I want to look over the mound but tell myself not to, as they're probably scanning the fields. Eventually, I can't stand it any longer, so I climb out of my harness and peer gingerly over the mound but no one is to be seen.

It's time to get back to the guide wire on the other side of the road to collect my bag. I decide to do a huge loop but, as I'm running, I spot that Frank, Mike, Nigel and their crew have returned. I race over to them but there's no time for celebrations. The guys are amazed that I'd used a reserve parachute, and I explain I sold my square parachute three days ago to raise the funds to travel here.

We drive a huge circuit so I can approach the guide wire from behind but, on reaching it, I discover my Para bag has gone. There's no time to dwell on it as we need to put some distance between us and the police.

We arrive back at Netheravon and enter the bar, and immediately a voice shouts out, "Did you jump the TV antenna?" I look at Frank and ask him how the hell everyone knows about it. I'm really angry they've mouthed off about it as it was supposed to have been kept under wraps. A short while later, someone tells me my brother is on the phone.

"Hi Pete, what's up?" I ask.

"Congratulations," he says. "I've heard what you did."

This takes me by surprise. "I know the jungle drums are good, but how the hell did you hear about it? We only did it three hours ago."

"Well, let's put it this way. The armed police surrounded Mum and Dad's house," Pete says calmly.

"What? That's way over the top!" I reply.

"What did you leave in your Para bag?"

I start to get a real bad feeling about this. "My sleeping bag," I say, but I just know I've missed something as Pete is pausing, waiting for me to finish. I say nothing.

"The police found one of your letters with their address on it."

"Oh shit."

"It gets better, Andrew."

"In what way?" I ask.

"You also left your Afghan souvenirs in there."

It hits me like a sledge hammer as I picture the police pulling out part of a rocket, chunks of anti-personnel mines, as well as spent bullets.

"I suggest you call them, Andrew, as Suffolk police have been called into work to search all prominent buildings in the area."

I make the call to the police station near my parents' house, but they tell me it's the Suffolk police I have to speak to. I'm given a phone number for the station close to Mendlesham TV Antenna. With a deep breath I call them.

"Good afternoon," I say, and introduce myself. "I believe you're looking for me but, can I just say, this whole thing has been blown out of proportion, and had I remembered what I'd left in my Para bag I'd have contacted you sooner." My voice is trembling, more than likely due to shock.

"All we want to know is, are you coming in to collect your stuff?" the policeman says.

He's being far too nice and I wonder what game he's playing. "Can I call in on Monday?" I ask.

"We look forward to seeing you," he replies.

Yeah, I bet you do, I think, cursing myself. I'd made a clean getaway and buggered it up with the bag. This friendly exchange seems weird and unsettles me; I was expecting a furious reaction.

I return to my parents' house and apologise.

"Not to worry, son, these things happen," my mum says.

"No, Mum, having armed police surrounding the house doesn't normally happen, but thanks for your understanding," is all I can think to say.

On Monday morning my father drives me to Suffolk and parks up in the police station car park. I'm keen to create a good impression so have put on a suit, shirt, and tie. The police doors seem to grow in size as I approach them, and I wonder what's going to happen to me. I take a deep breath and stroll into the station to see a police sergeant at the desk.

"Good morning," I say. "I believe you're expecting me. It's Mr. Guest."

He smiles at me like he's an angler pleased with his catch. "Yes, we are. Please go through that door," he says in a pleasant voice, but he isn't fooling me. All hell is about to break loose very soon.

The room has a table with two chairs, and I take one of them. The sergeant enters the room by another door and asks if I would like a cup of tea. I'm taken aback but tell him, hesitantly, that a cup of tea would be very nice.

"Who's that in the car?" he says, and I tell him it's my father. "Would he like a cup of tea?" I try to work out his game plan and tell him that my father's a coffee drinker. "Okay, we'll have a coffee taken out to him," he tells me with a cheery smile.

This must be leading up to the 'good cop, bad cop' routine, I think. Whatever game it is, it's working as I feel uneasy. I'd prepared myself to be given a hard time by aggressive policemen, but not this.

As I sit and wait for the sergeant to return, two other policemen arrive, each one stopping in the doorway to look at me with a smile on his face before entering the room. It doesn't take long before the place is full of policemen who line up on all four sides of the room. With no idea of what's about to happen I feel intimidated and try not to let it show, but my imagination is having a field day.

As good as his word, the sergeant returns with a cup of tea and a plate of biscuits. As he sits on the chair he looks me straight in the eyes.

"Well, Mr. Guest, it must have been very exciting. Tell us all about it."

I look around. Is this really the reason all these policemen are here? I tell them that my plan had started four months previously, as I had to research and prepare everything. I also tell them I was celebrating my 1,000th jump, thinking it sounds good, when in fact it was my 1,015th jump. When I finish there's a pause before he speaks.

"You know you broke the law, Mr Guest."

"Which law?" I ask.

"Trespass to land." His voice is calm but the words are delivered in a way that has my full attention.

"It isn't a criminal offence unless there's criminal damage," I tell him. All I did was climb up a ladder; nothing was damaged at all."

"Civil Aviation Authority," he replies, with his eyes firmly locked on mine.

"They govern aircraft, not fixed objects," I say, meeting his gaze and trying to get a handle on where this is taking me.

He smiles. "Well done, Mr. Guest, you've done your homework. Now, what was all the stuff in the bag?"

I explain I've just returned from filming the Russian war with the mujahideen, and the items are just souvenirs I was showing to a friend on route to the TV antenna.

"You do like to lead an exciting life, don't you?" he says with a smile. "You're free to go, and to take your stuff with you."

"Before I go," I say, seizing the opportunity, "would you sign my log book for the jump I did?" I also hand him a copy of *Skies Call*, a book of skydiving photographs, and apologise to the policemen in the room for the extra work I've caused them. The sergeant signs my log book and thanks me for the gift.

When I return to my father's car he asks me how I got on, and I tell him they were very nice, and were interested to hear all about it. My father, not sure how to take my comment, chooses not to pursue it and we head home.

At last I hear about the oil rig floor man's course I'd applied for through the job centre, and an interview has been arranged in Dundee, which is quite a trek from the south coast. I make the journey, have an overnight stay at a B & B, and then make the short trip there.

It's the classic 'panel of three' interview technique, with one guy being overly nice, one rather aggressive and throwing out questions in an attempt to trip me up, and the third being rather quiet and indifferent. It's something I'd been told about by a friend who had previously attended the interview, so I'm prepared for it. Once the interview is over, which doesn't take long, I head to the railway station with no idea about how I did.

A few days later, I receive a phone call from Frank.

"Andy, I've found a bridge we can jump. Can you meet us in Clifton, Bristol this afternoon?"

"I'm on my way," I tell him, with no hesitation. "It should take me about three hours to get there."

This is only to be a recce so the parachuting equipment is left behind. I load up my motorbike with a grip, a change of clothes, and a sleeping bag, and am soon driving across the counties, intrigued as to what this bridge is going to look like and how high it's going to be.

My first thought on seeing the Clifton Suspension Bridge is that it's a great looking bridge but there's not a cat in hell's chance of it being anywhere close to eight hundred feet. Frank, Mike, and I walk across it and peer down, and it seems even lower from the top then it did from the ground. I spot a plaque which tells us the bridge is two hundred and forty-five feet at high tide. We return a few hours later to check the situation when the tide is out, and it's obvious this will have to be done when the tide is in.

The height of the bridge is cause for much discussion, and we reach the conclusion that it will have to be jumped using a round reserve parachute. The reserve parachute will have to be transferred on to main risers so once we hit the water we can release the parachute from our harness. We agree to come back in two weeks' time.

The following day we meet up at Netheravon parachute centre to do a couple of fun jumps and chill out over the weekend. On one of the jumps we do some CRW and link eight parachutes, but one of the guys docks hard. His parachute collapses and he asks to be dropped, whereupon his parachute inflates. His next dock is a better one.

Later, I'm having a cup of tea when I'm asked a question.

"Andy, on the CRW when the guy's canopy collapses and he's dropped, how far does he fall before the parachute inflates?"

"No more than thirty feet," I tell him. As soon as the words leave my mouth the penny drops and my face lights up. I've just found the solution to low altitude BASE jumping, and it feels as if I've found the pot of gold at the end of the rainbow. I go and find Frank.

"Mate," I say, with excitement in my voice, "I've just resolved the height problem with the Clifton Suspension Bridge." I look around to ensure no one is listening in. "We pack the parachute without using the slider that slows the parachute opening, and just keep the slider down by the risers. We 'S fold' the parachute so it doesn't have to unfold, and attach a static line to the top of the parachute with a cord that breaks at 100lb pressure. As we get line stretch, the cord snapping will be like a pair of hands releasing the parachute. We should be open in about thirty feet, just like in CRW when we drop the bottom guy."

Mike McCarthy has joined us and is nodding in agreement, and we're all grinning like Cheshire cats that have found the cream.

During the week I repeatedly get the butterflies each time I think about trying this new packing method for the Clifton Suspension Bridge, as the stakes are high. I deliberate about how the parachute should be packed, and imagine what will be happening on the opening. I put into the packing a way of checking to ensure the parachute can't be packed facing the wrong way. The closing of the container has me thinking hard; I'm not keen on any pressure being applied before the parachute comes out of the container. Eventually, I settle for attaching an elastic band to the closing loop, but even then I use a pair of scissors to make it thinner. That's it, I'm all ready to go, the idea is brilliant, and I know I'm correct. The only problem is, someone will have to make that first leap and it's going to take bottle.

On Friday night Frank calls me to say that they did it – they jumped the bridge - and everything worked fine, exactly as planned. He says he'll meet me the following morning to show me the pictures. I'm a bit peeved they did it without me, especially as the parachute packing method was my idea, but I let it go.

I arrive at Clifton and look at Frank as he strolls towards me. I study his facial expression and I know they've done it and, sure enough, the pictures confirm the fact. They used a different method to close their container and attached a second 100lb break tie to the closing loop. It's the one thing I feel really uncomfortable about and I choose to go with my gut feeling and stick to my own method.

The wind is howling and it's obvious the conditions are totally unsuitable for the jump. I'm frustrated, but there's nothing I can do. I tell Frank I'm sticking around and if the weather proves suitable in the evening I'll go for it then. Frank tells me to let him know if I do it and, with that, we part ways. I visit a friend, Dave Grindley, a skydiver who lives in Thornbury which is just a short distance from Bristol. Dave offers to assist me as he's keen to see the fear on my face, and recruits Bonnie Wilkens to help as the getaway driver.

Early that evening I tell them what the plan is. Dave is to assist me on the bridge and take a photograph as evidence that I did the jump; Bonnie is to have her car parked at the end of the tow path. Just in case I end up in the river, Bonnie will have a rope with her to help me climb out.

The time arrives and the two vehicles set off, and my friends seem very enthusiastic at the idea of seeing me throw myself off the bridge. My heart beats faster each time I think about the jump, and I find myself doing a lot of soul searching. We arrive at the top of Clifton, and Dave and I approach the ticket barrier and purchase our two pence tickets. Once we are out of sight of the ticket booth I pull out my equipment and life jacket and start to gear up. Dave is grinning like mad and I really want to say, "this isn't funny... it's a very serious thing I'm about to do." The walk out on to the bridge makes me feel like a condemned man taking his last journey. I'm not very talkative and keep peering over the railings for the ideal spot to jump from. At last I pick my spot, but there's a breeze in the air and I ask Dave whether he thinks it may be too windy.

"It's breezy up here, mate, but there'll be nothing down on the ground," he says with full conviction.

I'm not convinced, but on the other hand it could well be my nerves starting to get the better of me as my mind game is in full swing. I take a deep breath, tell Dave that I'm going for it, and start to tie on my static line. Dave asks for my knife as it will be a quicker getaway if he can just cut the rope off the railings, leaving no evidence. My mind is somewhere else as I hand it to him. A quick whistle down, and Bonnie turns on the torch.

"Where the hell did she buy that?" I ask Dave. It's one of those fifty pence market stall bargains, and it hardly lights up the ground. Something is wrong as it seems extremely dark and Dave remarks that it's bloody typical - they haven't turned the bridge lights on tonight.

I climb up onto the railings and stand up. Only my soles are touching the railings but my balance is there. Bristol is in the distance and all lit up; people in their cars are travelling in all different directions. I know this will work, I tell myself, and the guys proved it yesterday. A calm hits me as I feel myself leaning forward, and I know I've reached the point of no return. I manage to utter the words "I've gone," and feel myself fall away.

There's just enough time to start to feel myself accelerate when the canopy cracks open, sending an echo down the gorge, and at the same time it feels as if someone has just hit me hard in the back as my feet go past my ears and kick the risers. The canopy is open and I grab my steering toggles and release the brakes, just in time to see the torch headlight shoot underneath me. *Dave you arsehole, it's still windy down here, and I'm running with the wind like a bloody express train.* All I can see are dark shapes looming up as I edge the canopy away, before hearing it clip part of an overhanging tree, and I splash into a freezing winter's river that cascades over my body. I quickly carry out my water drills by releasing one side of the parachute, as I'd been taught in the past. The sudden shock of the cold affects my breathing and I'm only able to catch short breaths. The embankment wall is too steep for me to climb out so Bonnie throws me the rope, and I instruct her to pull me further down the tow path towards some rocks.

I arrive at the rocks and make a grab for them, digging my heels in, but as I'm about to haul myself out I'm suddenly pulled back into the water. Unlike a round parachute, the square parachute I'm using has cells, and they've inflated in the water and caused the drag. The pressure on the harness in immense, and on the side the parachute is still connected it's pulled off my shoulder and has my arm pinned. My left hand can't reach around and I make a grave error by pulling my arm out, which allows the remaining parachute release system to disappear behind my back. I can't undo the chest strap as there is too much tension, and my brain works overtime for solutions. I think about going for my knife but then it hits me that I handed it to Dave. The parachute is pulling me hard and I'm slowly losing my ground as the water keeps rising. My right hand searches behind my back but the cold has got to me and I no longer have any feeling, just complete numbness. Bonnie stares down into the darkness, trying to see what's going on.

"Andy, do you want me to do anything?" she eventually asks. The answer is obvious and my ego takes a huge hit, but I've run out of options.

"Bonnie, let's put it this way. I'm losing the battle here, so unless you get your arse in this water I'm going under very soon."

Bonnie, fully understanding the urgency, jumps in and there's a gasp from her as she exclaims, "Bloody hell, it's freezing!"

"No shit," I reply. It's strange that the water is only up to her waist but it's up to my chin, and I fight hard not to be swept away. The tension is so powerful; it's like being on a tug rope with two guys at the other end yanking at me.

"What do you want me to do?" she asks.

"Reach behind my back and see if you can find the parachute release," I say with urgency in my voice.

A few seconds pass that feels like an eternity.

"I've got it!" Bonnie shrieks, as if she's won a prize.

"Pull it, woman!" I yell at her. As she does, my body leaps half out of the water. The parachute is lost but, hey, I've got away with it after making two fundamental errors.

The cold hits me hard. Running is difficult as my legs feel numb, so it's more of a slow jog. We jump into Bonnie's car and accelerate away. She's excited and says, "You did it," but I can't reply as I can't stop my teeth from chattering. Bonnie apologises that her heater isn't working, and parts of my body retreat inside of me.

Eventually we arrive at Dave's house and enter the kitchen via the back door. Dave is there with a can of beer, which he cracks open, and looks us both up and down.

"Why are you both wet?" he asks, oblivious to the fact I landed in the river.

An hour later I've warmed up, and now I can smile and take in what I've achieved, but with lessons learned. In the future, I decide, I'll listen to myself when I have reservations about the wind conditions, because other people have nothing to lose. And there needs to be better planning to ensure the recovery team have everything they need – an extra knife, for example. BASE jumping is very unforgiving, and this time I've been fortunate.

The following day we go back along the tow path and, to our amazement, the tide is out, and there on the mud is the parachute. A rigging line had snagged a rock. Dave has the picture printed that he'd taken of me and he's done me proud. I phone Frank to tell him the news - that the very first British night BASE jump has taken place. Both Frank and I know what we've achieved by jumping the bridge; it has brought us both within one BASE jump of being the first foreigners to qualify for BASE membership, having already conquered El Capitan and the TV Antenna. Word is spreading of our jumps and the old school within the British Parachute Association are not impressed. There's talk about repercussions if we're caught.

It's not long before Frank calls me again, and he sounds excited.

"Andy," he says, "I've just been talking to Mike and he's found a building in London for us to jump."

"How high?"

"High enough, mate, so best get yourself up here."

It's not long before I'm back on my bike and hammering up to London. Walking this dangerous path is like a drug and I'm getting a kick out of it.

I finally pull over at an address in Notting Hill Gate where I'm greeted by Frank, Mike and Nigel. They're keen to take me straight away to see this building to get another opinion, but their body language suggests they have a genuine tender and I can't help but get sucked into their enthusiasm.

My first impression of the building is that it's too low; it seems lower than the Clifton Suspension Bridge. I question Frank about the height and he tells me its three hundred and thirty feet, but I can't see it. There's only one way to find out, and I enter the building and make my way to the rooftop above the lift shaft, taking my altimeter with me. Frank is right about the height. When there's an open space beneath a structure - as in the case of the bridge - it gives the impression of height, whereas a building is a solid object reaching all the way to the ground, and it gives a totally different perception.

Logic says that as we were able to jump from two hundred and forty-five feet off the Clifton Suspension Bridge then this building is jumpable, so we return that evening with plans to go ahead but find the access door leading to the rooftop is locked. Compounding the problem, the area is thick with fog. We scour the building and find a potential exit point on the top floor in the corridor. One of the windows is unlocked and we establish it would be possible to pivot the window, climb out onto a very narrow ledge, then pivot the window back in order to launch.

Although something may be possible, it doesn't necessarily mean it's safe or practical. I envisage having a bad launch, which would put me too close to the building, and then being faced with the problem of finding the landing site in fog. Mike says he's happy to jump after me, and I laugh at his request that I should go first. I've learned my lesson from the bridge jump and this time I'm going to listen to my gut feeling, which is telling me not to do it. We agree it's jumpable, but the exit point has to be the rooftop above the lift shaft. We also agree not to break any locks, which would be a criminal offence, so the access door needs to be open.

For a couple of hours we talk in depth. It's strange ... it was only a short while ago that Frank and I spoke about having to go back to America in order to find a bridge and a building high enough to jump, yet, here we are having taken the lowest base jump from five hundred and eighty feet down to two hundred and forty-five feet, and now we're looking at jumping off a three hundred and fifty feet building, and all within the UK. We agree to come back on Saturday to do the jump, and go our separate ways.

The following Saturday I travel back to London, where Nigel and I discover that Frank and Mike had jumped the building the previous day. Frank had become the first person outside of America to be awarded his BASE number, and was awarded BASE 12. I'm envious of Frank - not because he's been awarded his BASE number before me, but because he now has no pressure. He's done his jump and is able sit back, relax, and watch someone else do it. Mike, having completed his too, hasn't shown up.

The three of us head into the building and Nigel and I hide our gear in our Para bags, aware that people will have heard about the jumps the previous day. Luck is on our side as the access door to the rooftop of the lift shaft is open. My heart rate accelerates, my mouth is dry, and my brain tries to suppress the fear within me as we climb the stairs. As we pass through the door onto the roof and see the sky, there's a deep sense of trepidation and my senses are in turmoil. I tell myself to take deep breaths to try and slow everything down as the mind games have already started, with voices in my head holding court like a jury behind closed doors.

The rooftop is surrounded by high walls with slits in them, and I peer out and view the vastness of London beneath me. Well known landmarks dominate the skyline. As I contemplate what I'm about to do there's a deep, sickening feeling inside me as I imagine standing on the edge. The sense of dread is overpowering, and I try to remind myself that I'm doing this because it's fun.

As I gaze out through the slit, my face is met with a strong breeze. Nigel paces up and down, voicing his concern about the wind, and I can't help but think Nigel is right. It feels too strong. I push my hand through the slit expecting the wind to be even worse on the other side, but something strange happens and it eases right off. Of course, wind will accelerate through narrow passages, and that's what is happening.

I'm caught between two emotions: Relief, because I now realise the weather is on my side, and fear because I'm terrified. I'm the only one who has put his hand through the slit; the only one who realises that it's safe. I have my get out of jail card and can say 'the weather isn't good, so let's go'. We would all leave and no one would be any the wiser. But there's a massive flaw with this thought… I would know, and I know my head wouldn't let it go. My mind would tell me I'd bottled it, and I know it would haunt me. I curse the fact that I have this burning need to know more about myself, which constantly puts me through this mental turmoil. Why can't I be a normal nine-to-five guy? Deep down, I know why. I don't just want to exist, I want to feel alive, and there's a price to pay for that which requires me stepping outside my comfort zone.

I pick up my parachuting equipment and start to put it on. Nigel looks at me.

"What are you doing?"

"I'm scared as hell," I tell him, "and I'm searching for any excuse I can to walk away, but I know it's not the wind. Put your hand through the slit; it's perfect out there. I can't bottle it, Nigel, I'm jumping."

Nigel is quiet for a moment. "I'm not being funny, but I'd feel a lot happier if you went first," he says. I'm unable to reply as the jury in my head are still out, hoping for the letter of reprieve.

I'm all geared up; I've triple-checked myself, and have checked Nigel out. It's strange… I feel alone but I'm not alone, my head is somewhere else and voices are evaluating the situation I'm in. It's like having constant companions, although they don't always tell me what I want to hear.

I climb up the pole to stand on top of the wall and check my static line is still tied to it, which is going to help deploy my parachute. It's the fifth time I've checked it. The London landscape is before me and people are all around, going about their business, dashing here and dashing there. I'm about to experience something exhilarating and I feel it enticing me over the edge. I look at Frank who is lying on the wall with a camera, and a feeling of peace washes over me.

It's time to go.

I bend my knees and explode over the edge, punching my arms forward. *Was the one test jump off the bridge enough?* The parachute snaps open, the adrenalin pumps hard, and the voices in my head scream, *You've done it! You've bloody well done it!* I can't stop smiling as I steer the parachute down and land on the grass in front of the apartments. As I look up I see Nigel launching himself off the building. What crazy madness to jump off a three hundred and thirty feet building, I think, but I feel out of this world.

Frank greets me with a massive smile and congratulates me. I have now qualified for BASE membership so we call America to speak to Carl Boenish, the founder, who tells me I'm the fourteenth person in the world to qualify.

A week later I arrive at the Clifton Suspension Bridge with some friends, with the aim of BASE jumping it with Taff Jones. It'll be Taff's first, but my second time off this bridge. The landscape is pure white and there's a chill in the air, with snow falling from tree branches onto the ground. While we're passing the time and having a snowball fight, waiting for others to arrive, a shout goes out.

"Look at that!"

We watch as a red parachute descends gracefully from the bridge and the jumper lands on the tow path side, picks up his parachute, and runs away.

"I wonder who that is?" someone asks.

"I know exactly who that is," I say, having recognised his parachute. "It's Graeme Henderson."

Two hours later, Taff Jones and I venture onto the bridge, and once in the blind spot of the CCTV cameras that are just around the corner from the sign displaying the Samaritans hotline number, we take our equipment out of the Para bags. We get dressed quickly before proceeding to walk out to the exit point, and are thankful there are not too many people around on this cold, snowy day. As I peer over the side I see icebergs floating down the river and shudder at the thought of entering the water, telling myself today is not the day to miss dry land. I climb onto the railings which have small vertical spikes on them, making foot placement awkward, before taking the leap. As my parachute snaps opens with the echo going down the gorge, I release the steering brakes but the left brake line hangs up, which turns the parachute over the river. I know I'm about to join the icebergs but there's nothing I can do now, so I take a deep breath and grit my teeth. It's a shock when I enter the freezing, murky water with a splash, resulting in a sharp intake of breath and the words 'bloody hell' coming from my mouth in pants, but I have a pressing situation to worry about as the parachute lands over my head. I manage to pull it off as I drift with the current, aiming for the side. Gary Lawry is dressed in a wetsuit and is acting as our lifeguard.

"Gary," I shout, "I think the lines are entangled with my legs. Get in here!"

"Mate, you're doing really well. Just keep swimming," he shouts back as he continues to watch me. There's no doubt he has also seen the icebergs floating past and thought shouting encouragement was the prudent decision. Taff also has the misfortune of landing in the river.

Later, we're at a friend's house in the warm with tea and coffee being served, and the mood is buoyant with laughter and jokes when a comment about Graeme Henderson jumping before us is made. I suggest we call him and have Gary speak to him, as Graeme would not recognise his voice. The call is made, the room goes quiet, and Graeme answers the phone.

"Mr. Henderson, it's the Avon police. We have had an incident this morning and found something that has suggested you were at the scene. Can you explain to us what you were doing on the tow path below the Clifton Suspension Bridge this morning?"

"I was walking the dog," Graeme replies.

"He hasn't got a dog," I whisper, and we all try to hold back our laughter.

"Mr. Henderson, you live in Oxford. That's a long way to come to walk the dog," Gary says, and after a short while we can't hold back any longer and fall about laughing. I take the phone from Gary.

"Graeme, it's me, Andy Guest. We were at the bridge about to jump it ourselves when we saw yours. Nice one, mate!"

"You bastards, you had me going there!" he says.

It's a great end to the day.

Two months later, my brother Pete tells me he's found a cliff to jump. This is the last of the four BASE objects yet to be completed in the UK. We do our recce and look at this majestic white chalk cliff - Beer Head - from all angles, and we check the height. Everything says it's jumpable; it's just a question of proving it.

We come back another day and I watch with Ken as Pete prepares himself to jump. I'm nervous for him. If he succeeds he'll have jumped three of the four required objects. He takes his run up and leaps over the edge, and to our relief the parachute opens and we watch as he floats down. He becomes the first person to BASE jump a cliff in the UK.

I step up to make my jump, the mind games start, but something isn't feeling right. Fifteen minutes later I'm still stood there and gazing out to sea from this cliff top. It's a beautiful sight but my adrenalin isn't flowing; it appears I've used it all up watching Pete. Ken tells me I don't have to jump.

"Too right I don't," I reply, and I walk away.

I try to come to terms with the fact I've walked but it's hard to take; it's like listening to a court case in my head, both sides giving their evidence. I know the decision was right but it still eats away at me.

Two weeks later I'm back. I take a deep breath on Beer Head and run for the edge, leaping off without hesitation, as if I were on fire. As soon as the parachute opens I have closure. I'm at peace with myself.

From the moment I started the UK BASE scene I'd had a dream, and now it's come to fruition. I've just become the first person to complete the four required BASE objects in the UK.

I am British BASE #1.

SEND ME ANOTHER MAN

One of the many twisting paths in my life leads me to the oil fields on Thistle Alpha platform in the North Sea. As I remove caps and dope the threads of a thirty-two feet long pipe, tasting the salt of the sea in the bitter wind, I think back to the floor man's course I attended at Montrose in Scotland a few weeks previously. It only lasted for a fortnight and I wonder if it was enough to prepare me for working in this environment. Time will tell but I'm thankful that, at the end of the course, I was given an envelope that offered me a job working for Santa Fe. As a roustabout I'm at the bottom of the pecking order. My job is to maintain all things on the oil platform, which basically means I have to do a lot of cleaning and painting, most times in the cold.

"Get off my derrick!" I hear someone yell. My eyes are instantly drawn to the drilling rig where I see a man marching down the stairs. There's a slight pause before a figure appears in the V-door - an opening at floor level in one side of the derrick used as an entry point to bring in drill pipe, casing, and other tools – and I see it's the driller. "Crane op, send me another man, "he shouts.

Later in the day I'm blasting dirt and mud off the floor with a pressure gun. The flare stack soars above the oil platform, burning off the gas, and the heat radiates down and spreads out. At night it creates a glow that sends shadows leaping across the floor.

"Get off my derrick!" I hear someone yell. My eyes are again drawn back to the staircase where I see a man descending. There's a slight pause before a figure appears in the V-door. It's the driller again, who shouts, "Crane op, send me another man."

Over the next two days I'm introduced to chipping paint off, and repainting various items, and several times my work is interrupted by more shouts of, "Get off my derrick!" Each time my eyes are drawn to the staircase where I see a lonely figure making his way down. It's always the driller and he always shouts, "Crane op, send me another man."

I know the derrick is where the drilling crew work but I've never seen what goes on up there as roustabouts are not allowed on the derrick floor unless there's a very good reason to be there. The derrick dominates the oil platform and Thistle "A" has two of them that work twenty-four seven. The noise emanating from them is relentless: the clanging and screeching of pipe sections being run into the hole, the ear-splitting shudder and vibration of the drilling, and the escalating 'hum' of the pipes being retracted before being split and racked. My derrick has taken the form of a monster that's constantly spitting out men and has the added, unwelcome sound of the driller's growl.

I'm happily painting away when I'm approached by the crane op.

"Andy, how do you fancy working on the derrick as a roughneck?" he asks.

Who would choose to go into a monster's den? I think. "In the last three days," I tell him, "I've seen five men kicked off the floor, and you're asking me if I want to go up there?"

Like a salesman, he goes into his pitch. "There are two routes for a roustabout to move up. You can go crane op, or you can go roughnecking on the drill floor and eventually become a driller," he says. I recall a conversation I'd heard just the day before: *'Only wimps become crane ops'* and, being Royal Marines, I'm thinking I'm no wimp.

The crane op interrupts my thoughts and points out that roughnecks get paid more, so my salary will increase. On that note I tell him I'll do it. If this is to be my new career I'll have to go up there at some point, I think. Even so, I have deep reservations as I head to the door that leads to the drill floor. I wonder what I've let myself in for as I climb up what appears to be a never-ending staircase.

When I enter the monster's domain, eyes from four dirty, muddy individuals - two roughnecks, the assistant driller, and the driller himself -

look over at me. There are no welcoming smiles, just cold stares. I take a deep breath. "The crane op has sent me up here," I tell them.

"Stay there and don't get in the fucking way," the driller shouts. He looked scary from a distance on his own, and now there's a pack of them.

I'm frozen to the spot as I watch the guys in action. A ninety-six feet long section of pipe is lifted into the air, with a guy hanging onto it, and it swings towards the middle of the floor. He stabs it into the top of the drill pipe and a second man throws a chain. The coils of chain rise from the bottom pipe to the top pipe and, spinning it at the same time, the guy jumps back. Two other guys with big-jawed tongs clamp the pipe, another chain leaps into the air, and the driller tightens the pipes together. Slips are lifted off the floor and are kicked in to suspend it while the drill pipe is added. Finally, the slips are lifted and drilling can continue. It's hard and fast and, frankly, bloody frightening, and I'm aware that the movement and immense weight of the equipment could do some serious damage.

Instead of taking charge of the heavy equipment as I work on the drill floor, the drill pipe tongs manage to take charge of me. There's no slick action on my part and, at times, it feels as if I'm being led in a waltz across the floor as I fight to gain control of them. Each day at the end of the twelve hour shift I retire to my room utterly exhausted, wondering what tomorrow will bring.

The room has a bunk bed, and the person I share with is on the opposite shift so we never meet. In a way it's a blessing to have a sanctuary that I can escape to, to be on my own. Each day I climb the stairs to the drill floor I feel embarrassed as the other roughnecks make things look so easy. I continually wait to hear the words, "Get the fuck of my drill floor," but they don't come.

It's a wonderful feeling to board the helicopter at the end of two weeks of gruelling work. I'm not worried about the expanse of sea below me as the helicopter flies two hundred and seventy-five nautical miles to Aberdeen; I have only one thought: I'll be on land soon, and heading home, and by the weekend having some well-deserved fun.

We arrive at Aberdeen airport where I'm met by a representative of the company and given £200 in cash in hand and the rest of my pay in a cheque. Quite a few of us travel south on the train and most guys grab a beer as it's an alcohol-free zone on the rig, but I stick to the tea.

The driller sits opposite me on the train and I wonder, as I look at him, how on earth I'm still working on the drill floor as a roughneck, considering my performance. A part of me thinks, *Keep your mouth shut*, but I can't.

"I have a question," I say. "In the first three days I saw you kick off five guys from the drill floor, so how is it I'm still there?"

The driller looks at me. "You have no idea what you're fucking doing," he says, "but you get stuck in and that's what we need. The other guys were holding back. I can work with you, and in time you'll improve. If you don't, you're off the fucking floor too." He sits back and laughs, and I smile, not sure if he's joking, but my gut feeling says he isn't.

It's nice to hit the drop zone flush with money in my pocket; now I can have unlimited jumps and I don't have to make a single pint last the entire night. The only annoying thing is the weather isn't playing ball, so we sit in the club house drinking tea and coffee, swinging the lamp and telling stories, but it's not enough. As we try to decide what to do the wind outside whistles past the club house, playing its own piper's tune.

"The wind!" a voice shouts out. "Let's do some parascending!"

Everyone bursts out of the club house, excited we're about to have some fun, and we embark on a treasure hunt for a long piece of rope. I run around like a headless chicken wanting to be the first one to find it so I can have the first go, but I'm out of luck as Sam Leighton beats me to it. We head into the kit store and emerge with a Para Commander, and venture out onto the drop zone. Parked up outside the club house is someone's mobile home; a perfect anchor point. One end of the rope is tied onto the caravan, the other to Sam's chest strap. We stretch out the canopy and ask Sam if he's ready.

"Let it go!" he shouts.

The canopy instantly inflates and Sam sails into the air. There's a lot of laughter, all of us wanting to be the next person to give it a go. But it's short lived. A strange, eerie sound behind us has us spinning around and, to our horror, we see the large static caravan lift at the front, do a one hundred and eighty degree turn and start to roll, being dragged away by the parachute. We hadn't taken into account that the strength of the wind would be enough to pull it.

"Get me down!" Sam screams.

We race forward, some chasing the caravan, others attempting to untie the granny knots on the rope. There's a slight lull in the wind and the caravan pitches forward and buries itself in the ground.

"Get a knife!" someone shouts, and we all dash off back to the club house in search of one, but once inside we fall about in laughter and decide to stop for a drink, leaving Sam hanging in the air.

Ten minutes later Sam saunters through the door. "You bastards!" he shouts, which makes us laugh even more.

"How did you get down?" someone asks.

"As soon as I was five feet off the ground I released the parachute and landed on my arse," he says.

My two week break passes quickly and once again I'm back on the train for the long journey up to Aberdeen. I arrive late in the evening and head to a very tired looking B & B the company have booked. It's an early start in the morning, a quick breakfast, and then we're on the minibus to the airport.

Once I'm back on Thistle "A" platform, it's not long before I'm out to start my twelve hour shift. I'm determined to improve my performance with the tongs and decide the best way for me to learn is to study the other roughnecks and analyse what they're doing that makes it seem so easy. I soon realise that gaining control of the tongs is all to do with body position and gravity, and when it's my turn I copy them. A smile spreads across my face when, instead of being led in a waltz across the floor, I perform a smooth, seamless action.

While the drilling takes place I must be seen to be keeping busy, so I'm constantly cleaning or painting, or hosing the mud off the floor. In the mornings I'm allowed a five minute coffee break, which is timed from the moment I leave the drill floor. I'm surprised we're only allowed five minutes as it takes a minute to get to the coffee room and another minute to get back. Lunch break is only thirty minutes but well worth it as the food is outstanding. I often have trout for a starter and a steak to follow, as well as a pudding. During the second part of the shift I'm allowed another five minute break.

Each shift finishes with a vast darkness surrounding the platform, and as the second crew take over I head for the shower and for something to eat. There are no TVs but the platform has a small cinema, where the first person in there will call the control room and request the film they'd like to watch. It's quite common to walk in and find someone has opted for a porn movie, unsatisfied with the rather tame Page 3 calendars that are dotted about the place.

I spend little time socialising as I know it's going to be another hard twelve hour shift the following morning, so heading to bed usually seems like the right thing to do. The oil platform operates twenty-four seven and the noise of someone's hammer drill is incessant. I plug earphones in and listen to my Sony Walkman in the hope I'll drift off to sleep.

By April, 1982, I'm no longer the weakest link in the drilling team, having mastered the various techniques for different situations. During one morning tea break I see from the newspaper headlines that the Falkland Islands have been invaded. The name rings a bell, and I'm certain it's a place that a lot of guys in the Royal Marines tried to avoid being posted to. None of my friends expect the war to happen, and nor do I, as we feel the Argentineans will leave before the British troops arrive, so we're somewhat surprised when it kicks off and both sides engage in combat.

I'm still on the military books as I have to serve three years of Royal Naval Fleet Reserve time, and a letter arrives from the Ministry of Defence that states I may be called up should we take heavy casualties. I write back and give them my company's phone number, and tell them if they call the company they could have me off the oil platform in twenty-four hours. To my surprise they reply, thanking me for volunteering, and say they've been inundated with ex-Royal Marines throughout the world who have been turning up at embassies and saying they're ready to go. I feel guilty that I've trained for this and men I've served with have been deployed and are putting their lives on the line. I promised to serve my country and here I am, safe.

News filters back as the fighting intensifies that two people I served with in R Coy were killed when their landing craft was bombed and sunk by Argentine Skyhawks. Their faces are before my eyes: Royal Marines R.J. Rotherham and A.J Rundle, two great guys whose lives have been cut short. I lift my glass, stare out to sea, and drink a toast to them.

It's the beginning of June and I head out to start my shift to see the drill string is being pulled out. The previous crew had just started so we have another fourteen thousand feet of pipe to go, which is broken off in ninety-six feet sections and racked back in the corner. When my five minute break arrives I dash off to grab a tea and pick up The Sun newspaper from the table, which I flick through as I drink. As I turn the pages I see a picture of Trellick Tower, the building I BASE jumped off in London, and my eyes focus on the headline: 'Skydiver Falls to his Death'.

There's only a handful of us BASE jumping in the UK, and my eyes dart left and right to speed-read. I'm stunned when I see the name Frank Donnellan. It's a huge shock. I've lost a friend, and my brain is in a daze as questions fill my head, but I know I won't get answers until I'm back on the mainland. I hurry back to continue my shift and there's no time to think about Frank as we're working flat out, extracting the pipe, in the most physically exhausting job I've done.

When I'm back in my room I reflect on Frank. I see his face, his infectious smile, and the energy and enthusiasm he had for adventure. Sadness creeps over me knowing that he has now paid the ultimate price. I tell myself we all know the risks, as Frank did, but I have so many questions as to how it could have gone wrong, which have to be put on hold. A part of me wonders if I've just been lucky, and I wonder how long it will last.

As soon as I'm back on the south coast I contact Nigel and arrange to meet him. I have to find out what happened to Frank, to get an understanding, and to find answers to the questions that keep spinning in my head. At our meeting Nigel tells me Frank went to the building to jump it with two others and, as they entered the rooftop, Frank's container burst open and his parachute landed on the floor. A comment was made, something along the lines of, 'That's a shame, you won't be able to jump now,' but Frank said it was okay, that he could put it back in the container, and he proceeded to do so. A cord is used to pull the flaps together and help close the container, but Frank had forgotten to remove it. With the cord jammed in the flaps, the container couldn't open.

I'm shocked and confused, and I ask Nigel who checked him before he jumped. Nigel tells me that no one did because he was an experienced skydiver. The words bounce around my head and I have huge problems taking it in.

There were two stupid mistakes made. Firstly, when his container accidently opened, Frank should have cancelled his jump. Secondly, everyone should have been checked before the jump. Had Frank been checked, the cord would have been picked up and he would still be alive today to see his child grow up. I'm so angry that such a simple thing, that was completely avoidable, has taken his life, and I decide from now on I will go my own way and separate from the group in all things concerning BASE jumping in the UK.

As I make my way back to Thistle "A", I read the newspaper reports that say The Falklands war is over. Seeing pictures of the Royal Marines hoisting the Union Jack outside the Governor's house fills me with pride. All the British armed forces have done an outstanding job and it's nice to see the country united, waving flags on their return. Sadly, two hundred and fifty-five British military personnel lost their lives and, together with Frank's death, it sits heavily on my heart.

I manage to join the Royal Marines Free Fall Parachute Display Team as a guest jumper for my upcoming two week break in July. This cheers me up no end because I'd joined the Royal Marines CRW team to train for the 1982 World CRW Championships in France but, unfortunately, the dates clashed with my work on the oil platform so I had no choice but to drop out of the team. It was going so well, too. At Headcorn in Kent, we managed to build an eight-stack from three and a half thousand feet due to the speed we were docking at, and I was really looking forward to the world championships. Although being a guest jumper isn't on the same level, it softens the blow.

July arrives and I need to fly to Norwich airport and then try and find transport to get me to Butlins in Clacton. One of the crane operators lives in Norwich and suggests his wife could pick us both up from the airport, I could go to his house for a meal, and then he'll drive me on to Clacton. I can't believe my luck. The helicopter flight from the oil platform to Aberdeen is on time; we catch our second flight to Norwich and, true to his word, his wife is there to collect us and greets us with a smile.

His wife very kindly cooks a meal and afterwards the crane operator talks about his railway set while we're sat in his lounge. I'm not that interested but I feel, out of politeness, I should listen. Time ticks on and I realise I've missed any chance of a night out with the Marines, which is disappointing.

"Andy, it's late," the crane operator says. "Why don't you stay the night?"

This is deviating from my plan but I consider it ... until I turn around to see his wife standing in the doorway wearing a see-through nightie and smiling at me. The alarm bells go off in my head and I'm reminded of a story I'd heard on Thistle "A" where the assistant driller had sex with the crane operator's wife while he watched; a story I'd dismissed as nonsense.

"Thanks for the kind offer," I tell him, "but you did say you'd drive me to Clacton. I could be jumping first thing in the morning so I really need to get there tonight."

It's a relief that, reluctantly, he does drive me to Clacton, leaving one very disappointed wife behind.

I enjoy being back on the road with the Marines parachute team and being amongst friends, with the buzz of pushing the limits on displays as we free fall, followed by hooking up our parachutes. The weather at Clacton defeats us but we carry out displays over Newcastle, Dagenham, Filey, Yeovil, Southsea, and the Commando Training Centre at Lympstone, before I have to head back to the North Sea.

On my break I visited a joke shop and bought some exploding triangles that are inserted in the end of cigarettes, as an opportunity to bring some laughter to the oil platform. Once I'm back any packets of cigarettes are fair game, and I prime quite a few of them. One day, after our shift has ended, our crew has to attend a safety meeting in the cinema. The driller is giving a speech when the crane operator offers him a cigarette. He takes a drag or two and in the middle of the speech there's a loud bang and everyone in the room jumps. The end of the cigarette has peeled back, the driller's eyes are wide open, and the crane op is pleading he doesn't know anything about it. Over the next week all I have to do is smile at someone smoking and they're ditching their packets all over the place, when in fact I haven't touched them at all.

When the year draws to an end I leave Thistle "A" for my two week Christmas break, and on arriving at Aberdeen airport the company rep meets me. I'm handed £200 in cash, the rest of my salary in a cheque, and am given an extra gift. It's a nice gesture, but having to travel six hundred miles with a twenty-four pound turkey sat next to me is a burden I could have done without, especially when back at my parents' house we discover it won't fit in the bloody oven. My mother donates it to an old people's home so it doesn't go to waste.

I escape the English winter for a short period and head to Zephyrhills in Florida for a skydiving holiday, which is a great opportunity for me to skydive in the sun and chill out around the bonfire at the end of the day. We sink a few cold beers before moving out to the bars in the town where we play pool with the local rednecks.

I'm on my last jump of my holiday and in free fall when, as I'm about to link up with a group of skydivers, I feel a sharp pain across my face. I move away and open my parachute. When I land, Ian Graham approaches me.

"What's up?" he says.

"I think a cord came out of someone's container and hit me in the face," I reply, and show him where it hurts.

"Your sinuses have gone," he tells me.

Three hours later I'm on a flight heading back to the UK, and as the aircraft climbs away and pressure rises in the cabin I feel an intense pain and have a nose bleed. The air hostess dashes off and fetches a pack of ice, and while I'm holding it to my face she says, "Don't worry love; it happens to some people who aren't used to flying."

It was a welcome break, but now it's back to Thistle "A". It's a long helicopter flight out to sea and as I look down I see huge waves crashing and rolling on top of each other. The helicopter noise drowns out any thoughts as we bounce around in the turbulence. It's getting mentally harder returning to work; it now feels as if I'm working on a factory production line as the job is so repetitive. The two weeks off feels like two days, while the two weeks on feels like a month. When we land there's just enough time for a quick cup of tea and to get changed before we head out to the drill floor to replace the other drilling crew.

I'm only a few minutes into my shift when we spot mud fluid, which is used to lubricate the drill bit, oozing out of the drill string, and it doesn't take long before the fluid becomes a fountain. It's clear the derrickman has got his mud viscosity wrong and the pressure in the well is building up. A shout goes out to get the blow out preventer on, and time is critical; taking too long could result in a huge explosion which would flatten the derrick.

By the time the BOP arrives on the drill floor the fountain of mud has grown in size. Someone needs to take charge of the BOP and stab it into the drill string, but we can't see it through the mud fluid. Self-preservation takes over and I dive into the fountain, trying to locate the top of the drill string and the bottom of the BOP. The mud has had caustic soda added to it and it's burning my skin, my eyes are stinging, but I eventually manage to do it and the fountain stops when we turn the key in the BOP.

I need to bring up a section of pipe from the lower deck, and as I stand by the V-door covered from head to toe in mud with my skin burning, I see the crane op in his cab with his feet up, eating a sandwich and listening to music. It's quite clear the man is a wimp but right at this moment I'm wishing I had been, too. I still have eleven hours to go and I'm not permitted to leave to get changed. This shift is going to be bloody miserable.

Time passes and I hear about a table tennis competition taking place outside of our working hours, and to help pass the time I decide to enter. My crew and I are having our last cup of tea before we go out on shift when a guy from another crew walks in. He says we should have the balls to support 'our man' and asks if anyone is going to put some money down. There's a quick response from my crew who tell him to 'fuck off'. Once he has left, the crane op pipes up.

"Who's in this final, then?"

"I am," I say, to their surprise.

"Have you played before?" the assistant driller asks.

"Yeah," I tell him. "I used to play in a league and was just reaching county standard when I joined the Marines."

No more is said and we go out to start our shift, most of which involves running the pipe into the hole. There's a gale force wind outside and the rain is horizontal, coming at us in sheets. Even with the heat from the flare stack, it's freezing. The waves, breaking white, look threatening and I spend much of my time with water streaking down my cheeks and soaking into the pores of my skin.

The following night when I finish my shift I play my table tennis final and to my surprise some of my crew come to watch. My opponent is an attacking player and his style suits me to the ground. The guy who offered the bets strolls in, just in time to see me play the winning shot. He asks if it was the first game and my opponent tells him it was the last, and that I've won. He looks horrified, whereas my crew are overjoyed. I'm surprised at how happy my crew are for me, and it's not until the following day I discover they put two grand on me to win. When we return to Aberdeen they all insist on buying me a pint and, before I know it, I'm shit-faced, miss my train, and have to spend the night at Aberdeen railway station.

Once I arrive at my parents' house I pack up my bike and set off for Netheravon. I'm meeting up with the Royal Marines who are attempting a European stacking record, and as a former Royal Marine I'm going to be a part of it. The first person I see is Mike Wills, one of my best friends, who started skydiving at the same grass roots parachute school as me. The first time I met Mike was just after I completed my Royal Marines training and he mentioned he was looking at joining as an officer. Our paths have followed very similar paths since then. We have a Royal Navy Sea King helicopter and Mike and I discuss how many jumps we're likely to get. We're hoping for at least twenty, as the jumps are free.

The following day we have a brief on the jump - we're going for a European 15-Stack record - and are put in our docking order. I love doing big stacks … there's something impressive about them and it's nice to be in the elite, a team considered to be the best in the country for stacking.

On our very first jump everything goes according to plan. I dock twelfth underneath my brother, and three more dock under me, and we now have our European 15-Stack record. There's jubilation on the ground and each guy congratulates his team mates. I overhear the Navy pilot talking about leaving so I seek out Mike to tell him what I've heard, and we're both concerned that we're going to lose out on all these free jumps we were expecting to have. I tell Mike we need to come up with a reason for the helicopter to stay so we can get some more jumps in and suggest we go for the British Free Fall Star record, which is when skydivers hold hands in a perfect circle in free fall. Mike agrees and we approach the pilot, but he looks confused.

"I thought you guys were just going for the one record," he says, and we laugh.

"No sir, Royal Marines are always up for a bigger challenge," we tell him.

We don't have enough bodies to go for the record so we recruit five army lads who are on the drop zone; however, we have to wait two days due to the weather. Mike and I are smiling as we board the helicopter – we'll get our twenty jumps after all.

To everyone's amazement, we get the record on the first attempt. Everyone is buzzing about it but Mike and I sit on the club house steps and look at the pilot in the helicopter as he fires up his engine to depart for Yeovilton.

"Can you believe it, Mike?" I say. "Two jumps and we've got one European and one British record. I should be ecstatic, so why do I feel I've been robbed of eighteen jumps?"

"Yeah, in a way it sucks," he says. "Come on, let's go get a beer."

October arrives and I meet up with Nigel to fly to America to attend Bridge Day – an annual event which commemorates the 1977 completion of the New River Gorge Bridge by closing it to vehicles and opening it up for pedestrians. It's the only day of the year that BASE jumping is legal there, and that's exactly why we're going.

We land in Washington and Carl Boenish, the founder of BASE, along with his wife Jean, picks us up from the airport. We head south and during each rest stop Carl gets out a Frisbee or his pogo stick. When we arrive at the bridge, Nigel and I instantly love the height of it at eight hundred and seventy feet, having been used to jumping from two hundred and forty-five feet. Others who will be BASE jumping will consider this a low jump. Most of the people here – around three hundred - are skydivers doing their first BASE jump; the hardcore BASE jumpers only number around thirty.

Carl introduces us to some of the top American BASE jumpers and I get to meet Phil Smith, BASE #1 in the world. Carl mentions our British BASE packing method and how quickly the parachute opens but, more importantly, how it's beneficial for opening on heading – helping to ensure the jumper has a good opening and is facing in the right direction, which lessens the chance of a building strike.

As I take up my position there is no fear. BASE jumping has become a normal thing for me; it just feels as if I'm doing a swallow dive but instead of entering the water my parachute snaps open instead.

Over seventy-five thousand people have come to watch, and it's a carnival atmosphere with people chanting, "Go for it!" We exit off the bridge and Nigel does a five second delay while I do a three. When my parachute cracks open on heading, I quickly unzip my jumpsuit and pull out a Union Jack, and then drop it so it stays inflated, trailing behind me. I wanted the Americans to know the British were here.

Nigel and I do two further jumps off the bridge and just before my last one I cast my eyes over someone's parachute container in front of me. The equipment is packed as if he's about to jump out of an aeroplane, and it worries me.

"Have you lengthened your closing loop?" I ask him.

"Why would I do that?" he says, staring at me.

"You're jumping sub terminal, not from an aircraft."

"I've never had a problem doing hop and pops from the plane, so why don't you just worry about yourself?" he says.

I watch him jump off the bridge. He throws his pilot chute, which promptly tows behind him, and he pulls his reserve parachute. The main parachute starts to come out at the same time and I watch him land in the river. The main snags on a rock and the reserve takes him under the water.

Later on, we hear there's been a drowning.

It's sad, and his death prompts many questions, the first of which is, why weren't there more safety boats at this event? There was just one, and it was busy with another jumper and couldn't make it to the guy in time. The second … why are some people not open to advice?

Nigel and I are offered various places to do a BASE jump from, but the one that catches my eye is jumping off a skyscraper in Miami. On route, we stop off near Orlando. We've become friendly with Jon Stark who offers us an opportunity to see his workplace, where they refurbish Boeing 727s for the wealthy, and we accept his offer. Nigel and I are blown away by the sheer luxury in one of the planes being revamped for an Arab - from the king sized bed to the gold taps. It's an eye-opening visit and we thank Jon, who decides to come with us to Miami.

Once there, we walk around the outside of a building still under construction and see our landing area will be the car park below it, and we head to a nearby green to pack the parachutes. The Americans, on hearing about my pack job, ask me to pack theirs too. We book into the Holiday Inn opposite the building and ask for a room that looks onto the construction site. I arm myself with a pen, paper and a cup of tea, and record each time the security man appears to do his rounds. What I note is that he's a very bad security man as he has predictable patterns. He comes out at 9.00 p.m., 10.00 p.m., and 11.00 p.m., and each time there's a forty-five minute gap before I see him again.

As soon as he disappears we grab our gear, make our way over to the construction site, climb the stairs and reach the fifty-fifth floor. Before my eyes the whole of Miami is lit up, and it's a breathtaking view. We exit in pairs doing three to five second delays to ensure height differences between us. There's a silence as I'm airborne with the lights of the city flickering all around me. I start to feel the acceleration, hear the noise of speed picking up, and then all too soon it's over. When we land in the car park our getaway van is waiting and we climb in and roar off. It's a fitting end to our BASE trip and I love the fact I managed to jump a skyscraper.

Back on Thistle "A" I'm the senior roughneck and coaching the new guys, something they're appreciative of when they discover I was left to find my own way when I started. I'm about to be promoted to derrickman but I make the decision to quit. I'm not saddened by the idea of leaving as this path seems like a dead end, and there's something inside of me crying out for more, so my journey needs to continue elsewhere.

I'm out on my last shift when it occurs to me my crewmates may grab me at the end, strip me, and cover me in dope, which has been known to happen and would be a nightmare to wash off. So, with an hour to go I walk off shift and head back to my room. I grab my washing kit to clean my teeth and, as I do so, I discover the water is salty. There's a reaction from someone walking past the door that seems unusual so I carry on as if nothing is wrong. As soon as he's gone I spit everything out of my mouth and on closer inspection I notice salty grains in the toothpaste. Someone has got to my wash bag but I'm confused as it was in my locked cabinet.

I head into the shower and wash all the mud, grime and sweat off my skin and then grab a handful of shampoo and rub it into my hair. Straight away I sense something doesn't feel right, and when I look at my hand I'm horrified to see it's not shampoo but engine oil. I hold up the bottle and can now see both are the same colour but the oil is floating on the top. It takes me an hour using a soap bar to get it out of my hair.

I head back to my room, puzzled as to how anyone was able to access my wash kit. My door is ajar and, as I push it open, a paper cup of water lands on my head.

It's not long before the whole crew and I are gathered together and waiting for the helicopter. The crew tell me I'll be missed, along with all the practical jokes I used to play on them. I congratulate them on getting me on my last day and ask how they managed to get their hands on my wash bag. Apparently, someone saw where I hid the key.

"It's nice to know you can take a joke too, Andy," one of them says. "No hard feelings, eh?"

"Course not," I say, laughing.

He offers me a coke and I accept it, pulling the ring off. I take a huge swig only to find it's full of salt, which makes me gag. I lift up the can to see they'd drilled a hole in the bottom, added the salt, and then had the welder close up the hole. The whole room is in stitches.

As I fly away from Thistle "A" I look back at it. I've worked with the company for two years and a whole year of my life is embedded in that platform. As I see the distance growing between us a smile stretches across my face. I've had some fun times there but I've found another, more thrilling path to venture down and I'm excited about it.

RECORDS TUMBLE

Now I'm unemployed I spend a little time pondering my future and decide to take some time out. Armed with the cash I have, along with a bank loan and two credit cards, I book a flight to Florida with the intention of living the dream – becoming a DZ Bum and living permanently on a drop zone. It's perhaps not the most sensible decision, however, after two years on the oil rig I feel I deserve a little fun.

I arrive at Zephyrhills, pitch up my tent, and can't wait for the good times to begin. I skydive during the daytimes and party in the evenings, but it's not long before the funds begin to run low. There was a flaw in my planning: I'd not taken into account the exchange rate. America, as far as I was aware, was in a deep recession and had always been a cheap place to visit. But by the time I arrived the economy had bounced back.

I resort to eating just once a day at 'all you can eat' buffets and leave feeling sick to my stomach having crammed in breakfast, lunch and an evening meal in one sitting. Days pass, and it gets to the stage where I can't afford to eat out at all. I borrow a rod and catch catfish in creeks, and then grill them for supper, but it's not enough and I'm bored of eating them every day. The reality of my situation finally sinks in and I realise my time here has come to an end. It's been a great three months, I have forty-one jumps under my belt and I've made some amazing memories, but it's time to go home.

Back in the UK, with my credit cards shredded and a large debt to pay, my urge to rejoin the military intensifies and I decide to pursue it, however, I'm keen to secure a position that will give me interesting, high profile missions. I rule out the Special Boat Service – the Special Forces unit of the Royal Marines - due to not being a strong swimmer, so the obvious option is the

Army's Special Air Service. I know I have to get fit before I can apply, and so it begins.

I start to run to get myself back up to speed, slowly building myself up. Being unemployed is limiting, preventing me from spending time on the drop zone, and not being able to do the things I'd like because it's being dictated by my bank balance is depressing. I take my frustration and turn it into a positive – dedicating as much time as I'm able to physical training. The runs are lonely but I daydream as the landscape passes me by. More often than not I'm a solitary figure running through the countryside, but I have the odd nerve-wracking moment when a car grazes past me. As much as I'd like to shout out *Idiot*! I don't; there isn't an idiot in the world who realises he is one. Instead, I run and focus on what the objective is, and remind myself my fitness will improve and it will get easier as I progress. I have time on my side and push myself. The quicker I get my fitness up to speed the sooner I'll be in a position to apply.

The Royal Marines invite me to join them on another British stacking record attempt, and my spirits are lifted because I know there'll be some fun coming up and the jumps will be free.

When I arrive at Netheravon there's a deep chill in the air and on our first practice jump it hits home. There's no door on the aircraft and I'm in the cold seat while we climb to twelve thousand feet. No amount of clothing is going to keep me warm so I take a sleeping bag inside the plane to deflect it. It crosses my mind that if we have engine failure which requires us to exit quickly then this sleeping bag may hamper me, but fighting the freeze takes priority.

On our fourth attempt I dock fourteenth, and the stack builds to seventeen to set a new British record. We try to improve on it and come close when the eighteenth guy docks, but it fails to hold together long enough to be a record. However, a new British record is nothing to be sniffed at. The film footage appears on the TV show *Record Breakers* hosted by Roy Castle, and we're all invited onto the programme.

In the evenings at the bar on the drop zone I have a great time and the camaraderie between skydivers – Royal Marines or not – is fantastic. I spend time socialising with Jackie Smith, a charming lady and a great ambassador of the skydiving sport. I was a student learning ten second delays when I first met Jackie; my friends and I had spotted her and remarked she'd been in the British skydiving magazine and was a British champion. Jackie walked over to us and said hello, and my immediate reaction was to look behind me to see who she was talking to. I was somewhat surprised to find there was nobody there.

"You're talking to us?" I said.

Jackie smiled. "Who did you think I was talking to?"

Feeling rather foolish – I was only nineteen at the time - the only thought going through my head was, *Wow!* Not only was she attractive, she had a gorgeous smile. Jackie spent over half an hour chatting away to us and as she walked away we all talked about what a lovely lady she was. A year later, in 1978, Jackie became World Accuracy Champion, becoming the only person ever to hit ten consecutive dead centres at a world meet. During my time with the Royal Marines Free Fall Parachute Team our paths crossed with mutual respect, but now I was getting to know her more and our friendship was growing.

Jackie had been a member of the Red Devils - our greatest rivals - and was the first woman to serve full time in a military parachute display team. Wouldn't it be great if the Royal Marines put the Red Devils' golden girl in a Royal Marine parachute eight stack, I think.

I'm pleased to see Jackie is up for it and has faith in me, and so I recruit another six Marines to join us. We exit the aircraft from twelve thousand feet and I fly my parachute next to Jackie's before I make my approach and take hold of hers. This doesn't faze her as Jackie has taken part in some smaller stacks previously, and as soon as I slide down her lines the other guys dock on.

So here we are ... me and Jackie Smith in a Royal Marines eight stack over Netheravon, with Stonehenge in the distance. The world looks stunning. What could be more perfect?

Once we reach the cut off height I give a shout out to the guys to start dropping off and I manoeuvre myself to be next to Jackie while holding her harness. Our parachutes fly side by side and, using as much strength as I can, I pull her towards me. Jackie responds by leaning forward for what is likely to be the first kiss in a stack in the UK.

The things a man has to do!

My physical training is ongoing and I reach the stage where I run ten miles at breakfast, ten miles at lunch, and ten miles in the evening, as well as doing a load carry on another day with a Bergen filled with stones. The time feels right and I apply to join the SAS through Reservist 21, one of two Reservist SAS regiments. My interview comes up and I head to Hereford.

The gentleman conducting my interview is called Staff Sergeant Hassle, and I can't help but think it's a fictitious name. The interview seems to be going well, especially as I've seen action in Afghanistan against the Russians.

"Mr Guest, are you thinking of joining us full time?" he asks.

"Totally. That's why I quit the oil rigs. All I've been doing is training to get myself ready," I reply.

"Well, the thing is, we don't actually like the back door route," he says, clearly referring to the fact that my plan was to go through training as a reservist in order to make my way in to the full-time section.

I point out that the Royal Marines are not the army so I'd be unable to transfer from there, which leaves me with no option. He tells me the rule has now changed and Royal Marines *can* transfer. I leave the interview with the words 'back door' in my mind. Although he didn't say it, he implied that part-time reservists who are selected to join the SAS are inferior to full-time soldiers who transfer from a regular unit.

I head up to Dunkeswell but the weather is too bad for any skydiving. One of the guys asks if I'd like to join him on a quick two-mile run around the airfield and I dash off to get changed. We start trotting around; there's no real pace to the run which enables us to chat along the way. We're a quarter way in when I feel a sharp pain on the outside of my right knee, which causes me to hop. I rub it for a while and set off again only to find my leg keeps collapsing, and an alarm bell sounds in my head.

After returning to West Sussex I arrange an appointment with a top sports specialist in East Croydon and he questions me about my training. I tell him about my three daily ten-mile runs.

"You're a wanker," he says, looking me straight in the eyes. "You've over-trained, and everything will have become so tight that something had to give."

I thought he'd be impressed with how much training I've done, not insult me. I learn a ligament has snapped on the outside of my knee and clearly I have to put my SAS selection course on hold. I'm angry with myself and can't believe it's happened, especially as I hadn't even broken into a sweat.

The injury allows me time to think. Maybe it was meant to be, and has put me in a position not to be accused of coming in through the back door. I go to the Brighton Royal Marines career's office to apply to rejoin but I'm told I have no chance, so I go on my way.

Later, I speak to Rod Boswell, a serving captain in the Royal Marines and a fellow skydiver, who also participated in the last Royal Marine British stacking record. He tells me he'll make some enquiries regarding the situation. Rod tells me the following week to go to the Brighton career's office and see the same guy again, who'll be expecting me. He tells me there's no way I should have been turned away as the Royal Marines have a man power shortage.

The guy in the career's office is not too impressed with me. "You went over my head," he says.

"Apparently you were mistaken," I reply.

He drags out the process and it takes me four months to rejoin.

It's October 1984, I'm back at the Commando Training Centre at Lympstone, and as I walk through the gates I have flashbacks of going through my training. Over the next few days I'm processed and find out my draft is to

Scotland. A week later I arrive in Arbroath and join Comacchio Group. I've not heard of this part of the Royal Marines before as it didn't exist when I was previously serving, and it's a shock to discover Comacchio Group RM has been responsible since 1983 for protecting the nation's nuclear deterrent, so in essence I'll be doing guard duties. I don't feel it's a problem as I have a plan: I'll be heading out of this guard duty environment to Hereford for an SAS selection course that will challenge me. I send a letter to Hereford explaining I've rejoined the Royal Marines and am now in a position to enter through their front door, and I ask what I need to do to get on the selection course. I receive a letter from Hereford with instructions to 'ring this number'. I'm excited - I'm just a step away from getting on the course - and I find a quiet payphone in a corridor, ensuring I have plenty of coins for the call. After I explain who I am, I ask what I need to do to get on the selection course, and there's a long silence.

"Are you still there?" I ask.

"Yes," the guy says. "I'm just reading a memo in front of me that says Royal Marines can't transfer."

I pause, letting it sink in. "What the hell do you mean, I can't transfer? I've just signed on for five years based on the fact you guys said I could."

"I hear what you're saying. Yes, that was the case, but I'm afraid it's out of our hands. The Marines have a man power shortage and have disallowed it."

I'm devastated. After all that physical training all I've achieved is to be the fastest runner in my troop.

The guard duties are in two locations and each is as boring as the other. This isn't the excitement I signed up for so I turn to two things, the first of which is running. We're allowed out of the secure area if we're training so I grab every opportunity I can to keep up my fitness while most of the troop watches soaps on TV. But it's not enough; I need an adrenalin rush. My whole body is crying out for that natural fix.

Cheddar Gorge, in the Mendip Hills in Somerset, soon becomes one of my favourite BASE sites. The jump is easy but the canopy control calls for quick reactions. One of the first groups to jump Cheddar messed up when a person who was not up to doing a free fall was allowed to. He was very tall, and after a poor exit he proceeded to flip over onto his back, which is a big no-no. His parachute opened but stalled after the pilot chute snagged on something, and he impacted hard causing a potential broken back. A second guy jumped to get down and check on him, and meanwhile, a third person who was low in experience jumped using a static line. He took so long to take control of his parachute that he hit the opposite side of the gorge and broke his leg. Both injured parties were loaded into a mini and taken to hospital.

Aware there are a couple of groups having incidents, I decide that if a friend approaches me to BASE jump I'll no longer turn them down but accept the responsibility and take them on the BASE circuit in order for them to qualify for their World BASE membership number.

The year passes and another one begins. The day-to-day routine at work is monotonous and the months roll by. My fitness improves and I set myself a challenge to run a marathon when I hear that a nun of fifty-six has just completed one in less than three hours. It's the incentive I need.

I enjoy my runs; they're an escape from the compound. It's just me and my thoughts as I run alongside the River Clyde from Coulport to Kilcreggan, Garelochhead and Faslane, and then take a short-cut back to my starting point. The run around the water's edge with rolling hills surrounding me is so picturesque, and the tarmac roads are quiet and give me a good surface to run on. All in all it's around twenty-two miles, and although I'm putting in the mileage my timings are not improving and I feel slightly disillusioned.

By chance, I come across a running magazine with the headline: *Putting a lot of mileage in does not improve your time.* The article talks about Fartlek Training – a combination of interval and speed training that can improve speed and endurance – and I decide to give it a go on six mile runs, although I'm not convinced it will work.

As I run through Kilcreggan one day I notice a TV antenna, and on a later recce I see the compound is deserted. This has my attention and I know I'll be back because I've just found a way to break up my boredom. Perhaps doing guard duties on this side of Scotland won't be so bad after all.

With our scheduled guard duties over we head back to Arbroath, home of 45 Commando and Comacchio. As soon as we're stood down and given a week off I'm on the first train out of there and heading home. Scotland is a beautiful country but my social life is in the south of England and I can't wait to get back.

Gary Lawry, a close friend of mine who I met on the Royal Marines Free Fall Parachute Display Team, has opened a parachute school at Eaglescott in North Devon, so a few of us decide to pay him a visit. On arriving at the club house I notice a young, pretty girl packing a parachute, and as my friends head off to chat to Gary I decide to introduce myself to her. I discover she's called Alison Watts, and we talk for a while.

At the end of the day we all go to the local pub - The Royal Oak - and it's quite clear Gary's club members tend to be rather subdued, so it must be a bit of shock for them when they see how loud we become as the beers flow. The landlord is ex-Royal Navy so isn't fazed when we strip off. He's seen this plenty of times in the Royal Navy Mess and joins in on the laughter.

Each time I travel back to Scotland I find it harder to leave my social scene where I have so much fun. On this journey back I bump into Esther Reynolds, someone I've become friends with. The first time I saw Esther was when she jumped at the skydiving school I started off with at Ford Airfield in 1976. We never spoke back then but Esther, I seem to recall, was doing fifteen second delays while my friends and I were on static lines. She has now become one of the top female accuracy jumpers and is National Champion.

I tell Esther in passing that one of my problems when I come down from Scotland is the train connection, as quite often I arrive in London too late to catch the last train heading south. To my surprise she offers me a key to her house and tells me I can stay over whenever I want, whether she's at home or not. Her generosity is very much appreciated as hanging around railway stations in the early hours of the morning isn't much fun, and I'm indebted to her.

As much as I hate doing guard duties back in Scotland, the down time allows me to run. I spot a poster advertising a short distance race around the Royal Navy establishment at Faslane and decide to enter. As soon as the race starts I push to the front and am leading right up until the last four hundred metres, when I'm passed by a Royal Navy runner who competes in marathons. I'm disappointed that I'm beaten but, fair play to him, he paced it well and I'm happy with second place.

On returning to the south I'm given a slot on a parachute display at Barnes in London and find myself in a Royal Navy helicopter climbing to altitude. I can see my old secondary school, St. Marks, below me – the one I quit at fifteen years of age. I feel no fondness or attachment to it; in my eyes the school let me down badly. Here I am about to leap out of a helicopter over London while serving in the Royal Marine Commandos. Life hasn't turned out so bad, I think.

Three days later I'm on my travels again and arrive in the heart of Berlin for another parachute display. It's the Allied Forces VE Day celebrations and, with Britain hosting, we have the centre stage in front of the top officials. It's an unusual display in the fact we'll be landing in an arena on a dual carriageway that will be constantly moving. The slot we're given is after the marching troops and before the tanks, and we're told if we fail to land on time the tanks will not stop for us. Tall trees on either side of the road are a hazard, but being run over by a tank seems a lot worse. The French and Americans also have parachute teams jumping, who will be at either end of the road.

I love the idea of doing a high profile display. We're not an official parachute display team but a team made up from club members of the Royal Navy Royal Marines Sport Parachute Association. I've been nominated to be jumpmaster for the team, and our aircraft is an American military Huey helicopter.

It's the day of the display and the weather is kind to us; it's sunny with a light wind and hardly a cloud in the sky. We board the helicopter and climb away. I'm positioned near the edge of the helicopter and take charge of the parachute load, and conduct a wind drift indicator run (dropping 22' crepe paper with a 3oz plasticine weight) to calculate the wind direction and strength and determine where the exit point will be. I tell the pilot what I require and the direction we need to fly prior to dropping. Over the next forty-five minutes we hold off, and as there's no door on the helicopter we're freezing. The Berlin Wall is so clear to see from the air and it's such an intimidating structure. We're not that far from it so I guess the East German guards will see our display, too.

The pilot receives the call and we start our approach. There's only one cloud in the sky below us but, unfortunately, it's obscuring my view. As we get to the other side of the cloud I catch sight of the landing area and Bobby Scoular, one of the jumpers, asks me what we're doing. I have to make a quick decision as it's a moving arena and there's no opportunity for a second attempt, so I scream "You're gone!" and push Bobby out of the helicopter backwards. I dive out after him, laughing my head off when I see the stunned expression on his face.

Another guy behind me trails smoke so the spectators can pick us up from the ground. After a short free fall we open our parachutes, I call Bobby over and make my approach, and grab hold of his parachute. I slide down his lines and position myself just above his shoulders.

"Drop the flag!" I shout out to Bobby, who pulls out a large Union Jack and lets it go, and when it unfolds it's a beautiful sight. The other guys link up behind me so we have three pairs in a bi-plane formation (two parachutists linked up with one person stood above the other).

I make my approach to the landing area, fly over the trees and turn down the dual carriageway to land just thirty feet away from the high brass, who are officials from four different countries. As my feet hit the tarmac I spin around to see the remaining jumpers land on target, but I also see the tanks are rolling towards us. We just about have enough time to drop our kit, salute the high brass and jump to one side before the tanks rumble menacingly past us.

Afterwards, we receive congratulations for our display from the senior officials, many of whom had not seen canopy stacking before. It's a job well done and we head out in the evening to celebrate, which for some reason seems to involve drinking lots of beer.

The following day, dressed in our various Royal Marines and Royal Navy uniforms, we're taken to Checkpoint Charlie – the best known crossing point of the Berlin Wall - as permission has been granted for us to pass through. It's such a special but extraordinary moment and evokes a lot of feelings in me. Once we're through, the contrast between East and West is unbelievable. Someone seems to have stolen the colour … it's like stepping from the glitz and glamour of a Hollywood movie to a low budget film noir. Everything is muted, sandy or grey in colour, and people don't smile but stare. I feel guilty knowing that some are envious of us as we can cross back over to the west at any time we want. I'm reminded of how lucky we are.

We head to some shops to find a place to eat and a man races across the road, opens his jacket, pulls out a camera and snaps a picture of us before he runs away. We're told by our guide it's the Russian KGB who will print the picture and identify which branch of the military we are. Again, it feels like something out of a film.

At the restaurant the waitress cannot do enough for us and we're shocked to see how cheap things are, which validates how poor the east is. Our five course meal costs us a little over two pounds.

Once back in the west we visit Checkpoint Charlie Museum. It's very moving, and when I read about those that escaped, and those that died trying, I can almost feel their lost souls in the room.

We return to England but within a week I'm back in Germany for a competition in Bad Lippspringe. After the competition I persuade a couple of friends to drive to the Kocher Viaduct, which towers six hundred and seven feet above the Kocher River valley. We arrive and pull over, and when we walk over to view it the sheer size and height of it excites me. I no longer feel fear but a deep exhilaration - like a kid who's found the candy store. From jumping all the low stuff in the UK I feel spoilt.

Mike Wills joins me to jump the viaduct and Nigel Watson-Clark has come to be the getaway driver but decides, on seeing it, that he wants to jump it too. One thing's for certain - all three of us can't jump at the same time as both Mike and Nigel need to be overseen by me, so they toss a coin, which Nigel wins, much to Mike's dismay. We grab a coffee and a snack, and then find a quiet spot where I pack all the parachutes. The guys watch me closely. As much as they've put their faith in me they want an understanding of how my packing method works. It's decided that Nigel will jump with me at sunset, and Mike at sunrise. They'll use a static line fixed to the viaduct to deploy the parachutes, and I'll jump free fall.

Sunset arrives and Mike drives the car, drops us off on the bridge, then heads to the valley floor. I can see Nigel is a bit nervous as this is his first jump, but for me this has become normal. The tremendous fear I had in the early days of BASE jumping has gone.

Nigel has a text book exit, his parachute deploys, and I know he's buzzing and will do for some time to come. Jumping at sunset is always incredible – there's something about the pink and orange hue of the sky and the stillness in the air that somehow makes it more special. I push off and pause, feeling the acceleration, before I throw my pilot chute and watch the parachute crack open. When I land we depart the scene and get something to eat before pitching the tents.

The next morning, just before sunrise, we wake up and grab our gear. This time its Nigel's turn to drop us off on the bridge. I can see Mike really wants to do this but the look in his eyes tells me, like Nigel was, he's nervous, as this is considered a low jump for both of them. Mike has a great jump too, and all three of us celebrate on the ground. I know one thing ... these memorable moments will live with us forever and will crop up time and again in conversation.

On returning to Scotland I'm on a high and feel that my time off has been productive, challenging and enjoyable: a perfect combination. The guard duties continue and it's just a question of counting down the days until my next break. Work is work, it's a necessity as it brings in a wage, and it's just a question of getting on with it. I throw myself back into running, my only real form of escape while I'm up here. My need to feel I've pushed myself never ceases and the sense of achievement afterwards makes it all worthwhile.

A few days later I drive out in the Landrover to check my running route and to get an accurate mileage, and after a quick warm up it's time to see if this Fartlek Training has achieved anything. I set off along a flat, winding road and am thankful the traffic is light as the location is off the beaten track. As I run my lungs and legs work in unison, and I pick up the pace because I feel I have a lot of reserve. It feels good, and I enjoy seeing the marker points go past as I encourage myself to keep pushing. When I see the finishing line it feels like Heartbreak Lane at the Marines training camp; it's all or nothing so I give everything I have left. As I cross the finishing line I hit the stop watch, and while I walk around catching my breath I see I've just completed ten miles in fifty-five minutes. It takes me by surprise … this Fartlek Training actually works. I start to apply for marathons. My goal is to complete one in less than three hours.

On my return to London I meet up with Esther, who expresses an interest in doing a BASE jump, and also Mike, who decides he'd like to obtain his BASE number. I plan to take them to Mendlesham TV antenna and dispatch both of them on a static line while I'll go free fall. I'm concerned about Esther's parachute as it's an accuracy canopy that has a different design in performance and hasn't been used before on a BASE jump. I'm not comfortable with Esther jumping for the first time with it, and my compulsion to protect a woman surfaces. I tell Esther she'll use my canopy as it's reliable and has been BASE jumped a number of times, and I'll jump hers. My mind feels more at ease with this decision.

On arriving at Mendlesham the weather conditions are suitable, so I tell the pair of them to gear up. We scale the fence before hurriedly proceeding to climb the ladder. It's not long before I'm cursing my fear of heights which makes this climb harder for me. I'm so nervous but try not to let it show.

We reach five hundred feet when I notice a flash breaking up the darkness, almost like a streak of lightening, and it confuses me. By the third flash I realise what it is. I tell Mike and Esther there's been a change of plan because we have other jumpers on the antenna, and we'll exit from here instead.

"Okay, here's the score," I tell them. "We're at five hundred feet and I'm jumping free fall. If I'm happy to do it then you'll both be fine on static line."

I give them both a bit more encouragement before dispatching them, with Mike going first. I feel more pressure with Esther, as I have the responsibility of a woman. I often wonder why I feel this way; perhaps it's just an act of being chivalrous that's been instilled in me from my father.

Esther takes it all in her stride and I observe them flying away under their parachutes into a field close to the road where the car is parked. I launch myself off the antenna, happy to know my BASE pilot chute is far better for the job compared to the one I had on my first jump off this antenna. When the parachute opens I grab my toggles, but the drag from my fifty-two inch pilot chute virtually cancels the little speed I have on this accuracy canopy and I only just land outside the compound. It's a pain as I now have further to run while wearing all this gear.

Back in the car, we travel a short distance and watch the other jumpers. I see a parachute open and recognise it as belonging to Nigel Slee, who would have recognised mine as well. Two hours later I bump into Nigel at Pampisford.

"You scared the hell out of us," he says. "We thought we were on our own. And Jesus Christ… who the hell was that on the accuracy canopy? That opening was horrible."

I laugh. "Yeah, you're right. It was pretty bad."

It's been a good day. Mike is now half way to attaining his BASE number and Esther expresses an interest in getting hers, too.

A while later I'm back at Dunkeswell for another attempt at the world stacking record, and it feels like a reunion. Some of the guys haven't jumped for a number of years but we know the skill they had is still within them. After a few practice jumps to blow the cobwebs off, the world record attempt begins. Our objective is to build a twenty-four stack and on our first attempt we break the British record with a nineteen stack. The issue we have is when we reach the lower heights where the cloud is, as it creates turbulence that causes the stack to swing and parachutes to misbehave, resulting in the stack breaking up. We go for an early start just after sunrise to try and get clean air; the lower valleys have sea fog but the airfield is clear as it's on top of a hill.

We exit the aircraft and the stack seems to be building well, however we reach the break off height and only secure another British record. I can see the sea fog has risen and is sweeping over the airfield, and as I enter it I reduce the speed of my parachute, my ears straining to hear the other skydivers around me. I check my altimeter and it shows zero, but I'm still under my parachute and descending with everything around me eerily white. I'm quite clearly in a valley with the airfield a few hundred metres above me, and I have no visibility. Suddenly, the fog clears and the ground rushes up, and I flare my parachute just in time to land safely. To my right is a set of power cables and to my left a tree; deer have bolted and there's a quietness in the chill of the air. As I stand there taking in how lucky I've been, I wonder how the others have got on.

Still wearing my gear, I walk along a country lane and ponder the best way back. I spot a house with a light on in the distance so I make my way there and knock on the door. An elderly lady greets me, curiously looking me up and down.

"Sorry to trouble you," I say, "but could I use your phone? I've been attempting a world record and need to get back to the airfield."

"Oh! I've just been watching you on the news!" she says rather excitedly. "Please, come in. Would you like a cup of tea?"

"Thank you, that's very kind," I tell her. I'm never the one for turning down a cup of tea.

With the call made, I sit and wait, sipping my tea and chatting to this lady who treats me like royalty, and eventually a van pulls up and takes me back to the airfield. The driver informs me everyone has been accounted for safely, which is a relief.

The days have been productive. While chasing this record we have secured three British records, two European records, and a twenty-two stack night world record. But that twenty-four stack is proving to be elusive.

We're towards the end of our final attempt when I see Jeff James dock twenty-three, which equals the world record. I'm beneath him and make my approach but the bottom is swinging wildly. I can't understand why twenty-two isn't coming down the lines, which would help to dampen the swing. It's so bad that all I envisage if I try to dock is Jeff going through my canopy, resulting in an entanglement. I peel off to try again and it's looking good. In my head I'm yelling, *we've got it,* but as I close in voices in the stack start shouting to break off as we've reached the minimum height. To my horror I see Jeff drop off, followed by everyone else one at a time. I can't believe it.

When we land some of the guys celebrate the fact we've equalled the world record, but I feel totally gutted. It doesn't help when Jeff approaches me.

"Mate, I thought you were going to be on."

"Not a chance," I tell him, "it was swinging so badly."

"You should have just hit me," he says, leaving me questioning my decision, and making the excitement of our achievements over the last few days slip away.

The following day we disperse with talk about how close we came, and that we should come back the following year and try again. I arrive back in Arbroath half a day late and explain the record attempt went on until sunset, and there was no transport to get me back in time, but it falls on deaf ears. I'm given galley fatigues for two days.

The following month our work schedule changes. My previous request for time off to enter the British National Championships was turned down, but this sudden change allows me to enter. The next day I'm on the telephone trying to pull in a scratch team, and am chuffed to bits when I manage to achieve it.

The Nationals are fun; there's nothing quite like competing to get my adrenalin flowing. Everyone seems to have had a great time and is now feeling relaxed as the competition is over with no major incidents. For the presentations, we're told to be in uniform. The guys aren't keen but as there has been a strong turn out by the Marines, someone has decided we should. I meet Herman Landsman who has come over with his Dutch team to compete. Herman looks at me in my uniform with my Royal Marine Commandos flashes on my shoulders and he seems surprised.

"Andy, you are Marines?" he asks.

"Yes," I tell him.

"You are Commando?"

"Yes," I say again.

"Really? You are green beret?"

By the time I answer back for the third time, I feel I've grown a foot in height.

It's been an enjoyable British Nationals and I've come away with three medals: two silver and a bronze. I'd have preferred a gold thrown in to complete the set, though.

On my return to Scotland I decide to jump the TV antenna at Kilcreggan, and my aim is to do a night jump with less chance of detection. It's also a chance to log a new site that no one else has jumped. Spence, one of my marine colleagues, agrees to drive me out to the TV antenna. I hide my parachute in a Bergen but I'm seen by my troop officer loading it into the Landrover. We're only permitted to leave the compound if we're training, and the officer calls out to me.

"Guest, you're going to knacker your knees training with a Bergen."

"I'll be fine, Sir," I shout back.

Spence and I drive off. *Phew!* I think; that very nearly ruined my plans.

I climb the TV antenna, reach the top and open the trap door. It's not a particularly high mast, but it's high enough. I tie my static line off, which will help to deploy my parachute quickly, climb over the railings and peer down. All I see is darkness, and I wait for a moment in the hope my eyes will adjust. I'm sure when I get closer to the ground things will become more obvious so I push off with my head held high and my hands reaching for the stars. The parachute opens on heading and I grasp my steering toggles, staring at the ground. Everything is black but as I glimpse to my left I see the faint outline of a tree and estimate my height is around ninety feet. As I prepare for landing I suddenly hit the ground hard at a speed of 20 mph. It winds me and my legs hurt from the impact. I'm confused as to what happened and I slowly stand up only to find I've impacted on a hill - a bloody hill that's the same height as the tree. I limp back to the Landrover reflecting on what lessons I've learned, as all mistakes are to be learned from. The answer is obvious: next time I'll jump with torches strapped to my legs that will shine down like headlights.

The following morning I'm still suffering from the impact – I'm stiff and I'm limping. My troop officer spots me.

"Guest! What did I tell you about training with a Bergen?" he shouts. "I told you you'd knacker your knees."

"Yes sir," I shout back.

If only he knew.

With guard duties over, we board the coach back to Arbroath. It doesn't take long to sort out my locker, wash and iron my uniform and polish my boots. I'm good to go and before long I'm flying out the main gate and heading to the station. It's Christmas leave and my plans are in place; now it's time to implement them and have some fun.

I arrive back at my parents' house and within a couple of hours the Honda Superdream is fully loaded and I'm riding the one hundred and fifty miles to Dunkeswell.

It's good to be back with fellow skydivers and talking the same language. I have nothing in common with the guys in my troop, except for two who are also into sport and understand my passion.

A couple of the guys from the Royal Marines Free Fall Parachute Display Team are at Dunkeswell and looking for people to replace them on a demo over the Christmas period. I tell them they have no chance but, out of interest, I ask where it is.

"Chelsea Football Club," one of the guys says.

I used to live a short distance from the club and this demo instantly feels special, so I agree to do it. My name is put down for the display and I'm delighted.

The week passes quickly and before I know it we're doing a practice jump on the outskirts of London on a small airfield. There's total cloud cover, which put doubts on whether the display can actually take place. Of all the days, I think, cursing the British weather. On the practice jump we scrape our minimum exit height of fifteen hundred feet and, as we're repacking the parachutes, one of the guys watches me.

"Andy, why are you packing like that?" he asks.

"That cloud is as far as we can see," I tell him. "We're not going to get any more height so I've BASE packed it so I know I'll be open sixty feet under the aircraft."

He pauses, looks skywards, and then turns to me. "Will you BASE pack mine?" he asks.

Before long I've BASE packed all but one of the parachutes, as the team leader isn't here. When he arrives he discovers I've BASE packed the canopies, and asks if I can do his.

"I'd love to," I tell him, "but looking at the time we should be boarding the aircraft now," and with that comment we start to gear up.

As we fly over Chelsea I gaze down on the streets I grew up in as a teenager. Images flash through my mind of kicking a ball around with my mates and shooting each other with air pistols, never thinking it could have taken an eye out. I can see Chelsea Power Station, where I caught my fantail gold fish in the river Thames, and it seems surreal. Who would have thought that eleven years later I'd be flying above it, about to parachute into Chelsea Football Club? Diane, my old school friend from primary school is in the football stadium as I managed to arrange tickets for her. The moment feels special.

We get the shout from Gary Lawry, my former Royal Marines Display Team colleague, that we're running in. My brother, Pete, is sat next to me. We haven't got a lot of height and some of the young guys on the team are expressing their concerns.

"They're not happy," I tell Pete.

Pete smiles at me. "I guess they're sat in the wrong place." By sitting at the back of the aircraft away from the door, they have two choices: Follow the old school out of the door or stay in the plane.

Gary looks at me and shouts, "Out you get!" and I exit the aircraft, deploying my parachute in the first two seconds. The opening is very hard, and I yelp, feeling slightly winded. My ears pick up that the others have exited and I hear each one yelp as their parachutes crack open. Well, there's no doubt some have been shocked at just how hard the opening is, and I can't help but chuckle. The last person out doesn't yelp at all and opens lower. Quite clearly, it's the team leader.

It's a wonderful feeling to parachute into Chelsea stadium, the first football stadium I ever visited as a kid. After we land the crowd roar. Wow! I'm on centre stage in the middle of the football pitch and I love it. It feels special; as if I've come home.

We gather behind the football stadium to pack the parachutes so they're easier to carry and an old school friend, Mark Saunders, comes around the corner. We haven't seen each other for ten years and it's great to see him. We chat a little before I head off to meet up with Diane and her boyfriend. It's been a fantastic day, and one I'll treasure. More importantly, it's been a fantastic year.

I'm being constantly enticed to step outside my comfort zone for the thrill and the rewards, emotionally and mentally, of these experiences that make me feel so alive. But some of what used to be very much outside my comfort zone has now become normal for me. What this means, and where this will lead me, I don't know. The only certainty is that I'm not going to stop chasing this incredible feeling.

LET'S DO IT

It's the start of a new year and I have unfinished business, but military work is taking up my time and I'm becoming disillusioned with all this guard duty. Those higher in the chain in the military have done nothing to stem the flow of people leaving who, like me, have become disheartened, so our company of men constantly has man power shortages. My new CO asks me what I think of the job and I don't hold back, telling him morale is at rock bottom and nothing has been put in place, such as adventure training, to lift it. Twenty minutes later I'm told to see the company commander who tells me he's had reports that I'm a trouble maker. I remind him it was only twenty-four hours ago that I was standing here in front of him and he'd praised me, telling me promotion was just around the corner.

Due to the man power shortages our work schedules keep altering. I've entered five marathons and haven't been able to run a single one due to these late changes, and it's very frustrating. I spend a lot of my time trying to think of a way to get myself out of Comacchio. There has to be a way out as I have no wish to be one of these guys who have spent five years doing guard duties. Someone has suggested applying for the Falklands patrol vessel as it's only a six month draft but I'm not convinced my request will be considered.

It's been a while since I've managed to get away and see my friends in the south of England, but at last I'm able to. My motorbike is still my only form of transport, having never got around to taking my driving test. At times it's an endurance trial, fighting the cold in the winter, and I set myself a challenge of riding for thirty miles before I get off to defrost, having to scream into my helmet from the pain of the cold to finish those last couple of miles. It takes a while to be able to run and jump to try and warm myself up; my fingers are in such pain as well as my knees. It's now that I look at car drivers with envy, having the luxury of heaters, but I'm thankful I'm mobile.

I meet up with Esther Reynolds again in London and plan to do another jump with her to advance her towards her BASE number, and having already taken Mike Wills to Cheddar I decide to take Esther there as well. It's also an opportunity for me to qualify for my night BASE number as, for the last three years, I've only had the cliff jump left to do. It's going to be a full moon tonight so it should be ideal.

We arrive at Cheddar and the weather is perfect. Still, it's quite a daunting jump to do, falling into a gorge that is confined in space, and our brains will have to think fast. Throw into the picture the 'what ifs', and thoughts can become overwhelming. If the parachute opens the wrong way it, along with your body, will have a cliff strike. The impact will hurt, the parachute will start to collapse, and your rate of descent will increase as you try to salvage the situation with minimal seconds left before the impact with the ground does serious damage, if it doesn't kill you. If the static line fails to work correctly, you will hurtle to the ground knowing this is the end and there's nothing you can do. The risks are high; there are no second chances. There have been three BASE fatalities already in the UK, all three, in my opinion, due to human error.

I set up the static line that will deploy the parachute by using a tree as the strong point. Esther puts my equipment on and I check her twice over. When I look into her eyes I can see her mind is on a journey, evaluating everything. She seems distant. I talk her through the jump, what she needs to do on the canopy control and where she is to land, and I move her to the edge and again remind her to dive for the sky. Everything around us is peaceful; it's a lovely location but it goes unnoticed. Esther is in deep thought, the clock is ticking, and she's taking longer to jump than normal.

A point is reached while standing on the edge when calmness sets in and the moment feels right, but there's also a point when the moment can pass and it's not going to come no matter how long you stay there, the mind remaining in turmoil. I know we have passed that time; I've been there and experienced it myself, and I tell Esther to step back because today is not the day. Esther is reluctant; her determination doesn't understand walking away, but I know the time slot has gone for her to feel confident about it.

"Esther, you don't have to go. I've walked away before," I tell her.

"What?" She seems shocked and turns her head towards me. "You've walked away?"

"Yes. If it doesn't feel right you don't have to do it. We can come back another time. Remember, there is always another day."

Esther seems relieved - if I was able to walk away then it's fine for her to do so, too. I wasn't aware she was feeling unwell, and I reassure her she's made the right decision. It would have been really stupid of her to jump with her health not at its best.

I send Esther down to the landing area below us with strict instructions to put the car headlights on at the sound of my whistle. It's not long before darkness smothers me, and all features seem to be swallowed up. It's lonely as I sit on the rock on my own and wait for the full moon, deep in my own thoughts. Again, I question why I am here but I suppress it; I have no time for it right now.

My equipment is fitted and I check myself three times over, twice checking the static line. There's something beautiful about tonight, I think, as my thoughts drown out any outside noise. It seems perfect for my jump but, as time passes, a problem arises. The moon is behind me but on the wrong side of the gorge, and although the sky above me is bathed in moonlight, when I look into the gorge all I see is an unfriendly, featureless darkness, all the dangers hidden. I whistle down to Esther who flicks the headlights on. I was expecting the whole gorge to be lit up like a concert stage but I only find two very weak beams just bright enough to light up a courting couple in a car.

My brain races and evaluates the risks, and I remain seated on the granite rock to contemplate what I'm about to do. Logic tells me to walk away but it clashes with my ego. Although I told Esther it was okay for her to walk – and she was right to do so – for some reason I'm struggling with taking this information on board for myself on this occasion. How it will look if I walk away from this bothers me more than the risks. I know it's going to take all my concentration to focus on the job in hand.

I stand up, breathing deeply, and take in the beauty of what this night has to offer. Village lights flicker in the distance, stars shine above me, and a full, silver moon hangs in the sky. I peer down into the void and see two dim lights illuminating the ground about fifteen feet in front of the car. My nervousness returns. Any mistake is going to have dire consequences.

The time arrives. There is nothing more to gain from waiting; the thoughts will just continue to circle in my head. I shout, "Here I go!" and leap for the stars with all my strength exploding from my legs. There's a pause when the realisation hits me that I've committed, and I start to feel the acceleration before I'm jolted upright with a loud crack that echoes down the gorge; the silence broken. I grab my steering toggles and pull the left one down hard, swinging the parachute around. There's nothing but darkness as I peer into what seems to be the grim reaper's domain. I know I'm heading back towards the cliff so I yank down the left toggle again and find myself flying over the car and across the weak beam of light, flaring the parachute for a tip-toe landing next to the driver's door of the courting couple, elated and relieved I've got away with it.

The car window winds down and a nervous voice says, "Do you do this all the time?"

"When one has the urge," I reply, and by looking at their faces I know I've ruined the moment for them.

As Esther and I drive away my elation has gone. I feel angry with myself that I've broken my golden rule of walking away if it doesn't feel right. I allowed my male ego to compromise common sense and I promise myself this is the last time it happens. Esther is happy for me as I've qualified for my night BASE number, and she's impressed with how well I dealt with the jump, but inside I know I let myself down in my judgement.

Later, I phone America to be told I'm Night BASE #28 in the world.

I need to get Esther going again. Time is passing and I need to choose an easier site, so we travel to the Clifton Suspension Bridge. Once there I talk to her about the by-law that concerns throwing objects off the bridge, which is illegal, however all we will be doing is stepping off the bridge and there are no signs to say we can't do it, so it's not a problem. We won't be sticking around though, I tell her, which elicits a nervous laugh.

I brief Esther on the jump and practice her in an off-heading opening, and then talk about the landing area, which is a very small patch of grass by the road. Esther has found another parachute but, yet again, this strong desire to protect her resurfaces. I tell her that I know my parachute works smoothly and has been consistent so far with on-heading openings, so she will jump mine and I'll jump hers. As we walk out onto the bridge I can sense her nervousness and know how she's feeling. There's a time to talk and a time to allow a person to have their thoughts in quiet so they can reach deep within themselves for that extra bit of mental courage, and so we don't speak.

I dispatch Esther who, yet again, does a text book jump, and knowing time is critical for a quick getaway I follow her off. As my parachute cracks open it veers to the left and out to the middle of the river, which is tidal, and unfortunately the tide is out. I turn the parachute around using back risers and to my horror I see a lot of mud, which I know is waist deep, between me and that patch of grass. As I flare the parachute I lift my legs up as high as I can, land on my arse on the mud, and slide onto the grass. It was a quick reaction and it helped me today.

Our getaway is smooth and we park up, laughing with our driver. Esther has grass in her hair from falling over on landing and my Russian military belt buckle has scooped two pounds of mud down my trousers, giving the impression I'm a big boy. Once back at a friend's house the wine flows and I see in her eyes the same feeling I had when I started BASE jumping - that buzz, and the need to feel it again, to have that natural high.

The following morning we decide that since we're in the south west of England it makes sense to go back to Cheddar, having just had the bridge jump to build Esther's confidence. When we arrive I'm all too aware that

Esther has to face her demons on this jump, having walked away before, and the mind game will be harder for her. She will need to reach deep as only she can win this battle; I can only be an observer.

Esther is checked three times over and I repeat the instructions: "Dive for the sky and remember what I said about the canopy control." After a few seconds of gathering her thoughts Esther leaps off this three hundred and thirty feet cliff, her canopy snaps open, and then, to my astonishment, she throws my canopy instructions out of the window as her instinct in being a British female accuracy champion takes over. I observe her go on to deep brakes, backing up the parachute, and then she flies perfectly into the landing area. I've just been educated by my student in how to fly a canopy in to the Cheddar landing area in a more controlled manner.

Esther is now only one jump away from her BASE number but it may well be the hardest jump yet for her, as she has to get her head around jumping off a building. I know from experience it's not an easy task to master.

As I head back to Scotland I reflect on my time off and feel content that I've had these mentally challenging moments. Success brings its rewards but I know if a BASE jump were to go wrong, having taken on the responsibility of my friends, it would devastate me. However, if my friends were to jump with other BASE jumpers and something went wrong I'd feel guilty for not being with them, so I'm in a catch 22. I close my eyes and choose to think of the smiles and the laughter after the jumps, and how close I've become with my friends, and before I know it I'm asleep and in the land of no pressure.

I finally reach Arbroath and arrive at the camp. It's dark and a long walk to the portakabins that serves as our accommodation. I soon meet up with Spence.

"Andy," Spence says, "I kid you not, the bloke who shares my room makes me nervous."

"In what way?"

"Get this. Yesterday I was writing a letter and I could hear this swishing noise coming from his corner, so I walked over and looked around the corner only to see him dressed as a Ninja with a Samurai sword."

"You're having a laugh," I tell him, whereupon he takes me to the drying room and, sure enough, on the clothes line is a Ninja outfit with a pair of funny shoes alongside it.

"On a Friday night," Spence goes on, "he dresses as a Ninja, tells me to leave the window open, hops out and comes back again on the Monday morning at 5:00 a.m."

"Where does he go?"

"He tells me he goes into the woods and survives," Spence says.

I laugh and walk off, telling him, "You've every right to be nervous, mate. And on that note, sleep well."

The following morning, once again I board the coach to head over to the west coast of Scotland to start my guard duties, still calculating in my head how to escape this job. Before long I'm on duty and admiring a nuclear submarine bomber parked alongside the jetty. The sheer size of it amazes me; its potential as a killing machine just seems crazy. And then something else catches my eye, and not for the first time: a tower at the end of the jetty that I've already climbed with an altimeter to gauge how high it is. An idea forms in my head of a possible, though a drastic way to get me out of this soul-destroying job. BASE jumping is new. Most of the public don't know what it is, so anyone parachuting off a structure will just be considered mentally unbalanced. So I picture this... a Wednesday afternoon, when a lot of military people take the afternoon off and call it 'sports afternoon'. I gear up and can do it in the open as no one will know what I'm doing and will think nothing of it as I'm in a secure location having passed all the military security checks. I climb the tower, tie off my static line, and jump at a forty-five degree angle between the nuclear submarine and the loch. The parachute cracks open, I turn forty-five degrees, flare the parachute, and land on one of Britain's nuclear submarine bombers. The story would become legendary in the Marines. As for me, I'd be marched in front of the commanding officer who would certainly not be too impressed and would undoubtedly yell, "What the fuck do you think you were doing?" whereupon I'd reply, "Wednesday afternoon, Sir, is sports afternoon, and my sport is BASE jumping." One of two things would happen. They would deem me mentally unbalanced and say I should not be working near Royal Navy submarines, or, they would discharge me from the Royal Marines. Either way, my career of doing guard duties in this soul-destroying job would be over, so it would be a win-win situation. I love the plan; it appeals to me immensely. It's the stuff of legends.

As I run the eighteen miles around the loch, my head drifts from thinking about what I'm going to do when I'm back south again, to landing on this nuclear submarine. The thought makes me burst into a smile every time I envisage how cool it would be.

I'm back to having some time off and decide to visit Dunkeswell. I see my friend, Raymond Marks, otherwise known as Radar, and persuade him to come with me to go skydiving at Netheravon. We have a fun day there and afterwards hit the on-site bar. Radar asks for a vodka and, unbeknown to him, I buy him a double. I introduce Radar to some of the skydivers I know, the stories flow, and there's much laughter. Each time Radar wants a drink I buy him a double. Later in the evening I notice he has disappeared but someone hands me a pint and I soon forget about him.

In the morning there's no sign of Radar and I remember I was buying him double vodkas, which at the time seemed funny, but now I'm concerned he's still missing. I go on the hunt for him and eventually find his tent. When I unzip it and peer inside I can see he's asleep but looking extremely worse for wear, so I head to the canteen to get a tea. I join a long queue which appears to be moving slowly, and as I look behind me I see an extremely good looking girl. Immediately, a thought enters my head and I grin before looking away.

"What are you grinning at?" she asks, and I turn back to face her.

"Never mind, we probably have a different sense of humour," I say.

"Try me."

I tell her my plan and to my surprise she bursts out laughing. "Let's do it!" she tells me. I have just been handed a wonderful wind-up opportunity.

"I'm Carol Smith," she says, as we both race off.

I'm leading and Carol is hot on my heels, and another person shouts out, "Where are you going?"

"To wind up Radar," I shout back, and he joins us.

On reaching the tent I quietly unzip it, and Carol slips inside and undoes a few of the buttons on her top. I zip the tent back up, leaving just enough space to peer in. Carol gives Radar a nudge and he groans as he stirs before finally opening his eyes, which widen as soon as he sees her. Carol starts to do up her buttons.

"Thank you for last night, you were wonderful," she says.

There's a long pause and Radar replies, "You're welcome."

"I'm going for coffee. Would you like one?"

Radar nods. "That would be great."

Carol climbs out of the tent; I count to five then dive in and shout, "Not a chance, matey!" The three of us burst out laughing.

I head back up to London to see Esther again to tackle her qualifying jump, having recently found another building which I've jumped with a good landing area in front of it. We're joined by John Murray at Esther's house, who is also looking to qualify for his BASE number. I pack my parachute that Esther is going to use, while observing John to ensure no mistakes are being made. This time I won't be jumping but I'll control the jumps on the rooftop and remove the static line from the strong point.

Once at the building we tip-toe up the stairs as all around us people are asleep, and when we reach the lift-shaft rooftop I watch them both putting on their gear and then prepare the static line. I check them twice over to ensure everything is correct, but we all know there is still a huge risk when your foot leaves that edge and you've put your faith in the parachute snatching you from certain death.

"Okay, you're both good to go," I tell them. "Now it's down to you to win the mind games. Don't think of it as a building but just a launch platform, the same as the other three." Although I'm not jumping I feel nervous; it's the responsibility I feel that they've put their trust in me.

John goes off first and I help Esther to climb up the wall to get into position. This building is the mirror image of Trellick Tower, the very first building I jumped. I watch Esther leap off and can't climb the wall quick enough to check on her. It's a welcome sight when I see her under my parachute, floating down to the landing area. I quickly disconnect the static line and depart the rooftop, leaving only our footprints, excited for the both of them.

I look at Esther with her beaming smile. This lady and I have been on an incredible journey that has challenged us mentally. We've both had to step outside our comfort zones, dig in deep, and find that courage to commit our lives to experience the adrenalin-charged thrill that leaves us feeling so alive afterwards. We both know this experience will stay with us for the rest of our lives, as will the friendship. Back at Esther's house we telephone America and Esther is awarded World BASE 113, the same as her door number. The three of us pop a bottle of champagne and celebrate.

I return to my parents' house in Rustington and it's a chance to relax and unwind and devour one of my mother's curries, a recipe taught to her by the native women in Malaya. The aroma in the house is wonderful and I know I'm going to be rewarded with a delicious meal.

I keep my antics a secret from my parents so as not to worry them. To have three sons who all do things that put their lives on the line, either through work or on a quest for adventure, must be a nightmare. My parents continue to be the rock I can turn to, and to know I have their support in whatever I choose to do is a comfort.

I'm only at my parents' house for a couple of days to regroup and wash my clothes, and then I hit the road again. This time I'm meeting a friend, Leo, who is making a spoof movie, and I've agreed to make two BASE jumps for it. To add to the fun aspect of the video I've decided to make the first BASE jump in a Hawaiian shirt, shocking American golfing shorts, an Afghan cloth-ribbed, tank crew helmet and, to finish off, a pair of glasses attached to a big plastic nose and a black moustache.

I gear up in the blind spot from the booth that sells tickets on the Clifton Suspension Bridge. I check myself over, ensuring no mistakes have been made, and establish communication on the radio with the cameraman who is filming from another location. Strangely, as I walk out onto the bridge, pedestrians who pass me don't give me a second glance, and here I am thinking my dress sense is outrageous. Not in Bristol, apparently. I peer over the top of the railings to choose my exit point and hear a shout, "Look at that wanker!" On looking up I see they're painters working on the bridge. I give them a wave and continue my walk.

I choose my exit point, proceed to tie off the static line, and inform the cameraman I'm ready to go. All of sudden a shout goes out, "Grab him!" and I look over my shoulder to see three of the painters are sprinting across the road towards me. It's a shock as this has come from nowhere, so I shout on the radio that they're after me, and I'm exiting. I haul myself up with no real time to steady myself, yell, "three, two, one, exit," and on looking back I see a hand reaching out for my shoulder. But he's too late; I'm falling away. I no longer find BASE jumping scary, but the moment gets my heart racing.

We find a secluded spot and I BASE repack my parachute, but this time for free fall. A couple of hours later I'm climbing a very tall electricity pylon. There's a gentle breeze, the sun is out, the rumble of traffic can be heard in the distance, but what really captures my ears is the buzz of the electricity. It's not a ladder I have to climb but a stairway, and I'm thankful for how easy it is compared to what I'm used to. I decide to go from the top and, once there, it's apparent I'm going to have to free fall past the bottom suspended cable before I can deploy the parachute. After a quick talk to the cameraman I receive the clearance to jump and go through my regular swallow dive position, looking at the sky. I start to feel the acceleration, throw the pilot chute out, and before I know it I'm floating down and choosing my landing area.

With the two-jump task complete I head down to Dunkeswell. I'm grateful I'm on leave and have a few more days off, as the Marines club has a Sea King helicopter coming in. I meet up with Radar and tell him about my jump off the Clifton Suspension Bridge when the painters tried to grab hold of me. He laughs.

"That was you? I was up there in the afternoon to do some work and spoke to the painters who told me about it. They thought you were about to commit suicide as they saw you tying up the rope."

Over the next four days I manage to get twenty-nine jumps out of the Royal Navy Sea King helicopter.

I travel to meet Mike to complete his BASE circuit and we enter a block of flats in London to find access to the rooftop is open. It's a strange thing but when I head into these public places to do a BASE jump, I can't but help feel that all those around me know what I'm up to. This adds to the pressure, even though I know it's a ridiculous thought.

I reassure Mike I've triple checked everything and will be hot on his heels when he jumps. A deserted building site will be our landing area, which means we can exit close together.

"Take deep breaths, mate," I tell him. "Focus on the sky, bend your knees, get a big push off and punch above the horizon."

I observe Mike taking that deep breath, his knees bend, and then he's gone. The parachute opens and, to my surprise, it turns, resulting in Mike landing on a bush around the corner. I put myself on the corner of the building to give myself more clearance, check my static line for a final time, take a breath and push off. The parachute opens and I steer down to the building site. Mission achieved; Mike has just qualified for his BASE number and I've shared this journey with him. I feel my responsibility for him is over now and in a way I'm relieved.

As I pick up my parachute I clock two figures entering the building site via the open gate. I'm in no mood to get into a debate with someone about whether BASE jumping is legal or not so I bolt for a hole in the back fence. A quick glance over my shoulder alerts me to the fact they're giving chase, and as it's awkward to run with my gear on they are gaining on me.

I have no time to step through the hole so I opt to dive through it instead. To my dismay, part of the parachute snags the fence and as I pick myself off the floor one of the guys grabs my parachute for a tug of war. His friend is like an excited school boy, jumping up and down and yelling, "Come back through the hole!"

"Stop pulling my parachute, you're tearing it!" I shout, but he carries on. My anger rises and I contemplate punching him, as perhaps this is the only thing he understands. Charlie, my getaway driver walks towards me and I think when they see the odds are even and they don't outnumber me two to one they'll perhaps rethink their actions. It's at that moment I see something glittering on one of the guy's shoulders and I spot numbers. I now take stock, look this guy up and down, and realise he's a copper. My brain screams, *Plan B*, but what the hell is plan B? Before I know it I'm throwing the parachute over his head and I turn to run, jettisoning my parachute from my harness at the same time. When I look back I can see the policeman is totally tangled up with it and going nowhere.

I arrive at the getaway car and open the door to find it's a left hand drive and Charlie is already in the driving seat. Without thinking, I jump on the side and scream, "Go, go!" and Charlie hits the throttle to the floor. How crazy, I think, that I survive the jump and here I am hanging outside this car and screeching off down the road.

Mike and I celebrate afterwards. We're already good friends but this BASE journey and the experience has no doubt made our friendship stronger.

My brother Ken kindly goes to the police station to retrieve my parachute and is told to wait. The two young policemen arrive and know he's not the one who jumped, so there's a standoff. The policemen disappear and, as Ken leaves, he thanks the duty sergeant for their advice to sue the police chief constable for the return of his goods.

Three days later Ken receives a call to go and collect the parachute. It appears the bluff has paid off. Back at the station the desk sergeant says, "Do you realise we had lawyers look into this and there's no law against it?"

"I could have told you that," Ken tells him.

In my experience, some police officers will accept there is no law against BASE jumping, while others will be peeved about the fact and will try and find something else to push on you, perhaps disturbing the peace, hence it's better to run away to avoid the hassle.

Mike phones America and is awarded world BASE #138. It has been a very satisfying leave.

I return to Scotland but my tasking for guard duties this time doesn't take me back to Faslane on the west coast of Scotland; instead I travel the length of the UK visiting various military establishments, as well as doing more training. My jump onto the nuclear submarine will just have to wait until my next trip there.

It's a month before I get to visit the south again but before I leave I manage to jump the Erskine Bridge, at around one hundred and ninety feet, that crosses a river outside Glasgow, which is a new site for my logbook.

On returning to the south I can't afford to go skydiving. I do have some spare cash to socialise with and have a few beers, but I mostly try to save what money I have. I visit my friends, Jackie Collins and Charlie Jakeman, whom I've known for some time and have had a lot of laughter with in the past, especially with Jackie whom I've known since I joined the Royal Marines Free Fall Parachute Display Team. I spend some time at their place, drinking and swapping stories as we recall past times. In the morning Charlie asks me what I'm doing.

"I'm heading back to Scotland via Blackpool," I tell him.

Charlie looks puzzled. "I thought you still had a couple more days off?"

"I do, but ever since seeing that double glazing advert on top of Blackpool Tower on the TV, I've wanted to check it out to see if it's still jumpable."

Charlie pauses for a moment before his face lights up. "Let's go now!"

This takes me by surprise, and as my brain is registering what he's just said I can hear Jackie laughing in the background.

"Okay, let's do it," I reply, thinking it'll sure beat travelling on public transport.

We hastily pack, and Charlie decides to take his parachute with him just in case he decides he wants to jump as well. The three of us climb into an overloaded car and roar off down the road laughing our heads off, as we know we're about to start an adventure.

After many hours of driving we finally arrive in Blackpool and head straight to Blackpool Tower. We're all excited – there's a sense of mischief about us, like children who want to do something but not get caught. As I gaze up at the tower I think how nice it would be if I was the first person to jump off it.

We head inside and make our way to the lift - there's nothing of interest for me downstairs; I'm only interested in getting to the top and having my question answered. When we exit the lift I see nothing but windows and curse the fact the double glazing company got here first. Looking at the horizon with a thick plane of glass separating us, I feel disappointed.

A noise behind me has me turning around and I see Charlie pointing to a stairway, which we head up. To my total surprise we are now outside, my spirit is lifted and the excitement returns, my body tingling. I look over the side to identify possible landing areas and see only one, which faces the beach. After studying the enclosure it's apparent they have CCTV in operation, and after careful examination I hit the jackpot and discover a blind spot. I tell Charlie that this is where we'll gear up, and from here we'll hit the corner. We'll use climbing carabiners to lock on to the railings, which will act as the strong point for the static line. There are no signs to say we have to catch the lift down, so we'll descend by our own unique route.

We decide to leave before we attract attention, and I ponder how we're going to bypass the security on the door with our gear when we come back. As we head to the streets behind Blackpool Tower in search of a café, I notice all of the tourist's shops with their corny slogans, and an idea hits me. We purchase two kiss-me-quick hats and then head off to find accommodation. Once settled in, we go in search of a multi-storey car park whereupon I BASE pack both parachutes, as Charlie has decided to join me. In the evening we go out for a meal and discuss the plan, the aim of which is to keep it simple. We'll arrive at the tower when it opens and while it's still quiet, with not too many people on the ground who may hamper our getaway.

Now it's time to play the waiting game, and it's a restless night as I'm excited, my mind repeating the climb up to the exit point like a video on a loop. I'm so thankful when it's time to get up. I shower, dress, and go for breakfast, but I'm not feeling hungry. I can sense the atmosphere has changed. Yesterday this was nothing more than an idea but today we're planning to do it. We put both the parachutes into dustbin liners and then pack them into a Bergen.

"Right, let's do it," I tell Jackie and Charlie, and we grab all we need and head off to the front of Blackpool Tower, where I'll be entering. Charlie and Jackie will enter from the rear.

As we approach the front there's a lack of activity, something isn't right, and I head up to the main door to discover the premises don't open until 2:00 p.m., which we hadn't planned for. Frustrated, we grab a drink in a nearby cafe and realise we'll now be jumping at the busiest time of the day. The time seems to drag, and the anticipation sends my thoughts into overdrive.

Finally, the little hand on the clock drags its way to the two and we set off. I approach the main building and enter the front door with a little guilt, but I shrug it off. Meanwhile, Charlie and Jackie arrive at the other door and, as per the plan, stand next to the doorman in their kiss-me-quick hats, looking like holiday makers, and go into their role play.

"I want to go to the top of the tower," Jackie says to Charlie.

"No, we're not going to the top," he tells her.

Jackie continues to plead to be taken to the top with Charlie repeatedly saying no. Eventually, the security doorman pipes up. "Don't be so miserable, take her up there."

"I would," Charlie says, "but I don't want to leave the Bergen anywhere."

"Take it with you," the man says, and on that note they enter the building.

I'm stood close to the blind spot when they arrive, and I gaze out across the horizon knowing I'm being filmed.

"Okay, take the dustbin liners out and send Jackie back down with the Bergen," I say, not looking at them. I step back into the blind spot and look at Charlie, and to my surprise he says he wants to say goodbye to Jackie. I guess he's more worried about this jump than I'd thought. Time is not on our side so I tell him to do it quick. A few seconds later, and with a concerned look on his face, Charlie returns.

"The security guy was talking to the guy on the lift and asking about two men in leather jackets and a blonde woman. The lift man has just told him the woman has gone down and the Bergen didn't seem as full."

I tell Charlie not to panic but as I turn around the security man strolls around the corner. He looks at me, then looks at the two dustbin liners, and his eyes meet mine.

"How far is that building on the horizon?" I ask him, pointing to one in the distance.

"About thirty miles," he says.

I keep firing questions at him. "How far is that? How far is the one over there? When did they build this tower?" After fifteen minutes I thank him for his time and for answering all my questions.

"You're welcome," he says, and walks back down the stairs. I turn to Charlie.

"In a few minutes he's going to realise he didn't check the bags, so we need to be quick." We're both good to go but I insist we check each other out. "Are you ready?" I ask him when I've finished, and Charlie looks at me.

"Andy," he says, "I want you to know you're looking at a very scared man."

I smile. "I know, mate. My heart's thumping as well, but let's go."

We step back into view of the CCTV and climb up on the small wall, pass the carabiner over the railings and back over the static line before screwing it shut, and then climb the last bit of the railing to stand on the top.

"Get down!" a voice calls out, and I freeze, but I'm puzzled as no one is near us.

Charlie points out the speaker next to the CCTV. "It's coming from there."

"Well, that puts him on the floor below us so I'd say he's a bit late," I tell him.

Charlie tells me to go. I look down to see there is no one underneath us and I launch myself off Blackpool Tower with my classic swallow dive, but legs apart, with a smile on my face. I take in the view and the whole sensation of falling through the air, knowing no one can take this moment away from me. As I fly the parachute down to the beach I hear Charlie's crack open behind me, followed by a loud, 'Wahoo!' Well, the plan was to be quiet but who can blame him? We've done it.

Upon landing on the beach we gather our parachutes and make a bolt for it, running past Jackie who is armed with my camera. As we dash across the sand, up the steps and into the road, ground security is racing to check the beach to see where we landed. We make it back to the car park, throw the parachutes into the boot and slam it down.

"Walk away," I say. "That's it ... the evidence has gone. There's nothing they can do now; let's go for a walk." We stop for drinks and giggle like naughty school kids. It's been exhilarating.

On returning to London, Jackie processes the photographs and she's captured me perfectly, leaping off Blackpool Tower – the first person to do so in the UK. I carry the smile on my face all the way back to Scotland.

At Arbroath I pack for our guard duty deployment on the west coast of Scotland. My parachute is already BASE packed, and all I can think about is my plan to BASE jump a tower and land on a nuclear submarine bomber. However, doing it in the first week isn't an option as I'm at the wrong location. As I go for a fifteen mile run around the loch I think about what the consequences of my actions will bring. The worst case scenario is that I'll be discharged from the Marines but perhaps this will highlight the situation and improve things for others.

The following week I change locations, and now it's a just a case of waiting for Wednesday to carry out my plan. The excitement builds as the hours pass. It's Monday, and I'm bored, when I'm told I have a phone call. Somewhat curious, I pick up the receiver.

"Marine Guest speaking."

"My name is Colour Sergeant Steve Groves. I'm the admin sergeant working at the Royal Navy Royal Marines Sport Parachute Association at Dunkeswell. We're looking for an instructor and currently you're the only one who is available that has enough jumps to attend an instructor's course. How would you like to work here?"

I'm completely taken aback. "How soon can you get me out of here?"

"Leave it with me … I'll have an answer to you by Friday."

This has thrown up a possible escape out of this job, which I've wanted all along, and I ponder whether I should carry out the jump on Wednesday or give Steve Groves until Friday. The conclusion I reach to is to give Steve until Friday and, if it doesn't transpire, I'll do the BASE jump the next time I'm back at this location. I've been thrown a light; it's just a question of whether the light is going to show me an exit.

On Friday I receive a call from Steve. "What's the score?" I ask him.

"You're on draft," he tells me.

I'm over the moon. Not only have I escaped this job but I'm going to be working at a skydiving school at Dunkeswell - a place I consider to be my second home.

As I return to Arbroath I ask the Sergeant Major if a draft has come through for me. He finds this amusing.

"Guest, you know the score. No one escapes from here." He wanders down the corridor and on his return I can see he's holding an A4 sheet of paper. "Bloody hell, Guest, I don't know who you know but this has been signed by the admiral. You're on draft. Do your leaving routine."

A grin stretches across my face. I've escaped the system, and I feel like a prisoner who has done the impossible and broken out from Alcatraz.

I arrive at Dunkeswell and am given my own room in the old control tower. I can't believe it; I'm getting paid again to do what I enjoy and from now own my jumps will be free.

Within a few weeks the Royal Marines world record parachute canopy stacking attempt has come together again. Having come so close to the world record the previous year, can we finally get it?

On the first jump we equal the world record for the second time. It's a great start but on the following jumps we're frustrated to keep hitting the turbulence in the air close to the clouds when we have twenty-two people attached. Rod Boswell decides to change things - those lighter in weight are to dock higher up, which will hopefully result in the stack descending more slowly. I'm now docking as number seven as opposed to twenty-two, and I notice a huge difference as I'm holding more weight with more people hanging under me. I can almost feel my arm and leg sockets being pulled out.

I land from a jump feeling totally exhausted and wonder how many more it will take for us to nail it when one of the guys on the ground approaches.

"You did it!"

"Did what?" I reply.

"You just broke the world record with a twenty-four-stack."

My first reaction is, *Thank God for that; now I can have a rest,* but as I'm walking back it starts to sink in. We've just taken the world record back from the Americans and it's the second time I've helped to do it, having previously been on the world record thirteen-stack.

That night the party is in full swing. News at Ten screens the moment, having covered us for a few days, updating the public on our attempts. The beer flows and spirits are high, and it feels amazing. There will be no more galley fatigues for me this time around, as now I live on Dunkeswell Airfield.

It's towards the end of the year and I have to attend a British Parachute Association course close to the Scottish border at a place called Braunton - a windswept, cold airfield. My parents drive over to Dunkeswell to collect me, along with all the equipment I'll need.

I attend the Category System Instructor's course and after three days all seems to be going well. Today I was asked to take two lessons, with examiners observing, and was happy with my performance. I notice in the evening the chief instructor's attitude towards me seems to change, which puzzles me as we've been getting on well. On the last day, convinced I've passed, I enter the office where the chief instructor, who is also one of the five examiners, tells me I've failed the course, and I'm the only candidate to do so. My reaction is to think it's a wind up, however, I continue to listen to my debrief. I glance down at the document in front of the examiner and notice my original score, which was a pass, has been crossed out and replaced with a fail. It's disappointing and I'm confused as to why.

Later, still confused as to what is going on, I'm approached by two other examiners. They tell me the chief instructor discovered I was a BASE jumper and was not impressed, hence the fail mark. It was common knowledge I was a BASE jumper but no evidence could be pinned on me to ban me from being a member of the British Parachute Association.

We British BASE jumpers are like a secret family, and it has to be a secret because of the potential of being banned from participating in a sport we love. It amuses me that the chief instructor doesn't know that the two examiners he's been socialising with, and who have just spoken to me, are British BASE jumpers too.

As we sit drinking tea I'm aware I'm going to have to repeat this course, which angers me. It's a sad way to finish what has been an outstanding year due to someone, in my opinion, who cannot – or doesn't want to - see the birth of a new sport worldwide.

THE FRIENDLY GHOST

It's the start of 1987 and I'm so pleased to be living and working on a drop zone with no more guard duties and doing what I enjoy: falling out of aeroplanes and getting paid for it. I no longer have to pay for my skydiving and it enables me to pay off the debts I accrued from my '83 trip to America at a faster pace.

The old control tower, which is my new home, was built in World War II out of concrete and was the only airfield the American Navy were based at in the UK. I decide to make my bedroom as comfortable as I can: I paint my room in magnolia, and a local carpenter makes me a pine double bed, to my measurements. I have my own TV and a standard military wooden cupboard, but to give the room that finishing touch I put together a marine aquarium, finding it relaxing to watch the crabs and fish, each with their own unique characters. My fish tank cupboard is also complimented by being stocked with beer and wine, ideal for the parties I host when I invite people back. This room not only serves as my bedroom and social space, but also as a classroom, as I've taught myself how to teach skydiving to an imaginary class of students.

I travel up to Netheravon to attend the British Parachute Association Accelerated Free Fall Instructor's course, which will test my free fall flying skills in the air as well as my teaching skills on the ground. The course has a high failure rate as it demands a high standard of flying from the instructor candidates, and I know I'm in for some pressure as those at Dunkeswell who have completed it told me they only passed with the minimum twelve points needed.

Each jump on the course feels like going for gold at the National

Championships – there are no second chances. There are five jumps to complete and with no debrief I have no idea how I've fared on each one, which just adds to the pressure. The weather is just not working in our favour, and I still have one more jump to do when the week comes to an end. I overhear two of the guys from the Red Devils mention they're going to follow the National Safety Officer to Langar Airfield in Nottingham to complete their jumps, and I manage to tag on.

On my final jump I release the examiner, who is playing the part of a very bad student, and he carries out the drills I've instructed him to when, suddenly, he alters his body position to fall slower. The word *bastard* comes to mind and in that split second I see it happening: I respond. I'm at my maximum slow fall rate and just mange to re-grip the examiner and give him the pull signal. As his parachute deploys I move away horizontally, checking my altimeter to confirm the pull was in the safe zone.

With the course over, I enter the office for my results and it's with some relief I hear I've passed with fourteen points. I'm chuffed with my score but I now know it means I'll get to work with real first time students who are learning skydiving in free fall, and it feels both scary and challenging.

My work for the Category System Instructor's course continues, and I teach two courses a week on how to exit the aircraft on static line and steer the parachute to the landing area. There's a feel good factor when I take people through the whole course and after their jumps they tell me it's the best thing they've ever done.

The six months since I failed the CSI course pass quickly and I find myself travelling to Cranfield to try again, but I wonder whether I'm going to get the same bullshit concerning my BASE jumping activities and if I'll fail before I've even started. Once again it's a five day course and I present my two lessons and brief, this time with more confidence. On the Thursday evening I'm approached by one of the examiners - a fellow BASE jumper - who informs me, yet again, that my BASE jumping activities have become a topic of conversation behind closed doors. He tells me they've decided to award me my CSI rating with the view that on the day I get caught BASE jumping I will lose it, as the British Parachute Association will ban me for life. I don't understand this short-sighted view as people using parachutes for parascending are not punished, and it angers me that they cannot see this is the birth of a new sport. When people laugh at me when I tell them it will take off, I just tell them, *You'll see.*

I thank the examiner for giving me the heads-up, and the following morning I enter the office where all but one of the people before me is unaware that I know I've already passed.

Back at Dunkeswell, I'm told to report to the Commando Training Centre to speak to my company commander, and I'm unclear what it's about.

"Do you have a tendency to fall off objects?"

It's a question I least expected. "Yes, it has been known," I tell him, wondering how the hell he found out.

"Guest, here's the situation. While you are working at the RNRMSPA there is to be no more BASE jumping in the UK, because of the BPA's feeling towards it. If you choose to do it abroad then that is up to you."

My brain evaluates what he's saying: I'm having my right to choose what I want to do in my spare time being taken away from me. However, it seems like a fair compromise.

"Yes Sir, that seems fair," I tell him, and make my way back to the airfield.

The Berlin display comes back around and we're invited back again. The French are hosting it and we get to jump the French Transall C-160 on practice jumps, as well as on the actual display. The VE Day celebrations are watched by one hundred thousand spectators, and it's an awesome sight to see from the air. Knowing the East German guards manning the Berlin wall will be watching, I wonder if, should we get the exit wrong, we would we make the international news and what the repercussions would be of landing on the East side. I don't get to find out though because, once again, we manage to outshine the French and American military parachute display teams.

The American team decide to keep to themselves in the evening but the French colonel organises transport to pick us up. We're introduced to frogs' legs and garlic snails, and we're taken to a club where live sex takes place on the stage and where waitresses wear very little. It appears the small rooms I thought were toilets are where business and pleasure takes place, with a lot of money changing hands. All the guys are interested in the drinking, laughing, and joking, with only a couple choosing to watch the show.

Later, the colonel awards us French para wings for doing five jumps out of their French aeroplane, and it's a lovely gesture.

I return to Dunkeswell and twelve days later I'm allowed to take time out from working at the club to spend time with the Royal Marines Free Fall Parachute Team to help them out, as they're short on guys. I complete two complicated diamond stack formation displays over Den Helder in Holland, which gets my heart racing again. As the stack pilot does the steering I'm merely a passenger at his mercy, and my eyes are the size of saucers as they flick between watching his approach over the harbour and my own parachute, in case it starts to collapse.

We move onto the Royal Norfolk Show and do free fall bomb bursts in the sky while trailing smoke from our ankles, and then do the same under canopy building stacks, which looks great for the thousands of spectators below us. The short time with the display team has been fantastic and has brought back many memories.

Back at the RNRMSPA we get ready for another record attempt, the aim of which is to build and break our own world canopy stack record. Everyone is raving about the new French parachute called 'Contact' and we purchase thirty-two of them. There's much excitement as we put the first jumps together, but we encounter major problems with weight issues and struggling to hang on, as well as canopies misbehaving in the stack. We haven't come across such difficulties before, and when one of our riggers checks out the lines on some of the canopies we're shocked to discover that some of them are a different length, which explains why we've been experiencing problems. Some of the guys can't help but think this has been done on purpose to scupper our record attempt; it's either that or very bad quality control, but we'll never know the truth. It's so bad that we bring into play some of the old canopies we used previously and alternate them in the stack. It improves the attempt but we still have big issues, and ultimately it's too big a problem for us to resolve to be able to break the stacking record.

We decide to take time out and do a fun jump, just to chill, and I suggest we go for the British free fall star record, where skydivers link up in a perfect circle. We invite the British eight-way formation skydiving team to join us on the attempt. Both Skyvan aircrafts fly in, individuals fasten their helmets and put their goggles on, and with all eyes focussed on the job in hand, thirty-six bodies pile out of the planes. As soon as I hit the airflow my arms are thrown back and my legs are extended to increase my dive speed, as I have to catch up with one of the first jumpers out. I glance left and right and see others diving as well, and once I'm at the correct level it's time to focus on the approach, as star formations can be fragile to dock on to which can sometimes result in sending people tumbling. I observe the star formation increasing in size and it's a wonderful sight in the air but I know time is running out. I take my place in the formation and glance around the group, watching the last two skydivers dock. Smiles can be seen all around as, to our surprise, we break the British record with thirty-four of us linked up on our very first attempt.

A fortnight later at the Peterborough Skydiving Club, they build a thirty-two star formation and celebrate what they perceive to be a British record. They even have T-shirts made up only to discover, a little late in the day, what we'd achieved two weeks previously.

Work at the club continues and is enjoyable, as we run first jump courses week after week. It's what I live for, and to think I get paid to do this makes me extremely happy.

The end of the year finishes off nicely with a trip to Cyprus to compete in a skydiving competition and to expand my experience of eating world food dishes. We go to a restaurant in Larnaca one evening and enjoy a fish meze, and we're so impressed we go back the following night and try the meat meze. The waiter just keeps bringing out plate after plate, which we demolish, until I try something that tastes really horrible. Curiosity gets the better of me and I ask the waiter what I've just eaten. "Sheep's brain," he tells me, and my face mimics a chameleon and starts to change colour as his words circle around my head. The knock on effect is I now want a description of every dish coming out of the kitchen so there are no hidden surprises.

Over Christmas I manage to organise for some of my club members to spend the holiday skydiving in Spain, flying out in a private aircraft, and the owner agrees to do two trips so we can take more people out there. It's a trip everyone seems to be enjoying - skydiving in the sun, meeting other skydivers, and swapping fun stories. On Christmas day some of us stop off to have a quick drink before heading up to the airfield for the Christmas party and dinner. We're about to depart the small bar we're in when an influx of people arrive, and I'm shocked to hear that some people had started a food fight as soon as it had arrived. I ask one of the people what idiots started it and I'm told it was three of my club members. I'm deeply embarrassed. To make matters worse, I hear that one of my club members also kicked a door in trying to gate-crash a party. The next morning I let them know I'm not impressed and I make the guy who damaged the door pay for it. I tell myself it's the last time I organise a club trip abroad; I don't want to be associated with anything like that again.

My leave finishes in mid-January and the RNRMSPA open for the new season. Work is mixed in with teaching and dispatching first timers from the aircraft, but I also have the chance to fun jump with the club members. When the weekends come to a close and the club members leave, I observe the cars driving off as a shroud of darkness falls over the airfield. Some will have a four hour drive, but for me it's just a case of grabbing a cup of tea and walking upstairs.

It's apparent that the old control tower has a ghost, who the club members have named Simon. At times it's a bit eerie when I'm on my own with the building creaking and footsteps echoing on the stairways, and it becomes more so when I reflect on some of the things I've seen and experienced. Many times I've been working at my desk and items have suddenly gone missing just after I've put them down. I've heard the door rattle, seen the handle turn and the door open, yet the only thing there was an icy presence. Once I was in the shower and saw a shadow move past the shower curtain. I opened it to see who it was but, of course, there was nobody there. The worst moment by far was having my bed shake of its own accord, with me in it. I sat bolt upright and, thankfully, it stopped. I'm not the only one who has experienced these strange happenings - other people have told me about their ghostly encounters too. Sharing my home with something from another realm was never on my agenda but I become used to it and simply turn up the volume on the TV to drown out the creaking noises. At times, when he's being overly active, I find myself talking to him. "Simon, stop messing me about." But there's never a reply and that's a good thing, otherwise I could well break the British record for eight hundred metres.

I'm approached to do a display for a high class wedding for the Simcoe family from Dunkeswell, who have the distinction that one of their ancestors was the first Lieutenant Governor of Upper Canada in 1791. I carry out my recce and see the landing area is going to be on their back lawn with the wedding party looking on. The lawn is not that big; it has high trees at each end, the grand house on one side and a terraced garden on the other. What it does have is over shoots, so if the approach to the lawn isn't right there's the option to pull out and land in a field or tennis court. I agree to do it but I know this is going to be challenging and will test the nerve of each jumper. I have a family member sign the appropriate forms, giving us permission to land there, and they accept responsibility for crowd control. Other forms are filled out and sent to the Civil Aviation Authority and to National Air Traffic Services to issue a NOTAM informing anyone that will be flying in the area that a parachute display will be taking place at that location on the date and time specified.

The day arrives and the wind is howling on the ground at the airfield, so the club has put parachuting on hold. I check out the display landing area and go back up to the airfield to brief the jumpers: Graeme Henderson, Bob Sturtivant, and Raymond (Radar) Marks.

"Guys, here's the score. The wind is fucking howling, doing thirty plus knots at a thousand feet. The wind on the ground in the landing area is only showing five knots because it's on the other side of the hill and below the tree line. It's too windy to do our normal display so it's just a question of every man for themselves. Let's do it and keep the parachutes staggered so we're not coming in at the same time."

It's not long before we're in the Cessna 182 and taking off, and no sooner are we airborne the aircraft is bouncing around which isn't helping our nerves, even though we have eight thousand jumps between us. As we fly over the landing area I open the door and throw out the wind drift indicator, and the pilot starts banking which allows me to keep it in view. I turn to the guys.

"I'm going to take you so fucking deep you're going to think I've kicked the arse out of it. Trust me; the WDI is still going. Remember to keep the parachutes staggered. This, gentlemen, separates the men from the boys."

There's a nervous smile from the jumpers and my heart is thumping like mad.

"Here we go!" I shout as I exit the plane.

We appear to be around five miles up wind. I head towards the landing area and decide I need to try and hold my ground as much as I can, only to see I'm going backwards, as I expected. I calculate that due to the size of the lawn and the fact the wind is likely to suddenly drop below the tree-line I have to turn over the back of the lawn, just above the trees. My parachute stops dead and I'm cursing, my brain is racing, but there's not much time to decide the cut off height and when to pull out and side slip for the tennis courts for a safer landing. My parachute rocks and then surges forward, and I land dead centre of the lawn. I can't help but blow out my cheeks as my adrenalin is pumping overtime. As I grab my parachute and move to the side

I look across and see the bride with her white gown blowing in the wind, and the wedding party, which includes some extremely high-ranking military officers, the sort of which I'll never meet. All are enjoying this spectacle as they sip their champagne, laughing and smiling. I know three people who are not smiling and that's the three landing after me, and I chuckle to myself as I peer up to see Bob, another former Royal Marines Free Fall Parachute Display Team member, approach the lawn. Bob also nails it and lands on the centre of the lawn, and to my surprise he unzips his jumpsuit, pulls out a box of Black Magic chocolates, and hands it to the bride. I notice Graeme is trying to side slip but hasn't enough height and lands on the next terrace below. All eyes are now on Radar and to my surprise he decides to cut the lawn by half to allow for the high wind. He is about to realise his mistake. As the wind drops off, Radar goes on deep brakes to lose the forward speed, but he's running out of lawn. I hear him shout, "Look out!" and on turning around I see the wedding photographer has decided to sneak on to the lawn to grab a picture. Radar lands but has to take a step forward due to his momentum and he knocks the wedding photographer off his feet, much to the delight of the cheering crowd. It's a clear sign the champagne is doing its work. The wedding photographer picks himself up, much to his embarrassment, as he realises he was at fault and put the jumper at risk. The family and bride thank us, telling us how awesome it was, and we're presented with a few bottles of bubbly to take away with us. We all agree we should toast the bride and groom, but more importantly the fact we survived, and on the journey back to the airfield we relive our jumps with much relieved laughter.

The following month all the RNRMSPA instructors are invited to take part in a British Free Fall formation record, to take place at the Middle Wallop Air Show. We all have to wear the same rigs and jumpsuits in the army air corps colours of light blue, which means we have to purchase them. It seems like a good deal considering we'll get to go for this record as well as having free jumps. Practice jumps take place on Colerne Airfield in Wiltshire out of two Chinook helicopters: CH47s. They're fun helicopters to jump from as they have tail gate ramps.

The day of the air show arrives and we're gutted to see we have cloud cover at around six thousand feet, and we're hoping it will clear as we stroll around waiting for our time slot. That isn't our only concern - in the practice jumps one of the problems we encountered was the difficulty in finding our slots in the free fall formation, as everyone is in the same colour.

A meeting is called and we're told the cloud is not going to clear, however the pilots are happy to fly above the cloud that isn't as thick, using beacons to work out our exit point. We're asked if we're happy to still to go for it and of course we agree. There's excitement as we unpack, check the equipment over, then start to gear up. We're rallied up to go through the jump and walk it out so everyone can see how they are going to approach the formation. I have one coloured marker opposite me to give me my line, and I'm due to dock on to Dave Payne who I happen to notice has rainbow coloured shoelaces. When we board the helicopters and take off, the vibes are good with no pre-nerves showing.

We're at altitude and there are tiny gaps in the cloud as we position ourselves in the door and line up. "Exit, exit, exit," is shouted out in quick succession and when I run down the Chinook and dive out it's an awesome sight, as I see to my right the other helicopter spewing out its jumpers. As I close in on the formation I know I'm on the right side but I haven't a clue where my slot is as everyone looks the same. I can feel the seconds passing by as the airflow rushes past my body at 120mph. I frantically search for Dave Payne's rainbow shoelaces and to my relief I spot them and fly over. *Yes!* I shout to myself as I dock. All around me people are smiling and yelling out, and as the fiftieth person docks it's clear we've just built a British military and British free fall formation record. The formation hits a cloud and we break out of it directly above the thousands and thousands of spectators. They can hear us cheering and see us directly above them against the white cloud background for a few seconds before we bomb burst to find our own bit of air space. The noise of fifty one parachutes opening echoes over the airfield, and later, on the ground, there is a lot of back patting and handshaking taking place as we congratulate each other.

The team of instructors at the RNRMSPA have all become great work colleagues but we've also become good friends, sharing the workload and chatting about our experiences with first time students. At times the roll of acting Chief Club Instructor is handed over to me to cover the CCI who has had to disappear somewhere for a period of time. I start to appreciate the responsibility that goes with the title and the amount of documentation that has to be kept up to date. The British Parachute Association operations manual is quite clear: all responsibility stops with the CCI, including the flying side of parachuting.

I persuade a couple of friends to form a team with me and to go over to Germany to compete in the Rhine Army Parachute Championships. I tell my mate, who shall remain nameless, that the local town of Bad Lippspringe has an interesting swimming pool complex where all the saunas are mixed and everyone is naked. He laughs and is convinced I'm winding him up. "Just you wait and see," I tell him. The aim is to drive over there as that seems the cheapest option, and I cook up some food as well as four whole cooked chickens so not to be stung with the high prices at the service stations. Once we arrive at the campsite we set up our tents, and then set off to quench our thirst in the hot sun. Later in the day I need to fetch something from my tent and when I unzip it I'm hit with an unbearable stench, which I soon discover is one of the chickens that somebody has hidden there. I have a feeling who the culprit is and I hide the chicken in his tent before making my way back to the bar. For the next three days this slimy, bacteria-ridden chicken travels from tent to tent and the reek of it worsens as each day passes.

I take my un-named mate to the local swimming pool and we enter the complex, get changed, and head into the pool area.

"Andy, I knew you were winding me up," he tells me, looking around at everyone in their swimming gear.

"I said the saunas, not the swimming pool," I say. "We need to go up these stairs."

When we reach the top we pass through the double doors and there's no one to be seen.

"You were winding me up," he says, and starts to laugh, whereupon a woman walks through the door, peels off her bikini, places it in a locker and heads off to a sauna. His laughter has stopped but mine has just started.

"Mate, pick up your chin and let's get in there," I tell him, and we both strip off. I point out the facilities as we pass each one – a room which can only be described as a giant sun bed, another which has the strong scent of eucalyptus to clear the sinuses, and three separate saunas. "Through those back doors," I say, pointing to them, "is an ice-cold pool. And I mean ice-cold."

We walk into the first sauna where we're met with a blistering heat which soon has us back-peddling out again, much to the amusement of those in there. We enter the second one more slowly only to find that it's too bloody hot as well, and then find the last sauna to be just about acceptable. The only other people in there are two naked German girls, aged around twenty. The sweat is pouring off us and we chat away about different things. One of the girls sweeps away the sweat running off her breasts, and we manage to maintain our conversation, but then she parts her legs to wipe the sweat from her inner thighs.

"Andy, I need to go," my mate tells me.

I'm confused as to why he has a sudden urgency to leave but all becomes clear when he stands up. The towel wrapped around his waist has taken on a shape which is defying gravity. He rushes through the door and I watch him execute a right turn. Both girls giggle, and I'm convinced it was planned. I'm in complete control - I've never thought about British politics so much in all my life - and I slowly get up and exit the sauna to go in search of my friend. I find him in the ice pool which, he says, *is just perfect.*

The competition comes to an end, the alcohol flows, and we sit in a circle on the grass for a few hours with people of many nationalities, laughing and joking. Somehow in the dark I find my tent, and during the night I wake up with my bladder at bursting point. I'm having real problems figuring out the zip, which appears to be stuck, and knowing I'm not going to be able to hold back much longer because it's so uncomfortable, I have no choice but to rip a hole in the tent to get out. In the morning I'm curious to know what the problem was and I discover someone had a sense of humour and had tied my zip up. I can see the funny side but at the same time I'm peeved I have to buy another one.

Back at Dunkeswell I take the plunge and buy a house with my brother Pete. It's such a great feeling being on the property ladder and walking through my own front door. It's even better knowing I'll no longer have people knocking to suggest continuing the party in my room.

Some of the guys plan to visit Eaglescott in North Devon and I decide to go with them to see Gary Lawry. When his club closes all the members retire to the local pub and I meet up with Alison Watts, the pretty girl I'd met here four years previously, and we chat all evening. We're surprised at how quickly the time has flown, and there's a lot to catch up on, even though we've kept in touch as friends, meeting up a couple of times and exchanging the odd letter or postcard. At the end of the evening, realising there's something special about her, I ask Alison out and she accepts. I point out it's not going to be easy as I work at the Marines club six days a week, but Alison tells me she understands.

Not long afterwards I receive a call from Alison who says she wants to see me, and as it's my day off I invite her over. I know she should be working, so the fact she's chosen to see me instead leaves me with a nice feeling. An hour later there's a knock on the door and I open it to see Alison standing there and looking a bit upset. It occurs to me that perhaps she's having problems at work, hence not going in today, and in my mind I'm already preparing what I'm going to say to her to make her feel a bit better. After a hug we sit down, and I ask Alison what the problem is.

"I'm pregnant," she says.

THIS AMAZING EXPERIENCE

The words, 'I'm pregnant', echo in my head; all other thoughts have been obliterated. There's just silence, and the only thing I can think to say is, "I'll put the kettle on."

As I fill the kettle and flick the switch, the voices in my head start up. *Bloody hell, I'm going to be a dad.* I'm used to evaluating and making quick decisions but this is a whole new area for me and I'm at a loss as to what the right thing to say is. As the kettle is boiling it's buying me a few minutes to gather my thoughts, and it's the only time I'm glad I filled it to the top. I've heard stories and seen film clips of moments like this but it's only now I'm really appreciating the impact those words have. I spoon coffee into the mugs, and grab the milk from the fridge, all the while feeling slightly numb. Questions are popping up thick and fast, but I have no answers. The kettle clicks off and the silence surrounds me. I pour the water into the mugs and then it hits me. I'm thirty-one years of age, but Alison is only twenty-three. I need to stop thinking about myself and start thinking about how this is affecting Alison emotionally. I take a breath, walk into the lounge and hand Alison her coffee.

"So," I say, "the first thing I want you to know is you're not on your own; we're in this together."

I suggest that Alison stays for a few days so we can spend some time talking this through. I can't help but think if my head is all over the place what the hell must it be like for her?

We have a late night and when I wake up in the morning my first thought is, *Wow. That was a strange dream.* And then it suddenly hits me that it wasn't a dream at all and it's actually happening. It's a weird feeling to know this is going to change our lives forever.

Over the next few days Alison and I go for long walks, and I try to reassure her she's not on her own and that things will work out. Even so, I'm finding it hard to grasp this whole thing. I'm going to be a dad; it just seems surreal.

My thought process is going to have to change, I decide; I now have other people who will be depending on me. I try and think what needs to be done and it's clear the first thing to do is to break the news to Alison's parents. It's something that Alison shouldn't have to do on her own, so I tell her that I'll do it. Alison's parents have divorced and remarried, so I'm going to have to break the news twice, and it's something I'm not looking forward to. I'll also have to go through it a third time, with my own parents.

A day is selected and it soon comes around. I collect my car from the garage, having just had it serviced, and make my way to Alison's in Ilfracombe. As I enter the A35 I spot a car on my left failing to stop at a give way sign. The driver is looking left and hasn't seen me, and he shoots straight out and impacts into my car with a huge bang, spinning me ninety degrees and turning my car into a V shape. I'm thankful that it's on the passenger side and even more thankful Alison isn't with me. It's clear my car is a total right off and I'm so pissed off as the timing just couldn't have been worse.

My father loans me his car to drive to Ilfracombe. After telling them about the pregnancy it's clear my parents are reeling from the news that I'm going to be a dad. My mother had given up the idea of being a grandmother, with three sons in their thirties and all single, so I tell myself this is good news for her, even though it's a shock.

I meet up with Alison and we drive to her mother's house first. This journey feels like no other car journey I've been on as I wonder what the reaction is going to be. I've no idea what I'm going to say and it feels more nerve wrecking than my first parachute jump. I enter the house where formal greetings are exchanged, and the atmosphere is relaxed as we drink tea and eat cake, just chatting in general. Something doesn't feel right, I can sense it, and by the look on their faces I can't help thinking they're expecting me to announce an engagement. *Well, this is going to be interesting,* I tell myself. I notice the time is moving on and I still have her father to see yet, so it's time to break the news. I can see Alison is nervous, and she isn't the only one. I can only hope my throat doesn't dry up at the wrong moment because my cup's empty.

"Alison and I have some good news to share," I say, and on that note Alison's mother sits up and edges forward in her seat with an eager smile on her face.

"Yes?" she says.

"We're pleased to announce we're going to be parents," I say, "and I want you to know I'll be supporting Alison all the way."

I watch both her mother and step-father digesting the news with slightly open mouths, and they look at each other and then back towards me. Yes, it's clear to see that's not the news they were expecting to hear. I make my apologies and explain we have to go, as we have yet to meet Alison's father. As I leave the house I take a deep breath and tell myself there's only one more to go.

We arrive at Alison's father's house and I'm welcomed in. The cycle of tea and cake starts again. The process is running the same, so much so I can sense I'm in the same situation here and they're expecting an engagement announcement. I know Alison is relieved that I'm breaking the news and she hasn't been left on her own to do it. The moment arrives and I look at their smiling faces.

"Well, I've come here today as Alison and I have some news we'd like to announce." It almost feels like a scene from an intense drama, the big build up that has you sat on the edge of your seat. I break the news and Alison's father, Tony, looks at us.

"Well, we weren't expecting that."

I'm relieved he hasn't come for me swinging, but no one seems to be eating cake any more.

Before I leave I give Alison a kiss and tell her not to worry as it will all work out. As I drive home it all starts to feel very real, but I'm still trying to get my head around it. *I'm going to be a dad!* It's an amazing feeling but

I know there are now going to be some huge changes in my life, some of which I'll have to make myself. I make the first one that night: I decide to stop BASE jumping completely. I have responsibilities now to my unborn baby, and I recall what happened to Frank on his building jump when he left his child without a father.

Two days later I'm on the telephone to the driver who crashed into my car, and I tell him that his insurance company are saying he's refusing to accept responsibility.

"Yes I am; there are no witnesses," he tells me.

I'm really not in the mood for this and my voice shoots up in anger.

"You what? Are you serious? Well here's the thing. One: You'll need to explain in court why your car entered the side of mine and left it in a V shape when you were supposed to stop at your junction. Two: As for no witnesses, the first guy on the scene of the accident saw the layout of the cars after the crash, and by the way, he was the mechanic who just serviced my car. Three: If your insurance isn't paying then fine … not a problem. I'll play this fucking game of yours. I'll take you personally to court. In fact my neck and back is killing me … oh my god, it's getting worse all the time. Looks to me if your insurance is exempt from paying it'll come out of your pocket."

I slam the phone down on him and as I stroll out through my open office door I receive a round of applause from my club members, who haven't seen me lose my temper before.

"That was entertaining," someone says.

The following day I receive a phone call from the insurance company to say they're going to pay out. I'm gutted to discover they're only going to pay me a small amount for my car because it's old; the fact it has done very little mileage seems to have no bearing at all, so this will leave me out of pocket.

The Royal Marines ask me if I want to take over at the RNRMSPA as the full time Club Chief Instructor. I have the choice of either getting wet and cold and digging holes and playing soldiers, or carrying on doing what I enjoy, so

I accept the offer. It's all subject to me passing the BPA Advance Instructor's course, a rating I must have to run the club in a full time capacity. There's no one to coach me, so it's a question of phoning people I know who have attended the course for tips and advice. I learn the course will be in two parts, and I have to pass both. There are a number of lectures I have to prepare and present, including showing my ability to actually run a parachute school. I already have that experience due to covering my own chief instructor when he was away, so I'm happy on that side.

The pre-advance course is held at Netheravon and I feel the pressure of it right from the start. There's plenty of running around to do with me trying to stay one step ahead of the game, and it's with some relief when, five days later, I'm told I have passed the first course. It's excellent news; I'm still in the running.

Everything at the club is ticking over. Members turn up at weekends and I'm paying them more attention now in order to know what they're getting up to. I grab a bowl of chilli in the afternoon and think how rare it is to get something to eat during the day; it's the first time this season for me and we're already half way through the year. As I walk outside the clubroom with my meal, I see a dozen people running to one side of the club house, and I don't have to ask ... I just know it's a bad sign. I look up and see two people entangled and both parachutes spiralling out of control. They should have carried out their emergency drills by now but they have failed to do that. Someone on the ground is yelling for them to release their parachutes and this angers me; if they do it'll be certain death as they are too low now. Lady luck is shining on them as, on the last spiral, both parachutes separate and they land safely. I call out to one of the club members.

"When they get back send them to me."

I speak to the two guys involved to find out how they got themselves into that situation, and why they failed to carry out their emergency drills. Both have learned a valuable lesson and, as they walk away, it's apparent it's been a big scare for them and they're unlikely to do it again.

Leo arrives back at the club and wants to film some more unusual situations, one of which is of two round parachutes linking up. I suggest that once it's achieved, one person climbing down the rigging lines so both jumpers are next to each other would be even better. Neil, one of the civilian jumpers helping out at the club, approaches me.

"Andy, I've always wanted to do this adventurous stuff. Can I give it a go?"

I brief him for the jump and we discuss the parachutes we're going to use.

It's peaceful and quiet in the air, and I dock onto Neil's canopy, grabbing the material and rigging lines. The first stage is done but I'm finding it's extremely hard work climbing down the lines. There's every chance my parachute may collapse and I'll find myself hurtling past Neil. Fortunately, the jump goes according to plan and Leo has his footage. Neil tells me afterwards that he's never been so scared in his life and doesn't want to do it anymore. I like his honesty, and the fact he has a healthy respect for what he just did. What I don't do is tell him how scared I was of what could possibly have gone wrong, but I leave him to think it was all very straight forward for me. Creating an illusion amuses me.

The second part of the Advance Instructor's course is held at Bridlington and again, right from the word go, the examiners put me under pressure. It seems I must know everything - even to the point of knowing how many hours are left of an aircraft's propeller. I have assigned two syndicates on the Category System Instructor's course to two classrooms, and I check with the weather for a parachute program as I am expected to run one, but currently it's not good enough. All in all everything seems to be ticking over so I decide to go for a tea, and on approaching the tea room I hear the examiners mention my name, and the National Safety coach saying he has a question I won't have the answer for. I hide in the corridor by the open door and listen in, and then tip-toe away to an office to find a phone number.

Later that day the weather breaks, and I stop the classes to move into the parachute program. The pilot has been instructed to prepare the aircraft and I'm setting up the drop zone to ensure it runs smoothly. I have the first aircraft of parachutists on board and it's about to take off when I notice the National Safety coach and the other examiners have all come outside to watch. I observe the aircraft taking off and hear the National Safety coach calling out to me.

"Andy, I have a question." I listen as he sets a scenario of someone exiting the plane at twelve thousand feet whose round reserve parachute accidently opens and the upper winds are doing forty knots and heading east. I take in what he says.

"So let me get this right, twelve thousand feet, winds doing forty knots heading east, and the person is on a round reserve. I have to say there's every chance the person may land in the sea. They're likely to be in the air for around ten minutes, so I would call the coast guard, who would tell me they can be there in eight minutes."

I give the coach the coastguard's phone number, which I'd memorised, and the other examiners laugh and walk off with the National Safety coach muttering, "bastard". At the end of the course I'm awarded my Advance Instructor's rating, and my job as the RNRMSPA Chief Club Instructor has been secured.

Alison moves in with me full time. It's a big step for her to be away from her family but we need to be together leading up to the birth. I'm excited at the thought of meeting my child.

We notice, after one false start, how some of the neighbours seem to be watching our every move, so we decide to leave the suitcase in the car in case there's another one. I'm slightly nervous at the thought of it being my responsibility to get Alison to hospital on time, and I dwell on what would happen if I had to pull over to deliver the baby myself.

The time seems to come around so quickly, and Alison tells me we need to go, so we head to the car and make our way to the hospital. Alison is taken away, which leaves me standing in the labour ward listening to women screaming. It's an anxious time and I find myself pacing up and down and feeling extremely nervous. Anyone would think I was the one giving birth. A nurse eventually calls me to follow her and I'm led to where Alison is.

After a few contractions I start to realise just how hard Alison is able to squeeze my hand as it's causing my face to grimace in pain, but I grin and bear it, wondering if this is payback time. When the moment arrives the midwife calls me around to the bottom of the bed, and it's strange to be bonding with someone I haven't met yet, although I know I will very shortly. There's a slight sense of guilt as I'm able to enjoy this amazing experience and watch the birth close up and pain free, and it's the most wonderful sight.

I'm told we have a son who weighs nine pound five ounces. I'm so proud of Alison and of how well she's coped with it all. It's no longer a thought but a reality – I'm a father. I'm in a daze; so excited but not knowing what I'm supposed to do next. I call my parents to break the news, and the news is broken to Alison's parents who have also become grandparents for the first time. Alison and I had only chosen one name - a boy's name - and we call our son Westleigh. I notice how big he is compared to the other babies, and the fact he is looking so healthy makes me feel proud.

It's quite daunting when we bring Westleigh home, and the responsibility we have in looking after him fully sinks in. There is the odd panic attack at the beginning, after hearing so much about cot deaths. At times I look at my son in his cot, trying to confirm I can see him breathing. When I'm unsure I poke him slightly to get a response. The whole process of changing nappies I thought would horrify me but it doesn't; after all Westleigh is my son. What I do learn very quickly though is to be prepared for the unexpected at both ends. I am determined to show I will do my fair share with Westleigh and spend as much time as I can with him. Some friends comment that I never go out to drink anymore and it's true. My life has changed, but it's for the better.

A few months later I'm in a deep sleep on the couch in the lounge when there's an almighty crash coming from the kitchen; washed up plates have hit the floor and smashed into pieces, scattering fragments everywhere. I sit bolt upright and think, *what the hell was that?* and see a cat stalking across my lounge. As I leap off the couch I stand on a wine glass that shatters under my bare foot, sending glass across the room. The cat makes a run for it upstairs and I limp up behind him with blood pouring from my foot. The cat enters the bathroom, jumps onto the windowsill to find the bathroom window closed, and sends a clay vase flying, which punches a hole in the bath. The cat bypasses me and races down the stairs and out of the kitchen window. Alison arrives home a few minutes later to find shattered glass on the floor, blood up the stairs, and plates smashed all over the kitchen floor. As I appear on the landing I see Alison looking extremely nervous, as if I have had some sort of mental fit, and it takes her a while to relax and accept it was just a cat in the house that caused all this destruction.

Alison tells me she wants to attend the Eaglescott Christmas party, and after thinking things over for some time now I've decided to propose to her. As luck would have it, when the day arrives I'm burning up with flu and trying my hardest to control my coughing. My body wants to rest but it feels important that I propose now as it's been twelve months since I first asked Alison out at Eaglescott, and it feels like the right time. This has to be the least romantic proposal ever; however, it's nice to hear Alison reply with a 'yes'.

The mortgage on the house has gone ballistic; in one day the interest rate has gone up three times to fifteen percent. I'm now in the situation where having cleared one debt I'm going into another. My entire Marines wage is paying the mortgage, leaving me without a spare penny to pay for food or utility bills. There is no light at the end of the tunnel - I'm just going further into debt - and I tell my brother Pete (who I bought the property with) that I have no choice but to sell. Pete's girlfriend steps in and buys my share, and I lose four thousand pounds, but it feels such a relief to not see the debt accumulate each month. Now it's just a question of paying it off.

As a temporary measure I tell Alison she will have to return to her mother's house with Westleigh, while I return to living at the old control tower. It's very upsetting for Alison and leaves her feeling vulnerable; it's not a situation I'm happy with either, being away from the both of them. I come up with a solution to apply for military married quarters, the catch being we need to be married. I suggest we have a registry office wedding as soon as we can, and the planned wedding with family and friends can still take place later in the year but as a church blessing instead. Alison agrees.

I'm working at the club on a busy jumping day and tell my staff I need to disappear for a few hours. I meet up with Alison and we both head down to the registry office with Stan Wood and his wife - Stan has kindly accepted my request to be my best man. The ceremony doesn't take long and we go for a drink afterwards. The whole thing feels surreal as there are no family and friends present. I return to work later in the day and Radar approaches me.

"Andy, where did you disappear to this afternoon?"

"I shot off to get married, mate," I reply.

Radar bursts out laughing. "Yeah, right."

I hold up my finger and show him my wedding ring, and his face is a picture. To be honest, it hasn't sunk in for me, either.

A week later Alison and I are given married quarters in Taunton, and our family is now back together.

A FINAL GOODBYE

I've just returned from sunny Florida having completed a staff training camp, and it's back to running the RNRMSPA club. I'm looking forward to the new season. My friend Leo Dickinson arrives on the drop zone and wants to chat to me about a new documentary he's making called 'Dead Men's Tales', which involves recreating a number of parachuting incidents. As Leo tells me all about it I can see an opportunity to have some fun in doing the unusual and it appeals to me. The incident that really captures my imagination is one that, strangely, involved my older brother Pete and Gary Lawry, when their two parachutes became entangled. I tell Leo I'd like to recreate it and we discuss how to carry out the stunt.

"I'll get Dave Payne to do it with me," I tell Leo. "He doesn't know it yet, but let me work on him. He's very experienced – he has a couple of thousand jumps under his belt - and we regularly work with each other. We've built that trust." Leo agrees and I'm delighted, as I have something to look forward to that sounds scary and fun.

I catch up with Dave. "Mate, I've got some good news. Leo's making a documentary and one of the scenes involves two parachutes becoming entangled, so it makes sense that two experienced people in canopy stacking do it. I told Leo you'd do it with me."

Dave stares at me. "You're fucking off your head," he says.

Okay, that didn't go as well as I'd hoped. "Hear me out. We use cutaway rigs, and link up our two parachutes. I come down your lines, you give me your steering toggle, and I connect it to mine via a carabiner. I then release you as the parachutes start to fly apart. Because our steering toggles are connected this will cause the parachutes to stall and collapse. We'll start plummeting at the same time and spin out like a weight on a string, with both parachutes entangled in the middle. At four thousand feet we talk to each other, jettison the parachutes, and then we're back to normal in free fall." Dave is not looking at all convinced. "We get paid fifty pounds a jump," I tell him.

"Okay, I'll do it." he says.

A few weeks later Leo is back with the cutaway rigs and his cameras. The parachutes are all packed up and we're ready to go when Leo produces a chest mount 16mm camera and asks if one of us could wear it. Dave is having the same thought as me - it's a potential snag which could have dire consequences, but at the same time the footage would be great. We take ten minutes to talk this through to ensure all scenarios are covered. I emphasise that communication is everything, and no one jettisons their parachute without communicating with the other person, as it could endanger them. The one thing we have between us is trust.

"Hey, this is going to be fun. Let's do it," I say to Dave. Looking at him, I'm not sure he feels the same way.

We board the aircraft, a Brit Norman Islander, and climb to ten thousand feet, both in our own deep thoughts. At last we start the run in over the airfield and I stick my head out of the aircraft and shout corrections to the pilot. When we reach the exit point, I turn to Dave.

"Trust me, this'll be great. Here we go!"

Dave exits the aircraft first, quickly followed by me, both of us doing short delays before opening the parachutes. My mind just goes through the normal process of doing a canopy hook up and I grab Dave's parachute and slide down his lines until I'm just above his shoulders.

"Dave, give me you steering toggle," I shout out, and he passes it up. As I'm attaching the steering toggles together and locking off the carabiner I notice we have a slight inbuilt turn, which is expected. "Switch on the camera."

"Camera's on," he calls back.

There's a smile on my face as I shout, "Lets ride the wild ride... here we go!" and I release him. As the parachutes start to fly apart, Dave's immediately goes into a stall and collapses. For a short while mine stays inflated and we start to spin, and then mine collapse too. The trouble is, my whole theory that the parachutes would stay entangled in the centre with us spinning on the outside has just been blown out of the water. We're all over the place. We're both spinning over the Devon countryside with blue skies above us and Dave is higher than me, then lower than me; I'm on my back, and then on my front, and all the time I'm checking my altimeter to see what height we're at. I was right about one thing: the visuals are awesome and there should be some fantastic footage of this. I bloody well hope the camera is working, I think.

As we reach the cut off height, Dave shouts out, "Andy, are we sticking to the plan?"

"Yes," I call back, and Dave jettisons his parachute. I take a quick glance to ensure nothing is entangled with my body, and I pull the jettison handle and feel myself fall away from the mess.

After we land, Dave strolls over to me. "Mate, that was nothing like what you said would happen."

I don't reply but burst out laughing.

Leo asks us to do the jump again. "Well at least there won't be any surprises," I tell Dave. We know what's coming and it's another fifty quid."

Over the next three jumps all goes well and we're asked, yet again, to do another one. The novelty factor has worn off now and it's becoming mentally tiring.

Once again we find ourselves on this wild ride when, suddenly, everything stops. Somehow, Dave's parachute has re-inflated and we've stopped spinning.

"Dave, you need to collapse your parachute," I shout. All of his lines are twisted up and I can see they're preventing him for putting his head up.

"Bloody hell," Dave yells, as he keeps pulling on one single line.

Suddenly, we're off again and being tossed around: up, down, and all the time spinning. My steering line nearly catches me under the neck so I grab it and find that on every three-sixty spin I have to feed it over my head.

We reach the cut off height and Dave shouts out, "Are we sticking to the plan?"

"No," I shout back. Things don't look right and I can see the potential of our two bodies colliding. "You go first."

As Dave jettisons my worst fears are confirmed, as his discarded parachute hits me in the chest. I now have my own spinning parachute with his discarded parachute caught around my camera. I try frantically to untangle the mess, knowing my safety altitude is being eaten up. I manage to remove three lines and the picture I see seems to indicate I'm clear of the discarded parachute, so I jettison mine. Much to my relief I feel myself fall clear.

Once back on the ground Leo informs us that he feels he now has enough footage and won't need us to do it again.

"Thank fuck for that," Dave says, but we can't contain the grins on our faces.

Another incident that Leo wants to recreate is one that occurred in 1966 over Halfpenny Green in Wolverhampton, where a student had what is known as a 'hang-up'. He was unable, when jumping from the aircraft, to break away from the static line, and was suspended in mid-air. The jump master, Mick Reeves, climbed down the static line, cut it free, and did a free-fall with the student before deploying his reserve. He was awarded the George Medal.

I approach Si Clark, one of my instructors, and tell him how much fun it will be to do it together. I also mention the bonus of getting paid fifty pounds for each jump we do. Si tells me he's up for it.

A couple of weeks later Leo arrives to film it. He wants some free fall footage of the instructor, which will be me, desperately trying to open the student's front-mounted reserve. I tell Leo it didn't happen like that in real life, and Leo points out that he wants to make it more dramatic for the TV audience, as that's what they do in the movies. It's a simple jump; there's no need to go all the way up to altitude, so we agree to do it from seven thousand feet. Si and I talk about the jump and the cut off height, and as he's playing a student from 1966 his altimeter will be hidden inside his jumpsuit.

It's a beautiful, peaceful summer's day. The Devon landscape below me looks like a picture, and there are two bright, sparkling coastlines in the distance. We position ourselves in the aircraft with Si on his back and me holding onto his side, and we exit and enter the slip stream. Straight away I spot a problem. Si has lowered his hands by his side, which causes him to move horizontally across the ground, and with me hanging onto his side there is only one outcome: we go into a spin. The spin picks up in speed and the G-force prevents me from going into the role-play of pretending to struggle to pull Si's front-mounted reserve. I check our height and it's clear the short time we had has been used up, so I release Si in the belief that he'll know the filming has finished and it's time to open his parachute, as this was not in the plan.

I turn one hundred and eighty degrees and start to move horizontally away from him for separation, and I glance back expecting to see him opening his parachute, but to my surprise I see him still on his back with a smile on his face. I spin back to observe him, and to make sense of what he's doing. The reality of the situation hits me; he has lost his altitude awareness.

There is no more thought process. My body instinctively adopts the position to dive to get to him; I know we have passed our pull height and we're already behind on time. I pick up speed through the air, accelerating to 180mph, compared to his 120mph. The clock is ticking, the altitude is being burned, and I have no time to look at my altimeter. I can see what is before me. I slice through the air like a peregrine falcon focussed on his prey. My mind reads off the height: two thousand feet, fifteen hundred feet, and the ground is expanding. At one thousand feet my head screams, *this is shit or bust*. I'm so close, alarm bells explode in my head, but I have to continue. I can sense the grim reaper is close by, ready to take me to his domain.

As I come over the top of Si I bank hard to kill my speed, so as to equal his, and skid to a halt sixty feet away from him. He looks at me. I throw a hand signal that indicates to pull, and at the same time I scream, "PULL IT! PULL IT! PULL IT!" My face doesn't hide the severity of our situation and Mandy Dickinson, who is filming from the ground, turns and walks away from her camera in tears. She knows the outcome and doesn't want to witness it, but she hears my voice screaming at Si to pull.

Some people say that when death approaches it's peaceful, quiet, serene; but not in this case. It's a fucking fight to the end. Si pulls his reserve that was going to be cut away as opposed to using his last resort reserve, and I see the canopy start to deploy. I spin again to avoid a canopy collision, but don't know if I still have time. I'm on unfamiliar equipment because we're creating something from the sixties, and it's gear I haven't used for fourteen years. I'm out of time to use my front-mounted reserve, and instead I hit the ripcord of my main, simultaneously staring at a tree that is rushing towards me with every intention of impaling me. I don't scream, but in my head a voice shouts, "Bollocks." I feel a sense of it being unfair, but there's a small voice at the back of my mind that is desperately clinging onto life, and it tells me that people have walked away from this.

I'm one and half seconds from impact. I accept my fate and know there is nothing more I can do.

When I get snatched upright, hard, and see my canopy inflate above my head, there's no time to rejoice. I grab my toggles, release my brakes, and turn ninety degrees to avoid the tree, and at the same time I continue the flare to land in a field on the edge of the trees. It all happens in an instant.

Do I thank God? No. God plays no part in life and death situations. Today just wasn't my day. Whether it was luck, or skill in my reaction, I really don't care. All I know is that it was close; too bloody close. I'm in shock as to how a simple jump got to that stage.

Leo, I discover, was open at a thousand feet.

"I know exactly why I'm down and dirty," I tell Leo, "I made a decision to chase after Si. But why the hell were you below opening height?"

"I couldn't believe what I was seeing," he says, "so I thought I'd keep filming."

We walk away, each of us trying to take lessons from this.

Four days later I'm parachuting into Ilfracombe to attend the church blessing of my marriage. It's going to be a special day, with friends and family joining us. Alison and I had planned to parachute in together, however, the weather is terrible and time is ticking on, and it's looking unlikely we'll get to jump. I make the decision to take Alison off the jump so she has more time to get ready for the big day. Some hours later, those of us jumping depart from Dunkeswell, certain we are likely to divert to an airfield in North Devon, but to our surprise the only place that has a bit of height is Ilfracombe, so I'm able to jump from the aircraft with friends. Once down, I change into my Royal Marines Blues uniform. The church is on a hill and I have visions of sliding down it and being unable to stop due to my hob nail boots, so I ask a friend to help me across the road.

As I'm in the church waiting for Alison to arrive, I wonder if any of my skydiving friends are going to play any pranks on me. But the thought is soon forgotten as I turn around to see Alison looking stunning in her wedding dress as she walks towards me with a smile on her face. I wonder if our son, Westleigh, who is nine days short of his first birthday, will start to play up, but he is as good as gold. It's a special moment to be stood there, exchanging our vows in front of our friends and family, and everything goes smoothly. I leave the church feeling that we can now relax as we're not on centre stage any more.

After the wedding we're extremely lucky as the skies clear. It's a lovely sunny day and we hold our reception at a hotel above the cliffs, next to the sea. At the end of the evening we discover friends have managed to get into our room and apple pie our bed. It's a funny, if not slightly exasperating end to a beautiful day.

Before we start our honeymoon I have a parachute display to take part in from a Royal Navy Sea King helicopter in Bath, and at the same time I've arranged for Alison to go up in a hot air balloon. I leave Alison in Bath and arrange to meet her at the Royal Crescent. Once back home I load our car to set off only to discover I have no petrol, so I stop at the cashpoint machine to discover it's out of order. Panic sets in and I call Si to meet me and lend me ten pounds to buy some, and then I call Dave Grindley and ask him to go to the Royal Crescent and collect Alison, telling him I'll meet them at his house. I have no way of contacting Alison to explain what's going on and it frustrates me.

When I arrive at Dave's house he tells me the balloon people were conducting a gas burn so there were thousands of people in the Royal Crescent, and yet he somehow managed to find Alison, whom he'd never met.

We have a fantastic honeymoon and once we return from the Lake District it's back to work at the parachuting school at Dunkeswell, and to finish the filming I'm involved in with Leo.

We decide to use two planes, one of which will act as a camera platform to film Si's hang-up. Si exits the aircraft and is suspended below, and I climb down the static line fighting hard to hold my grip. The old parachute equipment is heavy, bulky, and awkward, which makes things difficult, and there's a danger of the parachute deploying prematurely, so I opt to not be attached to the static line. If my parachute did accidently pop open, I'd end up bringing the whole aircraft out of the sky with everyone being suspended on my parachute. I continue down the line, fighting the slip stream, and once down with Si we stay there for a while before being cut free and deploying our parachutes.

We move on to filming the free fall jump, determined not to have a repeat performance of our last close call. On the first attempt Si is aware where his arms should be and it goes according to plan, right up to the point when his cutaway reserve doesn't open. When he releases the canopy he can't find his main canopy deployment and opens his last resort reserve instead. Afterwards, I inspect the cutaway reserve and discover that Si had attached extra elastic bungies to slow the opening down. It did that alright; it failed to bloody open. Leo questions my choice in picking Si, because on paper we shouldn't be having these problems.

On the next jump the free fall goes to plan, and I pull Si's front-mounted cutaway reserve and bang it to see the canopy go up in the air. Strangely, Si grabs me and pulls me towards him, and I'm worried his knee may hit me under the chin so I throw my arm up to protect my face. As I look into his reserve tray I note the rigging lines haven't moved, which is confusing. I'm totally unaware the cutaway reserve has gone up and over my head and is all over my back and legs. I bang Si's arm to be released and, thankfully, everything goes back to normal.

The last two jumps are text book, as I expected the first ones to go.

Once again the novelty factor is wearing off, and while filming for the last hang-up there's another problem. Due to a combination of the aircraft speed being too fast and my own tiredness, I fall off, much to the amusement of Si who is left dangling. Our safety man releases him from the aircraft by cutting his static line.

A couple of weeks later I reflect on the incident with Si that saw me so close to being killed, and a sense of guilt washes over me that I can't shake off. I put Si before my family, and very nearly left my son without a father and Alison to bring up a child on her own. I can analyse it and say my actions were justified, and it all ended well, but it doesn't take away the guilt. It feels as if there's a dark cloud hanging over me, and my emotions reach a point where they bring tears.

This is not me.

Having a family has changed me, and has made me aware of a situation I have to address. I purchase a safety device, so if my main parachute isn't deployed by a certain height the safety device will activate the reserve. It makes sense to take the decision out of my hands as I know if the same situation arose again, I would do it again. It's in my nature to go to someone's aid and I have to accept that.

Life at the skydiving school returns to normal, and I qualify for another instructor rating, this time Tandem. It makes things more interesting being multi rated.

A month later it's coming towards the end of the year and I manage to organise a large group from the RNRMSPA to fly out to Honk Kong on military flights to attend a competition. Alison has joined the Royal Navy reserves and is able to come as well. It's a fun time to explore this city under British control; it's a city that never sleeps. The parachuting competition is fun and, to my surprise, I become Hong Kong accuracy champion. I also complete a night jump, take part in a Hong Kong movie where I have to have a fight and fall out of a helicopter dressed in a suit, and I complete my first tandem with a real student out of a scout helicopter from eight thousand feet, which is quite challenging to do as we have to climb out onto the skid rails to fall over the side. Before I leave I board a light aircraft from Kai Tak airport, and we fly in between tall blocks of flats while watching women hanging out their washing on the balcony above us. It's a fantastic couple of weeks.

Alison returns home before me due to a shortage of military flights, as serviceman are flying home for Christmas leave. A week later I arrive at my parents' house and as I enter through the back door that leads into the kitchen I greet my mum, and then see my son walking around the corner. It's the first time I've seen him walk and it's the perfect welcome home - a moment to treasure that still brings a smile to my face.

Eighteen months later I'm still working on the drop zone, and I've now added Instructor Examiner to my ratings, which enables me to help out on British Parachute Association instructor courses to evaluate candidates.

At the start of 1992 I find myself at Taunton hospital maternity wing and listening to the wailing and screaming of all the women giving birth, the sound of which resembles the scene of a horror film rather than a joyous location full of happiness. I'm here to see the birth of my second son, Daniel, and it's another magical moment that makes me hugely proud that I've become a father again. It's giving me a meaning to life; the boys will depend on me and it's a task I relish with pride, nappy changing included. I observe Westleigh looking over the cot with a smile on his face, and he seems as excited as I am. Alison and I now consider our family complete.

I see an opening for another parachute school on the airfield as the civilian school has closed down, and the airfield management agree to allow me to start up a skydiving school, which I'm delighted about. It's a new adventure for me, although I'm surprised by some people's negativity in telling me it will never work, and I choose to ignore them. The tandem side of the business flourishes and I continue to pay the RNRMSPA for slots in the aeroplane. It's of mutual benefit, as this military club is self-funding.

Another instructor qualifies for his tandem rating and this helps me utilise the two tandem sets of equipment, as I pay him for each jump. As my turnover is under the VAT threshold it means my profit margin is higher, and the extra income comes in very handy. Alison and I put every penny we have into saving for a deposit on a house, and the business grows, allowing us to buy a two bedroom property.

I'm approached by the Marines eight-man CRW team who are one guy short, and they ask me if I'd like to join them on the practice jumps, which I'm more than happy to do, seeing an opportunity to do some canopy link-ups. I fill in the spare slot as they do their practice jumps, and they offer me a slot on the team, which I accept. Later in the year we head to Bridlington for the British CRW National Championships and the team, after completing all the rounds of the competition, win gold. After four silvers and a bronze at different National Championships, I finally have my first national gold medal and I'm delighted.

Dave Payne and I are extremely busy running Accelerated Free Fall courses. The RNRMSPA has a system in place to pay civilian instructors for running courses or jumping AFF students, but as Dave and I are serving Marines we cannot be paid for the jumps, so our fee goes into the slush fund. By the end of each year the slush fund has a fair amount of money in it, thus enabling the club to put on lavish Christmas parties from boats, marquee tents, and hotels, providing coaches so no one has to drive. It looks as if the slush fund is going to be quite large for another outstanding party this year because we already have three and a half thousand pounds in it.

I hear that a friend, Kevin, who was my original instructor from the Ford Airfield days, is selling some gear which would be ideal for me. I give him a call.

"Kevin, I hear you're selling eight sets of static line equipment."

"Yes I am," he says.

"Well, I'd like to buy all eight sets but the only snag is I don't have any money," I tell him, and can't help but grin at my cheekiness.

"How do you expect to pay for them?" he asks

"If you give me the equipment I could run static line courses, and every penny I earn will go directly to you with the aim of paying you off as soon as possible," I say.

To my surprise Kevin agrees, and I can't believe my luck. Our business has just expanded again.

One day, as I'm monitoring the parachute operations, I observe a student who is about to put a set of parachuting equipment on while wearing a T shirt. I inform him that students are not permitted to wear T shirts when jumping, and tell him to go off and get a jumper. Shortly afterwards I'm approached by three Navy lads who ask me if the rule applies to them.

"No, you guys are experienced. You could go naked if you wanted," I tell them.

Half an hour later they approach me again with the news they've decided to jump naked. I tell them to go into the clubhouse and put their skydiving gear on with a pair of shorts over their leg straps, and after I dispatch the female student they can take their shorts off and jump. In the aircraft I dispatch the lady on static line and decide to stay on board and go to altitude to watch the guys, as this could be funny.

As we're passing nine thousand feet I can't help but notice how warm the air is, so I climb onto the co-pilot seat and start stripping off. The pilot is my brother, Pete.

"What the hell are you doing?" he asks.

"I'm going naked. Its lovely out there."

We exit the plane into warm air, and in free fall we link up, holding hands and laughing our heads off with the lush green fields of the Devon countryside below our naked bodies. Once back on the ground the parachutes act as sheets and are thrown over us as we walk back into the clubhouse to get dressed again.

Even Chief Instructors can have fun sometimes.

The Royal Marines are planning to draft me, which could result in me losing my business if I'm not around to run it. So, after fourteen years of military service, I make the decision that it's come to an end. There's no fanfare; it's just a question of handing back my equipment before I walk out through the door for the final time.

The business continues to grow, and Alison now has a horse - something for her to enjoy outside of the family, having stopped skydiving when Daniel was born. My extreme adventures have been put on hold since becoming a dad, but I feel a familiar urge inside me, my inner spirit calling me to be set free. I need something; it's been nothing but work and raising a family for a long time. I chat to Alison and express my wish to BASE jump off Angel Falls in Venezuela, which is a high jump, and to my surprise she tells me she doesn't mind. I'm thrilled, as it's now given me something exciting to look forward to that will get my heart racing.

The BASE trip has all been paid up and I'll be travelling with Andy Montriou, one of my former students, who is now an experienced skydiver. We're flying out from Gatwick, which allows me to stop off at my parents' house to visit them and stay the night.

When I arrive, full of excitement, I'm shocked to discover my father has collapsed and has been admitted to hospital for tests. I contact my brother Ken, who says he is on his way; our other brother Pete is out of the country. My immediate priority is to give my mother support. She hadn't contacted us so as not to trouble us, expecting my father to be released from hospital soon.

While I'm waiting with my mother at the hospital, Ken arrives and asks me for an update. I tell him there is no news yet, but we both agree we should try to hijack the consultant before he reaches my mother and father for a face-to-face. Ken and I spot the consultant and introduce ourselves, and tell him he can be totally open with us. I know by the look on his face that something isn't right.

"I'm sorry, your father has cancer," he tells us.

Well, we didn't see that coming. "Are we talking time periods?" Ken asks.

He nods. "From today onwards."

I've just been knocked down and run over by a double decker bus. His words echo around my head. Part of me is asking myself the question, 'Did I really hear that?'

"Next question," Ken asks, "how fast can we get him out of here?"

Three hours later we're driving our father home. I make a call to Andy to inform him I'm no longer travelling to Angel Falls, and explain why. We arrange to meet that night half way from my parents' house to London, as I'm holding all the documentation including the flight tickets.

For the next two weeks Ken and I take turns helping our mother to look after our father: the person who has raised me and supported me; transported me to drop zones; always been there for me. Loved me.

One evening, as I sit with my father, he places his hand on my knee. "Son, he says, I can honestly say life has been interesting and fun."

Two weeks later my father is transported back to hospital. I give Ken a call and advise him to come quickly. Pete is still working abroad. We sit with our father and he passes away.

And then it hits me. I am never going to be able to talk to him or see his smile again.

Back at home we comfort our mother, who is more concerned as to how we are. My parents' house now seems to have this empty feeling, and I need to get out. I can't hold it back any longer and the tears stream down my face. I try to compose myself when I come across a phone box, as I have yet to break the news to Alison, and I call her but I'm unable to utter the words that my father has died. My voice is choked; there's just silence. Alison puts two and two together and tries to talk to me, but I'm not able to. All I can say is, "I have to go", and I hang up as the tears start again.

I return home to comfort my mum and to talk to Ken, and we come up with a plan to monitor our mother and pay her regular visits. I create a spreadsheet to show my mother her income and outgoings, so she has a better understanding of her financial situation to give her comfort. I return to Devon and meet up with Andy Montriou who tells me about his BASE jump off Angel Falls, and I'm pleased he had a lot of fun. I don't feel disappointed as I'm so happy to know I was with my father for his last two weeks. Had I done the jump, I would have not made it back in time to see him.

The day of the funeral arrives and thankfully all three sons are here. I have managed to arrange for the Royal Marines to send a Royal Marine bugler to repay a debt: my father conducted a funeral in the jungles of Malaya for two Royal Marines killed in action. I told them my father was serving in the Malayan police force, and that he was Royal Marine, too.

The bugler does us proud. Every note is crystal clear, and it's so moving when he plays The Last Post. We offer the bugler two hundred pounds, which he declines, and says it was an honour for him to sound The Last Post for our father.

It all seems so unreal. Can it be true that our father is no longer here?

There is one final thing to do.

We all meet up at Dunkeswell, and the RNRMSPA allow us to take the plane up with Pete flying. My mother sits in the co-pilot seat, and Ken sits back in the aircraft with me. It's a beautiful sunny day, the visibility is clear, and as we approach the airfield I open the door and stick my head out. When I pull my head back in I see my mother and my brothers watching me.

"It's time," I shout out, and I exit the plane. As I fall away I unscrew the lid of the urn and my father's ashes stream out. My eyes are mesmerised at the sight as the ashes glitter and sparkle like gold, and there's a sense of joy that his wish has been fulfilled. I'm overwhelmed with emotion under this canopy and purposely land in an isolated part of the airfield where I drop to my knees. The tears can't be held back as I look towards the sky and picture my father.

I return to the clubhouse where we all meet up and go for a coffee. Pete tells me that after I exited he banked the aircraft over so everyone could observe me in free fall, and they all saw my father's ashes being released.

There is no quick cure for the pain I feel at the loss of my father. At times I reach for the phone and then realise he won't be there, and an emptiness engulfs me.

Life goes on, and it seems all around me nothing has changed. But I now have a better understanding of the pain someone feels at the loss of a parent.

Later in the year I conduct night jumps and choose to jump on my own. After exiting the plane away from the light pollution, I look towards the stars and see Hale-Bopp comet, and to my surprise I can see the tail. It's a wonderful sight and I feel at peace.

Ken calls me and informs me that Dad was due to attend a Malayan Police Force reunion and that it would be a good idea for us to go. A few days later we're in Earl's Court in London and find the restaurant where the reunion is taking place. We get signed in and choose to stand close to the door. After a short while we observe a gentleman who walks up to sign in.

"Have you heard Pete Guest passed away?" the secretary says.

"Yes, I have. It's very sad," the gentleman replies.

"His sons are here."

"Where are they?" he says in a slightly excited voice. "I need to meet them."

We're pointed out to him and he comes straight over.

"Let me introduce myself. My name is Jock and I wanted to tell you that your father gave me my best Christmas present ever."

I'm intrigued so I ask, "What was it?"

"I'd just arrived at the camp, totally new, and was shown where to drop my bags off before reporting for duty. I was told there had been some sort of disturbance which they wanted to check out, so I was tasked to lead a patrol there. Your father had been in the jungle for two weeks and that's a long time, let me tell you. He'd just returned with his patrol when he was informed I'd arrived. He asked to see me and was told I'd been sent to check out this disturbance, whereupon your father turned to his men and said, 'drop your bags, grab a twenty-four hour ration bag, we're going back in.' He instructed his men to run to catch up with me … not an easy task in that heat. We exchanged passwords and your father walked over to me and said, 'Pete Guest; I heard you were in town. This disturbance you're checking out, my gut feeling says it's an ambush. So what do you say we check it out together?' We approached the area and, sure enough, an ambush had been set up, so you father and I sprung a surprise attack on them. There's no doubt that had it not been for your father I would have walked into that ambush and been killed. It was Christmas day."

We meet various people throughout the evening and learn how respected my father was, and hear things about him that we never knew before. We leave the reunion with a sense of pride, and knowing our father would have been so pleased that we were there.

CHALLENGES AND MIND GAMES

1997 draws to an end with the closing down of the RNRMSPA, and I feel sad about its demise – there was history in that club and now it's all gone. It's short sightedness to save the man power of two billets when, in my opinion, the military needs adventure training to keep morale up. I'm now the only skydiving school left on Dunkeswell airfield, but what skydivers want and what I have to offer is two worlds apart. I take the plunge at the beginning of 1998 with a huge investment and purchase my own aeroplane - a Cessna 206 G-ATLT. Previously, my stress levels have gone sky high when the pilot has been over an hour late, leaving me with customers waiting to jump and me thinking there's a chance he has forgotten he's flying that day. It makes sense to go for my pilot's licence and then go on to qualify for my jump pilot's rating, as if a pilot is late again I'll be able to step in. I approach the flying school at Dunkeswell as it is only a four minute drive from my house, and the flying lessons begin.

Taking to the air without a parachute feels a bit strange but I'm keen to learn, and over the next few weeks I grab every opportunity I can to fly. It's a requirement to learn aviation law, aircraft general knowledge and principles of flight, flight performance, human performance and limitations, meteorology, navigation and radio aids, and radio communications, and once I have digested each one I'm hit with an exam at the end. Strangely, I'm not feeling the excitement I was expecting, but I persevere.

On one training day I've been doing circuits around the airfield, practicing take offs and landings with my instructor, and after carrying out several of these we vacate the runway and head back to the flying school. We stop behind two planes, and I assume we're waiting for them to move before we can cross the runway and park up. My flying instructor makes a call on the radio.

"Golf Delta Romeo Uniform Kilo, we're going to jump the queue as I have a student about to go on his first solo."

I hear the words, wondering who his next student is, and as my instructor lines up the aircraft on the runway I cotton on to the fact that it's me and my heart rate responds.

"Andy, are you happy?" he asks, jumping out of the plane.

"Yes," I shout back, without really acknowledging what this means.

I watch the instructor stroll back to the flying school, and then turn my attention to the gauges on my dashboard, but my mind is blank. *Oh, what the hell*, I think, and I push the throttle in. The engine of this Cessna 172 bursts into life and I feel the plane starting to roll down the runway. My feet push the foot pedals, keeping the plane straight, and my eyes keep glancing at my speedometer waiting for it to reach my take of speed. Before long I'm airborne and climbing away. Wow, I think … here I am flying an aeroplane on my own, and it feels special. I look down at the landscape below me. It's something I've seen over a thousand times before, but never like this. I constantly check my artificial horizon to ensure the aircraft is level, and also check my speed, and then call on the radio that I'm down wind of runway 23, then cross wind for 23, and finally that I'm on finals for 23. My speed is reduced and my flaps applied. I'm all too aware that there are many eyes watching me about to land this bloody thing. I can sense I'm nervous, not because I may crash and kill myself, but because of how embarrassed I'd be if I damaged the aircraft on a bad landing. The runway comes up and I start to flare the aircraft, keeping an eye on the speed and angle of my nose, and I feel the wheels touch down. A huge smile of relief spreads across my face. I've just completed my first solo flight, the aircraft is in one piece, and I walk into the flying school with my head held high.

Later, I'm doing DZ control and talking students down who are descending on their parachutes when I hear on the radio two aircraft calling finals for landing. On turning around I see an aircraft on the runway and the two aircraft flying towards it preparing to land. They're on a collision course, so I call them.

"Aircraft on finals ... there's two of you ... you're on top of each other!"

Thankfully, both aircraft peel off in different directions and the situation is averted, but it was a bloody close one.

The incident makes me all too aware of things that can go wrong.

The skydiving business is going well, although the hours are long. My own aircraft is up and running for skydiving, and I get an extra buzz jumping out of my own plane. I call two of the charities that I contacted at the beginning (when I sought their permission to promote them) and both the charities - Exeter Leukaemia Fund and Devon Air Ambulance - inform me they are now receiving fifty thousand pounds each year from the charity jumps. My survey from all the charity jumpers shows that in one year at my school, two hundred and fifty thousand pounds was raised for over a hundred charities. It's a great feeling to know we're making a difference to people's lives.

I'm invited to take part in a British free fall record, where the plan is to get one hundred skydivers linked up in free fall. The closest we get is having ninety-eight linked up; the last two docked a fraction of a second after one person released his grip when his audio alarm went off, an item we were told to leave on the ground. It's disappointing to be so close to a British record, but it has put me in the unique situation of being the only person to be on both the largest canopy stack and in the largest free fall formation to be built in the UK.

Time passes so quickly, and before I know it I'm into another year. It's a beautiful sunny day and I'm in the aircraft as jumpmaster with a female student to dispatch from five thousand feet. We reach the exit point, I shout at the pilot to reduce the power, and my eyes focus on the student. She exits the plane on my command and I follow her out of the door, staying close. Her body position isn't symmetrical, which causes her to go into a spin, and it's clear she has lost altitude awareness because when we reach her pull height there is no attempt by her to do so. I quickly fly over and grab her to stop the spin, then signal to her to pull, which she does. I turn and do a short track to move away from her and deploy my parachute, clocking the ground, and it's clear I won't make it back to the airfield as my mind is already deciding where I'm going to land. My main parachute starts to deploy but then snivels. This is not the time for a slow opening as I know I'm low. As the parachute finally cracks open I grab my toggles, eyeing up the field I have chosen to land in, and there's a strange sensation of being pulled back. I look over my shoulder and to my horror I realise my safety automatic activation device has fired, releasing my reserve parachute. My adrenalin pumps as I observe my reserve stalling and diving, hitting my main and nearly wrapping up with it. It's clear but scary to see that my reserve really doesn't like to fly with my small main. I hear the words *canopy transfer* enter my head - something experienced guys have talked about for years when faced with this situation. I wait for the reserve to stall and as soon as it does I hit my cutaway pad, which releases my main parachute from my harness. Job done.

But there's that strange feeling again, and as I look up my worst nightmare becomes a reality. The steering toggle of my main has snagged the centre line of my reserve, and the main is trailing behind it, the drag causing my reserve to lose its shape. I no longer have a flying wing-shaped parachute, but a very strange U shaped one, and the reserve is no longer flying but descending straight down. I scream out loud, "For fuck's sake, can my day get any worse?" I realise it's a stupid remark as the outcome of this has yet to be decided. The Devon countryside I love so much is now a threat to my very existence as it approaches, and I'm back on the stopwatch. In my head I hastily convene a committee, and I shout at these voices to give me options, fast. I look down and can see I'm on the edge of the woods, and hear a voice shout above the others, "Trees! Go for the trees!" I don't know what my rate of descent is but I do know my parachute has no glide, and it's coming straight down, which is not good. One could say it's hazardous to one's health.

There's a chance that as I go through the trees the parachute may snag on a branch before I impact with the ground, thus it would be survivable. The problem is, how to get over the bloody trees. I have nothing to lose so I pull on a toggle with this misshaped parachute, having no idea what's going to happen. The reserve stalls and throws me into a spin, and I let up on the toggle. *Well that was fucking scary,* I hear the voices shout, but they've forgotten the predicament I am in and the impact this may have on my balls if I come to a thundering halt in the tree, as the manoeuvre has worked. I'm over the last tree in the woods, next to a sloping field, and as the tree approaches something catches my eye at the bottom of the field: large tufts of grass. All the time I spent on Dartmoor with the Marines has taught me to recognise wet peat bog. My hand instantly pulls the toggle again, which throws this mess above my head off the tree line. There's no going back now; I'm out of time. I adopt the best parachute landing position of my life, my brain still evaluating. Yes, I am descending fast, and in a split second I contemplate how much damage and pain this is going to cause: ankle, tib and fib, femur, pelvis… "Relax!" they say. Well fuck that, all my muscles have gone rigid and I clench my teeth. Here it comes…

I hit hard and bounce two feet into the air. There's no pain. Are the senses in my body on some sort of time delay? I'm still waiting as I hit the ground a second time, but there's still no pain, which confuses me. I attempt to get up and find that I can, and I feel over my body and take a step, noticing the Andy-shaped indentation in the bog. I can't stop grinning.

"Yes, you bastard!" I have bypassed the grim reaper's clutches today, and I'm on a high as I head back to the drop zone, the euphoria carrying me.

I return home at the end of the day and make no mention of it to Alison so as not to worry her, but while having a cup of tea I find myself reflecting on it. I bought the safety device after the filming incident to save my life and yet again I find myself going after someone who has lost their altitude awareness. That safety device has just put me through this horrible scenario but I know, overall, they are brilliant and I would recommend everyone to have one.

"Are you okay?" Alison asks me. "It seems like your mind is elsewhere."

"Yeah, I'm fine. Just thinking about work," I reply.

The following day is just another day and I have my reserve to repack as well as my main, not forgetting all the club equipment that needs to be packed for the next jumping day.

The months roll past. The weather has been frustrating for my flying lessons; every time I'm booked in it prevents me from being able to do my solo cross country flight. As I turn up for one lesson I'm informed the aircraft is off the road and being fixed, and yet again the weather is unsuitable. Later, the flying instructor receives a call to say the aircraft is ready and it's brought over and parked up outside. I really can't see from the ground what the problem is as above my head is nothing but blue sky. I approach the instructor and tell him the weather doesn't appear to be that bad, and let him know I've been waiting for six months to do this cross country flight. I tell him that if I did encounter problems I could just turn around and come back. It's unfair of me as I'm putting him under pressure, but I'm so eager to get this in the bag. I can see he's thinking about it.

"Right, if you find the weather is bad, you'll come back?"

"Of course. It goes without saying," I tell him.

"Okay, you can go," he says.

It's not long before I have my flight plan completed, as well as my pre-flight checks. With the aircraft lined up on the flight line I make my radio call.

"Golf Oscar Foxtrot Echo Yankee, lined up, zero five rolling."

As I climb away I level off, and I'm on route to Bournemouth airport, my first check point Chard village. Wow! The weather is crap - I have no forward visibility due to the haze, even though I have a blue sky above my head, but I decide to push on to Chard as it's not too far. If all goes well I should see Chard appear with the lake next to it.

Bingo! There it is. I'm bang on. It's now decision time and I opt to push ahead and continue to my next check point, which is Blandford village.

As I approach I know it's important I get my radio call in to Bournemouth Air Traffic Control early. I give them a call and inform them I'm over Blandford. Bournemouth ask me to switch my transponder on to 4422, and I repeat it back. There's a slight pause and I receive a call back telling me I'm not over Blandford at all, but Dorchester. I'm horrified and put the aircraft into a turn, circling over the top. I'm confused as to how this could have happened. I have a quick look at my map and I can see I've deviated right massively, but I don't know why, which is concerning.

Bournemouth call me again and ask what my intentions are. Looking at the map I can see I need to head for the high ground, turn right, and follow it to Blandford, but this haze is making the job harder due to the lack of visibility. I tell Bournemouth I am retracing my steps and I start to follow the ridge, and at the end I arrive over the top of Blandford and turn for Bournemouth. As I look at my compass I spot my direction indicator is now reading inaccurate, and I reset it. To my surprise, within a minute it's giving another false reading. I've just discovered what was broken on the aircraft that was supposed to have been fixed, and why I deviated so much, as I've been following my direction indicator. I learn a valuable lesson and that is to constantly check my DI with my compass, something that was not really emphasised in my training.

On arriving at Bournemouth I have to venture up to the control tower and walk the corridor of shame, and have my book stamped to say I've arrived. Much to my embarrassment I hear the words, "You're the one." They have informed the flying school that I was lost, and the flying school has now told me I am no longer to fly to Cardiff but to return back to Dunkeswell. I find it odd that they're not happy for me to fly to Cardiff in this weather but happy for me to fly back. Once back at the flying school I inform them that the direction indicator isn't working properly.

Two weeks later I try again and this time I have such perfect weather that I can see where I'm going as soon as I hit my cruise level. I'm enjoying the flying now immensely; it's a wonderful feeling to be flying cross country on a day like today. The aircraft is in perfect working order and I complete the long solo cross country flight to Bournemouth, and then on to Cardiff, and back to Dunkeswell without a hitch. A month later I have passed the last phase - the practical skills test - and I now hold a private pilot's licence, something I never imagined I would hold.

A week later my pilot's licence arrives and it seems strange to see my name on it. I hold it in my hand for a moment, the elation filling me, and then I slap it down on the table with a smile. My first objective has been achieved. I have to build up my hours before I can jump fly, and it makes sense to be checked out on my own plane to reduce the cost of the flying.

The Cessna 206 is bigger and heavier and has a variable pitch propeller control that I need to learn. My first thought as I open the throttle is that this is a beast of an aircraft, as it roars to life and pushes me back into the seat with its 320hp continental engine. It's such a thrill taking the aircraft up and flying down the avenues in between and around the outside of the clouds, all the time looking out for gliders, which is such an awesome sight.

With another parachuting day completed, I check my watch to see if I have enough daylight time left to do a quick flight, and decide that I have. I'm flying towards a beautiful sunset when my friend, Radar, passes me in his Pitt Special bi-plane and barrel rolls in front of me with the sunset as a back drop. I call him on the radio.

"Mate, you just don't know how good that looked!"

After landing I put the aircraft to bed and join Radar for a tea. We seem to be living the dream - we're skydivers as well as pilots with our own planes.

A few days later I'm at home when there's a knock at the door. It's a woman asking me to sign a petition, and I ask what it's for.

"To close the airfield," she says.

I politely tell her that I own the skydiving school so I won't be signing it.

I've been aware for some time that new people who have moved into the village are complaining about the aircraft noise, even though they knew the airfield was here before they purchased their houses, and this list of 'complainers' has increased to seven people. Not long ago I had one of them rant at me outside the local shop, saying the community was suffering. An elderly lady who happened to be walking past us put her shopping down and poked this guy in the chest.

"How dare you say you're speaking on behalf of the community," she told him. "You don't know us…you know nothing about us, nor what we do. This young man," she went on, pointing at me, "has done more for the community than you'll ever do. What have you done, eh?" The man was starting to look slightly uncomfortable. "The community are happy with the airfield. You new people causing all this trouble… if you don't like it then go back to where you came from."

The man walked off in embarrassment; it was a lovely moment.

It's true – I've given the local scouts a day at the parachute school, I've helped raised money for the youth club, and I've organised a village litter picking day. But I didn't do any of these things for any kind of recognition; it seems natural to me to help the kids and support the community I live in, as so many others do. However, I did appreciate the elderly lady pointing it out to him.

I decide to contribute some articles to the Parish magazine explaining the history of skydiving on the airfield. I tell them about the world record attempts that have taken place there, the people who have gone on to represent Great Britain, as well as all the regular charity jumps that take place and the amount of money that's been raised, along with a list of the charities that have benefited.

A while later I'm told that the anti-airfield protestors are trying to get elected onto the Parish council, and without hesitating I dive into the car, head down to the Devon County office in Sidmouth, and pick up a form. Within the hour I'm back and handing it over. Having found someone to propose me and second me, it seems I've just put myself forward for the Parish Council elections.

Back at the club I tell someone what I've done.

"Why have you done that?" he asks.

"I don't know," I tell him. "I did it in on impulse after hearing the anti-airfield crew were trying to get on the council. I suppose if someone asks me why I didn't try to do something about it, at least I can say I did."

I focus on work, concentrating on marketing and running the skydiving school, constantly trying to improve on the year before. Time passes and the elections take place, and I don't think about it as work takes up a lot of my time. When the results are released, to my shock I discover I've been elected, and I now have a new title: Councillor Guest. I'm even more surprised to find out I've secured the third highest votes, and I can only put it down to the articles I wrote for the Parish magazine.

During the first four council meetings I don't say anything but I sit in my chair, observe, and listen to what is being said to get a better understanding on how things are done. On my fifth meeting, and to everyone's surprise, I speak up. There's an issue with a pothole that we've not been able to get Highways to repair, and I ask if I can take it on, to which they agree. In the next meeting it's commented that the pothole has been repaired, and I'm asked how I managed to get Highways to repair it.

"I told them a motorcyclist hit the pothole and crashed, and that I hope he doesn't sue."

There's a pause, and then one of the councillors pipes up.

"I hadn't heard about the motorcyclist crash."

"I must have been mistaken," I reply.

The penny drops. "Well," the chairman says, "the pothole has been repaired so that's a good thing."

Over the course of these meetings I tell the other councillors that it's a sad but true reflection of modern times that he who jumps up and down tends to get his own way, and what we need to do is get the East Devon department involved by involving the TV and press, as no one likes to be under the spotlight. Before long, Highways find extra money to put catseyes down on the main road leading up to Dunkeswell, and the speed limit in one part of the village is restricted to twenty miles per hour. This aside, what I learn is how frustrating it can be when we vote on something, only to have East Devon County Council do the opposite of what we recommend, when we are only acting in the best interest of our community.

I've been making frequent trips to see my mother, to ensure she's coping. The dreaded C word has cropped up and I have to take my mother into hospital for further treatment. Both my brothers also arrive at the hospital, and it's nice to have the three of us together to support our mother, who has been our rock, always putting us first. We're allowed to go into her room to see her, and she looks so weak and tells us she is not doing too well. Clearly, the treatment has taken a lot out of her. My brothers and I chat to one side when a deep sense of loss suddenly comes over me. I venture over to my mother and reach out for her hand, holding it in mine. I notice its cold, and I check for a pulse. Within moments I know she has passed away. I turn to my brothers and tell them, and it's a huge shock as we were not expecting this.

The doctor confirms our mother has passed, and the feeling of pain and loneliness engulfs me, knowing that both of my parents have now gone, along with that solid support we have always had. The next few days pass and I'm still taking it all in.

As our mother is Scottish we organise a bagpiper to play at her funeral. I remember both my parents mentioning how they were looking forward to seeing the year 2000 come in, but sadly cancer prevented that from happening for both of them, and with my mother so close, too.

It's the 2nd of February, the day before my birthday, and all three brothers have come together on Dunkeswell Airfield to carry out our mother's wishes. It's only two years since we last did this with my father. Pete is flying once again and Ken is also in the plane as I exit and release my mother's ashes in free fall. I take comfort in the knowledge she is now with our father, but the pain is still there. Later, we remember the fun times we had with our parents - there are so many stories - and recall the time we spent in Malaya as children. We talk about our father's exploits in the Malayan jungles, fighting the communists with the police force, and the awesome curries our mother used to make, having been taught by the natives. Her love of cooking continued throughout her life and she was never happier than when she was nourishing and looking after her family. With a husband and three sons who had a zest for adventure and often found themselves in dangerous and life-threatening situations, I often wonder how she coped with it all emotionally. But she did; and she never held us back. My mother was a pillar of support for us all, the matriarch of the family, the glue that held us together. And she was strong.

My brothers and I return to our parents' house to go through all of the possessions, and we come across a notepad. Within it we find messages our mother had written to our father stating how much she missed him and how lonely she felt since he passed away. It hits home, and we can't help but be moved by it. The three of us stand there in silence and dwell on her words. As much as we stayed in contact she never mentioned it to us, so as not to worry us.

At various times I have the urge to phone my parents only to remember I can no longer do that, and the overwhelming sadness returns. I now have a true understanding of what people go through with the loss of a loved one and hopefully, in the future, I can help to give them some sort of comfort by finding the right words and understanding their pain. My own family is the one thing that pulls me through my own grief as I return home and focus on work.

A year soon passes and I'm chatting to Leo who has been given a great filming job to do, and he asks me if I'd like to get involved. It's a chance to have a break from normal work, and an opportunity to do something different that will have great visuals, so I agree. Andy Montriou, Mandy Dickinson, and I are to be dressed as climbers and will have to tumble in free fall in front of the Matterhorn, a mountain that straddles the border between Switzerland and Italy. I'm looking forward to the buzz.

We arrive in Zermatt and my eyes gaze upon the Matterhorn for the first time. It's an odd feeling to know I'll be free falling past the face of it soon, but I'm looking forward to it. We bump into a friend of Leo's who asks Leo what brings him here, and Leo outlines what the plan is. To our surprise he says this is not possible, and he will explain all later this evening. We meet in a restaurant and Leo's friend introduces us to two paraglider pilots who fly in the area. They inform us that due to the winds at this time of year, the turbulence is so bad it causes the parachute to collapse in the air, so it's extremely dangerous. I nudge Andy and tell him the guy is talking about a differently designed parachute, which is built for soaring and not skydiving.

The following morning we get dressed for the jump, and Leo talks us through it. We're taking two helicopters, one of which will be used as a camera platform as we exit from the second. We'll be jumping from the same height as the top of the Matterhorn, and I note we'll not have long in free fall as we won't have that much height due to the mountain sloping away. We're supposed to be climbers that have fallen over the edge of the mountain, so I decide to jump with a length of rope attached to me to make it look more realistic. I attach the rope to the side of my harness by rubber bands, to enable me to pull it away from my body when I deploy the parachute.

We board the helicopter to start the journey to altitude and as the helicopter bounces around in the air due to the turbulence, this just heightens our senses. My eyes focus on the snow on the Matterhorn, curling and swirling away from the rough rocky edges. The mountain range stretching away before me is breathtaking; just to see this sight alone is worth the journey. Voices of our guests from the previous night echo in my head: "This is not possible. The turbulence is too bad for the parachutes."

The time comes, we position ourselves in the doorway of the helicopter, and the command to exit is announced. I give the exit count and all three of us roll out and start to tumble, counting the seconds. As I come out of the tumble I realise I'm facing the cliff, which is racing past me. *Bloody hell!* At the same time I notice Andy is underneath me and I need to separate away from him, but it catches my eye that during the tumble the rope has somehow wrapped around me. I turn away from the cliff face and go into a track position that allows me to manoeuvre horizontally across the ground, and at the same time I start to barrel roll in the track, which allows the rope to unwrap itself from my parachute container. I grab the rope, pull it away from my body, and deploy my parachute, noticing we must only be around a thousand feet off the ground, which is what we expected. As my parachute flies away from the cliff face my height above the ground increases due to the ground sloping away steeply. The views are stunning - it's an awesome sight to be descending next to the Matterhorn.

Suddenly, my parachute collapses on one side and goes into a spin. I yank on the toggles to try and regain control, and all thoughts of the stunning views leave my mind. Each time I regain control and continue to fly away, my parachute collapses again. It's a rocky ride. The last thousand feet is uneventful, but I'm not relaxed until my feet land firmly on the ground. It's only now I can laugh as I approach Andy.

"Fuck me, mate. Those guys knew what they were talking about."

Andy tells me he had the same problem, but I'm pleased to see Mandy has landed her parachute safely.

My nerves accompany me on each subsequent jump, knowing I'm going to be in for another rough ride. All together we complete five jumps and, unfortunately, Andy loses his parachute in a crevasse as it fails to fly correctly again after collapsing, forcing him to jettison the parachute and use his reserve.

We're invited to a private showing of the film 'Killing Me Softly' in London. Alison and I watch the film, and it only seems like ten minutes in when Heather Graham has her kit off and is rolling around naked with Joseph Fiennes. Alison leans towards me.

"You didn't tell me you starred in a blue movie," she whispers.

It's the first time in a cinema that I've seen a film finish and not a single person has stood up to leave, as everyone is checking out the credits to see their name on the screen.

September arrives and I'm already looking forward to the clocks moving back to make for a shorter working day. I'm busy hoovering the clubhouse with the TV on in the background, and on the screen I see an aircraft has crashed into the Empire State Building. It seems like the kind of film that might interest me, so I turn off the hoover. It's a peculiar film in the way they have gone about shooting it, and I'm trying to get my head around it when the awful truth hits me: I'm looking at the news. I know this can't be an accident when a second aircraft hits the tower live on TV. I have to sit down as I try to take this all in; the horror of what I'm seeing is hard to digest knowing the many lives that have been taken.

The following day the news is all about the twin towers. I'm at the club checking in the tandem students and getting everything ready to start the jump program, and I call into the flying school to check on the weather conditions only to discover that all flying in the UK has been grounded for the day, due to the events happening in America. The news doesn't go down too well with the tandem students, some of whom have driven for two hours to get to the airfield, as some feel I should have known this was going to happen.

Over the next month there is a lot of news coverage about the al-Qaeda training camps and the possibility of going into Afghanistan. Tony Blair has tasked an MP to find out more about Afghanistan due to MI6 losing interest after the Russians left. He is briefed by an expert on Afghanistan and the advice is not to deploy British troops on the ground, highlighting the previous two occasions Britain entered Afghanistan and lost, and also the fact that Russia, being a super power, also lost. Tony Blair decides to take us into Afghanistan. It makes no sense to go in and get bogged down in a long campaign which will cost lives. Common sense says we go in, hit the training camps and withdraw, rather than go in with no understanding of the culture. It raises the question: Is there a hidden agenda as to why America is so keen to enter, such as oil pipe lines? It's with disbelief and sadness that I see British troops on the ground. I've been briefed on the sequence of events by the UK Afghan expert and with a heavy heart I know he is right. Many a British family is going to go through heartache for an unwinnable war.

For the past year Alison and I have been training for a marathon. We apply for London but are rejected, and not wanting to give up on this challenge we go online and apply for the Paris marathon, which we're accepted for straight away. As part of our training we take part in 'The Grizzly' - a twenty mile race held on the East Devon coastline that incorporates shingle beaches, steep hills, tarmac, fields, and not forgetting the streams and boggy stretches. The race starts and as soon as I hit the fields I'm off, only to be called back by Alison to not leave her. It's frustrating but, to be fair, it's only right I stay with her. Further into the race we reach a steep hill, and I'm hit with cramp and am forced to walk.

"Alison, I've got cramp," I shout out to her.

"I'll see you at the end," she shouts back, and leaves me behind.

As hard as I try, at various times the cramp comes back and Alison beats me in the race. It's a hard pill to swallow.

On the start line of the Paris marathon I turn to Alison.

"Don't give me any of this 'wait for me' business. It's every man or woman for themselves."

And then we're off. I hit the water stops on the route and like the fact they display the distance that's been covered, so I know how much is left to go. The crowd cheer as we go around but along some stretches there are no crowds at all, unlike at the London marathon. I take in some of the eye-catching sites along the route but an unexpected sight has me speechless as a female runner in front of me stops, drops her knickers, squats, and has a pee in the middle of the road in front of me, which I have to step over. I hear a very British voice in my head saying, *you can't do that!* but it's great dedication on her part to try and get a good race time.

As I near the end things are starting to hurt but I keep pushing myself, all the time glancing over my shoulder to see if Alison is creeping up on me. I wonder if it's possible that she has passed me and I haven't noticed. At forty-one kilometres I notice not only bananas on offer but sugar lumps, and instantly have the idea that sugar will give me a burst of energy. I cram two sugar lumps into my mouth and to my horror it takes away all the moisture.

I reach down and pick up a used bottle of water that still has a little left in it and gulp it down.

The finishing line comes up and I cross it. *That was painful,* I think, but I've done it. I walk back to the rest area and I can't believe what I'm seeing: Alison is sitting there. There's some confusion as to who finished first, and it will have to wait until we return home and check out our microchip times.

I find in the evening that going out for a meal is a nightmare as my legs are so stiff. The pedestrian crossing lights seem to change back again when I've only managed to cross half the road, and the cars rev up their engines, urging me to hobble faster. Stairways feel like it's the last push on Everest, but the pain is mixed in with laughter as I know how silly I must look. Alison seems to be coping well, though. On returning home we discover I'd beaten Alison by only one minute, my time being four hours two minutes. Alison says it was unfair as she had to queue for the toilets during the race. All I can think is, thank goodness for that!

I'm invited onto a world record mass balloon jump, to be held at Sibson near Peterborough, the plan being for sixteen of us to jump at the same time. The most frightening part of this is not for the skydivers leaping from the hot air balloon into still air (unlike in an aircraft, there will be no slip stream hitting us), but for the balloon pilot who is staying on board. When the balloon loses all that weight it's going to want to shoot up, so to try and reduce the effect of it the balloon will be descending when we exit.

The wicker basket is huge as it needs to hold seventeen of us, and we all climb aboard. It's a tight squeeze. The balloon pilot fires up and we feel the heat coming from the flames. Slowly, the basket lifts off the ground, and there's much excitement from all the skydivers as this is going to be fun. We drift over the countryside, all the time gaining altitude, and a helicopter flies around us to capture the event. Finally we get the command to prepare to jump and we climb on top of the wicker basket and all leap off at the same time. I do wonder, right at this moment as the balloon accelerates up, if the pilot now needs to change his underwear, and I'm thankful I'm in free fall where I belong. On the ground there is just one thought: let's get the beers in and celebrate the world record.

Later in the season I note it's the Queens Golden Jubilee, so four of us decide to celebrate it by completing fifty parachute jumps each in one day. One of the guys secures sponsorship, which is fantastic as that will cover the cost of the jumps. Some of the club members offer to pack the parachutes to help us keep going, as we plan to use all the parachutes we have. On the day we're lucky as the weather is perfect and we're soon leaping out of the aircraft from two and half thousand feet. The day is going well but we're having to stop jumping to give the packers a hand to repack the parachutes, as they're finding it hard to keep up. As we reach jump number forty-two I'm feeling tired, and the novelty factor of doing so many jumps in one day is wearing off. We finally complete jump number fifty and there's smiles all around. We take some pictures and create a collage before sending it to the Queen. Two weeks later we receive a letter from Buckingham Palace informing us that the Queen was most impressed on how we chose to celebrate her jubilee, and that she thinks we're very brave. This causes much laughter as we reflect on what was an enjoyable day. We have to admire the individual who holds the world record for doing over four hundred jumps in one day, but we're happy to fly in at second place for the most done by an individual in the UK.

At last I have logged the flying hours I need to be checked out for my jump pilot rating, having learned heading, how to hold my height, and to have the correct flying speed, which is just above the stall for skydivers to exit the plane. I'm not only checked out for skydivers exiting the plane in free fall but also for students exiting on the static line. This 'flying for skydivers' sounds easy but having skydivers hanging outside the plane when you're just above the stall point has me very focussed; the last thing any of us in the plane want is for *that* to happen. I've added a GPS to the aircraft which makes dropping skydivers over the correct exit point a lot easier, as I can track myself flying across the airfield. There's a lot going on at the critical point as I'm receiving instructions from the jumpmaster and making the correct radio calls.

I qualify for my jump pilot rating and am now in the position of being one of only two people to also hold Examiner, Advance, AFF, CSI and Tandem ratings in the UK. Having these ratings expands my experience, and I feel it helps me in my position on the British Parachute Association Safety Training Committee when we discuss the safety of skydiving in the UK and any improvements that could be made. After all these years of being a Club Chief Instructor, I am now in the driving seat on the plane with my first load of skydivers. It feels so strange when the skydivers exit and I feel the aircraft kick with the sudden loss of weight. At times I wish I was following them out of the door to share the fun with them.

At times, due to the weather conditions, the flying is challenging, especially on landing when the wind is across the runway and gusting, and my head hits the ceiling due to the turbulence. The jump flying eventually becomes normal though. One day, my load of skydivers board the aircraft, and I depart the airfield to climb to ten thousand feet. I'm passing five thousand feet and heading out to Sidmouth on the coast when I feel a vibration coming through my leg. *There it is again.* This isn't normal and my concentration is heightened as my eyes scan the instruments. *And there it is again.* My heart rate increases as I peer out of the window. If this engine goes bang the skydivers will exit the plane over open countryside, but I will have no choice but to stay with it. It's unlikely I'll make it back to the airfield so I look for a potential alternative landing area that can take a Cessna 206. It's a very uncomfortable feeling as the shudder of the vibration keeps coming through my leg. As I'm thinking about what action to take I place my hand on my thigh only to feel the vibration at source. It's with a huge relief I realise my youngest son has turned the 'vibrate' feature on my phone on. I continue the climb to altitude and start to see the funny side of how close I came to telling the jumpers to get out early.

Alison and I have always encouraged our sons to be outdoor people and have supported them in sport, as we feel sport is good for their characters.

Westleigh is into race karting and competes, and Daniel is into his football and plays for a team. The end of the year approaches and I close the club for six weeks, looking forward to some down time. We've decided that rather than have a holiday each year, we will have a big holiday every two years instead. It's January 2003 and we decide to visit Florida with the aim of taking the boys to every theme park we can find. It's soon clear that both boys have a love for roller coaster rides. The thrill of adventure appears to be in their blood, and this trip just whets their appetites for more. We visit the Kennedy Space Centre and the highlight of the trip is on the sixteenth of January when we observe Space Shuttle Columbia launch. It's an amazing sight to see as we feel the power of the rocket taking it skywards. I'm in awe watching this, and can only imagine what a rush it must be to be on board. I can't help but think how lucky these astronauts are.

A few days later we're in Tampa, and I take the boys through their skydiving positions before driving them over to the indoor skydiving wind tunnel. Both boys do exceptionally well, and I'm impressed by how quickly they take to it. In my work I'm trying to train people to that standard, and they seem to have cracked it in two minutes. As both boys emerge from the wind tunnel their first question is, "Dad, is that what free fall feels like?" I reply with a "yes" and both boys talk about taking up skydiving for the first time. I have a gut feeling they will do well.

Back at the theme park on one of the last roller coaster rides, Daniel is below the height bar and is told he is too small. He's bitterly disappointed. He already has shoes with hidden roller blades that give him a bit more height, but I take him to one side and insert tree bark into them to raise him up a bit more. Once we see the change of personnel on the height bar we give it another go, and Daniel's head meets the bar and he's allowed through. On the ride I make sure he is sitting next to me so I can take a tight grip on him. He has now ridden all the rides and it's a great finish to our holiday.

Back at home in the UK I catch the news that the Space Shuttle Columbia has disintegrated on re-entry, killing all seven astronauts. I think back to the launch and recall how lucky I thought they were, and I wonder if I was wrong to think that, but I know I would have taken that risk to experience what they did in space.

Westleigh reaches his sixteenth birthday. As a present he is driven to the airfield where I take him up to ten thousand feet, strap him to me, and we exit the plane on a beautiful sunny day. It's a special feeling to share this unique free fall experience with my son, and once the parachute opens I hand over the steering toggles and we have some fun beneath it. Back on the ground Westleigh is beaming, and I'm chuffed he has enjoyed it so much, but he now wants to know when he can start his parachute course. I know what skydiving has given me over the years and how it's shaped my character, so Alison and I chat about it. We feel it has to be a good thing for Westleigh, and even though we're nervous at the idea, we feel it's wrong to wrap the kids in cotton wool if they want to get the best out of life.

I'm starting to appreciate what my parents must have felt but, like them, I'm not going to stop my children on their journey.

THE WORST SCENARIO UNFOLDS

I'm enjoying flying in my Cessna 206 but ninety-nine percent of my flying involves just climbing up to ten thousand feet, dropping the skydivers, and descending again back to the airfield. Other pilots tell me that flying in Europe is a lot easier as you don't have to talk to air traffic controllers so much. I feel it's time for another adventure, and going on a long distant flight seems to be just what's required.

I'm aware that Aaron Jones, a pilot friend who is also on low flying hours, has recently flown in Europe and, as a confidence booster, it seems sensible to take someone with me on my first trip who has flown there, so I give Aaron a call and ask him if he'd like to come along. We meet up and all the flight plans are activated. We check the plane out, we have our flight plan, map and GPS, the aircraft is full of fuel, there are two headsets, a life raft, bags with a change of clothing, and our passports. We're good to go.

The Cessna 206 roars down the runway and we lift off and climb away, turning onto our first heading. The weather is dry and sunny with good visibility as we head to the coast. Each time I see the English coastline from the air I realise how special it is, and as we fly out to sea I look back at it fading away behind us. There's something about flying a single engine aircraft across the open sea - seeing the waves that seems to heighten my attention, becoming tuned into the noise of the engine, and feeling my own vulnerability. My eyes peer down at that vast sea below me and I know we would just be a speck on it should we ditch. I make a note of the direction of the wind and of any ships in the vicinity in case we do have to ditch, as it would be better to do so in front of a passing vessel. This is a jump aircraft with an up and over door that would need to be opened prior to ditching, which means that no sooner would we hit the water it would be pouring into the aircraft fast. It doesn't pay to dwell on it, but after a while my heart is lifted as I see the French coastline, and I feel the sense of relief as a smile returns to my face.

We call up our first French air traffic controller and pass on our information as to who we are and where we're heading. The French landscape below us slowly passes and we're able to enjoy the views, now and then spotting a Chateau in beautiful surroundings and rivers crisscrossing the landscape. The map acts as a backup but the GPS certainly makes navigation easier as we can see the aircraft flying to our destination.

It's time to call up another French air traffic controller, and we use the international language of English. The controller doesn't respond so we continue our transit. At the next zone we call another controller who replies in French, and we ask for English but receive no response, so once again we push on. It's a comfort that the visibility is so clear and it's great that we can fly for hours and not talk to anyone on the radio.

We land at a French airport and top up with fuel before pushing on, and soon arrive at our destination, Empuriabrava airfield in Spain, which is on the southern coastline close to the French border. It's a skydiving drop zone so we look out for skydivers as we approach to land and see a few descending. We park up the aircraft, check into some cheap accommodation, and go out for a meal. The following day we have a chance to chill out and chat to skydivers we know, and in the evening we head out for food and a few beers. Aaron asks me if I fancy flying out to Menorca, one of the Balearic Islands located in the Mediterranean Sea. The idea seems to add to the adventure so I agree, and the next morning we get up early, refuel the aircraft, and head to Barcelona before turning and flying out to sea. Once again my senses are heightened as I listen to every noise the aircraft is making, which seem to be magnified. There doesn't appear to be too much shipping taking place as I've only seen two boats. I zoom out on the GPS and I can see my heading is taking me to Menorca which is a reassuring to know.

On reaching the island I have to cut across the international airport approach so I call up air traffic control who clear me to proceed, which surprises me. I point to a bloody big passenger airliner on approach and tell Aaron I'm not too keen to fly so close behind it in case I catch any wake and it flips us, so I opt to put in a couple of three-sixty turns to create a bigger time difference between us. Aaron is very laid back and I feel he thinks we could have made it. We cut across the main approach of this international airport and Aaron is concentrating, looking out for the small private airstrip he has been to previously. Eventually he spots it and, to my surprise, it's like no other airstrip I have seen before - it's essentially a dirt track that's made up of loose gravel. As I start to flare the aircraft for landing I cut the power to save my propeller from any loose stones that may get sucked up and cause damage, and when the wheels touch the ground we leave a trail of dust behind us as we coast along before turning to park up. I hadn't imagined we would fly this far when we departed the UK, and it's opened my eyes to just how far I could travel around Europe in such a short time.

There really isn't a lot to see and so after a quick drink and a stretch of the legs we're back in the plane and heading for the Spanish mainland. As I look down on the sea again I wonder how on earth the World War II pilots coped with the stress of combat over the waves without the fancy instruments we have, and they have my greatest respect.

We cross the Spanish mainland and fly up the coast to our next destination, which is Perpignan in France, where we'll refuel. Aaron tells me about a place he's previously stayed in which is close by, and how nice the huge steaks were, and he suggests we could fly there after refuelling and stop there overnight. It's a winner in my eyes. Perpignan airfield is quiet when we arrive, with a long runway. As I flare the aircraft I'm catching lift from the heat of the runway and the Cessna 206 keeps gliding, eventually landing with a bump. It's not my finest hour, especially when Aaron says, "Ouch." Once refuelled, we head over to the main building, taking our passports with us to pay for the fuel. It's fairly straight forward until we head back through the corridor to find the door to the active airfield is locked, but we notice a switch next to the door. Aaron presses the switch but the door doesn't open so he starts pressing a few more times and tells me it doesn't seem to be working. At that moment we hear someone coughing and turn around to see a customs guy with his arms folded and not looking too impressed with us as he demands to see our passports. It appears the switch is connected to a buzzer in his office. We're taken into his office and he seems in no rush to clear us.

"I think you pissed him off, Aaron, but to be fair even I thought that switch was to open the door," I tell him.

We're cleared to leave some hours later but on reaching the plane the time is troubling me.

"Mate, we don't have enough daylight hours to reach the other airfield and neither of us have a night rating."

Aaron agrees. We just lost our steak dinner, much to our dismay.

The following morning Aaron takes over the flying, and no sooner do we take off the GPS goes down. Aaron starts to get the map out as he throws in a quick orbit, and meanwhile I've climbed into the back of the plane, opened my bag and pulled out a second GPS. Once back in my seat I plug it in, and jackpot, we have a GPS and the map is playing second fiddle again. The weather remains clear and the landscape gently rolls back as we enjoy the flight, and on reaching Cherbourg airfield we land to refuel one more time. It's also time to change seats as I take over as pilot in command.

We depart Cherbourg and head across the channel - only one more time do I have to go through this anxious moment of flying across water. Up ahead I can see the weather is changing and, with it, the visibility. I look past the edge of the cloud and study the water, searching for any sunshine that that would indicate gaps in the cloud, but none can be seen. By now I've entered the cloud and it's thick. I'm not instrument rated to fly in cloud, and neither is Aaron, and the decision has to be made quickly as I'm aware this is the most dangerous moment for an unqualified person who can get disoriented and lose control. I no longer look out but focus on my instruments to ensure my horizon is level as I initiate a slow one-eighty degree turn to back track on my heading and get me out of this cloud. Aaron is in full agreement and I can see he is also watching my instruments to ensure I'm not screwing up, as I would if he were flying. I thought flying over water was bad but this is horrible, and it's a relief when we break out of the cloud and find ourselves in sunshine, heading back to Cherbourg.

We're kicking our heels at Cherbourg getting the latest on the weather forecast, and it's not looking promising as the clock continues to eat into our daylight flying hours. For us to make it back it's now or never, so we make a break for it and try again. This time we make further progress before we see the bad weather again, but this time instead of flying into it we try and stay below it, lowering our height. We started at three and half thousand feet and reach the stage where we're at a thousand feet above the sea. The visibility is shit but, again, the GPS offers comfort as we can see we're heading to the right crossing point.

As we spot the coastline we contact air traffic control and inform them who we are and where we're heading. It's a relief to have land below us, and once again England's landscape is a sight for sore eyes. We're heading to Netheravon to drop Aaron off and I glance at my watch to see how much daylight I'll have left to continue my journey.

"Aaron, as soon as I land, jump out and grab your bag as I'll need to get going fast."

"No problem, mate," he tells me, and we both talk about what a fun trip it's been.

As I come to a rolling halt at Netheravon, Aaron jumps out with his bag, I turn the plane and lift off, and I'm only too pleased to be going. I look at the sun and wish it was a bit higher, and increase the speed of the aircraft to the point I'm going flat out as there's not a second to lose. The sun has gone down and I'm just passing Yeovil when I call up Dunkeswell airfield, but it appears the flying school is shut. At last I can see the familiar landscape surrounding Dunkeswell and I spot the airfield. The light is fading fast but this is going to be a straight in approach having confirmed there are no other aircraft in the circuit pattern. I spot the windsock and there is no wind, which is excellent, and I choose my runway so I can maintain this heading.

It's with some relief when the wheels touch down, and as I park the aircraft up and tie it down I notice how dark it is. There really wasn't a minute to lose. I head home evaluating whether there are lessons to be learned from this trip, especially the return flight from Netheravon, and the answer is yes - and that is to qualify for my instrument rating as well as my night rating in order to give me greater flexibility and fewer nerve jangling moments that have my heart beating faster.

Back on the drop zone, another glorious weekend of skydiving finishes with both my own aircraft and the hire aircraft having been kept busy. Everything I wanted to achieve in the parachute program is completed, with customers commenting that it was the most amazing experience they have ever had. As we start to pack up, I feel great.

I'm chatting to one of my instructors about how the day has gone and what we have coming up the following weekend, and we're interrupted when the pilot of the hire aircraft walks in and asks to have a word with me.

"Andy, when I was descending after that last skydiving load, the engine started spluttering," he tells me. "It gave me a fright."

We both go out to the aircraft and, clearly, there's plenty of fuel, so I start the engine up and run it through some different power settings. After twenty minutes of running the engine we're unable to get the engine to recreate the problem; everything is the way it should be.

"Not to worry," I tell him. "This aircraft is going into Exeter airport tomorrow morning for maintenance and having its fifty hour service, so I'll mention it to them when I'm down there." The aircraft is tied up and put to bed.

The following morning I fly the aircraft down to Exeter, which is only a five minute flight, and park it up outside the maintenance hangar. I speak to the aircraft engineer and mention the engine was playing up. He suggests that as it was a very hot day it could have been a fuel vapour lock, and hence it sorted itself out, but they'll check it out. I return to Exeter airport on the Friday to collect the aircraft and chat with the engineer regarding the previous problem, asking him if they found anything. I'm told that nothing showed up - they had run it through a number of tests and all the power settings were showing that everything was correct, so it probably was just a fuel vapour lock, as he first suggested. I board the aircraft and fly it back to Dunkeswell over the Devon countryside on a beautiful summer's day. The engine sounds fine and the aircraft is flying normally, as I would expect having just come out of maintenance.

The following day both pilots arrive – Paul Norman, an experienced jump pilot who I've worked with on many occasions, who will be flying the hire aircraft for static line jumps, and Darren Clayton, who will be flying my own aircraft for tandem jumps. After the second parachuting load on the hire aircraft Paul mentions to me that the alternator light flashed on a couple of times, indicating that the battery wasn't being charged for a couple of seconds. We're not that busy to be able to put the hire aircraft up again, so Paul parks it up. We take the nose cowling off the engine to have a look at the alternator belt, as Paul wonders if the right one has been fitted. I point out to him that it's a new belt that was fitted, and I can't see the maintenance people fitting the wrong one. We can see the belt is tight, and we're both happy with it, and we put the cowling back onto the aircraft.

"Andy, what do you want me to do?" Paul asks me.

"Well, as we haven't got another load for you, refuel the aircraft now to save time, and when we do start to use it again later we'll have enough fuel for three loads," I tell him.

Paul strolls into the clubhouse twenty minutes later and says, "Andy, the aircraft is refuelled – it's good to go," and then goes off to grab a coffee.

Cloud cover has rolled in, which now prevents me from doing tandems on my own aircraft. Bloody typical! Time ticks on and, eventually, there's good news: we can see a clear line from cloud cover to blue sky, so I rally up the pilots and we discuss the hole in the cloud we can see. I tell them to climb through the hole, and by the time they reach ten thousand feet the blue sky will be over the airfield. My aircraft takes off, shortly followed by the hire aircraft. I calculate that we should just have enough daylight time to get all the tandems jumped from both aircrafts. I have my radio with me for communication with the pilots as I'm running Drop Zone control, and I walk away from people to ensure I'm not distracted and can focus on the job.

My aircraft calls for permission to drop, which I give, and my radio crackles a short time later. It's the flying school who inform me that my hire aircraft has just called a Pan-Pan on the radio and will be landing off the airfield. The 'Pan-Pan' call tells me that the pilot has a problem, so obviously he has decided he can't make it back to the airfield and has decided to put it down in a field somewhere. I can't believe it - the aircraft has only flown for an hour and ten minutes since coming out of maintenance. I need to organise transport to collect them and bring them back, so I call Darren in my own aircraft.

"Can you see where the other aircraft is and confirm everything is okay?" I ask him.

"Roger that. I have the other aircraft; it's in a field south of the airfield. I'll show you after I land. There appears to be jumpers walking around the aeroplane."

Well, that's good, I think. I now know where they are and will be able to get transport out there to pick them up. The only problem will be getting the aircraft back. Clearly it's going to be too late to get an engineer out, as it will be dark soon, so I'll have to try and get one out in the morning.

My mobile rings and I answer it. "Andy, it's Julian, Dan's football coach."

"Hi. How can I help?" I ask him.

"I was in the woods with my son and we heard an aircraft flying over the top with a rough running engine. The engine went quiet, and then we heard a loud bang. We've just got to the edge of the field and can see the aircraft. It's a bad crash, I'm afraid.

"How bad?"

"There may be fatalities," he tells me.

I'm stunned. I thank him for his call and immediately call the flying school to get it verified. They inform me they know nothing, but they're aware the police helicopter and the air ambulance have been dispatched from Exeter airport. I call Exeter Air Traffic Control, tell them I'm aware I have an aircraft down, and I'm hearing it's a bad crash with possible fatalities. I ask if they can they tell me anything more. They inform me they have no other news.

I'm numb. It's like I'm here but not here. I tell myself to take a deep breath and start thinking about a logical sequence to deal with this. By now, Darren has landed my aircraft and walks over to me. I tell him the hire aircraft hasn't landed but crashed, and I just have sketchy information at this time. I tell him to put the aircraft to bed.

There are six people on board the hire aircraft, four of whom are my friends. One of them, Mike Wills, is one of my closest friends. I'm worried about how they are and the word 'fatalities' keeps ringing in my ears. I call one of my instructors over and tell him I'm shutting down the parachute program, and ask him to apologise to the customers and tell them we've had to cancel the last two aircraft loads. I realise there are two boys on the drop zone whose fathers are in that plane, so I also ask him to get one of the girls to take charge of the boys and make sure they don't hear anything. I desperately want to go to the crash site but I feel I shouldn't leave as the two boys are now my priority. Also, I know the police will arrive very soon and will want to talk to me. I call Alison to warn her about what has happened and hear a loud bang before the phone goes quiet. Worried, I call her mother who lives four doors away and ask her to go around and check on her. Putting that to the back of my mind, I know what I must do is call the British Parachute Association and inform the national safety coach and technical officer of the incident, as I am required to do. I tell one of them about the situation the best I can, explaining information is sketchy, and let them know I'm not able to leave the drop zone. Their reply takes me by surprise.

"It's nothing to do with us. It's not a parachuting accident but an aircraft accident."

The conversation comes to an end. I was expecting some sort of support but I now realise I am on my own. I receive a phone call from Raymond (Radar) who tells me there's a fireman at the scene of the crash who wants to know how much fuel is on board the aircraft, because it's pissing out everywhere. I tell him it's just been refuelled so it's carrying over two hundred litres. Radar also tells me that Emma - a skydiver who is a paramedic and a friend - is at the scene. This must be dreadful for her to see skydivers she knows involved in this accident.

The Air Accident Investigation Board are on their way, and I'm still at the club waiting for the police to arrive. I was expecting them within the hour but many hours later I'm still waiting and feeling frustrated that I can't leave and go to the crash site. I keep hearing the words 'multiple fatalities' but the messages are unclear and I don't know who has died. After seventeen years of running a skydiving school I always knew there was a risk of a skydiving fatality at some point, but I never imagined my worst case scenario would unfold.

Alison's mum calls me to say Alison is okay now, but she fainted and collapsed on the floor. I'm concerned for her, of course, but it pales into insignificance. I just can't take all this in.

At last the police arrive and one of them approaches me.

"What we want— "

"Before we go down the road of what you want," I interrupt, "I have two boys here whose fathers were in the plane. Their mothers aren't here so they need to be looked after."

He calls on his radio for a female policewoman to be dispatched to deal with the boys. I'm relieved in the sense that they will now receive professional help. The policeman then produces a list of things he requires from me; clearly the AAIB have told the police what they want. All the various documents and fuel samples are taken away, and I know people are now going to go through me and the business with a fine-toothed comb. I have no issue with that as everything was, and always is, done by the book; my only concern is for the families of those involved.

I ask the policeman what he knows and he tells me there are three fatalities, but he doesn't know the names. However, he gives me enough information for me to work it out: Paul Norman - the pilot, Richard Smith (Smithy), and his seventeen-year-old daughter, Claire. There's an emptiness. I feel like in my head I'm in a vast space; I can't really connect with anything but I'm going through the motions. My eyes seem to follow my head a fraction slower, my pupils enlarge, and there's a huge, unbearable depth of sadness. There was one tandem student on the aircraft, Daniel Greening, who was going to be jumping with Mike, and before I leave the airfield I'm able to tell his parents that he has been taken to the hospital. Mike and another skydiver, Dan Batchelor, have also been taken to the hospital.

It's late at night by the time I return home and both my boys are in bed. I find it hard to talk to Alison as there is too much going on in my head. I want answers, and I go over and over in my mind the sequence of events, but no answers are forthcoming. I fall onto my bed but I can't sleep; my head is sore from thinking too much and I lie there and watch the darkness fading away and being replaced with the rising sun.

Some skydivers I know are at my mother-in-laws house so I head over there to see them. I can tell by their expressions that something is going on but I'm not sure what. The news is broken to me that my best friend, Mike Wills, has died at the hospital. Mike was the tandem instructor on the aircraft but so many other images of him pass through my mind as if they're on a slide projector that's out of control. No sooner does one image appear, it's replaced by another. We started skydiving at the same grass roots club; joined the Royal Marines; were part of the Royal Marines Free Fall Parachute Display Team. We took part in parachuting world records together; I took him through BASE jumping. I picture all the conversations and fun we had together, and each time I recall these moments I see his smiling face and hear his laughter. He was such a large character. I can't hold it back - my eyes well up and the tears start to fall. I'm the Chief Instructor; I'm the figure head at the helm of the ship who's supposed to hold everything together, I tell myself. I walk the four doors back to my house, still trying to take things in and trying to keep my emotions in check, but I'm hurting badly.

There's a knock on the door and when I open it a man introduces himself as a reporter from the BBC. He asks me if I would like to give a statement and I tell him that two minutes ago I just heard my best friend had died. There's a pause and he says, "What about a short statement then?" I just glare at him and close the door.

"You have to take the kids and go and stay with your dad; things are going to go crazy around here," I tell Alison. "There's nothing you can do; it's only me that can deal with this." Alison departs with the boys and I'm thankful they're away from it all.

As the morning continues, everything around me explodes with activity. My home phone constantly rings. Skydiving friends call to offer sympathy, others call to try to get information about what happened. The press call and want me to give a statement but I feel I shouldn't until we have answers. I receive a call to say a large group of press are on the airfield and one jumper is holding court with them, telling them, in his opinion, what happened, when he wasn't even there at the time. Other press are offering money to be told where I live. A person I know takes the money and sends the press guy all around the country lanes, but not to my house.

AAIB arrive to take a statement, which I have to write down. It's difficult as the page is a blur and I struggle to see through the tears. I find their questioning irritating as they suggest things when I want to stick to facts, but as irritating as I'm finding this I know they're just doing their job.

The next couple of days seem to roll into one. The BPA's technical officer arrives, which I wasn't expecting, to hear my version of events. I go through it all yet again, and feel it's a shame the support wasn't there on day one. Two of my club members, Gavin Horrell and Leanne Milligan arrive to help and man my home phone to give me a break from it, as it's ringing constantly. I'm truly thankful they're here. Rumours are flying around that are totally inaccurate and I consider whether to give a statement to the press, but I know at times the press misquote things to make for 'better reading'. As much as I'm angered by these inaccurate rumours and want to set the record straight, I can't trust these people; I don't want to be misquoted and cause any additional pain to the families.

Later, I'm at home when I see a police car pulling up, and I go to the door to greet them.

"You found the house okay?" I say to the policewoman.

"Mr Guest, I was here two days ago," she tells me.

"You were here?" I'm totally confused as I have no recollection of her being in my house. I start to realise I'm still in deep shock. I'm going through the motions but as if in a trance, and nothing is being recorded in my head.

I make a point to visit each family and tell them I'm here for them, and that they can ask me any questions they want and I will answer them the very best I can, so they have the information directly from me. It's a painful journey to make, and each visit is as hard as the first one. I visit Claire's mum at a pub near her home. What do you say to a woman who has just lost her seventeen-year-old daughter? I tell her the sequence of events and explain that the AAIB are conducting an investigation and hopefully we'll have answers soon. Mike's brother, Patrick, visits me at home and I try to put to bed some of the rumours, again going through the sequence of events. Each time I recount it I have to go through the pain of losing my friends, and it tears me apart. I tell myself the families' loss is greater, and I have no right to feel the way I do. I meet Mike's mother whose concern is about how I'm feeling and coping; it makes me feel humble that she's worried about me. I visit the survivors at the hospital and chat to their families, and I don't think my face can hide the pain I'm in.

I know things take their time but I want answers. The families need answers; and they need the peace of mind to know I did everything by the book. I wander around the house but feel the need to escape and have time on my own, so I head to the clubhouse. I've just put the kettle on when a stranger walks in. He explains he is a friend of Smithy and wants to know if I could tell him what happened. I once again go over the sequence of events. He tells me that the rumour he'd heard was that we had just one aircraft operating, that it had been flying rough all day, and as we had to get people jumped we carried on. I tell him that's not true and point to my own aircraft that is parked outside. I also point out that the AAIB have all this information and at some point a report will released, detailing everything. He tells me he found it hard to believe the rumours as Smithy only ever had good things to say about me, including how professionally I ran things, and says that he's pleased he came to see me and got the correct facts. It's hard to hear these rumours. People who start them never ever think about the pain it will cause; all they care about is having a good story to tell.

I have been closed now for two weeks and I decide I should reopen to help with the healing process of the skydivers who knew the individuals. I contact each family and tell them this is what I'm considering, however, I want them to know if they feel it's too soon to reopen then it goes without saying I will remain closed. Each family gives me their blessing and say it's what their loved ones would have wanted me to do.

Two days later I'm on the airfield with Darren. I decide to drain the fuel from my aircraft, flush it, and refuel from a different location, as I'm still waiting for the results of the tests on my own fuel. Darren is about to drain when I receive a phone call from a young female engineer from AAIB who tells me that in an hour's time I'm going to be put on a conference call. I tell her that's fine, however, right at this moment I'm about to drain the fuel from my aircraft. Surely by now, I say, they should have the results back on my fuel? She tells me they have the results and I will find out in an hour's time. I explain I don't have that spare hour, and there's a pause, and then she tells me it's best that I drain it.

The words hit me like a sledge hammer square in the face. I'm completely distraught as this can only mean one thing - they found a problem with my fuel. I walk over to Darren and tell him what the engineer has just said, and that I can't understand it as I checked the fuel sample myself that day, and the testing kit indicated everything was okay. Darren proceeds to pour around two hundred litres of my fuel onto the ground, and I feel completely numb. Was this the reason the engine was running rough? Am I responsible for the deaths of four friends? I go over and over it in my head and still don't understand it as the testing kit is easy to use and it showed the fuel was clear.

An hour later I'm feeling beaten up and as low as anyone can get. The sense of guilt is immense; it's tearing me up inside. When I receive the conference call from the AAIB I'm introduced to the people around the table and I ask the question.

"What did you find wrong with the fuel?"

"There's nothing wrong with your fuel; you can carry on using it," the man tells me.

His sentence bounces around inside my head; it's not the answer I was expecting and it takes time for it to sink in. Then it finally does … there's nothing wrong with my fuel.

A rage builds inside of me, and a voice in my head is screaming, "You stupid cow! Do you have any idea what you've put me through for the past hour?" I can't believe how totally irresponsible she has been. Did she not think about the impact her comment would have on me and of the mental torture she's just put me through? While half of me is trying to contain this fury, the other half is trying to digest what the man from AAIB is saying: they still don't know the cause of the crash and are continuing their investigation. It's disappointing as I want answers, but as least the contaminated fuel rumour can be put to bed.

The long awaited draft report is finally sent out by the AAIB, not only to me but to all the families involved. I'm delighted to receive it as this may give comfort to the families as well as give me some answers. As I start to read it, alarm bells go off in my head, and once I reach the end I start again at the beginning, thinking I must have misread it. There are so many inaccuracies and I'm livid. It's another sleepless night as the words in the report keep going round and around in my mind. I can't imagine how the families must be feeling, and what they're thinking, having read it.

In the morning I go through it again, this time noting the inaccuracies, and next to each one I state why it's incorrect. I now feel that rather than the

AAIB being a helpful body, I am now at war with them. I'm not going to take this lying down as I have a duty to the friends I've lost, and to their families, to get the correct facts. That afternoon I approach a solicitor and pay her to respond to the AAIB report on all the points I've raised, and there are many. The AAIB are now obliged to make the amendments to the final version of the report on the points I have highlighted, but I know the damage has been done. A few days later I receive a phone call from the AAIB.

"Andy, you've put a solicitor onto us," he says.

"Too bloody right I have; I can see what you're trying to do. You don't say it, but you're painting the picture it was pilot error, and it's morally fucking wrong. The pilot has a family … what are they supposed to think? All the families are entitled to the facts, and I'll make damn sure they get them."

"And you think there are facts missing from the report?"

"Yes, I do. The report said that no witnesses could be identified who saw the aircraft being refuelled, yet the pilot told me it had been refuelled, one of my staff saw it being refuelled, and the fireman at the scene of the crash said the fuel was pissing out everywhere. Why aren't these things mentioned in the report?"

I go on to mention that in the report they state they found the fuel filter to be 85% contaminated, but the source of the debris was not established. Considering they checked the filter in my own aircraft (which had flown for thirty-six hours since its last maintenance check) and it was clear, surely that contamination must have come from another fuel source and was already present in the aircraft's fuel tanks. I ask if they've checked the previous locations the aircraft flew and refuelled from, and I'm told they don't have the resources to do that. I also mention that in the report they say the contamination was considered likely to have been present at the time of the power loss on the flight prior to the most recent maintenance (when the previous pilot had encountered the aircraft engine 'spluttering', just before I took it to Exeter airport). Surely, as the same 'spluttering' noise was heard by witnesses before the aircraft crashed, this should have warranted further investigation? I talk about further points – too many to mention – but the conversation goes nowhere and I'm left fuming. It takes me a long time to calm down.

I receive the funeral dates of those who died in the accident, and I'm horrified that Mike's funeral clashes with the funeral of Smithy and his daughter, Claire. I want to attend both and feel that I should, but I know it's impossible. It's a terrible dilemma but Mike was my best friend. I speak to Claire's mother who tells me she understands, and says I should go to Mike's funeral as we were so close. I'm so thankful for her understanding but feel bad that I've had to make a choice. Mike's brother, Patrick, approaches me and asks if I would deliver a eulogy for Mike. It's an honour, and I'm touched he has asked me, but I'm also aware that, emotionally, this is going to be extremely difficult. Patrick tells me that Mike had a lot of respect for me, and I know that's the key to why we were such good friends - we had both earned the respect of each other.

I spend days writing the eulogy, wanting to make sure I get it right, but I have no experience in writing one; in fact I have no real experience in writing at all. I just hope I have the balance right.

On the day of the funeral I parachute into the Commando training centre, landing outside the Officer's Mess, where Mike used to go, and once I'm on the ground I get changed and head for the funeral service. It's very emotional. I don't feel I'm one hundred percent there in my head, and I'm concerned I may choke up. When the time comes I get up and move forward to give the eulogy. I tell myself to take a deep breath, not to rush, but to slow it down. As I read from the paper in my hand I can feel my eyes brimming with tears. I'm on the edge … it's surreal, and it doesn't feel like there is anyone else here apart from Mike's presence. I finish with a quote from Illusions by Richard Bach:

Don't be dismayed at goodbyes. A farewell is necessary before you can meet again. And meeting again after moments or lifetimes, is certain for those who are friends.

I'm relieved I have got through it and I take my seat. I can only hope Mike felt I did him justice.

I also attend Paul's funeral, and it's still extremely hard to take in that this has happened.

Life goes on for others around me, but two years later it's still ongoing with the AAIB and I feel I'm stuck. I still have people constantly approaching me, wanting to talk about the crash, not realising the effect it has had, and is still having on me. I just can't get away from it. Club members comment that I've changed, that I no longer have that spark and smile on the drop zone, and I know they're right.

This ongoing battle with the AAIB has knocked the stuffing out of me. With little thought about the implications this could have for my family, I decide to move to Spain so people will no longer keep asking me about the crash. We sell the skydiving school, Alison sells her horses, we sell our home, I resign as a parish councillor, and the whole family moves to a town just south of Granada. It's a rash decision and I don't really take the time to evaluate it. I just need to get away.

Eight months later I receive an email from the coroner, informing me of the date of the inquest. She's aware I am now living out of the country and asks me if I'll be returning for it, listing the people who will be there. It goes without saying that I'll be returning, I tell her, as I have a duty to the families. But I let her know I'm bitterly disappointed that key witnesses have not been asked to attend. I receive an email back asking me which key witnesses I'm referring to. The first, I reply, is the fireman who was on the scene of the crash and saw how much fuel was pouring out of the aircraft. The second is Leanne, the girl in the office, who saw the pilot refuelling the aircraft. Both of their statements support mine and confirm what the pilot told me - the aircraft was refuelled and ready to go. I receive another email stating that the inquest is being put back to another date.

I ask myself why the two key witnesses who cancel out the AAIB suggestion that the aircraft possibly ran out of fuel were not asked to attend.

It seems to me that the AAIB, being a small organisation and not having the resources to investigate further, are keen to try and close the file with the suggestion that they found the reason for the crash – pilot error, which sounds better than, 'We have no idea', and wouldn't reflect well on them. Is this the reason those key witnesses were not invited? My head is all over the place. I'm so angry at the suggestion that it was pilot error, and that the AAIB seem to be ignoring the witnesses' statements.

In my opinion, surely the fact that the fuel filter was eighty five percent blocked has to be the biggest indicator of a possible problem with the aircraft. Yes, they ran a test with that fuel filter and the engine worked, but how can they ignore the fact that the hard impact when the aircraft hit the ground, and subsequently removing the filter and transporting it to the test centre, could well have loosened off some of the debris found on the filter? If they took that into account, the filter could well have been more than eighty-five percent and up to one hundred percent blocked before impact. These questions just keep flying around in my head. I can't sleep at night; it's so important to me that all the facts come out for the families, and I owe it to my friends. I'm so tired at times. I just want to go to sleep, but I can't. At the same time I have to try and put a different face on in front of my family: a face that tells them I'm coping. But I'm not. I seem to have become two people. One is seen as a strong person who is holding the helm, but the other has turned in on himself.

It wasn't that long ago I was on the working party for the British Parachute Association, where one of my tasks was to review injuries in the UK and compile a report concerning the use of round parachutes. I had asked for the annual figures from the skydiving clubs to work with but there was an issue with data protection, so they gave me the details but with all the club names removed. It didn't take long for me to work out that the clubs were listed in alphabetical order, just as the BPA list them, so I then knew what each club had achieved within a course of a year. The figures showed I had the best safety record, and after eighteen years of running a skydiving school I was proud of it. Now I'm going through one of the worst fucking scenarios one could imagine and, in my opinion, the AAIB are not helping. Even though the aircraft had just come out of maintenance, and even though decisions were made on board the aircraft that were out of my control, I still have an overwhelming sense of guilt. Going through the 'what if' situations doesn't help; there's no turning the clock back.

The months pass and I fly back to attend the coroner's inquest that will have a jury who will decide the outcome. I'm humbled by the support of the families who have lost their loved ones. At the inquest all I'm asked to do is read out my statement that was taken at the time of the incident; I'm not allowed to say anything else. The fireman confirms fuel was pouring out of the aircraft, and Leanne confirms she saw the pilot refuelling the plane. The AAIB inspector reads his statement but then clarifies a few points and supports me in saying I kept the planes to a high standard of maintenance. He surprises me when he continues to say that the pilot found himself in a difficult situation, and the terrain was far from ideal. A lot of the small fields are separated by what are Devon embankments, which are made up of rock, stones, and mud: not ideal if you are over shooting. The area has a lot of rolling hills, and the pilot had selected the obvious field on top of a hill to land on, which was flat, but at the end of the field there was a steep drop. The AAIB also confirm my parachute school met all the Civil Aviation Authority requirements legally, and also admit they could not rule out that whatever caused the engine to run rough on the previous Sunday may have resurfaced. I'm thankful for his support, and also for his comments about the pilot. Though it is good for the families to hear, for me this change of tune is all too late. The British Parachute Association confirms we legally met all their requirements.

The verdict comes back that the crash was accidental. I feel relieved that the key witnesses attended so the families had a chance to hear from them, especially the fireman who was at the scene. This is three years after the accident. It doesn't bring back my friends, but I know they would have appreciated the work I put into this to ensure their families heard all the facts. The sadness and pain that they're no longer with us stays with me as I fly back to Spain.

It's clear that six months on from the inquest it's not sustainable for me to stay here in Spain, and I need to find a well-paid job. I return to the UK and work as a tandem and AFF instructor, but because of the British weather I know I'm not going to earn that much. I receive a message from my brother Ken and Ronnie Dunnett, a friend, asking me how I'd like to work in Afghanistan doing armed security, and I look at my current situation. I'm living away from my family in a caravan on a drop zone, and earning eight hundred pounds a month, but I could go to Afghanistan and be earning eleven thousand pounds a month. Yes, the risks would be higher, but the truth of it is we're running out of money, so there is only one answer. A few days later a country manager calls me and asks me if I'd like the job. I reply immediately with a 'yes'.

"Start growing your beard ... I'll have you flight tickets emailed to you in a fortnight," he tells me.

Two days later I fly back to Spain. I tell Alison not to believe all she hears on the news about Afghanistan and that I'll be fine, and we talk about the situation. I'm going to be working abroad, Westleigh has excelled in his A-Levels and Loughborough University has offered him a place, and Daniel needs to return to the UK too for his A-levels, as the International school doesn't teach the computer course he wants to study. I'm unhappy with the thought of Alison being isolated here, so we decide that she will go back too, to be amongst friends and family, which gives me some peace of mind.

I receive my flight tickets ten days later, and wonder how rough a ride this new path is going to be for us all. It does concern me as I have no idea what I'm letting myself in for, and the last time I was in Afghanistan I was nearly killed. I wonder if this is fate taking me back to finish a job it failed to do the first time round, but only time will tell.

INTO THE UNKNOWN

I leave Spain. A part of me is happy I'm heading off to do a job that will pay well, but I'm also nervous. *Where is this new journey taking me? Will it be a journey with a dead end?*

After a long trip I finally arrive in Kabul. It feels strange and slightly unsettling to be entering a hostile environment where men have big boys' toys that can kill, especially when I know they won't hesitate to use them. As I step off the plane and exit Kabul Airport I'm greeted by my brother, Ken, who has a huge grin on his face, and I smile back.

"Well, who would have thought that twenty-seven years later you and I would be back in Afghanistan together and, what's more, in Kabul," I say. It's so good to see him.

We jump into our vehicles and head to our guest house where the company we're working for takes in tenants. At the main gate the guards greet my brother with huge smiles and hugs. I'm not a man-hugging type of guy, and I look on. I'm shown into a spacious room with a double bed, wardrobe, and a table and chair, which is to be my new home, and after a few minutes Ken takes me downstairs and makes me a tea. I'm parched and it tastes wonderful. I have a thousand questions for him but it's hard to know where to start. Ken, who seems completely relaxed, suggests we go for a walk, and before I know it we're outside the compound and pounding the streets of Kabul, my flashbacks coming thick and fast of the last time I was in Afghanistan. Vehicles rush by, dust is constantly kicked up into the air, and drivers honk their horns expecting something magical to happen in front of them. The main road is in poor condition with litter strewn everywhere; stray dogs bark and roam around in search of a meal, and the smell of food being cooked doesn't disguise the putrid stench in the air. It's hard to believe how primitive the Afghans are now, when in the 60s the women walked around in miniskirts. Now they have to be covered up and are mostly hidden away.

Some of the Afghans who walk past stare at us out of curiosity as we dip in and out of the small, cramped shops that line the street. Ken always takes the first step in greeting them, using the little Pashto he knows, and I can see it goes down well. Some of the shops are filled with British Lee Enfield rifles and Ken tells me he would love to own one as he considers them to be antiques, but the problem would be transporting it back to the UK. On looking around I can see that carpets manufactured by hand in Afghanistan sell for four hundred dollars, which would sell in the UK for four or five times that amount. There are hats, blankets, and trinkets – items usually seen in tourist shops around the world – and the colours leap out at me. There are gem stones, with fake ones mixed in with them. Other shops stock Chinese electrical products, and there's a small shopping mall with armed security on the door who body search us. The shops here sell higher quality products and not many people visit due to the costs that are out of reach for most Afghans. The people continue to stare as we walk around and I remind myself we're in a hostile environment, which prompts me to ask Ken where his weapon is hidden.

"I don't have one," he tells me. "Not all of Afghanistan is at war, Andrew; ninety percent of the population are friendly."

I nod, but feel uneasy. I really hoped he'd had one.

As we head back, I observe one of our company vehicles enter the compound and notice the glare the Afghan guards give the British security personnel within it, compared to the greeting they gave my brother. Well, that settles it. It now looks like I'll be a man-hugger after all; one equipped with open arms and a heartfelt wish of "good life".

The following day I meet the country manager who talks about sending me to an area with a client to promote football amongst the women. This surprises me as it's not normally permitted for outsiders to see the women but, apparently, the client already has a dozen female teams who play behind closed doors with no spectators. Ken has already researched the area and all the feedback tells us it's under Taliban control, with the local Afghan police commanders warning us not to go there. The country manager seems to have adopted an, "it'll be okay" attitude, but with Ken's persistence in gathering intelligence reports the country manager eventually admits to the danger and the trip is cancelled. Instead, I'm given a project to manage the armed security on two American bases, using Afghans to man the security towers. I ask to see the paperwork for the project and I'm told there isn't any.

"I thought the project has been running for a year?" I say.

"It has, but we've been busy," he tells me.

I'm shown the contract and for the next two weeks I work eighteen hour days to create documents, as I've discovered we can be audited by the American Army.

With an extensive file completed it's time to head to an airfield camp, the first of the project's bases, where I'll have two hundred and seventy-five Afghan security personnel under my control. I'm not too impressed with the way my transfer there has been arranged as the journey is a one vehicle move, so I can only hope the vehicle doesn't break down. With each turn in the road my finger is on my safety catch just in case we run into a Taliban checkpoint, which has been known to occur on this road. With a steep drop to the left of me, rock face to the right, and no room to reverse, the outcome wouldn't be good; it would be a case of all guns blazing as we'd try to drive through.

I arrive at my guest house and hope it won't be attacked by the Taliban as the security set up is poor. I lie down with my weapon resting on the bed but tiredness wins, and I'm soon transported to another place in my dreams. The following day I arrive at the airfield camp and conduct payroll for two hundred and seventy-five guards. The guard commander tells me if I pay him then he will pay the men, but I decline; I want to ensure the men get their money and that he isn't dipping into it. I tell him I expect each man to produce his American ID card before wages will be handed over. Later, it's interesting to discover I have a man using his brother's ID who has bypassed the American security, and three other men have the same ID card number. One man, who I've just paid, immediately offers some of his wages to the guard commander, who shouts at him. Quite clearly, they are paying him a percentage for being given the job. The wage isn't great and amounts to around fifty-one pounds a month. Their living quarters are in a dire state, the heat is fifty degrees but my guards have no air conditioning, and they only have two toilets and three showers between them.

"Can the men speak to you?" the guard commander asks.

"Of course," I tell him. "I want all the men to know they can approach me."

As I'm having a green tea I watch as a single chair is placed outside and a circle of chairs is placed around it. It's not a good sign, I tell myself. After tea, I sit on the chair and am completely encircled by the men. Their spokesperson speaks in English and opens the conversation.

"Why do the Americans treat us like this? Unless the men get a pay rise, around seventy of them will leave today."

What a great start to my new job, having seventy guards quit, I think. "I understand what you're saying," I tell them, "but I've only just started this job and I can't do anything overnight. These things take time, but if you're not willing to give me any time then I'd like to take the opportunity to thank all those that are leaving for their efforts, and wish them well."

There's a brief discussion amongst the men and I'm told they will give me some time, so they won't be quitting today. It's been an interesting day, especially when I don't speak Pashto and often have to use a teenager to translate.

I receive a call from the deputy country manager, Aussie, who wants me to go out with him tonight, and he tells me to bring some extra ammunition with me. Darkness falls and I head to the main gate to meet him. I study the movements, not only to keep an eye out for him but to look out for a suicide bomber in a vehicle, or a shooter, so I clock potential escape routes. Aussie pulls up and I jump in the vehicle, whereupon he tells me to cock my weapon, just in case. We drive through the town and out into the countryside, and I have an uneasy feeling about it. We seem to be driving out into the wilderness.

"Where are we going?" I ask. "Why did you need me?"

"We're meeting a guy who is going to sell me ammunition. I'm picking up five thousand rounds," he says.

I can't believe what I've just heard. "So let me get this straight. You're carrying cash to pay for ammunition, and this guy knows you're bringing it, and he's chosen the meeting place?"

"Yes," he replies.

I can't help but think this is bad; very bad. We have no back up and we're on our own. The only thought in my head is: *what a wanker*.

The vehicle pulls up into a lay-by. I observe there's a thirty foot rock face to my left and I'm half expecting muzzle flashes to erupt and for our vehicle to resemble a cheese grater within a minute, but nothing happens. I continue to stare into the darkness with flickering stars above my head, watching for movement. From the shadows of the darkness, two figures emerge carrying boxes; a torch is switched on, and the boxes are checked. Brand new 7.62 rounds shine back at us, payment is made, and we drive off. Aussie is delighted but I'm still fuming at how irresponsible he has been, and for putting my life in danger. I tell him never to put me in that situation again - of carrying cash and meeting strangers in the dark in an isolated spot.

Back at the guest house I inspect the boxes and, to my surprise, I find the ammunition has come from the Americans, who gave it to the Afghan army. They are now selling it on the black market.

A high ranking American colonel arrives the following day to conduct a security review, which involves a walk around the airfield camp, and as the security project manager I've been invited along. Around sixteen military personnel with pens and notepads are on this walk, listening to the colonel as he explains his plans to expand the camp. At the main gate the colonel glances around and says, "All good here; let's move on." I turn to the

American major next to me.

"Sir," I say, "your main gate is flawed and you're going to be hit."

"Why do you say that?" he asks.

"Do you guys not learn from your history? You made the same mistake in Lebanon. When the gate opened, a driver hit the accelerator and drove his van straight through, right alongside the apartment building, and detonated. You lost two hundred and forty-two US Marines and fifty-eight French in one hit. The British have concrete blocks in place, making it impossible to drive straight through, as the vehicle has to go around a chicane. With something like this in place it will give your machine gunner time to react. You also need concrete blocks to protect your fencing. At the moment, with the main road only fifty metres away, a lorry could swerve off and crash through your fencing, close to where your C130s are parked up."

On that note, we move on to catch up with the colonel who is explaining he wants to push out the walls and make them higher. "Any questions?" he asks, but there is no response.

"I have a question, "I shout out.

"Who said that?" the colonel asks. There's a parting of the waves, which leaves an avenue between the American soldiers. At one end stands the colonel and at the other end myself. I can see he is looking me up and down, taking in my beard, Pawkul hat, Afghan scarf, and my AK-47. His eyes meet mine.

"Who are you?"

"I'm the British guy running your Afghan security guards," I reply.

"Thank you for coming," he says.

"You mention pushing out and building your walls high but, when you come under attack, how do you shoot back? I'll tell you how - by building shooting platforms and a ramp, so one of your armoured vehicles will be able to drive up and use the heavy machine gun if needed," I tell him.

"That's a very good point," the colonel says, and turns to his men. "And he's right, so we need to put in some platforms."

With that, we part ways.

The next day I'm picked up from the guest house to be transported to an outpost that is also a part of my security project, situated close to the Pakistan border. I'm in a car with three Afghans who I don't know, and driving through the countryside. I have my AK-47, but so do three of the others. The fourth is the young lad who acts as my translator. It becomes apparent that this route seems to be one way in, one way out, which increases the chances of being ambushed on the way back.

As we're driving out in the open desert-like features beneath a blue sky and with the scorching sun bearing down on us, we catch up with an American military patrol, and I order my driver to slow down. I'm cautious with any American patrol as I know they tend to be trigger happy. The American patrol comes to a halt and I order my driver to stop as well, putting adequate space between us. The Americans don't seem to be in a hurry as we sit and observe each other. Time ticks on, and I really want to get to my outpost before it gets dark. I tell everyone to stay in the vehicle as the last thing I want is for Americans to see Afghans carrying weapons in case they think we're the Taliban. I exit the vehicle and walk out towards them with my arms outstretched, having left my weapon in the vehicle. I've already removed my body armour through fear of them mistaking it for a suicide vest. I stop and very slowly start to strip off - waistcoat, shirt, boots and socks are all removed, followed by my trousers and lastly my pants - and I stand there naked with my arms extended and complete a three-sixty turn to show I'm not carrying anything.

"Can I drive past you?" I shout out in my best English accent.

"No," an American shouts back.

I'm not impressed. I get dressed again, and it's apparent by the look on my guards' faces that I'm now to be classed as the mad Englishman.

The American patrol moves on and we follow, but at a safe distance. A short while later they turn off and we head straight on. I can see an Apache helicopter circling up ahead and wonder what the pilot may be thinking seeing two vehicles heading to the outpost, recalling how in Iraq the Americans shot up a British patrol. I call the outpost and ask them to relay to the helicopter pilot that there are friendlies in two four-by-four vehicles heading their way.

When we reach the outpost I'm amazed to see high points looking down into the camp, which isn't a good start, as the enemy would have the advantage of dominating the high ground. I head to the operations room to introduce myself and the young commanding officer takes me on an orientation of the camp. The first thing that strikes me is that some of the walls are only chest high with a single strand of barbed wire on the other side, and the entire camp, which accommodates fifty men plus my fifty Afghan guards, has an unfinished look about it. I need to get the full picture because this makes no sense.

"Sir, what's the situation on these walls only being chest height?"

"A bit of a cock up," he tells me.

"In what way?"

"Well, when we were given the plans to build the camp and looked at the perimeter dimensions, it stated 350 in length, which is what we built. It became apparent we didn't have enough materials so we looked into it and discovered you Brits work in feet. We built it in metres and ran out of supplies."

You couldn't make this up, I think, and wonder what else I'm going to come across.

Next on my agenda I meet with my Afghan guards and chat with the guard commander about any problems they might have. They highlight the fact there is no area for them to cook in.

The following day I decide to train the guards on how to search individuals and vehicles, since they are manning the main gate, and I make if fun so they enjoy it. Quite clearly they have no idea what they're doing, but they're learning. I ask two of them to search my vehicle and I watch as one of them leans over and studies my engine. Suddenly he leaps back and utters something, and the concerned look on his face is clear for all to see. Intrigued, the others gather around to have a look, and find themselves peering at my fake bomb with a mobile phone attached to it. I call the number and when it rings a few of them jump back in horror. I sit them down and explain that had it been a real bomb, they'd be dead by now.

I stand the guards down for lunch and they invite me to join them. My head tells me not to as I know what will happen, however, accepting their offer will go down well with them. As we eat flies are everywhere and I'm constantly chasing them off my plate of food. The food actually tastes nice, though. As I'd expected, within half an hour my stomach is at war. I thank them for a lovely meal and make my excuses, walking off slowly when in fact I want to sprint. Stepping inside the portaloo isn't a pleasant experience, especially when there's fifty degree heat outside. Thank goodness for the six packets of Imodium tablets I carry; there's nothing worse than having gas build up when you have the runs.

I return to the guards and ask them to lay out all their weapons so I can inspect them as I'm all too aware some of them may have been dug up after twenty-six years of being buried from the Russian campaign. They lay five weapons in front of me.

"I want to see all the weapons, so tell your men to bring them over," I say to the guard commander.

"These are all the weapons, sir," he tells me.

I'm in shock. "The contract says each man must have a weapon, so where are the other forty-five?"

The guard commander explains that should the men be stopped by the Afghan Police, their weapons would be confiscated and sold on the black market. The men don't want to lose them so they keep them at home. It's imperative we get weapons on to the base, and we discuss the best way forward. It's suggested that two vehicles will leave the camp to retrieve them and that I should go with them, as the police checkpoint is likely to wave us through if they see me. I'm not keen on putting myself out on a limb; all sorts of things could go wrong and I'll be on my own with no military support and unable to rely on the guards – there's every chance that in the event of a firefight they wouldn't hesitate to run away. But I have no choice. I turn to the guard commander.

"Your man… he'll be stood by the road?"

"Yes," he replies.

"And he has a weapon?"

"Yes."

"Okay," I say. "Let's do it."

Two days later we drive out. I'm aware that danger can come from any direction but in what form I don't know, so my eyes are constantly scanning. I can see the driver's eyes flicking left and right, an indication we're close to one of my guards, I think. Sure enough, we spot him by the road. As we pull up he jumps in and we drive off, but I'm puzzled as I can't see his weapon. Before I can ask the question the vehicle veers off the road and we're heading out into the wilderness. The thought crosses my mind that I may have just been abducted, and my finger quietly releases the safety catch on my AK-47.

"Okay, where are we going?" I ask in a firm voice. There's a moment of pause which seems to stop time in its tracks and my only thought is that, depending on the answer, all hell could break loose in this vehicle. Being a hostage is not an option.

"Sir, now we go to his house to collect his weapon," the guard commander tells me.

It's an uncomfortable journey and I'm not willing to drop my guard so my finger never leaves my trigger. We park up in a village and the guard heads off with the driver and my guard commander, and I'm left on my own. Village kids appear and point at me - a foreigner in their territory - which doesn't help my anxiety. Time drags on and I know they've chosen to have tea and something to eat while I sit out here like a lemon.

Eventually they return and the guard has his weapon. This whole situation repeats itself eight more times. It's been an uneasy day and it comes as a relief when the guard commander tells me we can't get any more weapons today.

Before we head back to camp I brief the drivers about driving low profile, and feel slightly better when we're back on the main road. When we approach a police checkpoint my senses are heightened as it's difficult to know which ones are genuine and which ones are Taliban. Also, we're carrying weapons. We pass the check point smoothly without being stopped. One down, one to go, I tell myself, as I gaze out of the window at the everyday hardships faced by the people here in Afghanistan, and the donkeys and camels they have to rely on to transport goods.

I spot the second police checkpoint ahead of me and see there is a policeman flagging down vehicles. He has my full concentration and I check his surroundings for anything that may throw up a red flag. If we're stopped and he sees all these weapons in my vehicle I can see things will spiral out of control. I instruct my driver to keep going and not to stop and I wave to the policeman as we drive past. My eyes focus on my wing mirrors and I notice he has stopped my second vehicle. I'm not too concerned as the weapons are in mine. Further down the road I spot the second vehicle behind us and the driver is beeping his horn and flashing his headlights. Low profile, I told him, for crying out loud! He's attracting attention to us. We're approaching a bridge with a lay-by next to it, and the driver behind me is pissing me off so I tell mine to pull over. The second vehicle pulls over behind us, and the driver climbs out and races over. He talks to my guard commander for a moment and, as he does so, I decide to have serious words with him about low profile movements when he's finished.

"That's very bad; very bad," the guard commander says in English.

"Don't tell me his vehicle is breaking down."

"No sir. That policeman told them there is a bomb on the bridge and they're waiting for bomb disposal."

"Fuck me. Reverse the vehicles," I tell them.

The rest of the journey goes smoothly, and I arrive back at camp happy to have increased the weapons held by my guards by another nine.

Before I depart I speak to the American camp commander and mention that the guards need a cooking area. I also compare his camp to the Alamo and Rorke's Drift. He tells me he doesn't understand.

"Sir, in the Alamo when they lost their defensive wall, they all died.

Here, at night, it would be easy for the Taliban to storm in. You only have half a defensive wall and, being pitch black, you'd be in a blue-on-blue situation with your guys shooting their own. If you look at Rorke's Drift when the Brits lost the outer wall, they fell back on an inner wall. If you have an inner wall the men could fall back on, you'd know everyone on the other side would be the bad guys."

I make my way back to Kabul after an interesting two weeks, and once I'm settled in my room I decide to send the colonel an email highlighting my guards' plight on the airfield camp, reminding him they're depending on these guys for their security but they're not interacting with them.

Later, the country manager tells me another security manager is going on leave and I need to cover his project.

"What I am required to do?" I ask.

"Fill up some ATM machines scattered around Kabul, and transport some money around," he says.

So as not to go into this blind, I talk with a few people to get the bigger picture.

"You're supposed to inform the Afghan police when you're moving money around, but we don't," I'm told. "But there have been two recent attacks involving companies that move money around, so beware. The first attack was by men in civilian clothes who drove off in a police car; the second attack was by men in police uniforms also using police cars. So what does that tell you?"

I'll be moving anything from one million to three million dollars, in rucksacks. It's a three vehicle move with one going ahead to scout the road, me in the middle directing, and one at the rear as armed back up. I feel slightly out of my depth as this is all new to me and I don't know Kabul well at all. Some of the movements will involve passing high profile targets for the Taliban, such as a military camp or an embassy, and being caught by accident in an explosion attack is a possibility.

I arrive at the bank in one piece and order two men to stay by the vehicles and look out for any unusual activity, and for the drivers to remain in the vehicles with the engines running. Another two men will accompany me. I have a pistol hidden behind my back, not that it will be much use in an attack with AK-47 rifles.

As I enter the bank I notice two rooms adjacent to the corridor, and as I walk around the corner I'm gobsmacked to see a dining table with three million dollars stacked on top of it in full view of the public - who are walking around it - with just a single bank clerk standing guard. To make matters worse, I have to count the money before accepting it, which takes a considerable amount of time. Once counted, and as it's being stashed in our rucksacks, I wonder if this is a regular occurrence that has created a predictable pattern, therefore making it easier to launch an attack. I accept the money and tell the bank manager that next time I expect this to be conducted behind closed doors, away from prying eyes.

As I exit the bank I'm on high alert, and once in the vehicle I send my spotter on his way to scout the route ahead. The thought crosses my mind that I haven't chosen this route. Is this the same route they use all the time, which means our movements are predictable? Three million dollars! What would that be worth to my Afghan guards? It would be a life changing experience for them and their families, and I remember life is cheap and I mean nothing to them.

"Okay, take the next right turn," I tell the driver.

"Sir, that's not the right way," he says.

"Do what I tell you."

As the journey unfolds I constantly throw changes at the driver and can see it irritates my guards, but common sense says I am wise to do this.

At the second bank the money is counted again and handed over and signed for. I also have to collect some money from a company that used to transport money until they were attacked and had a guy killed.

"Do you inform the police of your movements?" the manager asks me.

"Ever wonder why they knew where to attack you?" I reply, and no more is said on the matter.

This task of moving money around goes on for two weeks before I return to my own project.

My country manager calls me into his office when I arrive. It seems Aussie and an American officer on my project on the airfield camp have had a massive falling out, so I'm told to go down there immediately to sort it out, and yet again in a one vehicle move in an attempt to keep everything low profile. This doesn't seem to be looking too good for me. As I'm the project manager the buck will stop with me, even though I'm the new kid on the block and have only been here for six weeks. I head down there with Jon, a former British paratrooper, with the aim of showing him what's involved, as he's going to cover me when I go on leave.

I arrive at the airfield camp and head to my point of contact where I'm escorted to a room and told to wait. Eventually, a home guard major appears with two other high ranking officers, and a gentleman I'm introduced to as an auditor. It appears I've walked into an ambush. There's a silence in the room and I can see people have pens and notepads, but no one is talking.

"Okay, who would like to start?" I ask.

The calm evaporates in front of my eyes, and a pit bull is unleashed as the major goes into a rant without stopping to catch his breath. What the hell did Aussie say to him to have him so riled up like this? The major demands to know my credentials to run security, stating he has never seen my guards doing any training and wants to know when that is going to happen. I pause as all eyes are on me. Clearly, this major is pissed off and wants revenge by attacking me and the company I work for. It appears my email to the colonel had him on the next flight down here and tearing into the major on the points I raised about the way my Afghan guards were being treated.

"Sir, let me tackle the points you raised one by one," I begin. "As for my credentials, I am a Royal Marines Commando. The Royal Marines have been established since 1664 and are a full time military service. I believe you will find them on the internet, probably under the title of 'elite' as regarded by many in the world, though those of us that are serving or have served tend to use the word 'professional'. So I need not say any more on that subject. I'd like to remind you, though, of the colonel's opening remarks, in that the best camp security he has seen has been run by the Brits, of which I am one."

The major says nothing, and so I continue. "I'm aware the colonel came down here and ripped a few heads, and I have to say I make no apologies. I tried to go through the right channels but my recommendations were being ignored, therefore compromising safety. At the end of the day I've been tasked with the security of this airfield camp, which means I have a duty of care to the military personnel here, and to their families, which I take every measure to implement. If this means I had to go direct to the colonel to have action taken, so be it. Now I can see these recommendations are being acted on, which can only improve the safety for those serving on the airfield camp. As for the training of my Afghan guards, I share your concern that training has not been conducted, and I have to say I'm bitterly disappointed that you haven't conducted it as required by the contract."

The major is taken aback by my statement and looks at me in disbelief. "You expect me to train your guards?" he shouts.

"Yes, Sir; as required by the contract drawn up by the US Army. Here's the thing. What the US Army did was to take the ex-pat out of the contract, so you guys don't actually pay my wages; another project does. The US Army did that to save money and wrote into the contract that you would conduct the training," I tell him.

I turn to the auditor and say, "Sir, correct me if I'm wrong, but I think you'll find that on page five, paragraph three."

There's a pause as the auditor reads up on it, and all eyes are on him. His head rises and he says, "He's right. The contract states that we will conduct the training."

"So let me finish off by presenting the documents," I say, handing them over. "However, there is one I'm unable to fill as I'm still waiting for the training of my guards to take place, so if you could let me know when that will be happening... Gentlemen, if there is nothing else I will go and inspect my men. I hope we can move on from this and work together as a professional team."

I stand up and the auditor and officers shake my hand. The major is silent as the others thank me for coming.

As I enter my guards' location I'm greeted with smiles and tea, and a chair is brought to me. They are keen to tell me about the improvements since my last visit: more showers, more toilets, and their accommodation now has air conditioning. There are plans to put air conditioning in the watch towers, too. I can sense they are pleased as I'm the first person who has managed to get improvements in over a year.

Later, I receive a call telling me to speak to the International Manager who wants to know what was said at the meeting, and the outcome.

"Andy," he says, "your approach may have been too abrupt. I should remind you they're our clients, even if they are the US Army. I'll speak to you in three days' time."

The following day I fly out to my outpost camp to check on things, and one of the guards sees me, smiles, and runs off to get the guard commander. Before I even have a chance to sit and have tea, I'm rushed off to see their new cook house that has been built by the Americans, and I can see how pleased they are.

As I approach the operations room I can see a lot of building work has taken place.

"Hello sir," the young camp commander greets me.

"What's going on here?" I ask him.

"I've had this idea ... building an inner defensive wall within the camp," he tells me.

"Very good idea," I reply with a smile.

In the early hours of the morning I go and check with my guards to see if they're awake in the watch towers, and as I cross the compound in the dark to approach the entrance area, the only American doing a security watch cocks his weapon and shouts, "Who goes there?"

I'm not impressed having a weapon cocked at me and I shout back,

"I'm the British guy running your security. I think you'll find the enemy outside the camp, so turn your weapon away."

My guards are manning a gate three hundred metres out of the camp. I don't like the idea of venturing out there but feel I have to show the men I'm also prepared to go out there at night. I stay with them for two hours drinking tea, but there is no chat as they don't speak English.

The following morning I fly back out to the airfield camp with Jon. For the past two days it's been playing on my mind that the International Manager is likely to sack me after the meeting I had previously. I'll be gutted to lose my job so soon as I need the money, and will have to somehow explain to Alison what's happened, but at the end of the day I know what I did was right and I'm at peace with that. The dreaded phone call arrives from the International Manager and I take a deep breath.

"Andy, that firm stance you took with the Americans seems to have gone down very well," he says. "You're right; perhaps rather than cave in to these guys we should be more firm with them and dictate. They've awarded us another contract to look after another American camp. Well done; keep up the good work."

It's a relief to feel I still have a job. I know I'll sleep better tonight.

Jon and I set off to return to Kabul only to find our vehicle is playing up, and each time his foot comes off the accelerator the engine cuts out. As we drive through a known Taliban village, Sarobi, we take a bend, and Jon eases off on the accelerator only for the engine to cut out just as three armed Taliban cross the road in front of us. It's with a huge relief when he pushes down on the accelerator the engine fires up again and we drive past the threat.

After three months it's a welcome break to return home for a month's leave. It seems strange to be back and I try to take in that I really have been working in Afghanistan. The month at home flies by and soon I am back on the ground in Kabul.

The deputy country manager calls me into his office and tells me to go with an Afghan they are employing to check out some weapons. The company is considering buying them but they want to know if they're serviceable. Due to the corruption that is so rife within the government, it's easier to purchase them on the black market then get the weapons registered. The cost of the AK-47s has increased; having first started at around a hundred dollars they now sell for five times that amount.

The Afghan has his own car and soon he's driving me down the back streets of Kabul in the dark, and through streets that have no lighting. We arrive at a compound and after a brief conversation between my driver and the Afghan security guard, the gate is opened and we drive in. I can see around a dozen men sitting inside and looking in our direction; there are no smiles just cold stares. We're ushered into a room where the one in charge talks to my driver but I have no idea what is being said. I position myself with my back to the wall while a group of men with beards and steely eyes stare at me. I feel it's a game of bluff, especially on my part as I try to look calm and confident, not that my height and slim build would intimidate anyone.

Weapons are brought out and I start to strip them down one at a time, checking them over. It crosses my mind that these guys could well be the Taliban. Like anyone else in Afghanistan, they're willing to do business for money.

They want paying now, and I have the driver tell them I have to report back first, and then the money will be arranged for payment. The driver goes on to say that I will be taking the serial numbers of the weapons and will expect the same weapons on the exchange.

I'm only too happy to extract myself from that location and leave the running shadows behind as our vehicle drives away. My driver tells me I made him nervous by not paying the money as these guys are very bad men, which is what I'd picked up. There's no doubt about it… there was a moment in there when my heart was beating faster. The Royal Marines taught me to have the posture of a confident person, and the art of bullshitting, but I could never imagine back then how useful it would be in this crazy, mixed up country I now find myself in.

That evening, Ronnie Dunnett - a friend and also a Royal Marine - invites me over to the house he is renting, and he has a few guests there from a charity. The young lady from the charity mentions how funny the American soldiers are.

"In what way" I ask.

"The other day we were in a taxi and came up behind this American convoy, and all the soldiers started shining torches at us," she says.

"Torches?" I reply, slightly confused by her comment.

"Yes, we had all these red and green dots all over our bodies," she replies with a smile.

"Those red and green dots weren't torch lights," I tell her. "Each dot was a weapon pointing towards you from a leaser sight. Don't let your taxi driver drive so close." There's a look of absolute horror on her face.

The following day the country manager calls me into his office and informs me there is a new project starting up, and they're giving me first offer on it. I would need to go to Northern Afghanistan to Mazar-e Sharif, recruit three Afghan guards, and run them as a PSD (Personal Security Detail) team, looking after an American client. A sister project is already in place up there who could assist me in recruiting the three guards I need. This new project would also pay me more. It doesn't take me long to process that I will only be looking after one client and three guards, as opposed to three hundred and twenty-five guards.

"I'll take it," I tell him.

"Okay, you're off tomorrow," he says.

And so another adventure begins.

INTELLIGENCE

I depart Kabul for this new adventure with kites flying high over the city. I have to take two vehicles, one of which is a four-by-four armoured vehicle with bullet proof glass and steel plates covering it, which makes it heavy. As the company is short on drivers I'm driving it myself, and following another. It's an eight hour trip that is testing at times, especially driving though some of the towns, as all those that use the road operate on a jungle rule basis and I have vehicles, camels, donkeys, and people coming at me from all directions.

My guards decide to stop for lunch but I opt to not eat and stay in the car, as the last thing I need is to end up glued to the toilet when we still have a long journey ahead of us. I feel very uneasy as it's clear for all to see I'm a foreigner. I have yet to grasp this new environment I'm in, operating outside a safe military camp, and my eyes keep rotating three-sixty around me. Finally the guards reappear and we set off again.

Further down the road we come across a bridge and my guard in the other vehicle pulls over; it appears he needs to pee. One of the Afghan guards who speaks English tells me the Russians helped them build this bridge.

"How?" I ask.

"Look over the side," he tells me.

I peer over and can't believe what I'm looking at. Russian military armoured vehicles are stacked on top of each other, spanning the gap, and concrete has been poured over the top to create the road. The guard walks off laughing. I've just witnessed Afghan humour and have to admit it was funny.

As the road winds its way to the top of the mountain the air gets colder, and the first sign of snow appears. There are no safety barriers, and steep drops to oblivion should we go over the side. We press on and I can feel the vehicle is sliding a bit as it tries to find grip, which is a bit concerning.

We arrive at the Salang Pass, which connects northern Afghanistan with the Parwan Province, and enter the tunnel, and it feels like rush hour with headlights trying to penetrate the dust. The road has gone; it's just endless potholes with vehicles struggling to pass each other as the exhaust fumes choke the air. At last daylight appears and I'm relieved, but what goes up must come down. I find myself on snow and descending a steep hill that has constant tight turns, and at times when I apply the brakes the vehicle continues to slide, which has my heart in my mouth. I eye up my door handle and ensure the door is unlocked: if the vehicle decides to continue to slide over this huge drop I may have to jump. It's with some relief when the road flattens out as my nerves have been tested more than I'd like.

I finally arrive in Mazar-e Sharif, which is to be my new home, and as I sign into the guest house I'm thankful the journey is over. It's nice to see they cook western food here, though I worry about the eighty-year-old man being their only security.

I think about my new role in having to drive around, sometimes in remote areas, and realise I am out on a limb and can expect no help. I reach the conclusion that what will be, will be, as that will be my kismet, so why worry about something I can't change? This enables me to focus on the job in hand.

Over the next three days I conduct interviews but have to call a halt. I'm frustrated as I'm being presented with family members who, to be honest, will be of no use to me; just not the right calibre to fill the role of armed security. I speak to the Afghan manager who works at one of our sister projects.

"Only send me individuals who can speak English, as if we get into a fire fight I need to be able to instruct them. Also, I want to know that you're telling me the next person through my door is as good as you."

This seems to do the trick and I'm able to recruit three guys: Abdul, Farhad and Ghafor. I sit them down and tell them our job is not about taking risks but avoiding them, and that I have a duty to their families to look after them, just as they have a duty to help me safeguard the client. I'm surprised to find out the client is already on site so I have no time to train the guys; we're straight into the job of escorting him around.

My client is an American construction engineer, and his job is to build accommodation for the Afghan Army. Our home is a small compound on an Afghan training camp called Camp Shaheen, based on the outskirts of Mazar-e Sharif. Alongside our camp is another - Camp Spann - which is a small American detachment. My accommodation is a converted shipping container and is en suite; it's basic but has air conditioning and is clean and tidy. The good news is that I have the internet in my room.

I download a manual of how to run a PSD team, and after reading it I start to put together a training program for my guards. When the client doesn't need me I carry out training and make it fun, giving out prizes for the best person at a particular task. I practice vehicle movements and teach them how to extract the client if his vehicle becomes inoperative, and also conduct fire and manoeuvre training – tactics used to cover foot movement in the presence of the enemy.

Before long the project is set up, the dust is settling, and things are falling into place. The guys come into work and move onto their first tasks which, as project manager, I've set for them. I choose Abdul as my deputy manager, who ensures these tasks are completed.

I could choose to take things easy when there are no road missions - put my feet up and watch TV, and drink tea all day. However, I'm all too aware there are choices in this job and the ones I choose will have an effect on how I cope with things mentally while working in Afghanistan. Over a period of time taking things easy can lead to mental boredom, and before I'd know it each day would become painful and bring with it the potential of becoming complacent, which could cost us our lives. I reflect that some people just can't cope mentally and will quit the job as they start to go stir crazy. There is nowhere to go; there is no night life; people work then hide themselves in their rooms. The next day the cycle starts again. So, I tell myself I must keep busy and keep looking for things to do.

I'm all too aware of the risks I face on a daily basis and that bad luck, as well as bad judgement, can play a big part in one's fate. As much as I wanted to, I was unable to emphasise to my family how much I loved them before I left for Afghanistan; the last thing I wanted was to highlight the risks and give them more reason to worry. I decide to write letters instead, in the hope that if something does go wrong my laptop will be returned to them, and they'll hopefully come across them in due time. It's not ideal, but it's all I can do.

Photographs of my family are pinned up above my desk, which bring me comfort at the end of each day when my work is done. I look at them for a moment before my fingers hit the keyboard; however, I hadn't taken into consideration the emotions I would feel in writing what are, in essence, goodbye letters. As I type to each member of my family I'm hit hard with the thought that I won't ever see them again, and I'm filled with an overwhelming sadness. At times I'm choked and have to walk away from the keyboard for a while before I resume typing again. It's a long and emotional process, fighting to find the right words to express to my wife and sons how much they mean to me and how proud I am of all of them, but once I've finished I'm left with a sense of peace knowing that, hopefully, the letters will bring them some comfort should the worst happen.

Work soon kicks back in and it's time to focus on the job in hand and evaluate my movements, as I need to transport the client. More military serviceman have been killed at a police check point and I tell myself to cock and load when approaching one, and to study the surroundings along with the body language of everyone around me. My Afghan team are full of smiles and at times, on the outside, I am too, but there's never a second that passes when I allow myself to get complacent. The letters stored safely on my laptop are enough of a reminder to me of the seriousness of the situation I'm in.

I spend some time networking and come across another Brit who is running IED courses for the Afghan National Army. The threat of IEDs has increased in the Balkh province, which is where Mazar-e Sharif is located, and also throughout the country, which has resulted in a lot of coalition forces being killed and maimed. On one of the roads I use regularly I can see the crater from an IED and I remind myself to constantly change our routes so no predictable patterns are visible. Tactics change all the time and it pays to try and stay on top of what the Taliban are implementing. As soon as the coalition forces design a method to defeat the IED, the insurgents will come up with a counter measure to our counter. The game of chess continues as each party tries to out-manoeuvre the other. There will be no hand shake at the end but broken hearts and tears, and somewhere in the world news will be delivered of a passing loved one.

I seize on the opportunity and organise a day's IED course, not only for my team but for three other security teams, teaching them about the latest methods used by the Taliban. They receive a presentation on tactics, the equipment used to make IEDs, and then a practical display that shows how they are deployed in the field. I also manage to organise a first aid course with the American Special Forces, as no one else will be around to treat us.

My next task is to put a map on my wall of the Mazar-e Sharif area and, using small red pins, highlight where incidents have taken place. The idea is that over a period of time I'll be able to see the bigger picture and where the hotspots areas are, which will help to determine where the Taliban are located.

I approach the Americans to see if I can get some access to their intelligence to improve the safety of my client's movements by being aware of what is happening around my location. I explain I'm a former Royal Marine and in my role of security I can access areas they can't, so I'll be able to gather information for them. I also inform them I was here during the Russian campaign with the Mujahideen. Before I leave I tell them I'm surprised they haven't cleared out Chahabolak village, just outside Mazar-e Sharif, which is a pro-Taliban village. The longer they leave it, the more confident the Taliban there will become, and sooner or later they'll launch an attack as the village is close to a major road.

Two days later I receive a call from the American captain.

"Andy… about that conversation we had the other day. We've just been attacked outside Chahabolak, as you said would happen."

So, it seems the Americans have just become interested in what I'm saying, and I'm invited back over. I propose we try and get all the security companies operating in Mazar-e Sharif to work together with us and share the Intel.

I drive over to Camp Marmal, an airfield which is run by the Germans, but which also has Americans on site. The airfield has high security and the first gate is manned by Afghans who, upon seeing me, just wave me through. Next, I have to stop while the vehicle is x-rayed, and on passing this I move to the next point. Dressed in my pawkul hat, a scarf, and with my long, unkempt beard, I wait for them to make the move. As the German guard starts to approach me I pull out a laminated picture of the British Union Jack and throw it on the dashboard, my expression serious. The German guard hesitates, takes a step back and talks to his colleague, and they wave me through without checking me. Sweet! They think I'm Special Forces. I drive past and only now give them a smile. It's all about looking confident.

I speak with someone from the German intelligence section and ask him if he's seen any unusual movements in the area.

"Like what?" he says.

"I was here during the Russian campaign," I tell him, "and the Mujahideen wouldn't move on this open ground. However, see that mountain range behind you? That's where they'd operate, so it's safe to say the Taliban would do the same."

He has a surprised look on his face. "We have an observation post on top of the mountain and last week they spotted twenty gunmen walking through the gorge."

I can't help but think it's crazy that the Germans can't engage unless they have been engaged upon. I pass on some details the Americans gave me - nothing confidential, but it might help to build a bigger picture - and we exchange our contact details.

My next port of call is the Swedish, and I chat with their intelligence section. I mention what the Germans told me and discover they had no knowledge of it, but they seem pleased to receive this information. I explain that what I'm trying to do is share intelligence to improve the safety for all of us. The Swedish pass on some information to me which they have gathered.

Information starts to flow - illegal checkpoints, various foreign nationals killed in an ambush, abductions, a police checkpoint killing two Swedish military soldiers all carried out by the Taliban – and it brings home to me the environment I'm in and why I have to remain on my guard and be alert.

Things are coming together. My network is growing but the long hours - up to twenty a day - start to take their toll. It's a welcome break when my three months is up and I have a month's leave, and once I'm home the exhaustion hits me. I try to switch off from being on high alert and for the first few days all I want to do is sleep.

It feels strange being back in a friendly environment and meeting friends who are living a normal life. Some complain about how hard life is treating them and I can sense I've changed by the way I think about their comments. Walking through the High Street, my head instantly engages, wanting to know who or what is around me. My eyes look at shop windows - not to see the products on display but to see the reflections of those walking behind me. When I stop, my back wants to position itself against the wall. I can sense I'm on alert and have to remind myself I'm in England so I can unwind. Life back home becomes busy to try and maximise family time together before I return. The month flies by and before I know it I have a feeling of loneliness as I board my flight in the knowledge that I won't be returning home for another three months, if at all.

By the time I clear customs in Dubai and arrive at my hotel it's two in the morning, and the double bed beckons me. This will be the first time I'll actually get to use it. I switch on my phone to set the alarm when it suddenly pings, indicating a text. The message is simple: *Urgent. Check your email.* I connect to the internet and in disbelief learn I have to catch a 6:00 a.m. flight and check-in is at 4:00 a.m. I curse and moan to myself that someone has a nasty sense of humour as I dash off to the airport.

Back in Kabul, the famous kites are still flying over the city, keeping the kids occupied as the dust continues to blow, and they dance across the sky as if to enjoy their freedom, as when the Taliban were here kite flying was banned. The city is noisy as people go about their daily routines in trying to survive from one day to the next. There's no sparkle in their eyes; they seem to be hollow. Certainly, with all the corruption, some Afghans are becoming prosperous and this is reflected in the new luxury houses being built, but the majority are struggling.

In the main office I'm briefed that Kam Air has changed the days they fly on. I'm told I will now be doing an eight hour road move to Mazar-e Sharif the following morning, departing at 5:00 a.m. and using one vehicle. Alarm bells sound in my head but I go for a cup of tea and reflect on this proposed move. Do the people in the operations room ever actually digest the security intelligence reports they receive and use common sense, I wonder.

I brief my driver and one shooter, and ensure an ex Ghurkha, Kamal and I are issued with weapons and that the entire team have more ammunition magazines. I report back to the office and inform them I'll be departing at 08:00 hrs, and not the time they have set. When questioned as to why, I point out that Anti Government Elements tend to do illegal checkpoints around sunrise, and they also plant their IEDs during the night. Therefore it makes sense to travel when more traffic is on the road so there is less likelihood of stumbling into one of these illegal checkpoints. Also, more vehicles travelling before me will help to ensure there are no IEDs or mines on the road as they would have been detonated by another vehicle before I arrive. Three Filipinos travelling on the same road ran into an illegal checkpoint and the Afghan driver tried to accelerate through it. The Taliban opened up, killing them all. Death comes cheap over here and no one blinks at the news.

I read out the movement orders before we hit the road so each person knows what to expect and what their role is. The journey is going well and we pass the police checkpoints without any problems. I tell Kamal that as much as the scenery is beautiful, it's wrong for the Kabul office to send us on a single vehicle move just because we're not escorting a client.

The road eventually starts to wind up the Hindu Kush Mountains to the Salang Pass, and it occurs to me it won't be long before this road will not be passable due to the winter snows. Built in 1964 by the Soviet Union, these mountain roads have seen their fair share of death over the years, from bitter fighting with the Russians to driving accidents. On 3 November 1982, during the Soviet occupation of Afghanistan, there was a huge fire in the tunnel which at the time was filled with Soviet military convoys, and a large number of the troops were killed. Last winter, an avalanche swept three civilian vehicles over the edge, killing a family of ten.

We reach the peak at 12,723 feet and start to descend the other side. I tell Kamal that once we are down at the bottom the landscape flattens off and we'll be able to make good time. There's no need to stop for lunch because it's Ramadan. As we descend I suddenly notice the vehicle has started to coast as the engine has stopped. My senses increase.

My worst fears have just materialised: we've broken down. This is exactly why we shouldn't be moving with one vehicle, I tell Kamal. The driver turns over the engine but it refuses to start. We spot a steel container fifty metres down the road and coast down to it, and stood next to it is a boy of about fifteen. Our driver climbs out of the vehicle with our shooter and opens the bonnet, and they stare at the engine before shaking some wires. For some strange reason they think this will change everything. They proceed to turn the engine over and I will it to start but it's just not playing. It dawns on me that that the driver has as much mechanical knowledge as the Guest brothers and my heart sinks. My brain moves into overdrive: no signal on mobile, Sat phone not picking up any satellites. Shit. I'm not impressed.

This is the wrong place for us to step out of the vehicle as we'll stand out as foreigners or, perhaps, as dollars to be sold to the Taliban. I tell Kamal to keep watching his side for anything unusual; meanwhile I watch the driver and shooter, as well as my own side. The thought crosses my mind that we may have been sold out by our own guys, so I watch them closely.

Seeing an opportunity to offer himself as a mechanic, the boy approaches us and points out we have a broken rear brake pipe. He promptly cuts it and seals it as he's unable to repair it, and they then try to start the engine. I'm even more convinced we have a major problem and start to think of our options as we're starting to attract attention. I observe five men, all with long beards, talking amongst themselves, and tell myself that not everyone with facial hair is Taliban, but I study them closely and wonder if I'm about to see a weapon being produced.

To my surprise they seem to be ignoring us, but I start to think they are just trying to be cunning and are waiting for support. It's an anxious time. I turn my head to look to the front to see what my two guys are up to and I see the boy has removed our fuel filter and is blowing into it. Oh, for goodness sake, this is not the time for a child to be playing at being a mechanic. He reattaches the fuel filter and our driver climbs back into the car and turns the key. I've already accepted that we're doomed when suddenly the engine roars into life. Damn it, I knew I liked the kid; I could tell there was something special about him. He asks for two dollars as payment and I'm only too happy to give him fifty. Kamal and I breathe a sigh of relief as we continue our journey, and nine hours later it's over. I'm greeted by my guards as a long lost friend.

Another day draws to a close and as I'm chilling out with a tea a pain develops in my stomach that eventually has me strolling up and down my fourteen by eight feet room, from my bathroom to my bed and back again, in a repetitive cycle. The pain is so immense that it eventually leads to me being sick, but the pain doesn't go away. Most of the night is spent pacing back and forth, but it eventually eases off a bit which allows me to grab a couple of hours' sleep. Over the next three days just the thought of food or liquid makes me feel queasy so I avoid it, but I know not having liquid in this hot climate is a big concern and will lead to complications, so I take a trip over to Camp Spann, which is a short walk from my compound. As I approach their main gate I greet the sentries with my best English accent, have a bit of idle chat with them, and they wave me through without checking for ID. I enter the sick bay, explain my problem, and they put me on an IV drip which also has something in it to relieve the sickness. As I head back later it's a relief to know I'm hydrated, and that night I go to sleep with the peace of mind that the medication will sort me out. In the morning there's a knock on my door, and as I open it I see it's Abdul, one of my security team.

"Mr Andy, you have turned yellow," he says in alarm. It's only then I realise my problem has got much worse. I quickly brief my security and head back to the sick bay, and they suggest I go to Camp Marmal and see the doctors at the German hospital, which I do. After an examination they tell me I have gall stones and I'm admitted into their hospital where, from my bed, I inform my company and my security team of my whereabouts.

The German nurse attempts to attach an IV to me but has a problem inserting the needle into my vein, and she gives up on her fifth attempt and scurries off to fetch the senior nurse, who takes over. She succeeds on her first attempt, and there is nothing I can do but just lie there as there is nothing to read and no TV to watch. I eventually drift off and achieve a good night's sleep. In the morning I wake up and notice the IV needle has come loose and the fluid that was meant for me is in a puddle on the floor. Eventually, the nurse arrives and we have to go through the 'stab him with the needle' game again. She's getting good and cracks it on her fourth attempt.

When I'm still in hospital on day three I give my company a call and they ask me what's happening.

"You're asking me what's happening?" I say. "I'm expecting you to do something about it."

They tell me they're going to send me a driver and organise a flight back to the UK for me whereupon I will have to sort out my own surgery, and when the driver arrives he informs me his instructions are to take me to Kabul. I can't believe the company wouldn't cough up fifty dollars to pay for a flight for me. It's a short trip back to my accommodation to pick up my weapon and ammo, and it's a one vehicle move with just me and the driver for an eight hour road trip that takes us over the top of the Hindu Kush mountains. It's an uncomfortable journey as every bump on the track causes me pain. If we're attacked it's not going to be much of a fight as I'm feeling extremely sorry for myself.

The sun slowly goes down; there is only darkness and shadows as we drive past small villages on the ever twisting road. We finally reach Kabul in the early hours of the morning and a few hours later I'm on a flight to Dubai where I catch my connecting flight back to the UK. I'm so pleased to be back.

Once home, time is of the essence if I want to keep my job, so I have little choice but to book into a private hospital to have an operation to remove my gall bladder by keyhole surgery. A woman I meet tells me she has had gallstones, and she equates the level of pain to that of giving birth, so it appears I can now relate to that experience. (My editor, a woman who has given birth, asked me to state here how much other women would admire me for making that previous statement.)

A few days later I'm on a flight heading back to Afghanistan after a two week turnaround time. The insurance policy the company has to have in place for its personnel doesn't cover me for the surgery, so I have to pay my own medical bills. The policy only seems to cover me if I'm blown up or shot. Well, that's good to know. I return to Mazar-e Sharif where my security team greet me with big smiles, and the client tells me it's good to have me back as the security ex-pat who covered me didn't go out of his way to interact with him or my team. As I return to work, still a little sore, I hope my stitches don't get infected, but it's nice to know that unbearable pain will not be returning.

There is no social life on Camp Shaheen so it's an ideal time for me to get back into running, utilising the 4.8km perimeter around the camp. I find myself huffing and puffing, with my breathing out of sequence, and it's clear I've been in self-denial about how unfit I've become. Over a period of time, though, my breathing becomes less laboured and I start to feel I'm in rhythm again.

One day, my client requests for my guards to not follow him around on camp. I tell him this isn't acceptable as I have a duty of care, and mention that I've noticed the Afghan officers have taken to carrying side arms.

"Why?" he asks.

"I'm not sure," I tell him, "but what I do know is that they've recently taken over one hundred recruits from Helmand. I'm asking myself what the chances are of sleeping cells." He looks confused. "Basically, they're a group of people assigned to live undercover until activated to perform acts of terrorism. So, as this is an Afghan camp and not an American camp, my guards will escort you." Steve doesn't look too happy but accepts my judgement, and we retire to our rooms.

The next morning I'm driving around the camp with one of my guards when we arrive at a scene, and my gut feeling tells me something is very wrong. People are gathered outside their accommodation and all looking in one direction, but there doesn't seem to be anything to look at. Suddenly, I spot some figures towards one of the observation towers, and then notice two or three people sprinting over there. I task my Afghan driver to talk to one of the men running back and to find out what's going on.

"Four Americans were doing some physical training around the perimeter fence, and as the they approached one of the observation towers the Afghan National Army guard shot and killed two of them:- one woman, Lt. Florence B. Choe who was in the medical profession, and one man, Lt. Francis L. Toner, who was an engineer. A second woman has also been shot in the arm. The fourth escaped by hiding behind one of the disused tanks."

I tell him to start driving as we're going to collect the client, go into shut down, and secure our compound on the camp. I catch up with our client and tell him to board the vehicle, and as we drive him away I brief him on the fatal shootings. He's shocked at what I've told him. Once we're back, I deploy my guards with their weapons and secure the compound. I make Steve a coffee and myself a tea, and Steve looks at me.

"Andy," he tells me, "whatever you say I won't question from now on."

It's a sad day today. Families are going to get some heart breaking news, but this is the reality of the environment we work in here. But for most people back home, this will have no impact at all.

We sit and chat and he tells me he was once a real cowboy; he's been stabbed twice and shot once. He's a nice guy who loves weapons, and he tells me he's stock-piling ammunition back at home in case of changes back in the states.

A month later, Steve informs me he has quit the company. This is a real shame. As clients go, Steve has been great and we've been getting on well, but his wife is ill and, quite correctly, his priorities have changed. He plans to route back through London for an overnight stay to give him a chance to visit Portsmouth and see HMS Victory. I ensure he has all the information he needs to make this happen.

Mazar-e Sharif continues to improve and I'm impressed by how much new road now has tarmac. Looking out of the vehicle I see many new trees have been planted. I'm told when the Russians were here they cut down all the trees for heating, as well as to take cover away from the enemy. But, improvements aside, from the intelligence I've gathered I can see the situation in Afghanistan is continuing to get worse as governments are at a loss as to how to approach the problems. Excuses are made and propaganda is pushed out, and they take advice from so called experts who have no real understanding of the grass-roots culture of this nation. This country is not governed by a central government but by regional tribal leaders who have been used to having power and earn a reasonable living out of it. As they have seen their powers being taken away, resentment has crept in. Some of those that were fighting against the Taliban are now fighting with the Taliban to demonstrate their resentment against the government and those that support it.

Through working here and seeing things first hand, I've formed an opinion that the Afghan government is corrupt, and everything seems to be based around how much they can milk the western nations for. There is a considerable amount of money going missing. It's been suggested that

President Karzai's brother continues to run the poppy fields. I'm told by other security personnel who have worked on projects trying to eradicate the poppies that they'd visited one of the president's brother's houses, and the basement was full of opium but they were not allowed to touch it.

I don't claim to be a political expert – far from it – but I do know that Kunduz is getting worse as the Taliban push more personnel up there, and they're doing it for two reasons. One: the Americans have opened up another supply route from Uzbekistan, and two: they're aware of the German's stance of not getting involved. This makes easy pickings and gives them the opportunity of positive publicity on their achievements. The Taliban are winning the media war as well; every mistake the international forces make receives a blaze of publicity, but when Taliban IEDs kill innocent children and women it doesn't make the news. This in turn encourages more people to join the Taliban. I despair at the lack of knowledge of those in authority and their inability to understand what needs to be done. I know from speaking to Afghans that they think western countries do nothing for them. The west, in trying to make it look like the Afghanistan government are standing on their own two feet, encourage the impression that the Afghanistan government is paying for everything. This has created the feeling amongst the Afghans that the western countries have done nothing to help them. Talk about shooting yourself in the foot. On the other side of me, Faryab is also getting worse as incidents of fire fights and IED use increases, and in between these two locations we have Mazar-e Sharif, where I'm located.

I attend a meeting with the American operations room and they inform me that an elder has come across thirty-two rockets and two RPGs lying on the ground on the edge of the city, obviously waiting to be collected. This is the second incident I know of in six months where rockets have been transported into Mazar-e Sharif. Yesterday, in the market in the heart of the city, gunmen tried to abduct an individual but the crowd turned on them and the gunmen beat a hasty retreat.

There is no doubt about the amount of fraudulent activity that has taken place during the elections, and all this does is to help change the climate for the worse. What is needed is a fundamental change in the approach to Afghanistan by the governments, and fully understanding the importance of involving the tribal elders from the different provinces. They are the key as they control their provinces and their followers.

I reflect on the politics as it helps to pass the time but I just find myself getting angry that Tony Blair entered us into this war when the UK-Afghan expert, when asked, advised us not to enter an unwinnable war. The British military death toll mounts up, as does the amount of British serviceman maimed when deployed to serve here. All these heartaches Blair has caused, and for what? Nothing has been achieved; it *is* an unwinnable war as the Russians found out.

I realise that dwelling on this isn't helping me as I can't change anything; it's just making me angry. So I change my thoughts.

I'm thankful that pirate DVDs are cheap and are available on American camps, but can't help thinking the American government pay for these shops to be set up. Back in America, those that promote a website that offers the facilities to download a film illegally are being prosecuted and it seems to me it's double standards. I have no guilt buying the pirate DVDs though, as they give me a little bit of chill out time when I'm stood down.

The internet is my life line, allowing me to stay in contact with my family. Alison tells me my eldest son, Westleigh, is getting stressed with his University exams, so I contact him and ask why he is pouring out his problems to his mum and not to me. He tells me he doesn't want me to get distracted in the environment I'm working in, which is so thoughtful of him, but I understand his fears. When I'm back skyping with Alison, tiredness overcomes me and I fall asleep, and when I finally open my eyes I see the words: *are you there?* on the laptop screen, repeated about twenty times. I apologise to Alison and explain what happened. "Well that's very nice," she tells me.

I'm cooking not only for myself but also for my client, and experimenting with the food. I have become his body guard, chef, and entertainment provider, occasionally taking him to the firing range to shoot the weapons. I also exchange a few messages with Ken who is working on another project in a different province, and we chat about the threats that we're both facing.

My guards are given a day off but when we're stood down at work I socialise with them, drinking tea and learning more about life in Afghanistan. They have warmed to me and open up to me, which is nice. They've seen I won't put them at risk. Once, after spotting cables poorly buried on the road, I stopped the vehicle. I informed them of my concerns and told them to remain in the vehicle as I ventured forward on foot to investigate whether it led to an IED. Ghafor told me, "Mr Andy, the Afghans respect you." I asked him why. "You give respect and in return they respect you back." He made me smile. "Let's have a tea, Ghafor" I told him.

Time passes and I now have the Norwegians sharing intelligence with me, so I'm coordinating intelligence with four countries. I've managed to set up meetings on Camp Spann with different security companies, as information is shared between us. One morning I receive a call from a security company who inform me they have just passed an IED next to a road. I call the Americans to warn them off and give them the location in case one of their patrols drives past. My situation suddenly changes, and rather than bluffing my way on to Camp Marmal, the Americans issue me with an ISAF (International Security Armed Forces) ID, along with one for my colleague who is working on a similar project to me, that will allow us easy access on to the airfield camp.

The following day I'm asked to attend a meeting on Camp Marmal, and my colleague assumes they're going to take back the ISAF IDs as, strictly speaking, we're not supposed to have them. We head to the camp where we meet an American major who thanks us for coming and introduces us to a German colonel who is in charge of RC North (northern Afghanistan).

"Let's go for a coffee," the colonel says.

As we follow him, my curiosity grows. At the meeting the colonel explains that he's aware I'm sharing Intel.

"Sir, nothing that is classified as secret is being shared," I tell him.

"No," he says. "I just wanted to ask if you could add me to your list, if you don't mind."

"Of course I don't mind, Sir. The whole idea was to improve the safety for all of us who venture out onto the roads." On that note we finish our drinks and part ways.

When I'm back in my room with a tea in hand - the only thing that seems normal in this country - I can't help but think the whole situation is crazy. Here I am… a civilian helping to coordinate Intelligence for four countries because they don't trust each other, but they will share Intel with me. At times I'm accessing classified areas with an escort and viewing things their own men are not permitted to see, and when requesting Intel I'm given files that clearly state 'classified eyes only'. On walking out of an Intelligence room a few days ago I overheard an American say to another serviceman: "You can tell the Special Forces guys; they all have beards." I do wonder if, because of my long beard and having been seen with one of the senior officers on several occasions, that everyone in the intelligence room has now just assumed I'm Special Forces, hence giving me these classified files without question.

My incident map now clearly shows the hotspot areas that surround me, and there have been so many incidents. My new client, Skip, appears to be an alcoholic who likes his whisky and every three days he wants more.

"Andy, can you get me another bottle? And not the Chinese one cos it's shit."

Alcohol in Afghanistan is banned, though the reality is Afghans, given the opportunity, will drink it. It's available but only on the black market. A bottle of whisky sells for one hundred and twenty dollars.

"Skip," I say, "you're setting me up with a predictable pattern, which is likely to lead me to being ambushed. Can I suggest you buy four bottles so I'm not repeating my journey to the same location so often?"

I go through my list: vehicle and weapon checks completed, guards briefed, and clients have been escorted around the construction sites. The day is ticking over smoothly but I ask myself what else can be done to keep one step ahead, and if there are any outstanding issues that need to be resolved. I decide to give myself a head start on the daily and weekly reports which will be rewarded with an evening off. I picture myself, tea in hand, and chilling out with a DVD, and need no more incentive. I get the laptop up and running and my fingers hit the keyboard, my brain putting things in a logical sequence. Suddenly, the door bursts open and two of my guards, Farhad and Abdul, run in. Nasir, a new guard who has replaced Ghafor, remains outside the client's door.

"Mr Andy! Mr Andy! We're hostages!"

My fingers freeze mid-flight as the words repeat themselves in my head.

"The labourers; they have locked the gate and will not allow anyone to leave or enter," Farhad says.

"How many?" I ask.

"More than I'd like."

I curse myself for thinking the day was going so well and I'm convinced I jinxed it, so I'm partly to blame for the change of events.

"Take my pistol and hide it behind your back," I tell Abdul. "Stay back, but keep an eye on Farhad and me." I turn to Farhad. "You come with me to translate ... we're going to speak to the labourers."

I'm only too aware that the labourers know we're armed, and my instincts tell me that to show force may inflame matters. It's a judgement call - dammed if you do and dammed if you don't. I can see the concern in my guards' eyes so I try and inject some humour.

"Abdul, if they grab me, produce the pistol and fire a shot above their heads. That should get them ducking. If they don't, I will, I know you're a crap shot." It works, and they burst into laughter.

Farhad and I head over to the labourers and we're soon spotted. A shout goes out and about a dozen more sprint over to support those on the main gate. They gather around and start yelling at me.

"Tell them I want one person to speak, and to tell me what this is all about," I say to Farhad.

It transpires that the Afghan subcontractor has not paid them, and they're about to go on EID (an Islamic religious holiday). The foreman did a runner last night after telling the men to meet him at one of the buildings to collect their pay. This is a typical stunt pulled by the Afghan company. The hope is that the labourers will travel home (some live 200km away) without their pay, and be so disgusted that they won't come back, thus saving the subcontractor money. Recruiting another workforce is not difficult as there are plenty of men looking for work.

I ask Farhad to translate what I am about to say. It goes very quiet as I speak and I can see the labourers are curious.

"The American company, who has always helped you, has paid the subcontractor for your work, and it's the subcontractor who has your money. Both the client and my boss are very angry as you guys have worked hard and deserve to be paid, especially as you are about to go on EID holiday to spend time with your families. We understand your desire to provide for your families and to make EID special. We fully support you and, because we are so angry, the Americans and I are joining your protest."

I can see their astonishment; they were not expecting this, and after a slight pause smiles appear on their faces. I spot my client, Skip, approaching us and I meet him half way to explain the situation. He is in full agreement and walks off to phone the subcontractor to read him the riot act. Moments later, my phone bursts into life - it's the chief security officer from my client's company.

"I've just heard you're being held against your will, which means you're hostages. Call out the military," he says. As he pauses to take a breath I dive in.

"Everything is under control. It isn't a threatening situation as we've joined the protest."

There's a high pitched voice ringing in my ear. "You've done what?"

I explain the situation and he calms down. I reassure him that as a precaution I had already informed the American military, who are based three hundred metres away from us, and they are monitoring the situation through me.

I return to the protesters and tell them to make space on the padlocked table they have placed in front of the gate, and I join them. There's a cold chill in the air so I instruct the protesters' spokesperson to delegate someone to make a large pot of tea; the protesters should have a hot drink and I will have one as well. Skip re-joins us, and two hours later the subcontractor foreman appears. Skip has strong words for him. The only way to get the message across is to tell him each minute this project is being held up it is coming out of his next payment as compensation.

We listen as the subcontractor informs the labourers he is going to go to the bank to fetch their money. Before he has a chance to leave the client tells the spokesperson that he and one other person should go with the foreman to ensure he comes back. Skip and I have no wish to find ourselves locked in any longer due to the foreman absconding again. Finally, six hours after this started, the foreman returns and the labourers receive their pay.

My DVD will have to wait for another day as I now have a report to write up regarding this incident.

The following morning Abdul and I head into the city to refill gas bottles; it's a one vehicle move, just the two of us. Abdul asks whether I would like to go to his house for tea as it's nearby and I take him by surprise by saying yes. When we arrive his six children, ranging in age from four to sixteen, are playing outside. A seventh child, an eighteen-year-old, is at college improving his English. I can see by the children's expressions that even with my beard I don't blend in, as the kids are wide-eyed as they look me up and down. I climb out of the vehicle and am greeted by Abdul's youngest child - his four-year-old daughter. She extends her hand and says, 'Salam Alaykum', their hello, which translates as 'Peace on you', and she's swiftly followed by the other children who do the same. I'm impressed by how well-mannered they are and feel, perhaps, that's what is lacking in some of the kids back at home who have things so much easier.

Most houses are in a compound surrounded by a high wall, and Abdul's house is no different. As we enter I'm shown to a room next to the main gate which is the guest room. The main house is located further back in the compound. The room has no furniture but has cushions laid out along three sides of the wall; there is a lovely carpet, manufactured by hand and made in Mazar-e Sharif, and the ceiling has a silk sheet stretched across it. The ambience in this room is peaceful and I feel comfortable here.

Tea and snacks are brought in by the children and the youngest daughter stays and plays with Abdul. It's clear to see there is a strong family bond, which is no different to my own family. Abdul's father joins us and I'm greeted with a hand shake. I learn that he will stay with Abdul for the duration of the winter, whereupon he will return to the hills. Abdul's wife remains in the house so there is no contact; it's not permitted.

After an enjoyable visit we leave the house and continue to complete the jobs on my list in the city. By the time we arrive back on base the day is over and I return to my room.

Being away for three months at a time can be hard. Some days are worse than others, but today has been a good day. Spending time with Abdul and his family was such a joy, and knowing the labourers have been paid, and will soon be with their families for the holiday, makes me happy. But it leaves me thinking of nothing other than Alison and my boys, three and a half thousand miles away. I console myself with the fact I'll be skyping Alison later tonight. It's become a crucial part of my day.

PREDICTABLE PATTERNS

As the months pass by, Skip moves on and another client arrives as a temporary cover, but he soon departs suffering with mental health problems. His replacement is a former American Navy Commander who takes over the construction as project manager, but he finds it difficult to understand the Afghan mentality and it's not long before signs of stress appear along with an inability to control his temper. I contact his country manager and inform him it's my duty of care to let him know that his construction manager has had a breakdown, and if he's not replaced he puts himself and my team at risk of being killed. He is replaced by Joe, and at last I have someone I get on well with who is able to deal with the difficulties we face here. I like the fact he chooses to understand the Afghan culture, and I think some of the decisions he makes are very wise.

Joe mentions he would like to see the Afghan national sport of Buzkashi, which takes place in Mazar-e Sharif throughout December and until the end of March. This is mainly due to the heat and the effect it has on the horses, so it's better to hold it through the winter months. I've attended three Buzkashis and I'm still no closer to understanding the rules; even the Afghans can't seem to explain them. The sport involves riding on horseback with the aim of carrying a dead goat along the length of the pitch, and trying to drop it into a goal.

What I do observe is that the rider who's holding the goat seems to take a whipping from other riders to try to make him drop it. Some men prefer to go to Bunny Ranch parlours and get whipped, while others seem to prefer to be whipped on a horse, and no doubt both get pleasure in what they're doing, but it looks extremely painful to me. It's obvious that some men are not there to compete but just to pose on their horses in front of the crowd as they're dressed in their best clothes, whereas the hard core players seem to be dressed as if they've just emerged from a coal mine, rough and dirty and wearing a thick type of mattress material which helps to take the sting out of the whippings. One or two even wear padded Russian tank crew helmets for head protection.

I take Joe down to watch a match. At one end of the pitch there's a small stand with tall embankments on either side. This end seems to be popular with the spectators, probably due to the safety element. The other three sides are full of parked cars with the spectators venturing forwards to get a better view. Young boys walk around trying to sell popcorn or nuts; another man tries to sell short whips. Goodness knows what they are used for.

I position my guys close to the vehicle and take a walk in front of the spectators in order to get a better view and to hopefully get some decent photographs. I find it very frustrating as the riders seem to stay in a huddle at the far end for long periods. On the odd occasion when they venture down to my end and I take a picture, someone seems to step in front of me. The clock's ticking and I'm not getting any decent shots so I walk away from the crowd and further onto the pitch, which is totally acceptable for the foolhardy. But hey, I have an excuse; I'm a photographer and sometime one has to go that extra yard.

I look around for what may make a good picture and notice a rider behind me. He's a poser but his horse is well decorated and so is he. I look through the lens and check my borders; the subject is well framed, the light is good, so I press the trigger. As I lower the camera I'm aware of a noise like rolling thunder, and as I turn around my eyes widen as I see twenty riders bearing down on me. It occurs to me I now know what it must feel like to be that lone cowboy having twenty Indians charging towards him, but at least he was able to draw his pistol. I realise all too quickly I can't outrun them regardless of the direction I choose, and my survival instinct kicks in. I stand my ground and face what is coming. Perhaps I'll have the option of jumping to one side at the last moment as I capture a glimpse of daylight between the riders. As the horses gallop past me through a cloud of dust I feel the ground vibrate under my feet, and the crowd roars, only to be disappointed that they missed me. As the danger passes it hits me with shame: I had the perfect picture in front of me and I let it get away. This is the difference between a professional photographer and an amateur. One thinks picture first, then survival; the latter thinks survival and misses the picture. I'm disappointed with myself.

I decide I need to make amends for my poor actions so I tell Farhad, who has come up beside me, that I'm walking half way up the pitch. I need to get a picture of the riders with the spectators as a backdrop.

"Mr Andy, I think this may be dangerous," he says.

"I think you're right," I tell him, "so while you're watching my back, if I should run past you, you follow me." There seems to be a difference in our sense of humour as he has a look of concern on his face.

There are other people strolling around on the pitch, and it strikes me these must be the adrenalin junkies. Sometimes the riders gallop straight towards the crowd who flee in panic, much to the amusement of the other spectators who roar in approval of the entertainment being provided. At various times the riders gallop past me but not towards me, and my camera fires off like a machine gun. The memory card captures the action that my lens sees, and to my delight I feel I'm capturing some good shots.

From the corner of my eye I see a horse has started to rear up and the rider attempts to get it under control. I spin around and in a fraction of a second the subject is framed and my finger is hovering above the button. As the horse rears up again my finger slams down. I hear the camera go through its motions and know the subject is captured.

All of a sudden the crowd start to run onto the pitch and I witness an amazing sight. What is happening all around me makes no sense: families are running onto the pitch, horse riders are galloping past the crowd and are joined by motorbikes, riders on donkeys, and even some cars. I look at Farhad and ask him for an explanation as to what is happening; he shrugs his shoulders as it is confusing him as well. In the past I've witnessed a pitch invasion at a football stadium back in England, but I've never seen a spectacle such as this before. Curiosity gets the better of me, and as everyone is heading down to the corner of the pitch we decide to follow. To my surprise there's camel fighting taking place.

As we return to the vehicles six men pass us. One glances at me, turns away, suddenly stops, and spins around. We've clocked each other. Well, well… six Taliban. My eyes search for any signs of weapons but there aren't any I can see. We seem to have a standoff as we're both aware we're on opposing sides, and all I can do is look them straight in the eyes and show no fear, though my heart rate has increased. I can see the hate in their eyes and know they want me dead, but it's not going to be today. Their leader is discussing us and is paying attention to our vehicles, so I tell my guards it's time to go and we load Joe into the vehicle. I have no idea if they've called for armed backup but I'm not hanging around to find out.

Once we're away from the scene and heading back on familiar roads, my thoughts drift back to the pictures. I can't get the fact I missed that earlier shot out of my mind and I question my thought process. Was there enough time for a snap shot and for evasive action if needed? The fact that the horses missed me without me having to take evasive action, I have my answer.

Months pass by and my leave period is all screwed up. I've now worked ten months straight, seven days a week. My beard impresses the Afghans who say I would make a good Muslim.

My guards return from escorting the client around the construction site, while I've been busy trawling through my emails, cursing the fact there seems to be a complete lack of management skills at the Kabul head office. Once again I'm being asked for documents that I've sent two or three times before. This is the fourth operations manager I've had and none of them seem to have taken the initiative in organising a workable filing system.

A text message comes through from Jason, a swing man covering someone on leave, and he informs me he's on his way with his client to attend a meeting at my camp. Being a typical Englishman I check the kettle is full and the tea bags are ready, even though Jason is American. At least I can grab a tea and Jason can have what he wants. Returning to my room, I decide to send the documents that Kabul has requested so I have nothing outstanding for the evening. My mobile rings and I walk outside for a better signal. It's Jason.

"Hi mate, how's it going?" I ask. The reply isn't what I was expecting.

"Dude, there's been a major accident. A motorbike shot out in front of us with two kids on it, and we've hit it. I think I'm looking at one dead and one injured."

"Where are you?"

He tells me his location and I can tell by the tone of his voice he's concerned. "I've just sent the client off in the other vehicle. I have one shooter with me and no means of transport, and it looks like the crowd is starting to turn ugly."

"I'm on my way," I reply.

I sprint into my guards' room and shout, "Grab your stuff fast; we're on the move, it's an emergency," and dash back. I throw my body armour over my head, and how I hate it when the metal plate smacks me on the back of it yet again. I go through a quick check - pistol in holster behind my back, AK47 magazine on, radio and GPS, scarf, hat, mobile - and I grab a bag of extra magazines in case of a fire fight before racing back to the guards' room.

"Come on guys," I shout, seeing they're still getting dressed. "Just grab your stuff and throw it in the vehicle; the other team are in trouble." The message sinks in and they get a move on.

We leave the compound and head off. I take the shortest track but it's still 10km away and the road is full of potholes. My driver slows down to try to navigate them and I look at him in amazement.

"Farhad, the other team are in trouble. Put your foot down and just hang on … this is going to be like a rodeo ride you've never experienced before." And that's exactly what we get as our heads hit the ceiling.

We approach a narrow road with shops on either side and I have no choice but to tell my driver to ease off the accelerator, just in case a child runs out. We eventually arrive on the scene, I can see a crowd of about fifty people surrounding our two guys, and after a quick evaluation I opt to drive a short distance past him to be able to swing the vehicle around the central reservation. We pull up a hundred metres behind Jason's vehicle, which is leaning over due to skidding into an irrigation ditch, and I give the orders for my three guards to deploy with their weapons. I position one guard by our vehicle, and one on the central reservation, and tell them to keep their eyes open and not to get sucked into just watching the crowd as the threat can come from elsewhere.

I tell Farhad to stay back ten feet and if the crowd grab me to fire a burst above their heads, but not at them. I repeat my instructions a second time to make sure there are no mistakes. The crowd parts as I approach, which allows me to reach Jason. Voices are raised and I spot an Afghan policeman twenty feet away and give him a look over. He has no weapon, which makes me feel better. I ask Jason for an update, and he tells me the motorbike shot across the road through the gap in the central reservation and straight into their path. He said one kid wasn't moving and the other appeared to be badly injured. I ask where they are. He informs me they flagged down a taxi and his driver, Sakhi, and the two kids plus their father went to the hospital.

Jason's phone rings. It's Sakhi saying he's requested at the hospital and that both kids are alive. It appears, by pure luck, they're apparently only suffering from bad gravel rash but are having further tests. Jason asks me what he should do and I tell him he needs to go and that I'll square things off with the policeman. I send one of my drivers off with Jason and study the faces from the crowd who watch him leave.

I approach the policeman with a greeting in Dari, with my hand extended, and inform him through a translator that Jason has had to go to the hospital and that I'll remain here until things are resolved. Some of the crowd push forward to try and listen to Farhad's translation of what I'm saying.

Someone starts a rumour which quickly sweeps through the crowd that Jason has done a runner, and that the kids weren't driven to the hospital but have been taken for their bodies to be hidden. I know I need to address the crowd and put this to bed as I can hear raised voices and sense the mood of these people is worsening. I tell Farhad to ask the crowd to gather round and to repeat exactly what I say. I inform them that both boys are alive and the doctor says they are not badly hurt and are expected to be released within the hour. One man comes forward and I ask Farhad who he is; the man explains he is the boy's uncle. I again repeat what I have heard from the hospital and ask him if the boy's father has a mobile phone, which he confirms. I hand him my mobile and tell him to call him to verify what I've said.

I pick up that two Afghans are being very vocal, and I check to see where my guys are and whether they're still in focus. My sixth sense is kicking in so I tell Farhad to get closer to these two guys and listen to what they're saying and report back to me. The uncle is talking away on my phone and I'm really hoping that the guys at the hospital have given me the correct facts. The uncle hands me back the phone and thanks me with a smile on his face. Well, that confirms Jason and Sakhi aren't crossing the Afghan border, I joke to myself. Farhad returns and points to one of the Afghans.

"That one's a good guy. He's trying to calm the crowd and is telling them it was the kids' fault. The other one is a bad guy and is trying to stir the crowd up by saying an American was driving, when we know it was an Afghan." I take an instant dislike to him.

I make a point of approaching the good guy to say hello, and have Farhad translate my thanks for his help in ensuring the truth was told.

The policeman is still writing up the accident when the guys return from the hospital with the boys' father, and at the same time Sakhi's family arrive in the form of his brothers and his father, Hamed. The policeman gives Hamed a warm handshake and it's apparent he is commanding a lot of respect. The boys' father and Hamed sit in the policeman's van to discuss things. I'm happier that Hamed is here; he is the ex-Chief of Police and is now Chief of Intelligence, and there's no denying it's a lucky break for us.

The Afghan troublemaker is back and I watch as he sticks his head into the van to give his ten pence worth, and after a brief exchange one of the brothers leaps to his feet to shadow him. Sakhi tells me the boys' father works for Hamed in the intelligence division. They are sweet words and I feel the tide is with us.

Some of the crowd disperses and I sense the mood has changed, so I stand my guys down. We put our weapons back into the vehicle and take the body armour off, but I keep my pistol. It's discreet and, more importantly, gives me comfort to know it's there.

Our trouble maker is still trying to stir things up and I can see Sakhi's brother is trying to counter whatever he is saying. He even approaches the boys' father and again tries to rally him into taking some sort of action. The father does react, but not in the way he was expecting him too: the man is pushed over with the father demanding to know why he's trying to stir things up. He's told to leave, otherwise he will be brought in for questioning to try and find out what his true motives are. The man is visibly shocked and I take some comfort from it. I can see the funny side, knowing he has no idea that Hamed and the boys' father are in the intelligence division.

Jason is feeling relieved as he only arrived three days previously and had no idea of Sakhi's family background. He'd heard the stories about how the Afghans have stitched up some of the ex-pats in sending them to jail. Even when a court cleared them they weren't released until a fee of around $40,000 had been paid, so I can understand Jason's concerns.

Before we depart, the good guy who helped settle the crowd comes over to shake our hands. Jason thanks him for his help and he starts to walk away.

"Mate, for his support I'd pay him $50," I tell Jason. It's the equivalent of seventeen days wages over here in Afghanistan. Jason agrees, calls him back, and hands him the notes. The man can't believe his luck, and a good deed has been addressed.

Sometime later I call into see the American intelligence section.

"Just to let you know, the bomb maker is back in town," I tell them.

"How do you know?"

"I've seen a spike of IEDs in the last week. The same thing happened last year and it's a predictable pattern. This means in a week's time, as he is normally here for two weeks, his parting signature will be a huge explosion. My gut feeling is that it'll be on the Camp Marmal side of Mazar-e Sharif," I tell them.

A week later there's a huge explosion that echos across the land. As the client and I venture out of our accommodation, a plume of black smoke can be seen towards Mazar-e Sharif.

Later in the day I go into Camp Spann to get an update on the explosion and they inform me it was a car bomb. Someone mentions there is a British four-man military team working out from Camp Spann, which is music to my ears, and I go looking for them. I meet Dan Allinson, and he welcomes me with a cup of Yorkshire tea. It's so nice to be able to speak to another British person and it lifts my spirits.

I head back to my accommodation to grab a shower and get all this dust and grime off me. I have shampoo in my hair and soap running down my body as I scrub myself, and it feels great. But when I open my eyes I see the water coming from the shower head is now liquid mud, and I'm not impressed. I head over to tell the client that the Afghan water man is not paying to take water from the well but is pumping it from the filthy river and pocketing the money. My eyes always seem to be stinging in the shower and I put it down to my soap, but my client tells me the positive news - he has been pouring bleach into the water tank to kill any bugs.

The day arrives when my client's country manager is coming to visit, so I rally up my team and brief them. Two are to remain with the client here, and Abdul and I will head to the commercial airport and meet up with the second team from the other project. The body armour is slung over my head and, as usual, there's a clunk as the armour strikes me again. I check my equipment: AK-47 magazine on, Smith & Wesson magazine on, and a spare bag with an extra fifteen AK-47 magazines. Between us, Abdul and I have thirty magazines giving us four hundred and fifty rounds each. The second team carries the same; all in all we have enough to buy some time providing we fire single shots. The words: 'the security guys died because they ran out of ammunition' still echo in my head. Exactly how many magazines did they carry, I wonder. I know some security personnel are running around carrying three, so I settle for this number as it gives me a little bit of reassurance to think I have more. Satisfied, I check the rest of my equipment: Sat Phone fully charged, GPS, mobile phone, hat & scarf, convoy orders, and drinking water in the vehicle for the client. It's time to go.

We jump in the 4 x 4 armoured vehicle and head off. The sky is blue, and the dust is in the air and trailing behind us. This time we don't come across any donkeys being chased by their owners, who normally resort to throwing stones as they can't catch them. Strange as it may seem, this encourages the donkeys to run even further. I cannot fathom why the Afghans do this. Neither are there are any signs of learner taxi drivers taking fare-paying passengers as it's more cost effective, however, I note there is a heavy police presence in the city. I deliberate as to what this is actually telling me; high profile visitor or a vehicle borne suicide bomber threat? My eyes scan left, right, forward, and mirror, yet I know in this traffic the best I could hope for is to utter the word *shit* before seeing the bright light and the 'this way' sign. I wonder if there will be two paths under the sign: 'sinners' and 'those that assume they're angels'. My thoughts are interrupted as I observe some kids playing with a tyre and a stick, making it roll.

We arrive at the airport and the second team arrive ten minutes after us. I brief them on the route back, the sequence of cars, and the distance to maintain between the vehicles, before radio checks are completed. I mention that should we be hit on route I expect support as per training, and also to cancel any thoughts about driving off to fetch help as we will fight through.

Afghan internal flights tend to run a flexi-time schedule, and once again this is confirmed by a call: the flight is delayed by an hour. This isn't unusual as Afghan flights can be delayed by up to four hours, unless the pilot decides he doesn't want to fly that day in which case it won't arrive at all.

We stand by our vehicles and keep surveillance on the antics going on around us, and I pick up on three of four PSD (Personal Security Detail) teams in the distance. The Afghan ones are openly displaying their fire power and the ex-pats are trying to look low profile but standing out, no doubt like myself, beard or no beard. A queue is forming on the other side of the road - passengers for the plane that hasn't arrived yet. The police won't let them into the airport until the airline staff appears, and as no one knows when that will be the queue lengthens and people become restless.

All of a sudden I hear music and my brain is confused. As the music bounces around in my eardrums I picture blue sea, coconut trees, and a cold beer, as this is Caribbean music I'm hearing. I turn to face the music and am greeted by two very dark gentlemen.

"Hey man, how's it going?" one of them says.

"Things are okay," I reply. "Where are you from?"

"Zimbabwe."

Getting into the beat of the music and standing next to two men whose skin colour is in contrast to those from Afghanistan is not my idea of low profile, though the music is very good. Boy, I think, I could do with having a cold beer next to a blue ocean right now.

People start to filter out of the building confirming the plane has landed and I call the client to brief him as to how he can find us, as we don't have passes to get into the airport.

"I have a slight conundrum; a policeman has stolen my phone," the client says.

"Did you say a policeman?"

"Yes," he replies.

"Stay there, I'm on my way," I tell him. "Abdul," I shout, "you're going to love this. We're going into the airport to accuse a policeman of stealing." The expression on Abdul's face says it all as he stares at me with an open mouth.

We head over to the policeman on the first main gate and I ponder how we're going to get through. I decide to start off with a friendly greeting and ask him if the Chief of Police is here. The reply, of course, is "no," but now I have his attention.

"I'm really sorry to miss him; it was good chatting to him the other day," I say. Now his brain is ticking over.

"You know the Chief of Police? How?"

I can sense he is starting to feel uncomfortable. We tell him we're going to the airport terminal to meet a very important person who is in charge of building the new large police base. The man's fear of being on the wrong side of the Chief of Police has made his decision: it is better for him to let us walk through.

I repeat this exercise at the second gate, and then we're in. I spot a very sad figure that looks out of place, and determine he must be my client's country manager.

"Scott ....Andy Guest," I introduce myself. "So, tell me what happened."

"I was sat on the bench," he explains, "and had placed my phone next to me. A policeman came over, sat next to me and said hello, and we chatted a little before he walked off. As I grabbed my bags I went to pick up my phone and it was gone." He tells me with confidence he would recognise the policeman if he saw him again.

"So, Scott, how long have you been in Afghanistan?" I ask.

"A week."

"Well, this is your first learning curve," I tell him, but my brain is actually thinking, *where's your common sense?* I think it's ironic they call it 'common' sense as very few people have it.

I enter the terminal building with the client and a policeman stops us. I tell Abdul to tell him we're going to see the Police Commander. This does the trick and he instantly steps aside so as not to get on the wrong side of him. It appears we're not the only ones who like to keep a low profile. Another ranked policeman steps forward, and the client starts to tell him that a policeman has stolen his phone. This isn't helpful and I'm annoyed, but thankfully the man doesn't speak English.

The Commander appears and I tell Abdul to translate for me.

"My client is the managing director of the firm that's building the big police base, and all his important telephone numbers are on his phone.

Unfortunately, someone has picked it up," I say.

At that very moment the client points to a policeman and says, "That's him." I catch a glimpse of a very worried looking face that scuttles around the corner; well he's now aware we're talking to his superior. I continue to explain to the Commanding Officer that it's very important we get this phone back, omitting the remark that a policeman has stolen it. Just as the Commander issues the orders for all his men to parade, the policeman reappears. He's had enough time to salvage the situation, and looks like he's handed the phone to the intelligence officer, who appears along with the phone.

"I know that policeman stole my phone!" the client says. A voice in my head is saying, *Think man... think about where you are and who you're surrounded by.*

This person could be a brother or a relative of the Commander and things could easily start to go down a slippery slope. This is not our home ground. The policeman says he found the phone and handed it in, and even though I know he's lying, when you're surrounded by sixteen policemen it's better to diffuse the situation. I step forward to thank the policeman in big gestures, and in turn face the Commander to thank him, too. As we walk away the client is still harping on.

"Just be happy you got it back," I tell him.

At the vehicle I complete the road movement brief to the client and we hit the road. While we're driving I give a running commentary of the area and the sights, knowing full well there will be no tip at the end of this journey. Scott only stays for a few days to get a grip on what's happening with the construction project.

One day we depart from another project, and in case the Taliban have set up a hasty IED roadside bomb I change our route and go the long way around, so as not to have a predictable pattern. We pass a compound that has a lot of young children hanging around the gate entrance, and I ask Abdul if it's a school.

"It's an orphanage, Mr Andy," he replies.

Later that day I'm in a meeting with the Americans on Camp Marmal airfield and I notice some huge boxes of sweets that have been donated by American schools for their servicemen. As I conclude our meeting I ask the major if it's possible to take two bags of sweets for the orphanage, and to my surprise he tells me to take a couple of the big boxes. His generosity is fantastic, and I'm excited at the idea of giving these kids, who have had a rough start in life, something nice. I arrive at the orphanage with my team and have Abdul explain to the woman who runs it what I would like to do. I take pictures of them receiving the sweets, and holding up a sign that bears the name of the school they came from. Some of the children are excited and curious, undoubtedly wondering who this strange person is amongst them, but others seem to have that lost feeling about them; their eyes are hollow. Others look bewildered and cautious at first, but they seem to warm to me slowly. Their surroundings are poor, the compound is muddy, and there's nothing nice inside the buildings - dirty carpets and paint peeling off the walls - but at least it's a roof over their heads and they're getting fed.

The following week I have another meeting with the American major and hand him the pictures of the children receiving their sweets. Three weeks later I have receive a message that the major wants a meeting with me, but no reason is given. I head over to Camp Marmal and knock on his door.

"Andy, thank you for coming. Follow me," he says, and leads me down the corridor. "I sent the pictures back to America for the schools to see, and the schools shared the pictures for the parents to see. It hit home as to how poorly the kids were dressed." He points to eight large boxes. "These are for you to give to the orphanage; they're full of clothes and shoes sent by the parents who held a collection."

A few days later I return to the orphanage to see some men leaving the compound, and am curious to know who they were.

"Abdul, what would those men being doing at the orphanage?" I ask.

"One or two of the men are probably looking for a wife," he tells me.

I can't but help think this country is screwed up - when a man can take a child for a wife. No doubt a small fee is paid to the woman in charge, which is unlikely to go back into the orphanage.

I observe the boxes of clothes and shoes being handed out to the kids. It's a nice feeling, and as much as I'd like to visit again I know I can't return in case the Taliban get to hear about it, as there could be reprisals. I do wonder, though, whether the men will return and if next week the orphanage will be missing one or two girls.

I try and break up the routine for Joe and escort him to a picnic he's been invited to, having first conducted a recce of the area so we don't move into it blind. I also take him out on the shooting range to fire some shots with the AK-47, and at the same time keep my guards up with the currency on their weapons. I always finish off with a competition with a fifty dollar cash prize, and it's with some relief that yet again I get to keep the prize money. I introduce Joe to Dan and the other three Brits; some evenings we spend at their location or on a Sunday afternoon we'll get together at ours.

Head office in Dubai give me a heads up that they may be sending me out on a road mission to check out an oil field, which involves driving through three provinces. I immediately start researching the route and contact the intelligence operations room of each country. I'm told that on one section of the road I'll be driving on there's been a number of fire fights, and the Swedish suggest I contact one of their camps in another province I'm driving to for an update on incidents. I visit one of the security companies who found themselves in a fire fight in that area to hear their version straight from the horse's mouth, as they say it was quite a fight with an RPG also being fired.

I receive a call from head office and am told I'm on an open conference on a speaker system.

"Andy, the clients will arrive at your location in two days' time and we need you to escort them to this oil field. Do you have any views on it?"

I'm shocked by how quickly they want this done. "If you're asking me for my view then I would say, at this short notice, it's foolhardy. All my Intel at the moment says we're driving into a Taliban stronghold, and if one of our clients is killed that will have a negative impact on the company. It would make sense to send someone to recce the route first so we know the layout of the land before taking our clients into it. The Taliban have just announced they're planning a major offensive, so use that as an excuse to put it back a week."

There's a pause and then head office come back. "We agree, so you're off tomorrow to conduct the recce."

Bollocks. When I suggested a recce I wasn't putting myself up for it. I'll have to leave a guard behind to look after Joe, but will pick up two guards from the sister project. Phone calls are made and timings are decided on. In the morning I brief the team.

"Guys, it's a two vehicle move. I want a thousand metres between the vehicles so we don't look like a convoy. Yesterday, a security team drove close together and were ambushed. Remember, the shepherd you see is probably a spotter for their main assault group further down the road. No uniforms, only normal clothes. Keep all weapons out of sight. We'll load the vehicle with three thousand spare rounds. No talking on the radio unless it's an emergency; the Taliban are listening in."

I think about my family and how this road mission may play out, and there's a tinge of sadness at the thought of no goodbyes. I insert the pictures of my family in my pocket as it gives me comfort to know they're with me. It's time to say goodbye to Joe and I tell him I'll see him in three days' time, and then I brief the remaining guard, Abdul, and tell him not to allow Joe out of his sight. I have picked Abdul to remain as he is a father and the others are single.

We load up and hit the road, and it's not long before we're outside Mazar-e Sharif and heading into the unknown. The miles soon fly by as the landscape before me slips away. At various times I look at individuals from the vehicle window with suspicion. Is he a spotter? I ask myself, and keep him in view until I can see him no more. We stop for a meal as I have to look after the men, but I choose to remain in the vehicle with my finger near the safety catch, constantly looking at my wing mirrors for anyone creeping up behind me. The road has many turns, up and over rolling hills in some places, and narrow dirt tracks in others. The country is beautiful and has so much potential but the Western world is blind to what is required and there will be no peace. Corruption has been so deeply rooted it's hard to see change. A certain large charity throws money into rural projects, such as chicken farming, in the hope to create jobs, but all that's required is to show a plot of land, a fence, and a hut with a few chickens running around, and then a large amount of money is handed over in dollars. However, it's common knowledge that in some cases, once the Afghan receives the money, the 'chicken farm' disappears the day after, only to reappear at a new location the following week claiming to be a new business. It's also common knowledge that some western individuals in charge of handing out contracts often meet in bars in Kabul. They ask the question to potential clients, "What's it worth to you?" Money is given and the contract is handed over.

The daylight hours come and go but we push on. It amuses me to see that a newly laid asphalt road already has a pothole, dug up by an Afghan who sits on a chair next to it. As we approach he waves us down to warn us of the pothole, and then expects to get paid for telling us about it.

We finally arrive at the camp and I instruct my men to put all their weapons in my vehicle before giving them money for their accommodation and food and telling them to head to a guest house. I watch them drive away before proceeding to the main gate, and an Afghan guard approaches me who, by the look on his face, is shocked at the amount of weapons I have in my vehicle. He disappears and a short while later, as I'm starting to feel uncomfortable being stuck outside, an ex-pat comes to the gate. I update him as to who I am, and it appears this village has two camps and I'm at the wrong one. Typical. All my guards have gone; it's just what I needed. My mental alertness increases. I have no choice but to drive on as I've been sat for too long here, and I know I'm more at risk the longer I stay. Thankfully, I arrive at the other location without incident and I'm soon shown to my room. I call my guards and explain I'm at a different location and we're still on for an early start.

The next morning I have two oil fields to visit, and my first stop is meeting up with a representative from the oil field who likes to be called Engineer Mohammad. We head out to look at Wellhead 28, and I take pictures to confirm that I've actually reached it for when I file my report. We drop off Engineer Mohammad and press on to the other oil field, which is on top of a hill. It's a single rough track that just seems to go on forever. As we approach the top I spot two gunmen and grab the radio and shout, "Two gunmen... go right on the next turn and we'll flank behind. Do not shoot unless they shoot."

Both vehicles part company. We race up our track, I order the driver to pull up short, and we disembark with weapons in our hands. I hear voices and poke my head up above the ridge to see two armed men engaged in conversation with my security team. Their weapons are lowered, so I approach from behind with one of my guards.

"Good day, how are you?" I call out.

The men turn around while my eyes are focussed on their weapons. It's not often I see fear on an Afghan's face, but at this moment their situation is unknown to them. I tell the guard to tell them they're amongst friends and to wish them good health, before asking who they are.

It appears they are two policemen tasked with keeping an eye on the oil wells. I continue my approach and offer my hand. Greetings are exchanged and the rest of the team join us. The two policemen board their motorbikes and roar off, and I take some pictures for the report as confirmation. The view from the hill top is breathtaking, the visibility so clear you can see for miles.

I've achieved what I needed to on this recce and it's time to head back, as I can't be one hundred percent sure those two policemen are not batting for both sides. I brief the guys and let them know that just because we're heading back this is the time we have to be more vigilant and keep a sharp eye for IEDs. My team head back to the Swedish camp to drop me off for an overnight stay.

That evening a Swedish officer introduces me to an American girl around twenty-two years of age who is serving in the military.

"Andy," he says, "can you give this young lady a lift back to Camp Marmal? Otherwise she's stuck here for another ten days." I tell her I'm leaving at 05:30 a.m., and she tells me she will be there.

In the morning as I'm loading my vehicle and preparing to move, the young lady turns up in her military uniform. I load her gear up in the back.

"Just so you know, our movements have to be low profile so you'll need to take your helmet off," I tell her. I take my scarf off and hand it over. "You'll need to cover your hair in case you're seen from the outside. My guards will meet us outside and one of them will take over the driving. We have a second vehicle that will have a further four Afghan guards in it, so it's a two vehicle move. As it's a low profile approach there will be some distance between the two vehicles. I can see you're carrying a side arm but I'll sit in the back with you with my weapon. Should we get attacked, what I require you to do is everything I tell you without hesitation or questions, as that costs lives. If we have to abandon the vehicle then you stick with me like glue. What I suggest you do is inform you superiors that you're departing this location. Are you happy?"

"Yes," she tells me.

On the journey back I chat to her with the view it may help make her feel more relaxed, as we're total strangers. Each time we approach a hot spot I inform her, as all eyes are looking out. I cannot believe and find it shocking that her superiors would allow her just to drive off with an unknown ex-pat and five Afghan guards without knowing my background.

We eventually arrive at Camp Marmal and I get her to phone her superiors to let them know she's arrived safely. What would her parents think if they knew their daughter was permitted to be transported without any military support?

I report to head office that in my opinion, based on what I know from the Intel I've gathered, I deem the risks to be minimal to conduct the mission. I call into Camp Spann and have a chat with them about it and tell them I've worked out a possible trail the Taliban are using to move men and supplies, and how I've reached that conclusion.

Two days later the three clients arrive, two from an oil company along with their security advisor. The road mission goes smoothly, and I even manage to get permission for them to set up on the Swedish camp to operate from. The clients are delighted and award my company with a contract. Initially I'm told I will head the new project but later I'm informed I've been rejected by their security advisor who wants a tall bouncer-type of guy to run it, and considers me to be too short. I find it strange as in this environment it's all about brains, not brawn. It's even funnier when they choose an ex-pat who is hated by the security Afghans.

My project has run its course and it's time to move to new pastures and another adventure. I'm touched by some of the Americans who thank me for my help, and by an email from a first sergeant which simply says:

Andy,
I wish you well on your new journey and want you to know you made a difference.
Thank you.

A CAPTAIN PHILLIPS MOMENT

I decide to follow a new path recommended to me by my brother, Ken, who has suggested working in anti-piracy security on the Indian Ocean. I learn that last year, in 2010, fifty-two ships were hijacked and twelve hundred crew members were held hostage, while the pirates pursued ransom money for the return of the ships and the crew. This sudden surge of piracy seems to have been triggered after pirates hijacked an oil tanker and demanded a one million dollar ransom, which was paid. Once it was paid it triggered a rush of attacks, which is one of the reasons the British government will not entertain paying ransom money. The ransom figure has now increased to seven million dollars.

Before I can work at sea I have to pay for and attend various maritime courses to complete my STCW 95 (Standards of Training, Certification and Watch keeping for Seafarers), the modules of which are: Personal Safety and Social Responsibilities, Fire Prevention and Fire Fighting, Personal Survival Techniques, Elementary First Aid, and Proficiency in Security Awareness. They're very simple courses and I almost feel it's just an attendance course, but they do throw me an exam at the end of it. I gain my maritime certificates and can now apply for work with one of the security companies who are looking for former Royal Marines. As we're Royal Navy sea soldiers, it's considered that our training as Commandos is of a higher standard, thus a big selling point when offering security to the shipping companies. The maritime security industry has boomed as shipping companies now request armed security teams on their ships to reduce their insurance costs, and to give their crew the reassurance that in the case of a hijack there are professionals on board.

I send in my CV that lists my experience and the certificates I hold, and

I'm offered an interview. After formal presentations I'm taken for a personal interview, and the gentleman interviewing me is impressed with my CV and what I achieved in Afghanistan.

"Andy, how soon could you be ready to go on the ships?" he asks.

"My suitcase is already packed," I reply.

"Great. You're going in two days' time."

I fly out from Heathrow and head to Egypt with no idea of what I'm in for, and I'm picked up at Cairo airport and taken to a hotel, paid for by the company. The following morning I'm driven to the Suez Canal and taken through customs, then onto the boat to meet the ship I'll be working on. It's a container ship run by an Indian crew and is around thirty-four years old; it's so decrepit it seems the paint is keeping the rust together. I meet the security team leader who explains our security routine and tells me this will be the ship's last voyage, after which it'll be scrapped.

It's an eye opener as we sit down to eat our meal, as the hygiene is poor. Cockroaches sprint across the table, and the air conditioning isn't working so we're all sweating. The smell of this, and oil, along with other things I can't identify, hangs in the air. As I work on my laptop that night a cockroach drops off the ceiling and falls into my t-shirt, which soon has me leaping around in an attempt to get it out. Sweat pours off me when I'm trying to sleep, and the cockroaches keep waking me up as they scuttle across my face. Breakfast is the same thing as we had for lunch and dinner the previous day: a rather bland curry. I just hope we're being served a fresh batch and haven't been given the one that was left out overnight, which the cockroaches feasted on.

As we enter the piracy zone our security watches begin. We're only a two man team, hence the watches are long: six hours standing on our feet in rotation, and they continue until we exit the piracy zone, which covers the whole of the Indian Ocean. My first maritime task runs smoothly and without incident, and after three weeks we return to the Suez Canal and depart the ship. On my return to the UK I pay the company a visit and ask to be made up to a security team leader. I point out that in Afghanistan I was in charge of three hundred and twenty-five Afghans, and that job was far more challenging than running a four man security team sailing across the Indian Ocean. It's not even debated, and I'm promoted to security team leader for the next tasking, which is an excellent result as I'll now be paid more. I understand the importance of ensuring all the documentation is correct, and the potential consequences if it's not. I have no wish to be jailed with my team somewhere.

A week later I'm back out on another tasking. Again, it's a two man security team on another container ship with an Indian crew. This time I fly into the Oman, and there's a delay in picking us up. It's a relief when we eventually get taken to the hotel as the last thing I need is problems on my first tasking as security team leader.

The following morning we're taken to Salalah Port where we clear customs, and the port authorities take me to the weapons store. I check the serial numbers of the weapons to ensure they match the documentation I have, and I count the ammo. With that done, our first job is to get the equipment and our own luggage aboard, tackling the steep gangway, which is difficult. The crew are very friendly and are delighted to see us, especially as we're armed. Once on board I meet with the captain for formal introductions, and then we're shown to our cabins. Once again it's a ship in poor condition, but I haven't seen any cockroaches running around so I count that as a blessing.

I carry out a survey of the ship to check what security measures they have in place. The most common defence to prevent pirates boarding a ship is to have razor wire surrounding it, but this doesn't always stop them, so I consider what measures we can put in place to prevent them getting onto the bridge, the area from which the ship is commanded. Should they reach the bridge, everything is about buying time, so I recommend to the captain ways in which we would slow the pirates down and prevent them from getting to the citadel. This is where the crew would head in the event of a piracy attack, and lock down. Water and food is stored there as rescue may be days away. The only people left on the bridge would be the security team and the captain; the security team would engage the pirates with the captain's permission.

We head to the Suez Canal and follow the coastline, sticking to the corridors that have been put in place by Navy warships from different countries. The warships escort the ships who don't have security teams on board; ships that have security on board don't tend to wait to be escorted by the military Navy, but keep going.

As soon as we leave Salalah the crew gather on the bridge, where I give a presentation on the security team and the pirate situation, and tell them what is expected of them if they hear the piracy alarm. There's a strict code on rules of engagement that we must follow before we can engage any pirates during an attack. We must display our weapons to warn the pirates we have armed security on board, and if the pirates continue their approach I must seek the captain's permission to fire warning shots. The aim is to give the pirates every opportunity to disengage, however, if they start to fire at us I'm able to engage as we have a right to self-defence.

My security colleague and I start to conduct watches on the bridge, which involves observing the sea for any unusual movements from small pirate skiffs. These are long narrow boats with very large engines on the back. Unfortunately, the same type of boat is used by fishermen and people smugglers, who we constantly come across throughout the transit. Fishermen will suddenly start up their engine and race to cut off the ship's approach. This gets my attention as I have to very quickly evaluate if it's a possible piracy attack or just fishermen trying to show us they have nets in the water ahead of us. The skiffs are hard to spot at times and we get a surprise when they suddenly fire up their engines and the white froth of the water appears behind them.

We pass through the Gulf of Aden in the black of night and approach the narrow entrance to the Red Sea at Bab-el-Mandeb, which is an extremely busy shipping channel with ships passing and overtaking each other in opposite directions. Adding to the chaos, there are skiffs racing around, and we use the night sight to pick up on them, as most don't seem to have a light on board. Often, a skiff is spotted when the night sight picks up on the small glow from someone's cigarette.

We continue our journey in the Red Sea knowing that in twenty-four hours we'll be outside the piracy zone and will be able to stand down and take it easy, which we're looking forward to. But as I'm on my security watch, the captain informs me that when we exit the piracy zone we'll be meeting another ship where we'll disembark, transfer onto it, and head back into the piracy zone again. We reach the rendezvous point and it's been decided we'll transfer to the other ship by lifeboat. The crew try to lower the lifeboat and find they're not able to use the motor crane as it isn't working, so they have no choice but to winch it down by hand, which takes some time. To my horror it's indicated we'll have to climb down the rope ladder, and I stare wide-eyed over the side of the ship. This is some height to be climbing down, and I note they position the lifeboat directly beneath the ladder so if I do fall I'll land in the wooden boat, which is likely to break my bones, but I won't get wet. I would have been a lot happier if they'd brought the boat in once I was down. It's a nerve-racking experience as I hate heights, but I try my best not to show it. I find that once I'm on the rope ladder the life jacket makes me lean back, adding to my concerns, and also the ladder swings around wildly in the wind. Thankfully, the manoeuvre is successful, and on reaching the other ship we find it's only eight years old and is crewed by Italians. The accommodation I've been assigned is called 'The Owner's Cabin', and it feels like I've just checked into a hotel as it's an en-suite and has its own lounge.

The whole cycle is repeated - briefing up the crew and running the watches. We call at various ports on route including Jeddah in Saudi Arabia, and then we head back to Salalah. When we reach Sri Lanka we disembark the ship and return to the UK.

The year, which took me out of the UK for nine months, passes quickly. I hear my brother was attacked by pirates but they managed to evade capture, and I meet the unluckiest security contractor who, on his first five taskings, was attacked five times. I also meet a lucky Ukrainian crew member who disembarked a ship only to hear it was hijacked by pirates after leaving port.

Corruption is common in most countries, and cigarettes seem to be treated like currency. To have a smooth passage through customs at ports, which all ships want, a large quantity of cigarettes are handed over with smiles all around. On one transit when I disembarked the ship in India at the chief of customs' office, my suit case was emptied and gone through with a fine-toothed comb, as I was not forthcoming in handing cash over. Eventually I was asked for a hundred dollars, which I refused to pay. We played the staring game and I assumed it was supposed to intimidate me, but it didn't work. Three hours later I was allowed to leave for the airport.

On some of the ships the captain was not always welcoming and I could sense a bit of resentment that he had to have a security team on board. It may have taken a few days, but once he had seen the security team were operating professionally and were polite, he would come round and become more approachable. As a team leader I had to try and win the captain over and try to find common ground with him. One captain loved to play table tennis and I was thankful for the days I played as a kid. He kept seeking me out to play as he was yet to beat me, though the games were extremely close. Another captain warmed to me as we shared a passion for photography.

The years keep passing and I find myself on different types of ships, sailing through the Indian Ocean. Oil tankers are very inviting for pirates due to their low freeboard (height from the sea to the upper deck), making it easier for pirates to board. Container ships offer more safety due to their height above water, but are still at risk. Pirates have found a way to bypass the razor wire by throwing a grappling hook on to it and then dropping a heavy anchor over the side that tends to rip the razor wire off. One has to be vigilant at all times.

One night on the bridge we hear on the radio a pirate attack taking place. The captain of that ship is giving a running commentary, and he is only twenty nautical miles away from us. An RPG rocket launcher has been fired as well as shots, but the ship has avoided being hijacked. I put the team on standby as we pass through the area but no pirates are spotted, and once clear of the area I stand down my team.

The ship calls into Durban and it's a chance to leave and go to the Mission for Seafarers, a place where we can get away from our surroundings for a while. The best part of it is the opportunity to use the internet, touch base with home, and grab a coffee. Although a beer would be lovely, once we depart a British airport it's company rules that we remain tee total, as the nature of our job involves working with weapons. I meet a priest and engage in a conversation with him, asking him what his role is.

"I give counselling to seamen who have been taken hostage," he tells me.

I find this interesting, and he goes on to tell me the horrendous ordeals some of the seamen have gone through at the hands of the pirates. He tells me that the last person he gave counselling to was a young Italian chef whom the pirates took a liking to, and he was raped by several of them. I also hear of a ship that was taken by Nigerian pirates on the West Coast of Africa, and every member of the crew was raped half a dozen times. It's horrendous to hear, and it appears not to be reported to the media so as not to scare seamen into not sailing in these piracy seas. I need no incentives to stop pirates boarding my ship but, if I did, this is it. No doubt, some of the seamen have heard these stories, hence they're delighted when my security team come on board.

On board the ship there's nothing to do but watch videos with the guys, who swap hard drives full of films, or do some physical training which seems to be popular with the security team. I understand why, as after a physical training session I get a feel good factor afterwards, and it reaches the point where I have a hunger for it. It's the one thing I look forward to, but at times it's not easy as the ship rolls about on the waves.

It's 11:00 p.m. and I head to the gym and set up to do some circuit training. I have some music playing on my headphones, and I grab the dumb bells and haul them to my chest. To my horror, someone has taken the nuts off and I see four weights shoot into the air. Time moves into slow motion and my head screams, 'No!' The 'Bang! Bang! Bang! Bang! as the weights hit the floor echoes around the ship, and I'm so embarrassed when the door is opened by a nervous crew member who has come to see what the hell is going on. I head to the bridge to apologise to the captain and to explain what happened. I'm told it sounded like gun shots being fired and half the crew had fled to the citadel, thinking pirates had boarded the ship. Two days later people start seeing the funny side of it and keep bringing it up, but I'd much rather they changed the subject.

On another tasking I'm on a container ship with an Indian crew, and my colleague returns from the gym. He has arms like Popeye and admits to having used steroids to bulk up his muscles in the past. He's not happy as he storms into the room.

"What's up?" I ask him.

"Every time I go to the gym to work out, the Indian crew come in and just sit there staring at me," he tells me.

I tell him I understand where he's coming from. The following morning one of the Indian crew mentions that my colleague has big muscles so I tell him he loves it when people feel them. Later that night my colleague returns from the gym looking very pissed off.

"What's the matter?" I ask.

"Now they're bloody well pawing my biceps," he tells me. I keep a very straight face but I'm laughing inside.

The days pass and each day our routine is the same, but eventually we're outside the piracy zone and our time is our own. I receive a message that the security team is to report to the officer's mess to see the captain, and I find my colleague in the gym and ask him if he knows why the captain has requested us, but he shakes his head. As we walk through the door we're greeted by half of the crew with smiles on their faces, a room full of decorations, a full buffet on the table with cans of soft drinks, and music playing in the background.

"Andy, the crew and I are aware it's your Christmas Day and we would like to wish the both of you a Merry Christmas," the captain says. I'm completely taken aback, as their faith doesn't celebrate Christmas, and I thank the captain and the crew for this magnificent gesture. I had completely forgotten it was Christmas day, and my thoughts are suddenly with Alison and the boys.

Some days whilst on watch we see some amazing sights. At times the ocean glows green or blue due to bioluminescent plankton; it's an incredible sight and my eyes are transfixed as we pass through it. One day, while anchored offshore, I watch close to one hundred and fifty dolphins playing in the sea, and the more I observe the more I notice things. Family communities play and work together. Young dolphins meet up in a line and have races, the mothers keeping an eye on their babies. Even dads join in and leap out of the waves. Sea World will never match this experience.

On another day I'm called to the bridge to speak to the captain.

"Andy, do you know what a Tsunami is?" he says.

"Yes, Captain," I reply. Why do you ask?"

"I've just received a signal that there's one on its way and it's heading towards us."

I pause to take in what he's just said. "When is it due to hit us?"

"Three hours," he says.

"Well, that gives me time for a cup of tea and a bit of sunbathing," I reply, and I walk away.

"Seriously, what are we going to do?" my colleague asks when we're on our own.

"Exactly what I said. Being on top of the bridge has to be the best place to be, riding the ship like a surf board when it hits us." He can't work out if I'm joking or not. "Mate, we're stuck on this ship. What else can we do?" I tell him.

Most of the ships are drifting offshore, which is common practice as they don't want to risk their anchors snagging on the seabed, and they now engage their engines and make a run for the open sea. The time arrives and passes but there is no great wave. Being out at sea we wouldn't have seen one anyway, as a Tsunami is an on-land surge. It transpires it's a false alarm.

A few days later we call into Mombasa and on the day we depart someone throws a hand grenade over a wall into a restaurant. The previous time I was here, someone walked into a night club and opened up with an AK-47 Kalashnikov Automatic Rifle. Nowhere is safe.

Five days into our next leg a fishing dhow is seen heading towards us and tries to intercept us. I keep an eye on it, noting its speed, and ours. It's a highly unusual manoeuvre and I can only consider it to be very suspicious. I'm fully aware that pirates hijack fishing dhows and use them as mother ships to launch skiffs from, as the dhow allows the pirates to travel further into the Indian Ocean and look for ships to hijack. On this occasion, our speed is greater and the dhow fails to intercept us. The rest of the journey goes without incident.

The highlight of the trip is getting to port and having access to the internet to touch base with the Alison and the boys, as my time periods at home are short before I am offered another tasking. I haven't had a Christmas at home for quite a few years as I've offered to work, allowing those with young children to spend the time with their families. My sons are grown up now, and it feels it's the right thing to do.

At the start of each year I have to attend a shooting course, which I must pass, and attend another FPOS (first person on scene) first aid course, as well as applying for another CRB certificate. Each of these I have to pay for, which sets me back a thousand pounds. The general feeling amongst a lot of the security personnel is that these yearly courses are only compulsory in order to enable the maritime security companies to claw some of their money back.

In the last year I have travelled to over twenty countries, but I've only seen ports and airports. This time I'm back on the Indian Ocean, having departed from Durban, and I'm heading to Dubai with a four man team in the piracy zone. I'm fast asleep in my cabin when the telephone in my room rings in the middle of the night. With bleary eyes I strain to look at my watch, wondering how on earth it could be possible that I've overslept when I have three alarms. I pick up the phone.

"This is the captain. We're being followed."

"I'm on my way, Captain," I reply, and leap out of bed. In a rush, as I'm trying to put my trousers on, I end up hopping around like a man possessed. Time is critical because, for all I know, pirates are on board and closing in. I sprint up the stairs, cursing the fact they accommodated me seven floors below, and as I reach the door for the bridge my lungs are bursting, sweat is already appearing on my forehead, and I'm fighting to catch my breath. I open the door and enter the bridge, and it feels as if I've entered a coal cellar with no lights. I'm aware of figures, but in the darkness I can't make out who is who. The room is kept dark at night so those on the bridge retain their night vision. I stagger forwards with my arms outstretched.

"Captain ... it's Andy, the security team leader. Can you give me an update as to the situation?" I head to the shadowy outline of some of the figures who are crowded around the radar in this darkened room.

"We're being followed," the captain says, pointing out a blip on the radar that's approaching from behind us.

"When did it start?" I ask.

"At twenty miles. Each time we've altered course they have too, and now they're down to a mile away," he replies.

My eyes watch this blip on the radar. It's clear something is closing in on us, and I'm aware it would be normal practice for a vessel to keep their distance at night. "Give me a new heading of three two zero," I ask the captain, and he carries out the manoeuvre. I can see the vessel behind us has also altered their course and continues to close in on us. *Anti-piracy drills at night, and seeing pirates, is going to be bloody tricky,* I think. "Captain, turn off your navigation lights; they're using them to zero in on us," I shout out.

The captain dashes off, turns off the navigation lights and returns to the radar. All our eyes are focussed on the blip on the screen. As we continue to observe the radar we notice the gap between us is growing; clearly they're no longer able to follow us. I remain on the bridge for two hours to ensure the situation doesn't change, and once I'm happy I return to my bed and try to grab some sleep, all too aware my shift starts in an hour's time.

During the trip I run the team through some training and record it in the daily report. I also request permission from my company to carry out some live shooting practice. Permission is given, and with the captain's permission and the crew informed, we conduct live firing, much to the excitement of the crew. Once completed I make a note of the amount of rounds fired, subtract it from my document, and give the captain a copy. When he notifies the port authorities about our equipment he'll have a true record, which is so important. If the captain's declaration doesn't match the amount of ammo on board there could be huge fines.

The ocean can be a beautiful place at times. I'm taken by surprise when I see a waterspout – a rotating column of water formed by a whirlwind - which at times reaches two thousand feet in the air. But, in contrast, I'm saddened to see tied up bin liners, crammed with rubbish, that have been tossed over the side of some ships.

Back in the UK I hear that our company has contracts on the west coast of Africa. It's connected with the oil industry so, if I'm to stand a chance of getting any work with them, I have to do an offshore survival course. I book myself onto one and head to Aberdeen to complete my BOSIET (Basic Offshore Safety Induction and Emergency Training). I mention to the company that I used to be employed in the oil industry, and it seems to work as I'm transferred onto that contract. I fly into Benin, which is a former French colony, and the good news is that I'm down as one of the team leaders to run security on one of the supply boats. It's an easy task; the guys who tend to have most of the work are the guys on the smaller vessel.

It's in the early hours of the morning, just past midnight, when I notice some of the crew seem to be getting excited outside the bridge, so I decide to go and investigate. I'm greeted by an awesome sight: a whale with its calf. As I peer down at the mother she's not moving but lying on her side, and she appears to be staring at me with her huge eye. For a long while I'm transfixed, and feel privileged to be given the opportunity to experience it.

There's no guarantee that we'll remain on the same vessel when we come out the next time and, sure enough, when I return to this project I'm moved onto another vessel, which is a small boat that runs the security. It's recently been acquired, and I note it's designed for inland rivers and not for the open seas, which can mean only one thing: it's going to be rough. From the harbour I can see how bad it looks out there, so I pop some sea sickness tablets, just in case. We depart the safety of the harbour and are thrown around all over the place. Sleep is almost impossible as I'm constantly rolling around, trying to use my pillows to minimise the movement in bed.

The following morning I'm on watch in the thick of a storm, and holding onto whatever I can as things are flying through the air. We have a security team on the drill ship, which we're protecting, and it hardly seems to be moving. My radio crackles and its one of the guys on the drill ship who is looking down onto my boat being tossed around like a toy in the bath.

"Is it as bad as it looks?" he asks me.

"No, mate; it's fucking worse than that," I tell him, amidst the sound of a loud crash as something else hits the floor.

As we're the lead security boat, it's our job to call ships that are heading our way and ask them to give us a ten mile separation. I've heard previous guys on the radio getting tongue-tied as they try to think about what to say, so I write up a script, get it laminated, and tell my team to follow it so the radio calls run smoothly, as the other security vessels are listening in. The radar gives us the direction of the ships and we can also see if their course will create a conflict. Once they reach a twenty nautical mile distance away from us the call is made. The hardest calls to make are the ones to Chinese ships, because there's no way we would get the pronunciation right, so we refer to their IMO ship identification number instead.

The boat I'm on is tiny and very cramped, and we have to spend two months on this, eating nothing but fried food. On the calmer days I venture out on to the bow with my rope and skip on a very small area the size of a man hole cover, aware that if I have one slip I'll be swimming.

On my return to the UK I discover this contract has come to an end as there has been a downturn in the oil industry. My next tasking takes me to Tanzania to provide security on a fishing boat that's heading to the Suez Canal. We're aware the risks are higher as we can't travel that fast, and we're not far off the Somalian coastline. While transiting, we hit a force ten gale, and the waves look like gigantic lurking monsters as I sit on the captain's chair and watch them. The fishing vessel is perched on top of a huge wave and it pitches at a steep angle, and as the boat slides down the wave and rotates sideways, the film 'The Perfect Storm' enters my head, which, I recall, didn't have a happy ending. Some of the security team are suffering badly with sea sickness and I can't help but feel sorry for them. The sound of three people vomiting loudly isn't pleasant, and I try and focus on something else, telling myself we're going to survive this.

When the storm eventually passes, the rest of the journey goes without incident in calmer seas, with both fishing vessels staying close together. We finally arrive at the Suez Canal and disembark the fishing boats, and I'm not sorry. It's so nice to return to the UK and have my feet firmly on the ground again for a while.

After a short break I fly back out again to start another transit from the Suez Canal, and when we reach Sri Lanka we have to disembark the ship at night from the rope ladder that hangs over the side. The sea is choppy and it's quite disconcerting to see how big the swell is as we watch our pick up boat being tossed up and down on the waves. People take to the rope ladder one at a time, trying to judge the precise moment when it's safe to descend, with a man in the pickup boat shouting, "Now! Quick! Quick!" When it's my turn I climb down four feet and hear a panicked voice shout, "No! Go back! Go back!" but it's too late, and I see the pickup boat rise up to me rapidly. To avoid my legs from being crushed I lift my legs up as high as I can, but the boat keeps on coming. It hits me in the arse and I let go off the ladder. *Well, I guess I'm on,* I think, and there's laughter all around, but mine is of the nervous type as I know I've just had a lucky escape.

After a few weeks at sea, and back at the accommodation, I say goodbye to my security team and join another team, bouncing onto another transit.

This one tasking has seen me bounce onto four different ships and I've been away from home for ninety days. I reach the Suez Canal and text Alison to let her know the pilot boat is approaching so I'll soon be at the airport and I'll see her tomorrow. As I'm gathering my possessions my mobile phone rings and I wonder if it's Alison, but it's the company I'm working for.

"Andy, one of the guys has just flown to Cairo; he's received a call to say two members of his family have been involved in a bad car crash and are in a critical condition in hospital. You're the only person that can cover him so we're asking if you will take over his tasking."

"It goes without saying I'll cover him," I reply.

When the call ends I realise I forgot to ask how long the tasking is for, so I call the company back and I'm told it's for ninety days, which is a shock. The words sink in and I text Alison to apologise and let her know it's all changed.

For the next three months I work with an Indian captain who likes to rule his crew through fear; he's the captain from hell and seems to get pleasure in intimidating them. The time drags with this man and it's such a relief when it's time for me to leave.

I've noticed on the last couple of trips that things are changing in the maritime security world, as more security teams are appearing from Sri Lanka and Croatia, and the salary has dropped by half. This tasking has been my longest time working at sea: I've bounced off five ships and have been away for one hundred and eighty days.

I decide I've reached another crossroads in my life, and after seven years of working nine months of the year away, I call it a day. I've had my fill of being in hostile environments and want to return to what I enjoy the most, and that's working at a skydiving school. I leave knowing I've made the right decision, and I can't wait to get started.

THE ONGOING JOURNEY

It's the beginning of 2015. I requalify for my skydiving tandem rating and I'm asked by the owner of the skydiving school at Dunkeswell if I would consider taking the Chief Instructor role again, which I accept.
"By the way, the British Parachute Association is coming to carry out an audit in two weeks' time," he tells me.

My first priority is to ensure the BPA are not able to find fault with anything, so I scrutinise all the documentation. Two weeks later, we pass the audit with flying colours. I'm not skydiving as much as I would like to as my priority is the safety of those skydiving at the airfield, and there are many things that need to be watched and kept an eye on. It doesn't take long for me to realise there's a huge difference in comparison to the days I owned my own school here, and what has made the difference is the aircraft. The Beech 99 aircraft is able to take twenty skydivers on a load, and the two powerful engines haul this plane to fifteen thousand feet in ten minutes. On one perfect summer's day I oversee eleven hundred skydiving descents in one day. In my time I used to oversee seven thousand descents in a year and considered that outstanding, but now the school is completing twenty-eight thousand descents in the same time period.

The sport has changed in the sense the social scene has changed; most people don't stay overnight on the airfield and drink in the bar any more. The nervousness that first time jumpers go through hasn't changed, but the skydiving equipment is so much better. Although there seems to be fewer characters in our sport of skydiving, there will always be the 'Walter Mitty' character at the club who wants to be respected and admired by people. They tell exaggerated stories in the belief that everyone accepts them as the truth, but they fail to realise that most people see them for what they are, especially the older ones who have seen it all before. I sometimes wonder if these characters have reached the stage where they actually believe their own fantasies. Compulsive liars they may be but, nevertheless, they remain a great source of amusement.

In the past as Chief Instructor, people built a trust in me and felt they could talk to me on a range of personal topics and seek advice. I never understood why they singled me out. Did they think I was an expert on the subject? Did they feel I was a good listener? Or was it because they knew I'd keep anything they told me confidential? I never did work it out. Once, one club member asked to speak to me privately, so I took him to one side.

"What would you like to talk about?" I asked him.

"I've just found out that my best friend is screwing my wife," he said. "What do you think I should do?"

I could see he was deeply upset and my concern for his welfare shot up.

"Well, the first thing you do is go over and take your name off the aircraft load," I told him, at the same time informing one of my instructors that he wasn't allowed to jump that day.

It was hard to know what to say to him, and I was confused as to why he felt I'd have all the answers. I told him it came down to how much he loved his wife and whether he felt he could forgive her. If the answer was yes, then he needed to talk to her. It gave him something to think about and he went on his way.

Here, the people are still getting to know me. I don't have any relationship problems to sort out; it's all about the skydiving.

It's a perfect day and I'm talking to some spectators who have family members doing their first jump when I hear someone calling my name. It's apparent there's a problem and when I look in the direction indicated I can see someone is down on the ground with the parachute spread out next to him. I sprint over and as I approach I can see the jumper is not on the grass but lying on tarmac, and I know he must be hurt. I quickly realise it's one of our instructors, Chris Jones, and it's a serious situation. Another jumper reached Chris a fraction of a second before me and he tells me he can't find a pulse. He starts CPR and then asks me to take over, which I do, but looking at Chris's face it's clear to me it's too late. The local doctor arrives on the scene having stopped his car to see if he could help. We tell him the situation and that the emergency services have been called, and he tells us to continue with the CPR. The emergency paramedics arrive and take over, and the doctor looks at his watch and informs the paramedics how long the CPR has been going on for. And then the paramedics call it - we have lost Chris.

People will be looking at me for clear instructions so I have to keep any emotions I have in check; I have no time to dwell on what has just happened. I instruct one of the staff to go back and shut down the parachute program and instruct another person to stay with Chris and ensure nothing is touched. I head back to the club, and the girls in the office are instructed on how to reply to any incoming calls regarding the incident. Two people are sent to start gathering all the documentation that will be required, as well as Chris's personal skydiving documentation. I ask for three copies: the police will want a copy of everything, as will the BPA, and the last copy is for the skydiving school. A call is made to the BPA to inform them, and I'm told the national safety coach and technical officer are on their way. I go back to the scene to meet the police, and while I'm there I look at the parachute, as one of the staff who was running Drop Zone control mentioned that he saw it spiral into the ground with what appeared to be an unconscious Chris slumped in the harness. I notice on the parachute riser that one brake had been released, hence the parachute started to spiral, and it seems to suggest that as Chris took hold of one toggle he passed out and his hand released the brake. Had the brake not been released the parachute would have flown in a straight line. I take some pictures of the riser to ensure this vital information is not overlooked further down the road. The police arrive and I explain the situation and inform them the BPA national safety coach is on his way and will work alongside them, as they will run their own investigation. I take them over to the parachute school where all the skydiving documentation relating to Chris on this jump is laid out on the table. The BPA national safety coach and technical officer arrive and are given a copy of everything for them to take away, and they then inspect the equipment. Finally, I check on the staff to see how they're coping with this tragic accident.

Once I return home I have the opportunity to reflect, and there's a sense of sadness knowing the effect this devastating news is going to have on Chris's family and close friends. The police and the BPA seem happy that the incident is purely a tragic accident. I spent years playing the 'what if' game and it's not something I'm prepared to go through again. It has happened, it's a tragedy, the sport has lost a really nice guy, and no amount of trying to make sense of Chris's last moments is going to change that fact. My mental barrier is up so as not to allow the emotions from the aircraft crash to resurface.

In the month of October 2016, and I hand the Chief Instructor role over to the owner who feels that, financially, it would be better if he took the role on again. I'm now working as a freelance Accelerated Free Fall and Tandem instructor. The jumping keeps me busy and I adore the whole feeling of free falling and doing what I enjoy. The great thing is I no longer have the responsibility of the drop zone; my only responsibility is for the people I jump with, and I love it.

Someone has suggested that a skydiver at the club, Elisabetta Launari, should speak to me on the subject of the Royal Marines, as her eldest son wants to join, and it's a subject I feel I'm more than qualified to talk about. I chat to Elisabetta about it to give her more insight, and also speak to her son, Matteo.

"Why the Royal Marines? The Army training would be easier," I tell him.

"I know, but I'm not interested in the Army. I want to join the best and prove something to myself."

I have to admire his answer.

Matteo completes a tandem skydive with me and, as I've decided to take part in the Berlin marathon, he joins me on my training runs. We switch the focus on the runs to ensure he meets the requirements for the Royal Marines, and sprinting after a seventeen-year-old who doesn't want to be beaten by me not only improves his mileage times but mine, too. After months of training Matteo passes the physical tests and is accepted for the Royal Marines Commando training. I'm delighted for him.

It's interesting to think about the difference between people who 'get up and do it' and those that just talk about doing it. Elisabetta, after much consideration, made the decision to leave her relationship and relocate to England with her two young children. This allowed her to be the person she wanted to be and continue her quest for adventure that now sees her as a skydiver. That decision created new paths for her sons.

These paths we choose in life can quite often have a significant effect in setting others off onto a life of adventure, but the desire has to be burning within them. That desire, I believe, is passed down to our children through a combination of genetics, the choices they see us make, and the risks they see us take. I mentioned earlier in the book that I felt perhaps it was my father who was responsible for my thirst for adventure and this constant need to test myself. But having my brothers drag me to the airfield to watch them on a skydive also kick-started something within me. My own sons grew up on a drop zone and were surrounded by thrill-chasers and, of course, they have the genes of two adventurous parents. It's the classic nature versus nature debate – is human behaviour determined by genetics or by environment? I believe it's a combination of both but, even then, if people want to chase exhilarating, adrenalin-pumping thrills, they have to step outside their comfort zone.

On April 25th 2017, my American client Joe, who I looked after in Afghanistan, messages me and asks if I've seen the news today about the Camp Shaheen attack. The Afghan news channel, TOLO, has reported that two hundred and fifty-six soldiers have been killed, and that the government is withholding the higher death toll. Joe tells me the Taliban drove up in two vehicles dressed in military uniforms, screaming at the gate sentries that they had casualties and to open the gate, which they promptly did. Once in they fired an RPG which took out the second gate, and both vehicles entered the camp with ten personnel and opened up with heavy machine guns, rifles and RPGs. Had we still been there this would have been a serious situation with my team attempting to hold back the Taliban and protect the client. Having lived on that camp for over two years I sense the helplessness of those caught in this horrific attack with no way of protecting themselves, as weapons would have been locked away. I keep my emotions in check, something I've learned to do over the years, as I can't change anything.

Alison and I have now been married for over twenty-seven years, and I ask her if she would mind if I started BASE jumping again. To my surprise Alison tells me she'll support my decision and I'm delighted at her reply. My eldest son, Westleigh, has already become the first son of a qualified BASE jumper to qualify for his BASE number, which is #1470. I'm not able to talk about BASE jumping with my son; the idea of him doing it makes me feel extremely anxious, knowing the risks that are involved, and it makes me realise how my parents must have felt all those years ago. I decide not to tell Westleigh about my plans, and I keep the reason for my forthcoming trip a secret.

I fly over to Croatia and meet up with Andy Callender who runs 50 Cal BASE Academy; he is an old time BASE jumper who has kindly offered me a free BASE jumping course. After a twenty-eight year lay off from BASE jumping after becoming a dad, I find myself on the edge of a bridge again with a three hundred feet drop below me. The nerves are there, and how I feel is exactly as I'd expected as I take a deep breath and take the plunge. The day before I had accepted a Facebook friend request from one of the guys I met, and he immediately posts a picture of me jumping off the bridge and tags me in it. Westleigh sees the picture and leaves a comment. So much for keeping it quiet! I do a further three jumps off the bridge, and it's so good to be back into it again.

Three days later we drive to Brento in Italy, just above Lake Garda, and I'm on top of a huge cliff with a sheer drop of two thousand two hundred feet. All the nerves kick in again and I get flashbacks from the past. I don't think my fear of heights will ever leave me, but I'm not going to let it get the better of me. I stand on the edge taking deep breaths and feeling very vulnerable, I check my GoPro is switched on, take another deep breath to help steady my heart which is beating out of my chest, and while focussing on the sky I launch myself over the edge. Five seconds into free fall I change my body position to start moving away from the cliff face.

Over the next two days I complete another three jumps off the cliff and I love every nerve-racking moment. I've missed this badly, but I know my decision to stop when I became a dad was the right decision, as my sons are far more important to me.

I return to Dunkeswell and continue to work on the drop zone, and a few months later I complete my six thousandth skydive. I think back to the day when I was working in the factory in Brighton, when the secretary of the social club showed me his Gold Wings for completing one thousand parachute jumps and told me it's something I would never achieve. I now hold Penta Diamond Wings for completing six thousand jumps, so I guess he was mistaken.

It seems to be that the skydivers on the drop zone seem to be less adventurous these days, so I decide to go up and do a couple of jumps and do the unusual. The first jump I do is with Chris Ware, an experienced skydiver who has a similar background to me in canopy stacking. I hook up with his parachute and proceed to climb inside one of the cells, and it's a bit like climbing into a sleeping bag but far more difficult. I achieve my objective and Chris captures the picture. On my next jump I jump on my own. I switch the video camera on and purposely collapse my parachute, causing it to stream for three thousand feet. I know it's going to look great from the ground, watching this parachute trying its hardest to open, while I prevent it as it throws me around in the sky.

With eight months of training finished, I fly to Berlin to take part in the marathon. This is my third marathon, my first being in Paris with Alison, and my second in London after being rejected five times in succession and for which I flew back from Spain at short notice in order to compete. Berlin feels special as I'll be running on the same dual carriageway that I parachuted onto at the VE Day Celebrations.

All goes well until the cramp hits me at eighteen miles, and I'm gutted; I was hoping to at least reach twenty-two miles before that happened. It now becomes a mental game as the cramp is painful, so I'm reduced to walking until it eases, and I start running until I'm forced to walk again. My pride is hurt when other runners pass me, but full credit to them. It's a wonderful sight to come around the corner and see the finishing line and know that my mental and physical challenge is almost over. I complete the marathon but I'm over my four hour objective, and it leaves me feeling my marathon runs are not over.

Back in the UK, it's a busy day jumping tandem students, and everything is straightforward until my tandem parachute opens with twists all the way up. It's unusual to have so many twists, and as I try to untwist the lines it soon becomes apparent that I'm on a loser. The longer I stay with this parachute the less height I'm going to have to use my reserve. I inform the young girl who is strapped to me to cross her arms and to keep her legs together, whereupon I release the parachute. We fall a short distance and the reserve parachute opens.

To my surprise, the girl, in a very calm voice says, "Didn't you like the last parachute?"

"No," I tell her. "This one's a nicer colour." It's my first reserve ride for over sixteen years, and my ninth in total.

The months pass. My two sons, Westleigh and Daniel are now grown up and doing so well. It's 2017 and they both have an exceptional year representing Great Britain in skydiving. Daniel wins a bronze at the World Cup; Westleigh wins gold at the Nationals, with Daniel winning three golds at the British Nationals. Daniel is chosen as the British Skydiver of the year; he attends the BPA AGM to receive his award and is told the Royal Aero Club have awarded him the bronze medal for aviation. I'm so proud of the young men they have become.

Alison continues to seek new challenges having walked from London to Brighton, which was sixty-five miles non-stop. We're currently walking different sections of the southwest coastal path together and are often surprised by the lovely hidden coves we encounter. I have had my best ever year for skydiving, having completed five hundred and thirty skydives. I'm looking forward to 2018 as, because the boys are now adults, I'm able to go back to having some more extreme adventures to rekindle that feeling I loved so much in the past.

Whilst working in security I was aware that a lot of my friends had a Facebook account, but I didn't think it was something I would ever want or need. But I eventually bite the bullet and am reunited with old friends I'd lost touch with, and cousins I didn't even know I had, which is amazing. I connect with current friends, too. Although the kitten and food posts are sometimes amusing, I decide to buck the trend and share a few of my life stories, along with some photographs, and I receive so many comments from people who tell me to stop posting on Facebook and to write a book instead. One of the jumpers at Dunkeswell, Phil Cane, approaches me and tells me he has a friend who's an editor, and he gives me her contact details. I dwell on it for a while but I know the seed has been sown, and I know it's time to put it all down on paper. I have a meeting with Elaine Denning, and it's clear we're on the same wavelength and she's someone I can work with. With the encouragement of friends I take the plunge and, well, here we are. I hadn't realised that writing the book would became a journey in itself.

It's hard to know how to conclude my story because the journey is still ongoing. I'm looking forward to having more extreme adventures in 2018 and rekindling that feeling - that zest for life, and for adventure and fun - which I love so much. There are a few things on the horizon for this year. I need another mental/physical challenge so I've applied for the New York marathon. I've also set my sights on BASE jumping off the Eiger which, due to my fear of heights, is going to make it extremely difficult for me to get to the launch point. For the unusual, and a first for me, I plan to BASE jump a zip wire and, to continue the unusual, I plan to be vegetarian until Christmas Eve.

Looking back, it's been quite a journey. Split second decisions have made the difference between life and death. There has been many a moment when I've had to dig deep inside myself to find something to help me overcome mental doubts or physical exhaustion. I've learned how to play the mind games with the voices in my head and have realised that nothing is ever achieved from being negative; all it does is kill dreams.

None of us know what the future holds, and which day will be our last. All I know is that the urge to follow the untrodden path is too great for me to turn my back on.

So, when I stand on the edge of the Eiger, one of the most famous peaks in the world at 13,000 feet, I'll have no idea what the next five minutes will have in store for me; no idea of what fate may have already decided.

But I know one thing.

There will be a very real fear in my belly, just as there was on my very first skydive forty-two years ago. I'll centre myself, I'll calm the voices, and I'll take a breath.

And then I'll jump.

ACKNOWLEDGEMENTS

This book would not have happened were it not for the help I've received from so many people.

I have to start, most importantly, by acknowledging my family. Even though, sadly, my mum and dad passed away before the idea for this book was born, had it not been for their love and guidance my life's journey could have been so very different. I have to extend that sentiment to include my brothers, Peter and Ken, who I was fortunate enough to have some amazing adventures with.

To my wife, Alison, and to my sons, Westleigh and Daniel, a massive thank you for your continued love, patience, support, and encouragement in all that I do. You have given me the best journey of my life, and I love you all.

My sincere thanks goes to my editor, Elaine Denning, whose knowledge, insight and encouragement kept me going to the finishing line, and to Kelvin Richards from Fathomdiving.com who very kindly loaned me a secluded office to work in when I was being continuously distracted at home by an over-excited puppy. Thanks, too, to Simon Ward and Leo Dickinson for giving me permission to use some of your fantastic photographs on my website.

To all of my friends on and off the drop zone – and there are far too many to mention – thank you so much for your continued friendship and support, not only during the process of writing this book, but always. You've given me a lifetime of memories to treasure.

Big thanks have to go to the followers on my Facebook page, for the likes, comments and shares, and for all the kind words. It really does make a difference. And a huge thanks to everyone who has bought the book. I really hope you enjoyed reading it as much as I enjoyed writing it.

If legends and myths are to be believed, I'd like to thank the Chinese Emperor, Shennong, who in the year 2737 BC had the ingenious idea of naming a bowl of boiling water 'tea' when a leaf floated into it. You, sir, have my respect.

And finally …

To Carl Boenish – the father of modern BASE jumping. Thank you for your inspiration, for having the passion for a new sport that was frowned upon, and for seeing beyond the limitations and restrictions that so many others wanted to put into place. And thank you for your kindness in saying we had just made the whole world jumpable. All those years ago I could never have believed that the way I chose to pack my parachute would have such an impact in the world of BASE jumping, and that I'd no longer be referred to as a rebel or a lunatic, but as a pioneer. Your energy, enthusiasm, and your soaring spirit, along with your infectious grin, will stay with me always.

28501674R00208

Printed in Great Britain
by Amazon